QUALITATIVE RESEARCH METHODS

QUALITATIVE RESEARCH METHODS
Public Policy and Evaluation

D.R. Kapoor
Puja Saigal

KALPAZ

First Published 2018

Published by

Kalpaz Publications
C-30, Satyawati Nagar,
Delhi - 110052
E-mail: kalpaz@hotmail.com Ph.: 9212142040

Printed at : G. Print Process, Delhi

Cataloging in Publication Data—DK
Courtesy: D.K. Agencies (P) Ltd. <docinfo@dkagencies.com>

Kapoor, D. R., author.
Qualitative research methods : public policy and evaluation / D.R. Kapoor, Puja Saigal.
pages cm
ISBN **978-93-5324-027-1**

1. Qualitative research. I. Saigal, Puja, author. II. Title.

LCC H62.K37 2017 | DDC 001.42 23

TO MY FAMILY

Mrs. Surinder Kapoor, Vikas, Puja, Navneet, Veedushi and Sahishnu, Vihaan, Praneel, Vihika

DEDICATED TO

Sahyog India School for Differently Abled Children, R.S. Pura (J&K State)

Contents

UNIT 3: QUALITATIVE TECHNIQUES

UNIT 4: PUBLIC POLICY

Foreword

A scholar, who is well versed with research methods and techniques and highly committed in his or her profession, can contribute to new knowledge, new theory, innovative practices, and new model for the policy planning, its effective and efficient execution and evaluation for impact analysis. It behooves on scholar to be methodical and use appropriate methods and techniques in order to find answers to research questions/objectives. He must have great concern for the validity of argument, and the soundness of evidence. Nonetheless, a scholar has to develop deep knowledge and research skills to find solution of the problems of poverty, socio-economic change.

In postmodern era, qualitative research has gained much significance as it is grounded to the field. Data are created by human efforts; put more prosaically, the way in which information is collected affects the content of the data themselves; scholar who 'produce data' are complex creatures whose perceptions and communications are shaped at every turn by the context in which they find themselves; and both the content and the quality of data are prime concerns. It is in-depth analysis of contextually–bound data. It involves the subjectivity of the researcher. All qualitative research methods adhere to certain themes such as qualitative data, content sensitivity, emphatic neutrality, inductive analysis and naturalistic inquiry.

Authors have made a sincere, exhaustive and intelligent attempt to elucidate the role of research in policy planning and impact analysis.

Various paradigms of research have been dealt nicely especially qualitative and participatory approaches. Qualitative Research design comprising sampling procedures and research tools (narrative and visual) for the generation of field data have been well elaborated with practical examples. Multiple techniques and perspectives have been described in the analysis of qualitative data. New emerging research areas in policy planning and its execution namely, ethics, good governance, social audit have been discussed thoroughly. For evaluation and impact analysis, various methods and techniques have been elaborated in a simple way. Question of trustworthiness and authenticity of qualitative data has been taken very appropriately. How to identify 'Most Significant Change (MSC)' by the people through participatory approach has been well taken up.

How to design, write and communicate the results in a logical ways have been well elucidated.

This book is expected to provide a practical research base for designing, remodeling of policy and its evaluation for impact analysis. The researchers, professionals, and generalists will find it useful, rewarding and worthwhile.

Dr Y. Pardhasaradhi
Professor & Director
Regional Centre for Urban & Environmental Studies (RCUES), GoI
Osmania University, Hyderabad
ADJUNCT Professor, UESTC, P.R. China

Preface

Qualitative research has gained much significance on account of its groundedness, 'contextually focused' and participatory. Generation of narrative and audio-visual data, analysis of data, and validation of results are derived through active participation of actors. Researcher and actors have been observed as proactive co-partners in research processes and evaluation. It recognises multiple views and multiple voices to understand the socio-economic-cultural and political initiatives for human development. However, the focus of research thus has shifted to its relevance, impact, and utility. It has also been recognised that all research must have "truth value", "applicability", "consistency", and "neutrality" in order to be considered worthwhile.

Over last few decades, research in different disciplines of knowledge has undergone various phases of change. This has led to the emergence of various research approaches which are shaped by different research paradigms. The various research paradigms have different criteria for epistemology, ontology and reality which have influenced research methods and methodology. The nature of knowledge within the rationalistic (or quantitative) paradigm is different from the knowledge in naturalistic (qualitative) paradigm. Consequently, each paradigm requires paradigm-specific criteria for addressing "rigour" for authenticity and trust worthiness.

There are consistent efforts to make the policy more inclusive, doable, quintessentially practical and epistemic, technological fit and cost effectiveness, participatory, and value for people. Implementation and governance is entrusted to generalists- bureaucrats and government servants. Therefore, all government policies, indeed all executive and administrative decisions, have to involve empirical predictions. Good governance is a master key to effective and efficient implementation of policy in order to ensure inclusive growth, social change, and justice. Socio-economic-cultural and political empowerment of "excluded, " "deprived, " or "vulnerable" are based on what the participants have experienced and reported in conversation, discourse and focused group discussion. Moreover, the policy implementers have, therefore, to pass through - virtue ethic, result ethic, universal ethic, public exposure ethic, and caring ethic.

Social audit has its own significance as a mechanism of establishing accountability. It is fact that huge investment is being made by the state, central and international agencies in various development programmes. It has become necessary to assess the impacts of the various development programmes on the socio-economic level of the people, especially below the poverty line.

Evaluation is a significant tool to assess the strengths and weaknesses in the system. Insights and cues from the evaluation provide substantial support to devise strategies to redesign our public policy or implementation plan and processes. Therefore, need arises to adopt more trustworthy and authentic or more reliable and valid method of evaluation. Preparation and presentation of a research report is the most important part of research process. No matter how brilliant the hypotheses are formulated and how well research study is designed, they are of little value unless communicated effectively to others in the form of research report. Moreover, if the report is confusing or poorly written, the time spent on gathering and analysing of data would be wasted. It is, therefore, essential to design, write and communicate the results in a logical way in a research report.

Preparation and presentation of a research report is the most important part of research process. No matter how brilliant the hypotheses are formulated and how well a research study is designed, these are of little value unless communicated and addressed effectively to the audiences. If the report is confusing or poorly written, the time spent of gathering and analysis of data would be wasted. Therefore, it is essential to design, write and communicate the results in a logical way.

All stakeholders/shareholders namely, policy-makers, service providers, managers, community, faculty, parents and students- could be well served by the development of tested knowledge. The purpose of the book is to enable the researchers and participants to work out their path independently and determine the right direction for overall benefit of the society.

We hope that the scholars, teachers, professionals, practitioners and policy planners, may find this book a useful, stimulating and rewarding.

D.R.Kapoor
Puja Saigal

Acknowledgements

We are highly thankful to Dr. Arun K. Gupta, Chairman, MIER Group of Educational Institutions, for his generous support, guidance and patronage. We owe our sense of gratitude to esteemed Prof. Y. Pardhasaradhi, Prof. N.R. Sharma, Prof. Lokesh Verma, Prof. Renu Nanda, and Prof. Ramnanna Dodifor their invaluable support.

We take this opportunity to express our gratitude to all authors whose works we have consulted or quoted in the book. We are also thankful to all National & International Institutions/Agencies whose research studies/works have been consulted and referred.

We duly acknowledge the moral support and stimulation by Sh. JeetLal, IAS; Sh. K.B. Jandyal, IAS, Maj. General (retd), M.L Sharma, Maj. General (retd) S.C. Sharma, and Dr. Ashwani Jojra. (Sahyog). Our heartfelt thanks go to Mr. Vikas Kapoor, for undertaking the cumbersome job of editing the manuscript. We are also thankful to Bharat Gupta for typing and designing of the book.

Last but not the least,we are highly thankful to Kalpaz Publications, New Delhi, for taking great pains in publishing this book.

JAMMU

D.R. Kapoor

Puja Saigal

Structure of the Book

The book '*Qualitative Research: Methods and Techniques' is based upon three significant areas namely, qualitative research methods and techniques; designing and implementation of public policy; and evaluation of policy / programmes to identify the impacts/outcomes.* It is further divided into six units; each unit contains number of chapters and is designed keeping in view the needs of the scholars, teachers, professionals, practitioners and policy planners.

UNIT-1 deals with ***'Research Paradigms'*** the emergence of various research approaches which are shaped by different research paradigms and characterised by three major premises namely, (i) epistemology, (ii) ontology and (iii) reality. Five main research paradigms discussed in the book are namely, (a) Positivism; (b) Constructivist (c) Interpretivism; (d) Criticalism, and (e) Post-Modernism. Nature of qualitative research vis-à-vis quantitative research (a) Ontological assumptions concerning the nature of social reality. (A person see social reality- as external, independent, given and objectively real, or, in stead, as socially constructed, subjectively experienced and the result of human thoughts as expressed through language has been explained with practical examples.

UNIT-2 deliberates on ***'Formulation of Research Proposal'***. Selection of problem, strategies for literature review, formulation of research questions/ hypotheses, research design and sampling techniques in qualitative research have been discussed with practical examples.

UNIT-3 deals with ***'Tools for Collection of Data***, Narrative tools such as diary, storey telling, focus group discussion, interview, observations; and audio-visual techniques have been described. The question of reliability and validity or authenticity and trustworthiness in qualitative research have been well taken up.

UNIT-4 contains ***'Formulation of Public Policy and Its Execution'*** Ethics in research, research and public policy framework, governance and execution, participatory approach and social audit as mechanism of accountability have been dealt in detail.

UNIT-5 ***'Qualitative Research Methods'*** includes namely, Ethnographic Method, Phenomenological Method, Grounded Theory, Field Studies, Mixed Method of Research, Ethnomethodology, Socimetric- Technique and Case Studies.

UNIT-6 deals with ***'Analysis and Evaluation'*** namely, the analysis of qualitative data, participatory approach for identification of the 'Most Significant Change', and methods of evaluation and style of report writing have been illustrated with examples. Criteria and benchmarks for evaluation of quality research have also been thoroughly discussed.

Unit - 1

Qualitative Research

1

Research Paradigms

1. What is a Research Paradigm?

Over last few decades research in different disciplines of knowledge has undergone various processes and phases of change. This has led to the emergence of various research approaches which are shaped by different research paradigms. Question arises what is research paradigm? A research paradigm is "the set of common beliefs and agreements shared between scientists about how problems should be understood and addressed" (Kuhn, 1962). Guba and Lincoln (1996) revealed that research paradigm may be seen as lay down of fundamental viewpoints about the natural world of realism and how it might be identified; and with the intention that these ideas are put into respite by three basic and interconnected questions. There is, however, the ontological question, "What is the structure and type of truth and, consequently, what is at hand that can be recognised and known about it?"; the epistemological question is: "What is the connection amid the knower or could-be knower and what could be known"; and the procedural and methodological question and issue is: "How could the investigator and inquirer set out regarding discovering whatsoever he or she deemed could be known in relation to?" According to Bryman (2001), epistemology refers to the ways knowledge is acquired. In other words, epistemology concerns what we know and how we can know the reality of the research subject (Wills, 2007). Ontological assumptions refer to the nature of the world and the human being in social contexts (Bryman, 2001; Wills, 2007). Methodology is - how do we go about finding it out?

Mertens (2005) has stated that the theoretical framework, as distinct from theory, is sometimes referred to as the paradigm and influences the way knowledge is studied and interpreted. The term 'paradigm' may be defined as "a loose collection of logically related assumptions, concepts, or propositions that orient thinking and research" (Bodgan and Biklen, 1998) or the philosophical intent or motivation for undertaking a study (Cohen and Manison, 1994). Mac Naughton *et. al.* (2001) also stated three elements in paradigm namely, a belief about the nature of knowledge, a methodology and criteria for validity. Subsequently, the fourth element has been added which is known as "Axiology". It is an indispensable and crucial, beside and alongside methodology, epistemology and ontology. The axiological inquiry asks what is essentially valuable and precious in individual life, in a more precise way, what kind of information and knowledge, if any, is fundamentally and inherently valuable and important. In this context, numbers of theoretical paradigms have come up and discussed in the literature. Some of these are positivist, constructivist, interpretivist, transformative, emancipator, critical, pragmatism and deconstructivist. A systemic relationship between epistemology, ontology, and methodology has been explained in Figure 1.1.

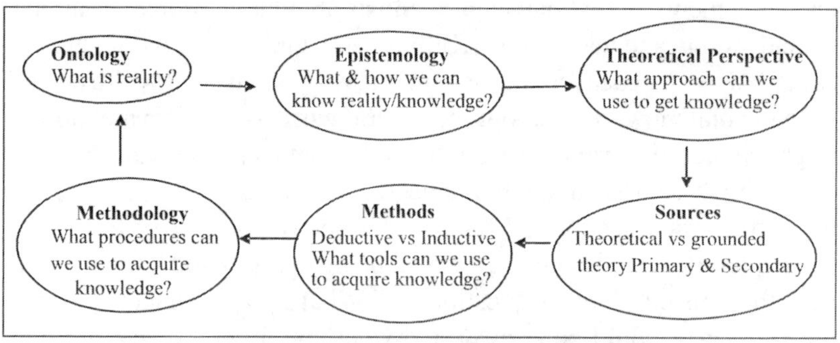

Figure 1.1: Systemic Relationship between Epistemology, Ontology and Theoretical Perspective.

The nature of knowledge within the rationalistic (or quantitative) paradigm is different from the knowledge in naturalistic (qualitative) paradigm. Consequently, each paradigm requires paradigm-specific criteria for addressing "rigour" for authenticity and trustworthiness. It is the choice of paradigm that sets down the intent, motivation and expectations for the research. Five main research paradigms namely, 1. Positivism; 2. Constructivist, 3. Interpretivism; 4. Criticalism, and 5. Post-Modernism have been discussed below.

(a) Ontological assumptions concerning the nature of social reality. (A person see social reality- as external, independent, given and objectively real, or, in stead, as socially constructed, subjectively experienced and the result of human thoughts as expressed through language).

(b) Assumptions concerning epistemological bases of knowledge. (knowledge is real, objective and out there in the world to be captured, researcher can observe, measure and quantify it).

(c) Assumptions concerning human nature and agency. (Do people respond in mechanistic way to their environment and the things that happen to them or do they initiate action and make choices? Is their behaviour determined by innate instinctual forces or by external conditions and forces, or do they act voluntarily and out of their free will?)

(a) Ontological assumptions concerning the nature of social reality. (A person see social reality- as external, independent, given and objectively real, or, in stead, as socially constructed, subjectively experienced and the result of human thoughts as expressed through language).

(b) Assumptions concerning epistemological bases of knowledge. (knowledge is real, objective and out there in the world to be captured, researcher can observe, measure and quantify it).

(c) Assumptions concerning human nature and agency. (Do people respond in mechanistic way to their environment and the things that happen to them or do they initiate action and make choices? Is their behaviour determined by innate instinctual forces or by external conditions and forces, or do they act voluntarily and out of their free will? Ontological assumptions concerning the nature of social reality. (A person see social reality- as external, independent, given and objectively real, or, in stead, as socially constructed, subjectively experienced and the result of human thoughts as expressed through language.

1.1 Positivism

The positivism paradigm contains two main themes; controlling the research condition such as human behaviour and investigating those through scientific methods (Douglas, 1973; Cohen, Manion, and Morrison, 2000). It is scientifically structured, and controlled through randomisation. The positivist's paradigm seeks to find the truth within controlled conditions that are scientifically observable. Because it is controlled, the positivist's paradigm tends to generalise findings with one truth. Hypotheses have to be tested to confirm or reject the thesis. In positivism, the main focus is on objectivity, verifiability and value neutrality. In addition, analysis uses metric data and statistics. Broadly speaking, positivism assumes that all sciences including the scientific studies have to observe a set of epistemological or fundamental guiding principles. These are:

- Link research to relevant theory - from top (theory) to down (field) model is followed (deductive approach),
- Pose significant questions/hypotheses that can be investigated empirically,
- Use methods that permit direct investigation and testing of the questions/hypotheses,
- Provide a coherent and explicit chain of reasoning,
- Yield findings that replicate and generalise across studies, and
- Disclose research data and methods to enable and encourage professional scrutiny and critique.

Positive paradigm is "a continuous process of rigorous reasoning supported by a dynamic interplay among methods, theories, and findings" (NRC, 2002, p. 2). It is based on logical positive paradigm which utilises experimental methods and quantitative measures. This approach involves (a) collection of data through questionnaire or tests or observations etc., (b) analysing of data, and (c) inferences from data, logical conclusions and generalisation. It can further be classified into:

(1) Inferential approach: Statistical methods can be classified into two categories: (i) descriptive statistics and (ii) inferential statistics. Descriptive statistics are used to describe, summarise, or explain a given set of data. Inferential statistics are used to infer from measured value based upon samples and population value (parameters) from which samples have been drawn. This means to form a database to infer i.e., to understand features of relationships of the population. Large researchers typically use a variant of regression analysis. They collect data on a representative sample of a well-defined population. Regress the dependent variable on a vector of independent and control variables, and assess the absolute size and relative magnitude of the estimated regression coefficient. In this process, the variables are measured correctly. The model is properly specified. The individual regression coefficients are twice the size of their respective standard errors. Derived sample value (statistics) approximates population value (parameter).

(2) Experimental approach: This approach attempts to establish cause and effect relationship among groups of subjects that make up the research study. It is characterised by a greater control over the research environment where some variables are operated to scrutinise their effect on other variables. For instance effect of ICT on learning outcomes. Experimental research concentrates on the control of variance: (a) to maximise the variance of the variables associated with research hypotheses; (b) to minimise the variance of extraneous variables that might affect the experimental outcomes, but are not themselves the object of study and (c) to minimise the error or random variance, including so-called errors of measurement.

(3) Simulation approach: This entails the creation of artificial environment within which relevant information and data can be produced. It is useful in building models for understanding future conditions. Simulations can serve as a tool to help researcher, evaluator, and methodologist address the complex interaction and analysis, statistical theory, and the violation of key assumptions. First, the simulation creates data according to a known model and then examines how well the model can be detected through data analysis. Sampling, measurement and analysis issues are dependent on the model that is assessed. The researcher can construct models of evaluation problems-making assumptions about the pre-test and programme implementation and see whether the results of data analysis provide answers to our research questions or confirm or disconfirm our hypotheses.

1.1.1 Methodology: The methodology frequently used by positivist investigators and researchers comprise: confirmatory analysis, nomothetic experiments, quantitative analysis, laboratory experiments (Olesen, 2004; Ryan and Julia, 2007).

Method: Deductive method linked with theory is used. **Hypotheses** are formulated and tested to confirm or reject the thesis. **Randomised sample** procedures are used to ensure control of variables and large sample is used to minimise sampling error. **Reliability and validity** of the instruments of data collection have to be established. **Inferences** are drawn through statistical analysis of data. **Results** can be replicated and generalise across studies. Since the focus of the positivist paradigm is to discover the 'truth' through empirical investigation, the quality standards under this paradigm are validity, reliability and objectivity.

- **Validity:** Anderson and Arsenault (1988, p. 257) explain that "validity refers to the extent to which what we measure reflects what we expected to measure [which] has two forms: internal and external namely, an experiment is valid if results obtained are due only to the manipulated independent variable and if they are generalisable to individuals or contexts beyond the experimental setting" (Gay and Airasian, 2000, p. 371).
- **Reliability:** Through statistical analysis reliability can be estimated. Internal consistency based on the correlation among the variables can be established by using Cronbach's alpha reliability coefficient (Brown, 2007; Newby and Fisher, 1997). The size of the data source is directly linked to quality standards. The larger the source of the data, the greater is the reliability of the results (Babbie, 1990).
- **Objectivity:** According to Guba and Lincoln (1989, p. 235), "objectivity responds to the positivist demand for neutrality. It reflects that a given inquiry is free of bias, values, and/or prejudice".

1.2 Constructivist Paradigm

Guba and Lincoln's (1996) mention that the real or factual is a mind construct of persons and these construct "do not live or exist external of the individuals who generate and grasp them". Consequently, there might be a lot of such constructed or structured realities; and they might be contradictory and mismatched. Constructions are not relatively "true", but to a certain extent; they are relatively complicated and conversant. Berger and Samuel (1966) have mentioned that reality or truth is a construction inside an individual psyche. However, reality is merely nothing but rather an internal mind construct and no merit can be given for assuming that researcher's point of view of them (participants) sufficiently stands for their own viewpoint of their circumstances and situations.

Guba and Lincoln's (1996) have explained that the mind constructions are connected to "physical or tangible entities", which could, as a result, emerge to contain some truth or reality free or independent of the constructions (Bailey, 2006). Consequently, their unambiguous or explicit idealist position seems to respite on an understood implied realism, and, thereby, leaves the paradigm in a condition of shake (Ayer, 1999). Constructivist assertions or views are liable to be lacking in any such acknowledgement of empirical understanding that is, grasping by acquaintance, by gathering, by experienced participation. Gephart (2008) thinks that researchers could not by any means be acquainted with a "real" world, and could not, in any way, even visualise it. It is due to the fact that individuals cannot imagine or envisage something existing with no notions of freedom and time, which are individual's own constructs (Gephart, 2008). Constructivists notably Guba and Lincoln admit that intangible constructs are connected to "tangible entities" and therefore emerge to believe "tangible" or empirical knowing. However, they do not articulate and coordinate the nature of empirical knowing and do not consider it as given any type of merit for the valid employment of theoretical and conceptual constructs.

1.3 Interpretivism Paradigm

- Interpretivism Paradigm is based on the assumption that truth is uniquely defined by a specific set of circumstances. In order to understand to know the reality, an individual is observed in different set of circumstances. Burnell (2016) states "Science is a quest for understanding. A search for truth seems to be full of pitfalls. We all have different understanding of what truth is. We are in danger of each believing, that our truth is the one, and only absolute truth. A search for understanding is much more serviceable to humankind and is a sufficiently ambitious goal of it. Therefore, the question of truth is not final. Professionally one follows the protocols of one's own discipline. For instance, positivists statistical analysis on the study of "wife-husband understanding" on a randomised sample reflected significant understanding. On the same sample the in-depth study was conducted using focus interview, and majority of them revealed that there had been little understanding between wife and husband.

Interpretive paradigms also study individuals with their many characteristics, different human behaviours, opinions, and attitudes (Cohen, Manion, and Morrison, 2011). The interpretive paradigm helps the researcher acquire knowledge by investigating the phenomena of the world. Therefore, its advantage is in finding a meaningful observation of objects. It gives opportunities to seek understanding and make sense of others' perspectives which are shaped by the philosophy of social constructions (Taylor, 2008). Through this paradigm, we can gain a fuller understanding of meanings, reasons, and insight of human action (Bryman, 2011).

- There can be no attempt to answer a question without deep knowledge of the specific contextual parameters defining those circumstances. Selection of themes, identification of locale, formation of groups, procedures and techniques of sampling, collection of narrative and audio-visual data, generation of data, analysis of data, and validation of results are derived through active participation of actors. The data comes from what people say and feel, how they interact with others and what they do in different situations, and these data are constantly cross-checked as fieldwork proceeds. As the researcher develops an understanding of what is going on, or an explanation for something, alternative understandings and explanations are considered, modified, incorporated or cast aside.
- It must be noted however that this subjectivity leads to results that are relatively complex to analyse and interpret objectively (Bryman, 2001). Nevertheless, it is generally acknowledged that it is more difficult to be objective in human research than

in scientific settings. Therefore, subjectivity is an integral aspect of such research. Through the interpretive paradigm, a researcher can observe a situation with different approaches to solving problems. Through this interpretive paradigm, a researcher can observe a situation with different approaches to solving problems. Through this, a multiple number of possible solutions and interpretations also emanate. Consequently, the function of epistemology in an interpretive paradigm is to acquire knowledge by investigating the phenomena in many ways, as the social context is different from natural science. The interpretive paradigm emphasises that the world is social phenomena and has different meaning. As a result, different researches can reach different conclusion for the same observation. The interpretivist paradigm seeks the understanding and meaning of people and situations which involves the subjectivity of the researchers. Therefore, the quality standards in this research paradigm are based on trustworthiness and authenticity of the researcher.

- Interpretive paradigm assumes that such deep knowledge comes only to those who have paid their dues. Data are created by human efforts; put more prosaically, the way in which information is collected affects the content of the data themselves; scholar who 'produce data' are complex creatures whose perceptions and communications are shaped at every turn by the context in which they find themselves; and both the content and the quality of data are prime concerns. It is in-depth analysis of contextually–bound data. It involves the subjectivity of the researcher. All qualitative research methods adhere to certain themes such as qualitative data, content sensitivity, emphatic neutrality, inductive analysis and naturalistic inquiry. For instance, "The Beautiful Tree" (Tooley, 2009) is an insightful, empathetic testament to the motivation and ability of the most underprivileged people on the earth to lift each other. "Behind the Beautiful Forevers" is the real life stories of Mumbai slum dwellers narrated by Boo, K (2012) with great sensitivity and skill, provide a uniquely illuminating window into larger questions of politics and social change.

1.3.1 Criteria of Evaluation

1. Trustworthiness

The trustworthiness criteria comprise four quality standards: the credibility (via member checking), transferability (via thick description), dependability (via outside reviewer), and conformability (conformability data audit) (Guba and Lincoln, 1989).

(a) Credibility: Credibility is parallel to internal validity. In credibility, the idea of similarities between constructed realities of respondents and the reconstructions attributed to them are measured (Gurba and Lincoln, 1989, p. 237). In interpretive research, different methods are applied to assess the credibility of the findings. According to Merriam (1989), multiple methods and perspectives, and members' checking are applied for improving credibility.

(b) Transferability: Guba and Lincoln (1989) describe transferability as a term that refers to the generalisation of research findings which can be applicable in different contexts.

(c) Dependability: In interpretive research, data should be trackable and results should be consistent. Therefore, a detailed audit trail should be given (Guba and Lincoln, 1989; Howitt, 2007).

(d) Conformability: The process of assuring data, interpretation and outcomes are rooted from the contexts and persons (Guba and Lincoln, 1989). According to Howitt (2007), conformability can be established by giving the readers clear track of data and interpretations.

2. Authenticity

Various viewpoints for measuring authenticity as mentioned by Bryman (2008) are: ontological authenticity which helps members to understand their social milieu. Educative authenticity helps members to appreciate others perspectives. Catalytic authenticity applies to provoke members to engage in action for circumstances change. Lastly, it is tactical authenticity which empowers members to take necessary steps for engaging in action. Natural personal and social setting will help to establish the authenticity.

1.4 Criticalism /Critical Theory Paradigm

Critical theory paradigm is "explicitly prescriptive and post/ positivist, entailing a view of what behaviour in a social democracy should entail" (Fay, 2000). There are three independent forms of scientific inquiry: empirical-analytic, concerned with prediction and control; historical-hermeneutic, concerned with understanding; and critical theory, concerned with emancipation (freedom from domination). The critical theorist focuses on 'interpretive understanding of systems of belief and modes of communication using methods of historical-hermeneutic science; the critical of these; and the investigation of their causes by the methods of empirical-analytic science' (Blaikie, 1993).

The critical paradigm promotes the notion of social justice in order to create the world which is "fairer, more equitable, more inclusive and more harmonious" (Taylor, 2008). In addition, according to Kincheloe and McLaren (2002), critical theory is concerned with the power and justice and issues in society such as poverty, race, gender and education. It considers the power of social politics and ideology which influence and control the research activities. This paradigm relates to "political agenda and that the task of the researchers is not to be dispassionate, disinterested, and objective" (Morrison, 2001) which involves self-criticism.

In critical theory, finding the issue is important and subjective. Its main objective is to improve existing situations which can be achieved through action research. The action can be continually changed to improve the quality of existing practices. This action shall then change and solve the problems. Therefore, the solutions are constructed by the reality. The predominant weakness of this paradigm is the difficulty surfaced when trying to conclude many interpretations. It also requires observational skills regarding the changes impacting subsequent actions.

In critical theory, practical issues can construct knowledge. The theory tends to change certain conditions through criticising practical, political and social issues. Therefore, the results are often subjective. The critical theory paradigm tends to see the world as something that has to change. It criticises social phenomena and changes them based on the interrogations of the phenomena involving both social and individual interactions.

Critical theory lays emphasis on progressive educational reforms, supports corporate ideology and the current free-market discourse or globalisation. Theory also advocates for effective policy formation, institutional restructuring, and other significant development that emerge alongside the imperatives of late capitalism. A critically informed in practice also calls for an interpretation of how social learning processes, institutional practices, and the role of teachers are being shaped.

Criticalism provides the opportunity to think critically and change the situations. Researchers engage in socio-economic-political-educational issues in the society. Therefore, the quality standard in this paradigm focuses on critical reflectivity, empowerment, and envisioning.

1.4.1 Praxis

According to Taylor and Wallace, (1996, p.1) "Praxis concerns the way in which the researcher attempts to stimulate the reader to take deliberate action towards changing practice." The reflection on researchers' practices, not as merely a self-evaluation, can be a learning process for the readers. According to Bain *et al.* (2002, p. 10), "reflection is an intrinsically good and desirable aspect of professional development." This paradigm employs writing as the process of inquiry for exploring individuals' own voices (Richardson, 2000). Therefore, it also can help researchers to understand and affect themselves emotionally and intellectually within their pedagogical practices.

(a) Pedagogical Thoughtfulness

Pedagogical thoughtfulness is a quality of research writing that engages the reader (and also the writer) in thinking about educational issues, especially teaching and learning (Ellis and Bochner, 2000; Howitt, 2008). Through writing, readers may be able to reflect on their own teaching practice and share with researchers working in the same context. Researchers may also reflect on their own pedagogical practices.

(b) Critical Reflexivity

Researchers' subjectivity could lead to overestimating their judgment on the phenomenon through the process of inquiry. The critical reflexivity helps the readers' to judge researchers' subjectivity, awareness and self exposure (Richardson, 2000). According to Johnson (as cited in Afonso, 2007), "reflexivity involves self awareness and 'critical self reflection' by the researcher on his or her potential bias and predispositions as these may affect the research process and conclusions". As a result, this criterion is powerful for envisioning the future and for empowering notion of educational process, not only to criticise, but also to act for the better future world.

(c) Re-envisioning

Re-envisioning is an important element of the criticalism in creating the changes. Imaginative thinking and envisioning can help to solve problems in life as well to think critically. According to Robertson and Gerber (2001), it is important for constructing the positive image of the future which could affect the future of society. Therefore, the envisioning is one of quality standards in the criticalist paradigm.

1.5 Postmodernism Paradigm

The paradigm of postmodernism focuses on seeking subject understanding through textual "reconstruction, without trapping on the certainty of objectivity" (Polkinghorne, 1992). Moreover, according to Taylor (2008), "postmodernism elicits both fear and favour via its basic principle: be suspicious of all grand narratives (including that of postmodernism, respond its critics, not without irony)." Research under the postmodern paradigm focuses on the importance of self reflections, envisioning, and lived experiences through impressionistic writing which stimulates researchers to express their emotionality in an engaging manner. Some of characteristic features of postmodernism are:

- Resistance towards certainty and resolution;
- Rejection of fixed notions of reality, knowledge, or method;
- Acceptance of complexity, lack of clarity, and multiplicity;
- Acknowledgement of subjectivity, contradiction and irony;
- Irreverence of for traditions of philosophy or morality;
- Deliberate intent to unsettle assumptions and presuppositions in ways of thinking;
- Disruption of binaries which define things as either/or;
- Refusal to accept boundaries or hierarchies. (Atkinsons, 2002a).

Denzin and Lincoln (2000), mentioned that the postmodern paradigm allows individuals to include their personal responsibility, emotionality, and ethics of care, multi-voiced texts, and dialogues to know something without claiming to know everything. Therefore, the postmodern paradigm will be powerful in facilitating research that is reflective, voicing and multi-perspective thinking.

Postmodernism employs the art based on research to empower and engage the readers. Through its impressionistic writing it is "intuitive and subjective" which involves personal voice and emotions (LeCompte and Preissle, 1993, p. 354). It includes a process of self-monitoring, and disciplined subjectivity that exposes all phases of the research activity to continual questioning and re-evaluation (Burns, 1996). According to Ellis and Bochner (2009), the idea of validity in the narrative research related to the researchers' work to engage the readers that the researcher experiences are lifelike and believable and help the readers to communicate with others different perspective and their personal experiences.

The postmodern process of deconstruction is one which seeks to interrogate these constructed 'texts'. The process might involve the deconstruction of language, drawing on linguistics and literary theory; of actions, drawing on anthropology and cultural studies; or of social patterns and constructs, drawing on sociology and social psychology. The effect of a deconstructive approach is to question the assumed educational, theoretical or moral superiority of particular world-views or dominant paradigms in educational research and practice. Some of the criteria or parameters of postmodernism are:

1.5.1 Representation

Taylor and Wallace (1996) state that, "representation concerns the challenge of representing others without reducing them to objects of researcher's gaze" This standard will judge representing of others voices during the inquiry process. Therefore, in this quality standard, how the researchers represent the reality and other voices become important.

The other concept which is important for representation criteria is crystallisation. The crystallisation recognises the different views of interpretations. According to Denzin and Lincoln (2000, within crystallisation process, the researchers could present the same tale in many different perspectives. The idea of crystallisation not only gives the space to recognise the different views, but also contributes the powerful interpretation for the research. According to Richardson (2000, p.934), within the postmodernism paradigm, "We do not triangulate; we crystallise. We recognise that there are a far more than "three sides" from which to approach the world". Therefore, this paradigm emphasises the plurality of the truth.

(a) Polyvocality

Polyvocality employs different genres on writing to create meaning and emotion. It is because there are alternative options to deliver information and feeling between researcher and readers' consciousness (Richardson, 2000). Thus, readers can gain emotional appreciation from the writing.

(b) Verisimilitude

The verisimilitude is the standard to judge either the idea or writing is similar with the reality and truth. According to Ellis and Bochner (2000), verisimilitude is presentation feeling of truthlikeness upon the reader who reads the narrative inquiry writing. Therefore, through the standard, researchers need to represent their writing in an engaging manner. Although the writing can be fictitious, the important point is truthlikeness.

(c) Criteria of Writing/Literary Criteria (Orientation, Strength, Richness and Depth)

Impressionistic writing becomes the way to represent the data in this paradigm. According to Richardson (2000), writing as a method of inquiry helps researchers to find out how the world, we, and others are constructing within our perspectives. Moreover, narrative inquiry engages the readers with the orientated, strong, rich, and deep textual representation. In addition, oriented text means, "the text should be oriented to answering the question of how the researcher as educator stands in relation of life" (Taylor, Gilmer, Tobin, 2002, p.31). This can be represented through involving value and teaching experiences in relation to the pedagogical context into research. In educational research, writing should represent "strong pedagogical perspective" (Taylor, Gilmer, Tobin, 2002, p.32) to interpret the phenomenon. The varies and meaningful description of phenomenon should be applied to create the rich text. Finally, the rich text should shape the writing to encourage the readers to think reflectively within their pedagogical experiences. Characteristic of Research Paradigm in Educational Research is shown in Table 1.1

Table 1.1: Characteristic of Research Paradigm in Educational Research (Lather, 2006 as cited in Howitt, 2008; Taylor, 2006)

Characteristics	*Post/Positivism*	*Interpretivism*	*Criticalism*	*Postmodernism*
Focus of Research	Discovery of truth	Creation of meaning	Emancipation (Power and agency)	Difference (self-other dialectic)
Reality	Objective	Subjective and constructive	Subjective (basis of issue of power)	Subjective (self and critical reflections)
Truth	One truth	Many truth	Many truth (socio-political power)	Many truth (sometimes no truth), challenges all grand narratives
Discourse	Structured, transparent, reflecting reality	Dialogic and creates the reality	Controlled by rhetorical and political purpose	Impressionistic writing, engaging, emotions
Objectives	Knowing the word, communication as transmission	Understanding the world Communication as transaction	Changing the world Communication as decision making	Understanding and Empowering the World Communication as engagement.
Findings	Precise, numerical	Comprehensive, holistic, rich description	Critique of power, privilege	Critique all grand narratives, self-reflections, empowerment
Quality Standards	Validity Reliability Objectivity	Trustowrthiness (credibility, dependability, confirmability, transferability, fairness) Authenticity (Ontological, educative, catalytic, and tactical)	Praxis (pedagogical thoughtfulness, critical reflexivity, and re-envisioning)	Representation (polivocality, verisimilitude, ambiguity, playfulness, paradox, literacy criteria)

Table 1.1 has been derived from the information gathered from various sources. It explains the comparative views of various paradigms. Each paradigm has its own characteristics, epistemology, ontology, methodology, and resources.

References

Anderson, G.L (1989). Critical theory status and new directions. Review of Educational Research, 59: 240-70.

Atkinson, E. (2000a). What can postmodern thinking do for educational research?, Paper presented at the annual meeting of the American Educational Research Association, New Orleans, 24-28 April.

Bogdan, R.C., and Biklen, S.K.(1998). *Qualitative research for education: An introduction to theory and methods.* (3rd ed.) Boston: Allyn and Bacon.

Boo, K. (2012). *Behind the Beautiful Forevers: Life, Death and Hope in a Mumbai Undercity*. New Delhi: Penguin Books

Bryman, A. (2001). *Social Research Methods*. London: Oxford University Press.

Bryman, A. (2008). *Social research method* (3rd Ed.) New York: Oxford University Press.

Cohen, L., Manion, L., and Morrison, K.(2000). *Research Methods in Education*. London and New York: Taylor and Prancis Group.

Cole, M.(2001). Educational postmodernism, social justice and social change. *International Journal of Theory and Research in Education,* 12 (1/2), pp.69-85.

Ceswell, J.W. (2003). *Research design: Qualitative, quantitative, and mixed methods approaches.* (2nd ed.) Thousand Oaks:sage.

Creswell, J. (2005). Educational Research: Planning, Conducting, and Evaluation Quantitative and Qualitative Research. New Jersey: Pearson Prentice Hall.

Denzin, N. K. and Lincoln, Y. S. (2000). *Handbook of qualitative research.* London: SAGE.

Howitt, C. (2007). *Quality standards associated with the post-positivist and interpretive research paradigms* (lecture notes). Perth: SMEC, Curtin University of Technology.

Mertens, D.M. (2005). Research methods in education and psychology: Integrating diversity with quantitative and qualitative approaches. (2nd ed.). Thousand Oaks: Sage.

Neuman.(2000). *Social research methods: qualitative and quantitative approaches*. (4th ed.) Boston: Allyn & Bacon.

Somekh, B., andLLewin, C. (2005). *Research Methods in the Social Sciences.* New Delhi: Vistaar Publications.

Taylor, P. C. (2006) Major research paradigms for science and mathematics educators *(Lecture notes).* Perth: SMCE, Curtin University of Technology.

Taylor, P. C. (2008). Multi-paradigmatic research design spaces for cultural studies researchers embodying postcolonial theorising. *Culture Studies of Science Education* (4), 1-8.

Taylor, P. C. and Wallace, J. (1996). *Doing qualitative research in science and mathematic education.* London: Sage Publication.

Tooley, J. (2009). *The Beautiful Tree. How the World's Poorest People are Educating Themselves*. New Delhi: Penguin.

Wiersma, W. (1991). *Research Methods in Education*. London: Allyn and Bacon.

Willis, J. W. (2007). World views, paradigms and the practice of social science research, (pp. 1-26). *Foundations of qualitative research:* interpretive and critical a

2

Qualitative Research: Meaning, Nature and Methodology

2.1 What is Qualitative Research?

The pursuit of knowledge has been construed in different ways at different times. The various research paradigms have different criteria for epistemology, ontology and reality which have influenced research processes, procedures and methodology. Purpose has been the generation of knowledge, theory, and practices. Evolution of paradigm proceeded from traditional approach to scientific and from scientific to modern, from modern to post-modernism. A Modernists or positivists followed and advocated quantitative research which is based on scientific principles of objectivity, verifiability, reliability and validity to substantiate new knowledge, or new theory. It involves rigorous data analyses that are adequate to test the stated hypotheses and justify the general conclusions drawn. The positivists also considered knowledge as independent of context, value-neutral and generalisable. Quantitative Research used 'hard' data and techniques and statistical analysis. Whereas, the 'qualitative' paradigm is contextual, locally embedded, and participatory, arising from reflection on experience and the 'art of practice' and 'skills of capturing narrative and audio-visual data and its interpretation. The qualitative research is seen as using 'soft' techniques. It is also in-depth study of a case. Most of the researchers agree that two approaches namely, quantitative and qualitative, in reality, are not necessarily incompatible. Reflection and locally embedded knowledge embody general propositions. On the other hand, the quantitative research cannot be value-free.

Qualitative research is like a prism which reflects multiple images of 'reality', reflects complexity, and fractures certainty. It recognises multiple views and multiple voices. It is methodology of ideas, and the deconstruction and reconstruction of ideas (Atkinson, 2007). It is contextual and there is nothing outside the text (Derrida, 1976) and reality is perceived as socially and culturally constructed. The process of deconstruction is one which seeks to interrogate these constructed 'texts'. It is 'opening up new imaginaries' in research and interpretation (Scheurich, 1996). For instance, each individual is unique and different from the other, therefore, he or she is observed in different circumstances to understand, and arrive at reality.

Qualitative research is a critical and systematic enquiry aimed at informing understandings of phenomena which are pertinent to the discipline. Thus, sociologists study sociological phenomena, psychologists psychological phenomena, economists economic phenomena, etc. (Bassey, 2005). Qualitative research is "to explore the complexity of the apparently simple, and uncover textual silences beneath the noise and splendour of social, political and educational rhetoric. It offers interpretations that are diverse, uncertain and polyvocal (Atkinson, 2005).

Qualitative research uses a naturalistic approach that seeks to understand phenomena in context-specific settings, such as "real world setting [where] the researcher does not attempt to manipulate the phenomenon of interest" (Patton, 2001, p. 39). Qualitative research, broadly defined, means "any kind of research that produces findings not arrived at by means of statistical procedures or other means of quantification" (Strauss and Corbin, 1990, p. 17) and instead, the kind of research that produces findings arrived from real-world settings where the "phenomenon of interest unfold naturally" (Patton, 2001, p. 39). Unlike quantitative researchers who seek causal determination, prediction, and generalisation of findings, qualitative researchers seek instead illumination, understanding, and extrapolation to similar situations (Hoepfl, 1997).

In brief, qualitative research is viewed as reflexive, intuitive, creative and professionally oriented exploratory scientific inquiry. It is more descriptively oriented, more dependent on context, and less cumulative. Qualitative research uses systematic procedures to discover non-quantifiable relationships between existing variables and their comparison to interpret the outcomes.

2.2 Cardinal Principles of Qualitative Research

- Each research question is uniquely defined by a specific set of circumstances.
- There can be no attempt to answer a question without deep knowledge of the specific contextual parameters defining those circumstances.
- Such deep knowledge comes only to those who have paid their dues.

2.3 Characteristics of Qualitative Research

- It is intuitive- it involves deep knowledge to explore the real world;
- It is holistic- research needs to explore systems because the whole is often seen as more than the sum total of the parts;
- It is subjective- researchers acknowledge being value-bound;
- Methods are often inductive- the process moves from specific observations;
- Dependable- uses systematic and rigorous approaches to research instead of method of reliability;
- It is auditable- verifiable through full and transparent explication of method;
- Its findings are idiographic- may not be able to generalise, yet have their own intrinsic worth;
- Naturalistic enquiry which phenomenology needs to be conducted in an open, naturalistic, parametric setting. The social science research can be better localised than universalised;
- Qualitative research cannot be conducted through a-priori samples only. Sampling goes on throughout research, through various sampling techniques, such as, typical case sampling, intensity sampling, critical case sampling, sensitive case sampling, convenience sampling, primary selection and secondary selection;

- Qualitative Research cannot be conducted through static tools and techniques, because very often the researcher employing qualitative research methodology does not have a sound theoretical base related to the reality. Theory in fact is the product of enquiry.
- One of the basic tenets of qualitative research is awareness of one's own biases. There is a need to address diverse issues, such as, gender, race, religion, ability, sexual orientation, and socio-economic status. The pursuit of knowledge has to be conducted with sincerity and care.

2.4 The Nature of Research

Qualitative research is contextual. Selection of themes, identification of locale, formation of groups, procedures and techniques of sampling, collection of narrative and audio-visual data, generation of data, analysis of data, and validation of results are derived through active participation of actors. Qualitative research is holistic in nature. It captures meaningful picture instead its parts. It not only cuts across the commonalities, but is inclusive of unique features of each constituent of the phenomena under study. Truth is to be understood in systemic circular relations. It recognises multiple views and multiple voices to understand structure, order and facts of the society. Assumptions of qualitative research are:

- Qualitative research has actual settings as the direct source of data and the actors (participants) are inspired, informed and involved in generation, analysis of data and validation of results. Most Significant Change is identified by the actors.
- Qualitative researchers go to the particular settings under study because they are concerned with context. They feel that action can best be understood when it is observed in the setting in which it occurs.
- Qualitative research is descriptive. The data collected take the form of words or pictures rather than numbers. The written results of the research contain quotations from the data to illustrate and substantiate the presentation. The data include interview transcripts, field notes, photographs, videotapes, personal documents, memos, and other official records.

- Qualitative researchers are concerned with processes rather than simply with outcomes and product. Qualitative strategies have suggested just how the expectations are translated into daily activities, procedure and interaction. The day-to-day process of interaction is richly portrayed (Rist, 1970).
- Qualitative researchers tend to analyse their data inductively. They do not search out data or evidence to prove or disprove hypotheses they hold before entering the study; Theory developed this way emerges from the bottom up (rather than from the top down), from many disparate pieces of collected evidence that are interconnected. The theory is grounded in the data. Constructing a picture that takes shape as you collect and examine the parts.
- "Meaning" is of essential concern to the qualitative approach. Qualitative researchers are concerned with what are called participant perspectives (Erickson, 1986). "What they (actors) are experiencing, how they are experiencing, and how they themselves structure the social world in which they live" (Psathas, 1973).
- Unpredictability and uncertainty is recognised as crucial aspects of the research situation. It reflects real world situations as they unfold naturally without any manipulation and pre-determined constraints or outcomes.
- All knowledge is partial, provisional, and contingent upon certain contexts and conditions. Revealing of a hitherto unrecognised mismatch between expectation and experience (actual or anticipated) that has far reaching practical and/or theoretical implications.
- It is assumed that ordinary men and women have the capacity to reveal the truth. Therefore, research is designed by the actors which is appropriate to their culture;
- Judgments are made on the basis of argument and evidence rather than whim, orthodoxy, and expediency. Reality can be presented by means of descriptive and argumentative language.

2.5 Identification of Problem

There are two significantly different kinds of problems-practical and theoretical- which require qualitatively different types of solution.

The test of a solution to a practical problem involves addressing 'What happened?' or 'What is happening?' whereas the test of the solution of a theoretical problem involves addressing 'Is this theory true?' or 'Is this argument valid?' (Swann, 2007).

2.5.1 Practical Problems

Four key areas are: identity and reflective practice; evidence and ideas; power, knowledge and language; social justice and social change and policy modification. For instance, learning and teaching are practical activities, and people who engage in them are necessarily involved in addressing practical problems, whether or not they are conscious of this being so. Participatory research can be viewed as a relatively pure form of research in practice. It privileges the experience and needs of project participants. The basic principles of the approach are based on recognition that ordinary men and women have the capacity to name their own reality. Actors (participants) are co-investigators in seeking solutions to the problems that beset them in their everyday lives. The investigative process is collective, dialogical, educative, and emancipatory. Expertise, whether from within the community or brought in from outside, does not direct procedures. The power of decision making is vested with the participants.

2.5.2 Theoretical Problems

Theoretical problems are those for which solution is a theory or set of theories. Such problems can usefully be divided into three categories: problems of value (what is good, what ought to be done, what is aesthetically pleasing); problem of facts (what is so in the world and why, what was so and why, what will be so and why), and problems of logic (what is valid and why). (Swann, 2008).

2.6 Research Questions

Generally speaking, research questions describe 'states' and 'processes'. In the first case, it explains how a certain given state (which type, how often) has come about (causes, strategies) and how this state is maintained (structure). In the second case, the aim is to describe how something develops or changes (causes, processes, consequences, strategies). Finally, researcher can assess or classify research questions as to how far they are suitable for confirming existing assumptions (like hypotheses) or how far they aim at discovering new ones, or at least allow this. Strauss *et al.* (1990) calls the latter generative questions and defines them as follows: "Questions that stimulates the line of investigation in profitable directions; they lead to hypotheses comparisons, the collection of certain classes of data, even to general lines of attack on potentially important problems".

2.7 Qualitative Toolbox

Toolbox is a set of ideas compressed into terminology. It provides valuable shorthand with which to communicate complex concepts. It is alleged that there is difference between dialectic and myth. But dialectic and myth have the same subject-matter, and the same goal in view but perform their functions in different ways; while dialectic investigates, examines and negates the hypotheses it makes in order to construct them, myth narrates, myth combines 'truth telling' with 'story-telling' through the power of transcendental imagination, myth puts what never was in time, makes old new, the past present, the ancient contemporary (Nikam, 1973).

Grand Narratives: These are big stories which history has explained itself such as pre-modernism, modernism and post-modernism. Postmodern thinking is concerned to read the silences in its own texts as in those of others (Stronach and MacLure, 1997).

Regime of Truth: Truth is linked in a circular relation with systems of power which produce and sustain it.

Discourse: Discover the diverse, complex and contesting discourses which pattern individual and social action.

Hegemony: It means dominance of an idea or set of ideas. Gramsci (1971) calls 'the organisation of consent' a process by which dominance is achieved 'from underneath' by enlisting the 'consent of the dominated.'

Governmentality: This concept reveals the means by which hegemony 'the organisation of consent' is achieved.

Contingency: All knowledge is partial, provisional, and contingent upon certain contexts and conditions

Sous-rature: "Since the word is inaccurate, it is crossed out. Since it is necessary, it remains legible." (e.g. mother, earner, lecture, researcher).

2.8 Qualitative Research Approach

Some of qualitative research studies are mentioned below:

2.8.1 Biographical Studies

The investigator begins with an objective set of experiences in the subject's life, noting life course, stages and experiences.

2.8.2 Ethnographical

This is concerned with studying an entire culture of the group of people or known as cultural anthropology. It is a method of field study that became popular in the later part of the nineteenth century. It is a method for carrying out qualitative observational research. An ethnography is a written description of a particular culture - the customs, beliefs, and behaviour - based on information collected through fieldwork. (Marvin Harris and Orna Johnson, 2000).

2.8.3 Phenomenological

It is concerned with study of the structures and essence of experience of particular phenomenon for people. It is personal experience of a phenomenon and the essential experience of others who have also experienced this phenomenon intensely. How X ideological perspective is manifested in this phenomenon. This focuses on the subjective experiences of people over a long period of time.

2.8.4 Case Based Research

This is concerned with case study. Case may be individual or institution. The case study is an intensive examination of "single case of a particular phenomenon". Andrew Bennett expanded the term to "include both within case analysis of single cases and comparisons between or among a small number of cases. In case based research a wide array of different data sources and a number of different analytic strategies are utilised. The case Study examines units of analysis that are not drawn from a well-demarcated population.

2.8.5 Grounded Theory

Grounded theory is a research strategy whose purpose is to generate theory from data. The focus of grounded theory approach is on the development of inductive, "bottom-up" theory that is "grounded" directly in the empirical data. Analytical and interpretive procedures are used for analysing and conceptualising data through coding (open coding, axial coding and selection coding), non-statistical sampling, writing of memos, diagramming of conceptual relationships, written and verbal reports. The findings of grounded theory are not arrive at by means of statistical procedures or other means of quantification, but are derived from data gathered by a variety of means including 'observation' interview, documents, and videotapes.

2.9 Qualitative Investigation Design

In a qualitative study, the activities of collecting and analysing data, developing and modifying theory, elaborating or refocusing research questions, identifying and dealing with validity threats are usually going on more or less simultaneously, each influencing all of others. In addition, the researcher may need to reconsider or modify any design decision during the study in response to new developments (Maxwell, 1998). Research is designed as such what is the problem? Why is the problem? How is the problem to be analysed and solved?.

The research design has to respond to the following queries:

- What will be the conceptual framework? (i.e. the conceptual framework that determines how much pre-specified structure of a study will have). It includes: (a) Identification of problem; (b) Research questions; (c) Research tools to be used; (d) Collection and analysis of qualitative data- subjects, contents and context; (e) Connecting research questions to data; and (f) Interpretations of results.
- What will be the methodology? This comprises: (a) sampling for the research; (b) approach-qualitative or mixed; (c) content and context, (d) tools and procedures for data collection.
- How data will be analysed? The main components are: (a) data reduction- without loss of significant information; (b) data display-the process to organise, compress and assemble information (graphs, charts, and Venn diagrams, causal models etc.); and (c) drawing and verifying conclusions.

They link theoretical frameworks, research questions, presentation goals, methods, and generalisation. Their realisation is the result of evidence obtained in the research process.

2.10 Planning of Qualitative Research

- Make decisions that narrow the study. At first, you collect data widely, pursing different subject, exploring physical and social spaces to get a broad understanding of the parameters of the setting, subjects, and issue in which you are interested. After you have developed a research focus, based both on what is feasible to do and what is of interest to you, narrow the space of data collecting.

- Decide what type of study you want to accomplish for instance, case studies, organisational studies, life history, and so on.
- Develop analytic questions. Assess the questions which are relevant in the field and which should be reformulated to direct your work.
- Plan data- collection sessions in light of what you find in previous observations. You will have to think about what you know already and what shape your study in taking.
- Write many "observer's comments" about idea you generate. Research records his or her own thoughts and feeling. Record important insights that come to you during data collection before you lose them. Whenever you feel strongly about an event witnessed or a dialogue engaged in, note the image that come to mind. When words, events, or circumstances recur, mention it in observer's comments and speculate about meanings. If you think you have a breakthrough in understanding something that was previously obscure to you, record and elaborate on it. If you notice that certain subject have things in common, point it out in observer's comments. The idea is to stimulate critical thinking about what you see and to become more than a recording machine. Try to relate what you are observing to ideas and finding in the literature.
- Write memos to yourself about what you are learning. After you have been in the field five or six times, force yourself to read over your data and write a one- or two-page summary of what you think in emerging. Develop links between research questions, themes and outcomes. Continue this practice of memos writing or summarising regularly. Identify patterns and the most significant change.

2.11 Sampling

In qualitative research:

- Features of the basic population are not known
- Extension of the basic population is not known in advance
- Repeated drawing of sampling elements with criteria to be defined again in each step
- Sample size is not defined in advance
- Sampling is finished when theoretical saturation has been reached

Therefore, purposive sampling method is generally used in qualitative research.

2.11.1 Purposeful Sampling

Purpose is to get insight about phenomenon, not empirical generalisation from a sample to a population. Qualitative research cannot be conducted through a-priori samples only. Sampling goes on throughout research, through various sampling techniques, such as, typical case sampling, intensity sampling, critical case sampling, sensitive case sampling, convenience sampling, primary selection and secondary selection.

2.11.2 Theoretical Sampling

Theoretical sampling is the process of data collection for generating theory whereby the analyst jointly collects, codes, and analyses his data and decides what data to collect next and where to find them, in order to develop his theory as it emerges. This process of data collection is controlled by the emerging theory.

Sampling decisions in theoretical sampling may start from either of two levels: they may be made on the level of the groups to be compared or they may directly focus on specific persons. In both cases, the sampling of concrete individuals, groups, or fields is not based on the usual criteria and techniques of statistical sampling. You would employ neither random sampling nor stratification to make a sample representative. Rather, you select individuals, groups, and so on according to their (expected) level of new insights for the developing theory in relation to the state of theory elaboration so far. Sampling decisions aim at that material that promises the greatest insights, viewed in the light of the material already used, and the knowledge drawn from it.

2.12 Tools and Techniques of Qualitative Research

Tools and techniques of qualitative research are such as, Observation, Interview, Triangulation, Focus Group Discussion, and Reflective Dialogue. Data also include materials such as field-notes, interview transcripts, diaries, photographs, official documents, and newspaper articles. Data are both the evidence and the clues. Gathered carefully, they serve as the stubborn facts. Data involve and inspire you to think soundly and creatively about the aspects of life you explore. This grounds the investigator to the empirical world.

- **Observation** is a technique of data collection in which one or more persons observe the happenings in a relevant situation on the basis of pre-determined scheme. It could be participant observation in which the observer participates himself in said situation. In non-participant observation the observer observes the behaviour in real life situation. Data from observations consist of detail description of people's activities, actions, and the full range of interpersonal interaction and organisational processes that are part of observable human experience.
- **Interview** is a two person conversation initiated by the researcher on content specified by research objectives of systematic description, prediction or explanation. The data from in-depth or open-ended interviews consist of direct question from people, their experiences, opinions, feelings and knowledge.
- **Triangulation** uses two or more methods to investigate to get a more complete, accurate picture of human behaviour. This can be done through convergence of gathering data from different sources through different methods. Therefore, reliability, validity and triangulation, if they are to be relevant research concepts, particularly from a qualitative point of view, have to be redefined as we have seen in order to reflect the multiple ways of establishing truth.
- **Focus Group Discussions** are organised group discussions which are focused around a single theme. The group is a purposive sample-based on certain pre-determined criteria. Statement(s) of one person initiates a chain reaction of comments/ responses from other respondents. When a group

deliberates over a theme/problem, many a time, there is an excitement among participants to put forward their views.

- **Email –Facilitated Reflective Dialogue** may be used to engage human service practitioners as partners in research about sensitive areas of front line work which otherwise can be difficult for a range of reasons, such as, time constraints, geographic limitations, trust in the research relationship, issue of privacy, and fear of professional judgment.
- **Written documents**: Excerpts, quotations, or entire passages from organisational clinical or programme records, memoranda and correspondence, official publications and reports, personal diaries, or open-ended written responses to questionnaires and surveys, autobiographies, personal letters, memos, minutes from meetings, newsletters, policy documents, proposals, codes of ethics, yearbooks, news releases, scrapbooks, letters to editor, newspaper articles, personal files are included in the data.
- **Field notes:** Field notes consist of two kinds of materials. The first is *descriptive*- the concern is to provide a word-picture of the setting, people, actions, and conversions as observed. The other is *reflective*- the part that captures more of observer's frame of mind, ideas, and concerns.
- **Transcripts from Taped Interviews:** As with field notes, a heading at the start of each interview helps to organise your data and to retrieve specific segments when you want them. The heading consists of the personal interviewed, the time the interview occurred, the site of the interview, and any other information that might help you to remember the content of the interview. Recording instruments have to be examined carefully before the start of the interview.
- **Photography:** Photography is closely aligned with qualitative investigation. It can be used in many different ways. Photographs provide strikingly descriptive data, are often used to understand the subjects, and are frequently analysed inductively. It is only an instrument dependent on the skill and insightfulness of the one who is holding it. Photographs taken by the investigator in the field provide images that later can be closely inspected for clues to relationships and activities.

Investigator has to understand how society affects and is affected by the photographic enterprise. Only when we do this more fully, we can explore in-depth the analytic worth of photographs.

Qualitative Research cannot be conducted through static tools and techniques, because very often the researcher employing qualitative research methodology does not have a sound theoretical base related to the reality. Theory in fact is the product of enquiry. Data are created by human efforts; put more prosaically, the way in which information is collected affects the content of the data themselves; scholar who 'produce data' are complex creatures whose perceptions and communications are shaped at every turn by the context in which they find themselves; and both the content and the quality of data are prime concerns. It is in-depth analysis of contextually–bound data. It involves the subjectivity of the researcher. All qualitative research methods adhere to certain themes such as qualitative data, content sensitivity, emphatic neutrality, inductive analysis and naturalistic inquiry.

2.13 Data Analysis

Data analysis is most comprehensive, the main components are:

- **Data reduction**: The objective of data reduction is to reduce the data without significant loss of information.
- **Data display**: Organise, compress and assemble information. There are many different ways of displaying data- graphs, charts, networks, diagrams of different types (Venn diagram, causal models, etc.)
- **Comparing:** Comparison is fundamental to systemic inquiry, whether data are qualitative or quantitative. Comparison is the intellectual activity in the analysis of qualitative data. Comparing is essential to conceptual development. Comparison helps in going from the first level of abstraction to higher level of abstraction.
- **Drawing and verifying conclusions**: Conclusions will be in the form of propositions, and once they have been drawn, they need to be verified.

2.14 Interpretation

The whole phenomenon under study is understood as a complex system that is more than sum of its parts; focus on complex interdependencies and system dynamics that cannot meaningfully be reduced to a few discrete and linear, cause-effect relationships. Interpretation of the data calls for:

- Revisit writings that helped you understand the basic ideas behind qualitative research. Start by going back to the first chapter in this book, the chapter that describes the basic theoretical orientations underlying the approach. What are the basic assumptions of symbolic interaction, for example, and how do the findings in your own data relate to those premises? Is the way you are thinking reflective of these ideas or are you at- tempting to use another theoretical scheme? What scheme are you using?
- Read published studies related to your own research. Study them to figure out how the authors explain their approach and contribution. How is your data similar to and different from that in the books and articles you are reading? What concepts, ideas, and theories do others use to frame their data? What is missing from their findings? From their analysis?
- Purposely try to be evaluative of your subjects and the situation you are observing! Although qualitative researchers usually avoid saying something is good or bad, for the purposes of getting a deeper sense of your own relationship to your data, ask: Is what I am seeing good or bad? What values, assumptions, and criteria do I use when I am evaluative? What do my subjects use?
- What are the implications of findings for practice? For current events for the theoretical orientation.
- Speculate about the assumptions that the audience you are writing for might have. Strategise about how to interpret to them what you have come to understand.
- Is there a story of an incident from your research that captures a major insight or understanding you have derived from your work? Tell that story. Try to work with it and think creatively about where and how you should tell it. How does it relate to theory, your findings, and so on?
- Work on writing a clear paragraph summarising what it is you want to tell readers.

2.15 Styles of Writing

2.15.1 Simple Front: Be simple and direct in the first section of a manuscript, laying the necessary groundwork for the reader to understand the more complex and detailed arguments and information later. If you want the very sophisticated reader to appreciate your knowledge and understanding of complex matters, reserve such information for later. You might also consider footnotes or appendices for such material in order to keep the manuscript moving.

2.15.2 Highly Convincing: Do you believe what the author is saying? Author can employ a number of strategies to be convincing. First, they can give a specific account of the research procedures used and the nature of the data collected. How many subjects did you have? For how long did you interview or observe them? You are also convincing when you effectively display good data to illustrate and prove your points.

There are several ways of reaching a decision about Most Significant Changes (MSC) in people's lives.

- **Majority rules:** A simple way of coming to a decision by the participants vote on the theme.
- **Scoring:** Instead of voting, participants can rate the value of a Significant Changes in the domains. The rating for each of the theme is then aggregated and with the highest rating is selected as the most significant.
- **Scoring by a group vote:** This method is suitable for groups who are short of meeting time. Prior to the meeting, participants are asked to read Significant Changes in theme and rate their significance. These ratings are summarised in a table and presented to the participants when they meet face-to-face. Participants discuss the scores and cast their votes.
- **Secret ballot:** Each person writes their choice of Significant Changes on a slip of paper, and then the total votes are presented.

The broad domains of Significant Changes identified by the actors (actual users) are given below:

- Significant Changes in the quality of social life of people (mutual support, trust, respect, and equality, interaction and participation, and social mobility) have to be identified.
- Changes in income of people and sharing of economic resources (equity in income and resource sharing, and upward shift from below poverty line) have been observed.

- Significant Changes in formal and informal decision-making and participation in political activities have to be assessed.
- The level of sustainability of people with regards to quality of life has to be assessed.

2.16 Criteria for Evaluation

Criteria are (1) Trustworthiness, (2) Authenticity.

2.16.1 Trustworthiness is the fundamental criteria because it is deliberated parallel to the positivist criteria that are internal validity, external validity, reliability and objectivity (Guba and Lincoln, 1989). The trustworthiness criteria comprise four quality standards: the credibility (via member checking), transferability (via thick description), dependability (via outside reviewer), and conformability (conformability data audit).

2.16.2 Authenticity is about conversation between researcher and participants, and the situations and emotional compassion that arise during the investigation (Ellis and Bochner, 2000). The authenticity criteria contain: ontological authenticity (understanding social milieu), educative authenticity (appreciating others' perspectives), catalytic authenticity (acting for change), and tactical authenticity (empowering members for action) (Bryman, 2008). Findings are qualitative, valuable and idiographic or transferable.

Then triangulation is defined to be "a validity procedure where researchers search for convergence among multiple and different sources of information to form themes or categories in a study" (Creswell and Miller, 2000, p. 126). Therefore, reliability, validity and triangulation, if they are to be relevant research concepts, particularly from a qualitative point of view, have to be redefined as we have seen in order to reflect the multiple ways of establishing truth.

2.16.3 Criteria for Evaluating the Building of Theories:

- Corbin and Strauss (1990, p. 16) have mentioned four points of departure for judging empirically grounded theories namely, (i) the validity, reliability, and credibility of the data, (ii) the plausibility, and the value of the theory itself, (iii) the adequacy of the research process which has generated, elaborated, or tested the theory, and (iv) the empirical grounding of the research findings.
- For evaluating the research process itself, they suggest seven criteria namely, (i) Are concepts generated? (ii) Are the

concepts systematically related? (iii) Are there many conceptual linkages and are the categories well developed? (iv) Do the categories have conceptual density? (v) Is there much variation built into the theory? (vi) Are broader conditions that affect the phenomenon under study built into its explanation? Has "process" been taken into account? and (vii) Do the theoretical findings seem significant and to what extent?

2.17 Quantitative Verses Qualitative Method of Investigation

Quantitative as orientations-reductionism and holism as qualitative- are obviously opposites. The former explains a whole by its parts, the later the parts by a whole (James, 1963). Both strategies can be useful, but both can also become hasty and dogmatic. In other words, each orientation becomes rigid and dogmatic when it is believed to be only true approach. For instance, reductionists tend to accuse holists of making unverifiable (meaningless) statements, where holists tend to accuse reductionists making invalid statements. Quantitative methods produce breadth but sacrifice depth; qualitative methods produce depth, revealing a complexity that quantitative methods miss, but they sacrifice breadth. Therefore, the best quantitative studies should be built on at least some level of depth, and the best qualitative studies also should offer at least some level of breadth. (Gottlieb, 2006). No method is good or, bad, scientific or unscientific in itself. Rather, it is the appropriate application of method to a particular problem that enables judgment about scientific enquiry.

Bryman (1992) identified 11 ways of integrating quantitative and qualitative research.

- The logic of triangulation means for him checking for examples of qualitative against quantitative results.
- Qualitative research can support quantitative research and vice versa.
- Both are combined in or provide a more general picture of the issue under study.
- Structural features are analysed with quantitative methods and processes with qualitative approaches.
- The perspective of the researchers drives quantitative approaches.
- While qualitative research emphasises the viewpoints of the subjective.

- The problem of generality can be solved for qualitative research by adding quantitative findings.
- Whereas qualitative findings may facilitate the interpretation of relationships between variables in quantitative data sets.
- The relationship between micro and macro levels in a substantial area can be clarified by combining qualitative and quantitative research.
- There is mixed form of research.
- There is a use of qualitative research in quasi- experimental designs.

The aim of evaluation in this approach is to assess research results that are characterised simultaneously by high and low inference levels. Instead of dichotomising research as quantitative or qualitative, we need integrative approaches that provide appropriate forms of knowledge needed by decision makers.

The World

Knowable ⟺ Ambiguous

Predictable ⟺ Variable

Single truth ⟺ Multiple realities

The Nature of Research

Empirical ⟺ Intuitive

Reductionist ⟺ Holistic

The Researcher

Objective ⟺ Subjective

Expert ⟺ Participatory & collaborative

Methodology

Deductive ⟺ Inductive

Hypothesis-driven ⟺ Exploratory

Reliable ⟺ Dependable

Reproducible ⟺ Auditable

Findings

Quantitative ⟺ Qualitative

Statistically significant ⟺ Valuable

Generalizable ⟺ Idiographic or transferable

Figure 2.1: Quantitative versus Qualitative Methods of Investigation.

Kadriye Erickan and Wolff-Michael Roth (2008) have given an integrative framework for evaluating research in education.

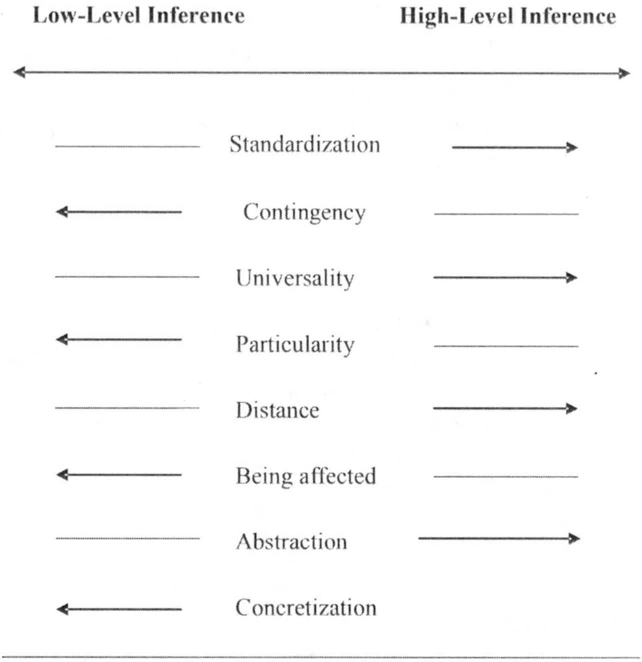

Figure 2.2: Integrative Framework of Research.

Johnson (2009) proposed a set of guidelines that is more inclusive and might better represent research in education. These guidelines are:

- Identify important problems and pose questions that can be investigated empirically or through other potentially useful approaches. Continuously generate, discover, describe, and construct new knowledge, and test knowledge claims.
- Separately and inter-connectively explore, reflect upon, describe, predict, and explain the natural world and meaningful social and personal 'world' and experiences.
- Explicate researcher and research values, purposes, commitments, and key background assumptions.
- Use method and strategies that, separately or in combination, can produce warranted investigation of particular research questions.

- Rely on sources of evidences.
- Link exploratory research to relevant theory through theory generation, theory testing, and ongoing theory modification.
- Describe nomological (i.e., general law like) knowledge domain, but also describe ideographic, local and contextual knowledge domains, and interconnect these to continually produce meaningful "practical theory".
- Replicate, document mediating and moderating processes, delineate conditions of generalisation, and identify broad generalisations when possible, but also identify complex contextual interactions to aid in particular understanding and practical application of education/social theory.
- Articulate, explicate, develop, and test "manualised models, "practice-based models, middle-level theoretical models, met-models (i.e., models of models) and transtheoretical and transdisciplinary models of educational phenomena, and interconnect these continually for scientific learning.
- Explicate creative and formal reasoning processes (i.e., deductive, inductive, abductive, critical- theory) to help situate and warrant findings and value choices.
- Fully disclose research processes and findings to encourage professional and societal scrutiny.
- Continually encourage self-examination and critique and on-going improvement of the programme and practices.

2.18 Seven Questions about Qualitative Research

1. Are qualitative research findings generalisable?

The question of generalisation invariably props up in qualitative research. It refers to replication of the results of qualitative research. Qualitative research is, however, evolved on different ethno-situations, ethno-groups, and ethno-themes. There is ample space for variations in the findings even in the similar situations between two researchers. Generalisation in qualitative research may, therefore, imply important implications of findings, either for personal use or others working in the similar areas or policy planning. Bassey (2003) draws a distinction between 'open' generalisation where there is confidence that the findings can be extrapolated (quantitative) and 'closed' generalisation which refers to a specific set off events (qualitative). Qualitative research offers interpretations that are diverse, uncertain and poly-vocal, and which do not necessarily lead to clear directions or sure answers, prediction or generalisation. It is this very uncertainty which makes it both challenging and exciting (Atkinson, 2005). Even positivists recognise multiple and contradictory findings as valid research outcomes.

2. Is qualitative research really scientific?

Scientific inquiry implies "a continuous process of rigorous reasoning supported by a dynamic interplay among methods, theories, and findings" (NRC, 2002). Scientific inquiry in social sciences including education is more descriptively oriented, more dependent on context, less cumulative, and more intuitive than the idealised model of experimentation. It recognises the importance of philosophical, historical, social and cultural context, participant involvement, political considerations, and ethical requirements as inherent features of the study of social and educational phenomenon.(Eisenhart and DeHaan, 2005). Qualitative research can only provide findings that are firmly embedded in social, cultural, economic, political, ethical contexts, in which case researchers would be restricted to using qualitative methods like narrative enquiry, or storytelling. It is the appropriate application of method to a particular problem that enables judgment about scientific enquiry.

3. Is qualitative research reliable and valid?

Without rigour, research is worthless, becomes fiction, and loses its utility. At one-technical level, rigour means being methodical, using appropriate techniques and attending to detail. At another-logical-level, it is expressed as a concern for the reliability and the validity of argument, and the soundness of evidence. Reliability and validity in qualitative research can be ensured through criteria of trustworthiness and authenticity. Trustworthiness is the fundamental criteria because it is deliberated parallel to the positivist criteria that are internal validity, external validity, reliability and objectivity (Guba and Lincoln, 1989). (1) The trustworthiness criteria comprise four quality standards: the credibility (via member checking), transferability (via thick description), dependability (via outside reviewer), and conformability (conformability data audit). (2) Authenticity is about conversation between researcher and participants, and the situations and emotional compassion that arise during the investigation (Ellis and Bochner, 2000). The authenticity criteria contain: ontological authenticity (understanding social milieu), educative authenticity (appreciating others' perspectives), catalytic authenticity (acting for change), and tactical authenticity (empowering members for action) (Bryman, 2008). Findings are qualitative, valuable and idiographic or transferable.

4. Is qualitative research ridden with researcher influence on participants?

Qualitative researchers are concerned with the effect that their own subjectivity may have on the data and papers they produce (LeCompte, 1987). It implies researchers own opinions, prejudices, and other biases and their effect on the data. In qualitative research, researchers have to conduct the subjective states of their subjects in objective way. It is in-depth analysis of contextually–bound data. It involves objectivity in the subjectivity of the researcher. It is to be ensured that the researcher own ideology or school of thought or experience may not creep in to influence the data and its interpretation. Researchers in qualitative approach be more careful in recording their field notes. In case any confusion or doubt, these field notes can be critically examined with other researchers. Researcher be quite sure that his experience, and thinking are informed by the data. The data argues with researcher general notions, so his thinking is necessarily shaped by the empirical world he is exploring.

5. Does researcher's subjectivity affect qualitative data?

It is generally observed that the presence of the researcher change the behaviour of the participants he or she is going to study. These changes are referred to as observer effect. A researcher is empowered with experience, knowledge and command over the language whereas participants are yet to be empowered. This gap between the researcher and participants may lead to observer effect. The intention is to enable the participants to express themselves freely and spontaneously in a natural setting in order to minimise the observer effect. The narration is to be based on real experiences on specific theme or themes. Since qualitative researchers are interested in how people act and think in their own settings, they attempt to "blend into the woodwork, " or to act so the activities that occur in their presence do not differ significantly from those that occur in their absence (Bogdan *et al.*, 2011). Therefore, participants are to be inspired, informed and involved to get their lived experience. Qualitative research explicitly requires clients participation "in the control of entire process" and defines all participants as "researchers" (Hall, 1981, pp. 7-8).

6. Can researcher use mixed method of research, qualitative and quantitative?

Quantitative Research uses 'hard' data and techniques and statistical analysis. Whereas, the 'qualitative' paradigm is contextual, locally embedded, and participatory, arising from reflection on experience and the 'art of practice' and 'skills of capturing narrative and audio-visual data and its interpretation'. Most of the researchers agree that two approaches namely, quantitative and qualitative, in reality, are not necessarily incompatible. Reflection and locally embedded knowledge embody general propositions. On the other hand, the quantitative research cannot be value free.

An empirical research that involves the collection and analysis of both quantitative and qualitative data is called mixed methods of research. It has been noted that such terms as 'multimethod', 'integrated', 'blended' and 'combined' have been used, along with 'multitrait-multimethod research', 'methodological triangulation', and 'mixed method research'(Creswell and Clark, 2007, 5-6). It is consistent and systematic use of the term 'mixed method' to describe research. A mixed method of research involves multi-paradigms-qualitative and quantitative.

Eisenhart and Howe (1992), proposed five criteria for mixed-method research namely, (a) ensuring a fit between research questions, data collection, procedures, and analytic techniques, (b) ensuring the effective application of specific data collection and analytic techniques; (c) being alert to and cognisant of prior knowledge; (d) being cognisant of both internal and external value constraints; and (e) assessing a study's comprehensiveness.

7. Which research approach is better, qualitative or quantitative

Quantitative as orientations-reductionism and holism as qualitative-are obviously opposites. The former explains a whole by its parts, the later the parts by a whole (James, 1963). Both strategies can be useful, but both can also become hasty and dogmatic. In other words, each orientation becomes rigid and dogmatic when it is believed to be only true approach. For instance, reductionists tend to accuse holists of making unverifiable (meaningless) statements, where holists tend to accuse reductionists making invalid statements. Quantitative methods produce breadth but sacrifice depth; qualitative methods produce depth, revealing a complexity that quantitative methods miss, but they sacrifice breadth. Therefore, the best quantitative studies should be built on at least some level of depth, and the best qualitative studies also should offer at least some level of breadth (Gottlieb, 2006). No method is good or, bad, scientific or unscientific in itself. Rather, it is the appropriate application of method, qualitative or quantitative to a particular problem to get the results.

References

Anfara and Mertz. (2006). *Theoretical Frameworks in Qualitative Research.* Thousand Oaks, C A: Sage.

Bailey, K.D. (1987). *Methods of Social Research.* 3rd. edn, New York: Free Press.

Bassey, M. (2001). A solution to the problem of generalisation in educational research:Fuzzy prediction. *Oxford Review of Education*, 27(10), pp. 5-22.

Cozby, P. (2009). *Methods in Behavioural Research.* 10th edition, Bemont: Wadsworth.

Denzin, N.K., and Lincoln, Y.S.(2000). *Handbook of Qualitative Research,* London: Sage.

Flick, U. (2007c). *Designing Qualitative Research.* Thousand Oaks, CA: SAGE.

Goode, W.J., and Hatt, P.K. (1990). *Methods in Social Research*, McGraw-Hill, New Delhi.

Guthrie, G. (2010). *Basic Research Methods.* New Delhi: Sage.

Hoepfl, M. C. (1997). Choosing qualitative research: A primer for technology education researchers. Journal of Technology Education, 9(1), 47-63. Retrieved February 25, 1998, from http://scholar.lib. vt.edu/ejournals/JTE/v9n1/pdf/hoepfl.pdf.

Kapoor, D.R. (2014). *Research Methodology: Methods and Techniques.* New Delhi: Regal Publications.

Marshall, C., and Rossman, G.B. (2006). *Designing Qualitative Research.* 4th edn., New Delhi: Sage.

Maxwell, J.A. (1996). *Qualitative Research Design: An Interaction Approach.* Thousand Oaks, CA: Sage.

Neuman, W.L (1994). *Social Research Methods: Qualitative and Quantitative Aproaches*. 2nd. Edn. Boston: Allyn and Bacon.

Patton, M. Q. (2002). *Qualitative evaluation and research methods* (3rd ed.). Thousand Oaks, CA: Sage Publications, Inc.

Punch, K. F. (2009). *Introduction to Research Methods in Education.* New Delhi: Sage.

Singh, J. (2008). *Methodology and Techniques of Social Research.* New Delhi: Kanishka Publishers.

Somekh, B., and Lewin, C. (2005). *Research Methods in the Social Sciences.* New Delhi. Vistaar Publications.

Strauss, A., Corbin J. (1990). *Basics of qualitative research: Grounded theory procedures and techniques.* Newbury Park, CA: Sage.

Wallen, N.E. and Fraenkel, J.R. (1991). *Educational Research: A Guide to the Process*. New York: McGraw-Hill.

Zeller, R. A. (1996). 'Validity', in J.P. Keeves (ed.), *Educational Research, Methodology and Measurement: An International Handbook.* 2nd edn. Oxford: Elsevier. pp. 822-9

UNIT - 2

FORMULATION OF PROJECT

3

Selection of Problem and its Sources

Selection of the problem is one of the most important phases in research process. Weak and ill conceived idea or problem will put a researcher in deep trouble. In such a situation, sometimes, researcher may resort to undesirable acts with stimulation to get degree. This may not be useful to the researcher (i.e. the pursuit of truth is compromised by disingenuousness or ineptitude on the part of the researcher) as well as to the society (i.e. wastage of resources). Beginners are likely to select problem that is too board in scope to manage or too narrow to get reliable results. The difficulty for many beginners in research lies in an insensitivity to the problems or "problem blindness" (Goode, 2008). Reasons of inappropriate selection of the problem are: lack of understanding of the nature of the research and systematic problem solving activity; impatience and hurry in selection; hesitation in consulting experts or peers in the field of research; poor reading habit; overconfidence; and picking up of area with no background knowledge.

Those who are more experienced know that research is often tedious, painfully slow, and rarely spectacular. They realise that the search for new knowledge and the solution of important problems take a great deal of time and energy and the intensive application of logical as well as divergent thinking. Researcher has to take it seriously because time consumed in the selection of appropriate and researchable topic will clear the path to conduct the research in smooth way so as to achieve the objectives of research. The researcher should have some of the characteristics of the ant, which brings its single grain of sand to the anthill. Researcher should clarify the following questions based on personal and social considerations.

3.1.1 Personal Considerations: The researcher should go through the below mentioned questions to clear his/her doubts

- Is the problem in line with researcher's goals and expectations?
- Is the researcher genuinely interested in this problem and free from strong biases?
- Does the researcher possess the necessary skills, abilities and background knowledge specific to his or her study?
- Does the researcher have access to the tools, equipments, field and subject necessary to conduct the investigation?
- Does the researcher have the time and money to complete the research project?
- Does the researcher have access to institutions, stakeholders and necessary skills to inspire inform and involve participants (actors)?
- Has the investigator earmarked the parameters of research ethics to be followed?
- Is the researcher familiar with his or her research design-What? Why? and How?

3.1.2 Social Considerations

- Are the investigative processes collective, dialogical, educative, and emancipator?
- Is it built on what is known and what is expected?
- How is it concerned for benefit to society?
- What is scope of the problem? Is it grounded to field? What is its significance? Is it contextually focused?
- Is it expected to empower the deprived and marginalised section of the society?

- Will it be helpful in the formulation of public policy?
- What will be the practical implications of the study in solving the problems of the people of specific locale?
- Will the study lead to the development of new theory or new practices?

3.2 Selection of the problem should be viewed from two angles:

3.2.1 Practical problems: Four key areas are: (i) identity and reflective practice; (ii) evidence and ideas; (iii) power, knowledge and language; (iv) social justice and social change and policy modification. For instance, learning and teaching are practical activities, and people who engage in them are necessarily involved in addressing practical problems, whether or not they are conscious of this being so. Participatory research can be viewed as a relatively pure form of research in practice. It privileges the experience and needs of project participants. The basic principle of the approach is based on recognition that ordinary men and women have the capacity to name their own reality. Actors (participants) are co-investigators in seeking solutions to the problems that beset them in their everyday lives. The investigative process is collective, dialogical, educative, and emancipator. Expertise, whether from within the community or brought in from outside, does not direct procedures. The power of decision- making is vested with the participants.

3.2.2 Theoretical Problems: Theoretical problems are those for which solution is a theory or set of theories. Such problems can usefully be divided into three categories: (i) problems of value (what is good, what ought to be done, what is aesthetically pleasing); (ii) problem of facts (what is so in the world and why, what was so and why, what will be so and why), and (iii) problems of logic (what is valid and why). (Swann, 2008). Identify important problems and pose questions that can be investigated empirically or through potentially useful approaches.

Key Points for the Researcher as Learner

- Seek mismatches (actual or anticipated) between your expectation and experience; turn (selected) mismatches into problems;
- When selecting a problem, be clear about what type of problem it is, and what type of solution will be required: practical (how

I can/we———?) or theoretical (What——?, Why———? and so on);

- Put into an accessible form, the practical ideas so that they can be criticised by researchers and experts and replaced with potentially better ideas;
- Weak and ill-conceived ideas can subsequently eliminated or modified through critical discussions with actors (participants to be researched).
- Don't be afraid to be dogmatic in the early stages of developing an idea, and don't abandon ideas in the face of premature criticism but subject the idea to severe criticism in order that the idea may need to modified or even abandoned.
- Work with other people, and draw on the world of public knowledge, but bear in mind the fallibility of all sources of ideas.
- Make judgments on the basis of arguments and evidence rather than whim, orthodoxy, fashion of expediency.
- The research should outline the basic assumptions.
- Find ways to defend and maintain your confidence in explaining your topic of research before the experts.

3.3 Sources

3.3.1 Field of Study

- Before entering into the field of research, the researcher has already acquired some basic knowledge of field in the academic course at graduate or post graduate level. A few of them may have even specialisation in a specific field at post-graduate level. Fields may be education, sociology, psychology, economics, history, languages or/and philosophy, etc. This background scholarship would help him to identify both the available evidence and the unsolved problems.
- It has been typical for the scholar to select a topic / problem in his major field of concentration. The researcher may feel comfortable and get stimulated in his own field of inquiry. Therefore, he can make use of his imaginative, creative and original thinking in the selection of problem.

- Researcher should go through priority areas in research as suggested by the centres of higher learning.

3.3.2 Professional Literature

- Researcher has to access the research studies conducted in the area of his/her interest. The study of professional literature will expose a researcher to pressing research problems.
- Research reports, bibliographies of books and articles, periodicals, research abstracts, year books, dictionaries, and research guides suggest areas that need research. Some specialised sources as the Encyclopedia of Research, Dissertation Abstracts, and the Hand Book of Research on Teaching, Psychological Abstracts and Surveys of Research in various disciplines provide rich sources of identifying appropriate problems for investigation.
- All published research reports generally conclude by making suggestions about further areas of research.
- Honing Research Skills:- **C**ritical reading, recording, accessing and storing of literature are the necessary skills which researcher must possess and utilised in identifying problems of research. Critical thinking demands intensive and extensive reading. "To be perfectly original one should think much and read little, and this is impossible, for one must have read before one has learnt to think" (Byron, 1935).
- This also involves purposeful (a) reviewing of the literature, (b) recording and storing of material related to the subject of study, (c) meta-analysis of researches, and (d) discussion of the results of various research studies to arrive at logical conclusion in finding appropriate topic for research.
- Use of 'Internet' or 'search engines' 'websites' are essential for the exploring the new areas or unsolved problems. 'There can be no knowledge without knower. Knowledge does not exist in an abstract sense' (Shera, 1970).

3.3.3 Experts and Senior Scholars as Source

- Stimulating contacts and interaction/discussion with professors and scholars inside and outside the classroom are helpful in identifying and designing of research proposal. Participation in seminars, conferences, workshops provides opportunities to discuss your problem with the experts, and senior scholars. The research can utilise their experiences in the selection of topic. Therefore, consultation with supervisor, senior researcher, practitioner and professional librarian would show you the way to treasure of new research problems to explore.

3.3.4 Researcher own Experience

- A mismatch between his expectation and experience (actual and anticipated) stimulates him to explore and investigate the problem. Sometimes, teacher may come across students having behavioural problems. These problems hinder the performance of individual and put a challenge before teacher to diagnose the causes and find out tangible solution through scientific investigation.
- One of the most fruitful sources of problem for the research is his own experiences. The researcher gains rich and varied experience during his/her interaction with peers, students, management, and other stakeholders. The researcher in the process of teaching and learning encounters number of problems. His professional experience prompts him to inquire or investigate the emerging problems. For instance, the scholar in the course of action in the field tends to identity reflective practice; new ideas; issues of power and status; social justice and social change and policy modification. In teaching profession, researcher is faced with the problems of "How to address the diverse population in the classroom?" "How to transact curriculum in an effective way?" "How can we enhance the quality of teaching and learning?" "How can we validate the examination results or external evaluation?" "How can we design our curriculum to address the needs of individual as well as society?" "How can we improve the system of evaluation involving peer, and stakeholders?" to what extent does one method yield more effective results than another? etc.

3.3.5 Analysis of Evidence, Practices, Trends or Needs in a Particular Area

- Meta-analysis of evidence would provide us insights into our weaknesses and strengths in our system, gaps and inconsistencies in our socio-economic-political system or in teaching- learning- curriculum design, mismatch between what we have realised and what is the potential. This can help researchers in identifying problems.

- Addition or modification in existing practices, methods, models, techniques and technologies provide ample scope for indemnifying new areas of investigation. There are also avenues for conducting research on developing new innovative practices to get optimum results.
- There is a need for good governance. There are also issues of availability, accessibility and affordably of quality education to the poor, deprived and differently abled children. There are socio-economic-political question of equity and equality of marginalised, deprived and their empowerment. Trends in social media, films, audio-visual, public discourse, conversation and genre analysis have given rise to numerous issues in research.

3.3.6 Inference from Theory

There are certain gaps and inconsistencies in the existing theories. These require further refinement and modification through generation of data in the field. Therefore, research studies can be identified in this context to fill the gaps or to clear the inconsistencies to get better results.

3.3.7 Completed Researches

Repetition of researches already completed is generally not welcomed. Sometimes, replication or extension of completed research studies can be a profitable and worthwhile activity. For example, the study can be conducted at different times on different groups, in different contexts and places. The findings of the qualitative research can be used for the purpose of getting additional evidence for the formulation or modification of existing of public policy.The study can be undertaken in case there are gaps, inconsistencies or weaknesses in design, tools, treatment and analysis of data. The purpose is cleansing of contradicting and refinement or modification or generation of viable and effective theory or practice.

3.3.8 Technological and Social Changes

- Socio-economic and technological changes have brought about tremendous surge in our lives. It has given rise to market-led; computer mediated world, a world where time and distance are compressed; a world where cross-cultural interaction has expanded the boundaries of knowledge; a world which is more modern than modern and has given new challenges and opportunities in research.
- Paradigm of producing different knowledge is replaced by producing knowledge differently, is 'opening up new imaginaries' in research and interpretation. (St Pierre, 1997).
- Validity of fixed curriculum, learning models, methods, and practices, are being challenged. Technology Rich Learning Environment has taken the place of conventional environment; this has given rise to new areas of research.
- The policies are being redesigned and reframed in the light of new emerging priorities. Question is how can the governmental programmes and schemes be made more effective on the evidence of researches? Government policy and commitment under 'Right to Education Act', that 'No Child is Left Uneducated' has attracted the attention of researchers as how to make it successful through the participation of stake holders.

Further Reading

Best, J. and Kahn, J. (2009). *Research in Education*. 10th edition, Needham Heights: Allyn and Bacon.

Corey, S.M. (1962). *Research in Education*. NCERT, New Delhi.

Cozby, P. (2009). *Methods in Behavioural Research*. 10th edition, Bemont: Wadsworth.

Goode, W.J., and Hatt, P.K. (1990). *Methods in Social Research*. McGraw-Hill, New Delhi.

Guthrie, G. (2010). *Basic Research Methods*. New Delhi: Sage.

Hillway, T. (1956). *Introduction to Research*. Houghton Miffin Co.

Punch, K. (2006). *Developing Effective Research Proposals*. 2nd edition, London: Sage.

Rummel, J. F. (1958). *An Introduction to Research Procedures in Education*. New York: Harper Brothers.

4

Review of Literature

The researchers get minimal formal training regarding review of literature. A little guidance from faculty or published sources, could not equip them as how to analyse and synthesise research literature. As a result, it is all alleged that most literature reviews are poorly conceptualised and written. Researchers may not be learning what it means to make and justify their claims. A literature review is a systematic, explicit and reproducible method for identifying, evaluating and synthesising the existing body of completed and recorded work produced by researchers, scholars and practitioners. (Fink, 2005). Krathwohl and Smith (2005) describe the essential tasks of a literature review for a research proposal is to a select group of studies that provide a foundation for the proposed project, understand their relevance and how they contribute to the study. "The writer task is to employ the research literature artfully to support and explain the choices made for this study, not to educate the reader concerning the state of science in the problem area" (Locke, Spirduso and Silveraman, 1999). It is not only to synthesise and summarise but also to inform and support some decisions.

Review of literature provides substantial intellectual inputs for the formulation of research questions, designing methodology appropriate to the field and action plan for the conduct of field study. Research questions need to be formulated on the basis of objectives of the field study. Most of the research questions are generated during the conduct of field study. The researcher must use his or her insight and experience while framing research questions. For example: in their introduction to the Discovery of Grounded Theory, Glaser and Strauss (1997) suggested that the researcher should start collecting and analysing data without looking for the existing literature in the field. *Tabula rasa* was the mantra, which was often used later on as an argument against scientific claims linked to qualitative research. This notion has still been pursued in qualitative research. It is also suggested by the experts in the field of qualitative research that there are several forms of literature which should be used in qualitative research.

Review of theoretical literature about the topic under study will help in understanding:

- What is already known about this issue?
- Which theories are used and discussed in this area?
- What concepts are used or disputed about?
- What are methodological controversies in this field?
- What has not yet been exploded in this field?
- Is research explicitly guided by some kind of theoretical or conceptual framework which seeks to explain the phenomena they are observing?

Documentary materials are also potentially valuable for generating theory as our observations and interviews (Glaser and Strauss, 1967, pp.162-63).

4.1 Use of the Empirical literature about earlier research in the same or similar field

Strauss and Corbin (1998, pp. 49-52) had listed nine-way of using literature.

- Concepts from the literature can be a source of making comparisons in data you have collected;
- To be familiar with the relevant literature can enhance sensitivity to subtle nuances in data;
- Published descriptive materials can give accurate description of reality helpful for understanding your own material;

- Existing philosophical and theoretical knowledge can inspire you and give you an orientation in the field and material;
- The literature can be a secondary source of data – for example, quotations from interview in articles may complement your own materials;
- The literature can be used beforehand to formulate questions that help you as a springboard in early interviews and observations;
- The literature may stimulate questions while you analyse your material;
- Areas for theoretical sampling can be suggested by the literature;
- The literature can be used for confirming findings or can be overcome by your findings.

4.2 Review of Methodological Literature

- Review of methodological literature will help the researcher in understanding the methods used. Is there any possibility or scope to modify or refine the methods?
- It will facilitate the researcher in understanding the procedures and techniques used in the selection of sample. What controls were applied to get accurate information?
- To see the distinctions, alternatives, and strengths or weaknesses of one technique over the other.
- What criteria were used for establishing reliability and validity of the tools?

4.3 Study of Theoretical and Empirical Literature for contextualising, comparison and generalisation of your findings

- How the existing literature is relevant for grounding the present researcher argumentation, or findings of the present study are in concordance with the existing research or the present findings contradict existing research.
- Comparison of outcomes of earlier research findings with findings of the present study will help us to identify the most significant changes over the time.
- The review of earlier researches will help the researcher in writing his /her research report.

- The literature can be used for confirming findings or can be overcome by your findings.

4.4 Internet as Source of Information

Introduction of technological innovations such as, the use of computers, e-mail, networks, teleconferencing and new software made possible for the researchers in India to collaborate globally and contribute more effectively towards research. Now it is possible to make the entire world's knowledge, or even just a big chunk of it, available to anyone and everyone, anytime, anywhere to compare his or her research findings with others to arrive at logical conclusion. It is now easier for the researchers to view and review a large array of research literature. Such a system could connect research studies not only to related work but to the relevant learning materials, state policies, teacher reflections, media reports and support organisations.

The range of electronic databases available today is widespread. There are databases that focus on research. They cover a wide spectrum of materials across disciplines. For example, Academic Search Premier (EBSCO) contains both full-text journal articles and abstracts, covering nearly every academic field of study. EDGE is a bibliographic data base that indexes and abstracts articles that provide international coverage on various themes. PsycINFO (OVID) is indexing and abstracting device produced by the American Psychological Association. Sources indexed include scholarly books, peer-reviewed journals, and dissertations (theses) all in the field of psychology and the psychological aspects of related disciplines, medicine, psychiatry, sociology, education, linguistics, and anthropology. Google Scholar contains academic journals, conference papers, books, professional magazines, reports, and abstracts of doctoral dissertations. Research-gate members can exchange their research experiences and literature with scholars. DELNET is a useful tool for researchers. Networked Digital Library of Theses and Dissertations, Directory of Open Access Journals provide free on-line service to the researchers. There are number of search engines through which one can access, and download the requisite information. The Internet provides extremely useful information. Searching materials relevant to research topic is complex. A specific skill is required for searching the creditable and appropriate materials. Therefore, numbers of books have been written to give practical guidance for how to use this source. However, it cannot be denied that Internet as a source is set with number of limitations. Therefore, it is essential that the scholar should make judicious use of Internet in conjunction with other sources of information.

There are several problems associated with the use of Internet. These are mentioned below:

- There is overload of information. In the mirage of information, researcher sometimes gets confused and cannot sort out what is relevant and what is not relevant.
- There is a question of accuracy or credibility of information gathered from Internet. Sometimes, information gathered does not reveal the original source from which the given information is acquired.
- It has been observed that the information on the web often changes quickly. For example. a very useful information once available may not be on the website or cannot be accessed. This causes unique referencing problems.
- Information gathered from Internet is sometimes misused. For example, information available on the Internet even though not relevant is twisted by the scholar to suit his or her theme under investigation.

4.5 Strategy for Review of Literature

4.5.1 Developing Research Skills: Reading, recording, accessing and storing of literature are the necessary skills which researcher must possess and utilise. This also involves (a) purposeful reviewing of the literature, (b) recording and storing of material related to the subject of study, (c) meta-analysis of researches and (d) discussion of the results of various research studies to arrive at logical conclusion. Use of 'Internet' or 'search engines' 'websites' are essential for the review of vast array of available literature on the subject. Honing involves two types of screening- substantive screening and methodological screening. Substantive screening is content screening i.e. relevant to your topic and question. Methodological screening – deals specifically with design, sample, data collection, and data analysis. Both contribute to your demonstration of mastery of the relevant literature.

Detail of strategy for working with literature is shown in Figure- as given below.

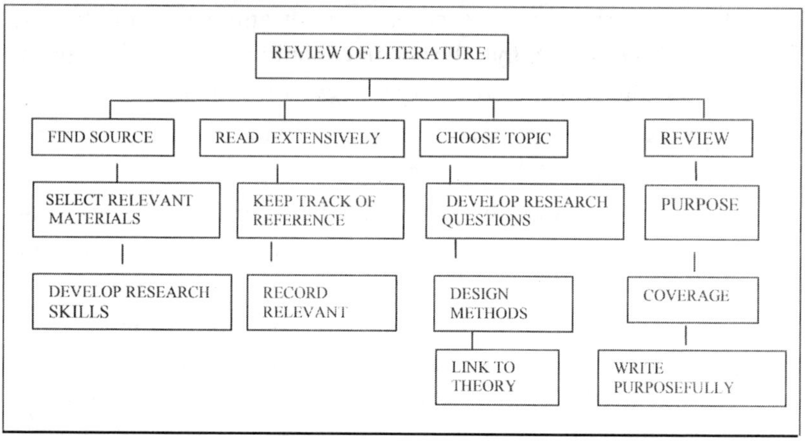

Figure 4.1: Strategy for the Review of Literature.

4.5.2 Efficient reading requires sorting grains from the chafe i.e. pick up what is relevant to your topic. Researcher should have focused and concentrated reading. It is to review the literature critically showing strengths, weaknesses and implications, as well as how various perspectives relate to one another and where they diverge.

4.5.2 Keep track of references so that in case of reexamination or need it can be accessed easily without the loss of time. Name all your sources and any point you like to make. If it is relevant include it in the text of your work, if it is not, leave it out. Keep details of every reference and make sure they include name, initials, date, title, publisher and page number. Keep references also on a separate word-processing file, which will enable to build these up alphabetically and simple paste into your work when you finish.

4.5.3 Writing relevant annotating: Use quotates only when they make a point strongly and clearly. Too many quotations can ruin the flow. And to be beware of the temptation to use quotations out of context, particularly where a quote seems to fit your work perfectly but you are aware that your point of argument is different from that of the writer you are quoting.

4.5.4 Informing your Study with theory: Purpose is to determine whether a particular theory can be translated into actual practice. People's views and positions are frequently not as clear-cut and researcher should bear this caveat in mind. Therefore, research has a great deal to do with: ontological assumptions concerning the nature of social reality; epistemological assumptions concerning the bases of knowledge; and assumptions concerning human nature.

Further Reading

Boyanov, M. I., S. D. Kelly, K. M. Kemner, B. A. Bunker, J. B. Fein and D. A. Fowle. (2003). Adsorption of cadmium to *Bacillus subtilis* bacterial cell walls: a pH-dependent X-ray absorption fine structure spectroscopy study. *Geochimica et Cosmochimica Act Pages.* 67, 18: 3299-3536.

Chan, Steve. (1997). In Search of Democratic Peace: Problems and Promise. Mershon *International Studies Review.* 41, 1:59-92.

Constance M. Winchell.(Eds) (1967, 1950). *A guide to Reference Books.* Chicago American Library Association.

Fink, A (2005). *Conducting Research Literature Reviews: From the Internet to Paper.* 2nd edn. London: Sage.

Goeser, C. (2003). On The Cross of The South: The Scottsboro Boys as Vernacular Christs in Harlem Renaissance Illustration. *International Review of African American Art.* 19, 1: 19-27.

Good, Carter V. (2008). *Introduction to Educational Research.* Second Edition. Surjeet Publications. New Delhi-7.

Hart, C.(2001). *Doing a Literature Search.* London: Sage.

Holt, Robert-R. (2003). Some history of a methodological rediscovery. *American Psychologist.* 58, 5: 406-407.

Keith, F. P. (2009). Introduction to Research Methods in Education. SAGE Publications India Pvt Ltd, New Delhi-110044.

5

Formulation of Research Proposal

5.1 What Research is Intended

Identification of the Research Problem requires lot of efforts and extensive reading on the part of researcher. Familiarity with the area and the sub-areas of the field is prerequisite. Researcher can take premise from specific field study. Identification of gaps/deficiencies of specific issue-educational, social, economic, cultural or political, that is what is anticipated and what is realised in the field situation would stimulate him or her to pick up the new topic of research. When topic of research is identified, need arises to explain and justify why do you like to undertake this research study? What are the expected outcomes of the proposed research study? What are its practical implications?

In their introduction to the Discovery of Grounded Theory Glaser and Strauss (1997) suggested that the researcher should start collecting and analysing data without looking for the existing literature in the field. Tabula rasa was the mantra, which saw often used later on as an argument against scientific claims linked to qualitative research. This notion has still been pursued in qualitative research. It is also suggested by the experts in the field of qualitative research that there are several forms of literature which should be used in qualitative research.

However, 'Comprehensiveness' and 'Broadness' are two of the criteria assessing the 'Coverage'. First, a standard for evaluating the literature review, and second the discussion part of the dissertation. 'The writer task is to employ the research literature artfully to support and explain the choices made for this study, not to educate the reader concerning the state of science in the problem area' (Locke, Spirduso, and Silveraman, 1999).

5.1 Statement of problem is one or two sentences claim that outlines the problem that the study addresses. Statement of the Problem should be specific, clear and researchable. A research worthy problem statement is the description of an active challenge faced by researchers and/ or practitioners that does not have adequate solution. The research worthy problem statement should address all six questions; what, how, where, when, why and who. Usually, a problem requires some reworking to get it into a suitable form for the study to proceed effectively. A good statement of the problem should provide the researcher with direction in pursuing the project. The statement should identify key factors in the research project.

Key themes in the statement of the problem should be elaborated i.e. made more specific. Therefore, considerable definition of terms (key-themes) would be necessary. An operational definition is a sort of manual of instructions to the investigator. It gives meaning to sub-themes by spelling out what the investigator must do to solve the problem.

Objectives of the study provide clear direction to research. They reflect the basic purpose of the study i.e. what we want to achieve. Objectives of the study provide necessary safeguards in collection of requisite information. Qualitative data thus collected are analysed and interpreted vis-à-vis earmarked objectives or outcomes of the research project. After selecting the topic and defining the research problem, the researcher should mention the objectives of the research. This means that he should explain what he aims to achieve through the research. His objectives should also explain the extent to which the research work is related to the specific field.

5.2 Research Question and Hypothesis

5.2.1 Research Questions

Research questions or hypotheses are more operational than statement of the problem, as such, lend more specific structure to the study. If a topic defines the general area, then the research question defines what aspects of that topic one plans to investigate. If a topic defines the general area, then the research question defines what aspects of that topic one plans to investigate. Researchable questions can be generated or developed through following sources.

- **Personal experiences**- sometimes our personal experiences of a particular phenomenon, or event can give 'insights' worth exploring;
- **Theory**- theoretical inspiration is most likely to happen when you find yourself relating theory to a real-world situation;
- **An observation**-Viewing the world through fresh eyes can provide powerful research angles;
- **Contemporary issues**- sometimes an old topic can take on fresh life. A topic might suddenly become an agenda or focus of global attention;
- **Gaps in literature**- one can explore whether an important aspect of an issue has been ignored, whether there are assumptions underpinning a body of work that need to be re-examined.

5.2.2 Hypothesis vs Research Questions

The hypothesis is the cornerstone of scientific method and that is necessary component of the research process. Hypothesis is logical conjecture, hunch or educated guess about the nature of relationships between two or more variables expressed in the form of a testable statement. Not all research questions can be easily 'converted' into a hypothesis, nor should they. A hypothesis may not be appropriate if:

- You do not have a hunch or educated guess about a particular situation;
- You do not have a of defined variables;
- Moreover, the researcher should ensure that the research questions are appropriate to the field situation and the research questions should take the cognisance of 'text' and 'Culture'. Your question centres on phenomenological descriptions; and on ethnographic study of a cultural group;

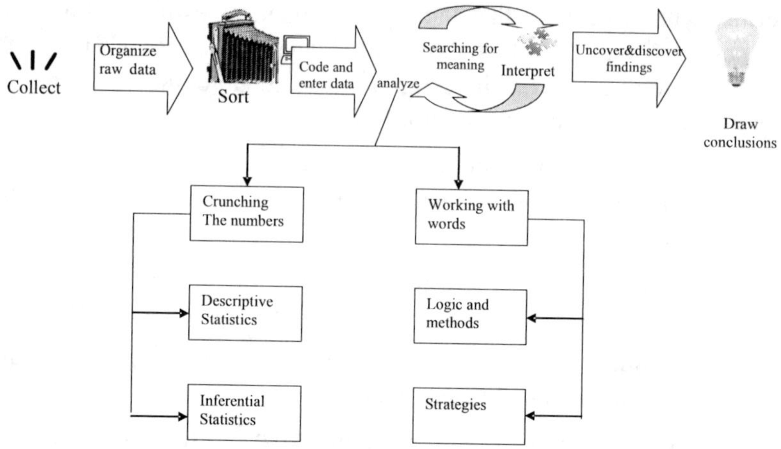

Figure 5.1: Objectives/ Research Questions/Theory.

5.3 How the Research will be Done

Research design gives the road-map to the research work. Research design is the plan, structure and strategy of investigation conceived to obtain answers to research questions and to control variance. Research design is framework for the collection, measurement and analysis of data.

5.4 Methodology

5.4.1 Method: A well defined problem points to a method of investigation. In qualitative research inductive method of investigation is used. This form is very powerful in generating concepts because it proceeds from particular observations to general conclusions.The researcher should explain the method he is going to use-qualitative, or mixed (qualitative and quantitative).

5.4.2 Sampling: Non-probability sampling design (purposive or judgment sampling) is used. Choice of locale and group is selected through participatory approach i.e. in consultation with actors (participants to be researched).

5.4.3 Tools: Instruments for collection of data are (i) Questionnaire, (ii) Focus Group Discussions, (iii) Semi-structured-Interview Schedule, (iv) Dialogues, (v) Observation, (vi) Case Studies, and (vii) Story Telling with Truth Telling.

The interpretivist's paradigm seeks the understanding and meaning of people and situations which involves the subjectivity of the researchers. Therefore, the quality standards in this research paradigm are trust worthiness and authenticity.

5.5 Standard Criteria

5.5.1 Trustworthiness: The trustworthiness criteria comprise four quality standards: the credibility (via member checking), transferability (via thick description), dependability (via outside reviewer), and conformability (conformability data audit) (Guba and Lincoln, 1989).

5.5.2 Authenticity: Authenticity criteria are: ontological authenticity which helps members to understand their social milieu. Educative authenticity helps members to appreciate others perspectives. Catalytic authenticity applies to provoke members to engage in action for circumstances change. Lastly, it is tactical authenticity which empowers members to take necessary steps for engaging in action. Natural personal and social setting will help to establish the authenticity.

5.6 Analyses: The main components are: (a) data reduction-without loss of significant information; (b) data display-the process to organise, compress and assemble information (graphs, charts, and Venn diagrams, causal models etc.); and (c) drawing and verifying conclusions.

5.7 Interpretation: The whole phenomenon under study is understood as a complex system that is more than sum of its parts; focus on complex interdependencies and system dynamics that can not meaningfully be reduced to a few discrete and linear, cause-effect relationships.

5.8 Limitations and Delimitations

A limitation identifies potential weaknesses of the study. Think about your analysis, the nature of self-report, your instruments, the sample. Think about threats to internal validity that may have been impossible to avoid or minimise or explain.

Delimitation addresses how a study will be narrowed in scope, that is, how it is bounded. This is the place to explain the things that you are not doing and why you have chosen not to do them—the literature you will not review (and why not), the population you are not studying (and why not), the methodological procedures you will not use (and why you will not use them). Limit your delimitations to the things that a reader might reasonably expect you to do but that you, for clearly explained reasons, have decided not to do.

Further Reading

Bacon Corey, S.M. (1962). *Research in Education*. NCERT, New Delhi.

Cozby, P. (2009). *Methods in Behavioural Research*. 10th edition, Bemont: Wadsworth.

Goode, W.J., and Hatt, P.K. (1990). *Methods in Social Research*. McGraw-Hill, New Delhi.

Guthrie, G. (2010). *Basic Research Methods*. New Delhi: Sage.

Hillway, T. (1956). *Introduction to Research*. Houghton Miffin Co.

Punch, K. (2006). *Developing Effective Research Proposals*. 2nd edition, London: Sage.

Rummel, J. F. (1958). *An Introduction to Research Procedures in Education* New York: Harper Brothers.

Campbell, J.P., Daft, R.L., and Hulin, C.L.(1982). *What to Study: Generating and Developing Research Questions*. Beverly Hills, CA: Sage.

Charters, W.W.Jr. (1967). Hypothesis in scientific research. Unpublished paper. University of Oregon, Eugene, OR.

Chaters, W.M. (1997). Hypothesis in scientific research. Unpublished paper. University of Oregon, Eugene, OR.

Good, Carter V. (2008). *Introduction to Educational Research*. Second Edition. Surjeet publications, Delhi -7.

Charters, W.W.Jr. (1967). Hypothesis in scientific research. Unpublished paper. University of Oregon, Eugene, OR.

6

Research Design

6.1 Research Design

Once the research project is identified and defined, the next stage is to design the research. The research design is the conceptual structure within which research is conducted; it constitutes the blueprint for the collection, measurement and analysis of data. It also contains time-frame work and financial aspect for the conduct of research. As such, the research design also includes methods and techniques for interpretations and its implications.

Following are the essence of a research design:

- *Selection of research approach*- qualitative or quantitative;
- *Design of sampling plan*- probability or non-probability sampling plan;
- *Design of experiment*- pure experimental or quasi-experimental;
- *Design of questionnaire*- Structured (reliability and validity), semi- or unstructured (authenticity and trustworthiness);
- *Data Collection*- Administration of test/questionnaire/scale or Conduct of in-depth interview/case study/observation;

- **Data analysis**- Statistical or in-depth analysis of contextually–bound data.
- *Interpretation of results*- inferences or interpretive.

Research design stands for advance planning of methodology and strategy to be adopted for the conduct of research keeping in view the objectives of the research and the availability of time and money. Methodology refers to method, sample, instruments of data collection and analysis of data, and strategy here implies to establish systemic link between research questions, data, method and techniques of analysis of data to get answer to research questions.

Ragin (1994, p. 191) gave a comprehensive definition of research design: "Research design is a plan for collecting and analysing evidence that will make it possible for the investigator to answer whatever questions be or she has posed. The design of investigation touches almost all aspects of research from the minute details of data collection to the selection of the techniques of data analysis".

6.2 Selection of Research Approach

If the research study happens to be an explanatory, wherein the major emphasis is on discovery of ideas and insights, the most appropriate research design must be flexible enough to permit the consideration of many different aspects of phenomenon. But when the purpose of a study is accurate description of a situation or of an association between variables (or in what are called the descriptive studies), accuracy becomes a major consideration and a research design which minimises and maximises the reliability of the evidence collected is considered a good design. Studies involving the testing of a hypothesis of a casual relationship between variables require a design which will permit inferences about causality in addition to the minimisation of bias and maximisation of reliability. But in practice it is the most difficult task to put a particular study in a particular group, for a given research may have in it elements of two or more of the functions of different studies. It is only on the basis of its primary function that a study can be categorised either as an exploratory or descriptive or hypothesis-testing study and accordingly the choice of a research design may be made in case of a particular study.

Table 6.1: Type of Study and Research Design

Research Design	Type of study	
	Exploratory of Formulative	**Descriptive/ Diagnostics**
Overall Design	Flexible design (design must provide opportunity for considering different aspects of the problem)	Rigid design (design must make enough provision for protection against bias and must maximise reliability)
(i) Sampling design	Non-probability sampling design (purposive judgement sampling)	Probability sampling design (random Sampling)
(ii) Statistical design	No pre-planned design for analysis	Pre-planned design for analysis
(iii) Observational design	Unconstructed instruments for collection of data	Structured or well thought out Instruments for collection of data
(iv) Operational design	No fixed decisions about the Operational procedures	Advance decisions about operational decisions

All qualitative research methods adhere to certain themes such as qualitative data, content sensitivity, emphatic neutrality, inductive analysis and naturalistic inquiry. Figure- summarises the research designs.

Research Design involves three processes namely:

WHY: What motivation they have to go for research? Why are the participants interested in the problem to be researched? What is the importance of the problem? Will it bring about substantial change in their lives? Will it empower them to be proactive in socio-economic, educational and political environment?

WHAT: The participant will decide what problem is to be undertaken for research. Professional researcher may facilitate them in identifying the problem. Two or more themes are to be identified by the participants in thc consultation with the professional researcher.

HOW: This comprises: (a) sampling for the research; (b) approach-qualitative or from qualitative to quantification;, (c) tools and procedures for data collection. How data will be analysed? The main components are: (a) contextual content analysis (b) data reduction-without loss of significant information; (c) data display-the process to organise, compress and assemble information (graphs, charts, and Venn diagrams, causal models etc.); and (d) drawing and verifying conclusions.

Table 6.2: Research Designs in Qualitative Research Approach

Research Design	
Design	Flexible design: Must provide opportunity to participant group and individual members to make choice regarding; • Selection of Problem • Research questions • Selection of Social Setting • Selection of Methodology • Mixed Method (Quantitative and Qualitative) (Researcher as Facilitator)
Method	Inductive Moving from bottom to top Modifying or reconstructing definition, phenomenon or research questions from new experiences from the field
Sampling design	Non-probability sampling design (purposive or judgment sampling) Choice of Locale and Group
Tools	Instruments for collection of data • Focus Group Discussion • Semi-structured-Interview Schedule • Dialogue • Observation • Audio-visual Techniques • Case studies
Operational Design	Of the participants, by the participants and for the participants focusing on: • Theme/Themes • Research Questions • Outcomes Decision
Statistical design	No pre-planned design for analysis • Comparison and Control • Development of Understanding and Awareness • Qualitative understanding to quantification • Graphs/ Statistical Matrix
Outcomes	Most Significant Change/Changes affecting their lives

Research Methodology: Methods and Techniques (Dr. D.R. Kapoor, 2014)

Outcomes: The focus is on the assessment (value added) namely (a) most significant changes in the situation; (b) increased knowledge base; (c) increased capacity among actors to inquire into and change their situation. Different levels of outcomes of participatory research to be assessed are ; (i) the actors in the research process engage in a common effort to transform their situation because they become aware of the causes of the present state and their own potential to be agents of change, (ii) the actors are empowered (increased in their capacity and knowledge base) to participate in decision-making process. In this research process their level of confidence is increased, (iii) awareness, increased in capacity and knowledge base, and collective involvement pave way for sustainability of programme.

6.3 Goals of the Study

Research is recognised as the basis of our personal, social, cultural, economic and political development. Therefore, goal of research is to improve our practices, re-design programmes and evolve new policies. Research is also undertaken for the generation of new theory or modification of existing theories. Researcher needs to be specific, and well informed. Therefore, deep knowledge and clear understanding of the goals are pre-requisite of research design.

6.4 Formulation of the Research Questions

Questions must be formulated as clearly and unambiguously as possible. This must happen as early as possible in the life of the project. In the course of the field visits, questions become more and more concrete, more focused and purposeful. Consequently, questions need to be viewed or classified in light of existing assumptions (for instance, whether they aim at new discoveries or confirm old existing one). Research questions are not to be kept very broad to miss the logical conclusion. Too narrow and sketchy research questions would bar to reach the truth or block rather than promote new discoveries. Questions should be formulated in such a way that (in the context of the planned study and using the available resources) they are capable of being answered.

6.5 Selection of Method

In qualitative research, inductive method is used. Of late, modified analytic induction approach is considered for collecting and analysing data. The procedure of analytic induction is employed when some specific problem, question or issue becomes the focus of research. Data are collected and analysed to develop a descriptive model that encompasses all cases of phenomena. Some of the methods used are:

6.5.1 Case Studies: The aim of case studies is the precise description or reconstruction of a case. You can take persons, social communities (e.g., families), organisations, and institutions (e.g., a nursing home) as the subject of a case analysis. Your main problem then will be to identify a case that would be significant for your research question and to clarify what else belongs to the case and what methodological approaches its reconstruction requires. Case studies may be Historical Observational Case Studies, Observational Case Studies, Life History, Multi-case Studies, and Multi-site Studies etc.

6.5.2 Comparative Studies: In a comparative study, you will not observe the case as a whole and in its complexity, but rather a multiplicity of cases with regard to particular excerpts. For example, data on the specific theme 'empowerment of rural women' may be collected using Focus Group Discussions Technique and In-depth Individual Interview. Data derived from FGDs and Interviews are compared. Here the question arises about the selection of cases in the group to be compared.

6.5.3 Retrospective Studies: The research is carried out retrospectively. Biographical research is an example of such studies. Certain events and processes are analysed in respect of their meaning for individual or collective life histories. A range of process-oriented procedures are also strongly related to the present and are therefore not interested in the reconstruction of past events from the point of view of (any of) them but in the course of currents from a parallel temporal perspective. In ethnographic studies, researchers participate in the development of some event over an extended period in order to record and analyse this in parallel to its actual occurrence. In conversation analyses a conversation is recorded and then analysed in terms of its sequencing, while in objective hermeneutics a protocol is interpreted in a strictly sequential manner "from beginning to end."

6.5.4 Longitudinal Studies: It is a method where data is analysed again at later times of data collection i.e., longitudinal studies with several periods of data collection. Implicitly a longitudinal perspective within a temporally limited framework is realised in ethnography by virtue of the researchers' extended participation in the field of study, and also—with a retrospective focus—in biographical research, which considers an extended section of a life history.

6.6 Design of Sampling Plan

A sampling plan is a mechanism by which the sampling units of a study are selected from the sampling frame of the population. The selection of sampling plan in a study in turn affects the cost and time to conduct the study, and the reliability -validity of the study. Hence, it should be selected with utmost care. In qualitative research, non-probability Sampling Plan is used.

Non-probability Sampling Plans options are: Convenience/ incidental sampling; purposive sampling; judgment sampling, quota sampling; and Snowball Sampling.

6.6.1 Purposive Sampling: Purposive sampling targets a particular group of people. When the desired population for the study is rare or very difficult to locate, purposive sampling may be the only option. For example, you are interested in studying cognitive processing speed of young adults who have suffered closed head brain injuries in automobile accidents. This would be a difficult population to find. Your city has a well-established rehabilitation hospital and you contact the director to seek permission for getting requisite information.

6.6.2 Theoretical Sampling: Decisions about choosing and putting together empirical material (cases, groups, institutions, etc.) are made in the process of collecting and interpreting data. Glaser and Strauss describe this strategy as follows:

- Theoretical sampling is the process of data collection for generating theory whereby the analyst jointly collects, codes, and analyses his /her data and decides what data to collect next and where to find them, in order to develop his theory as it emerges. This process of data collection is controlled by the emerging theory.
- Sampling decisions in theoretical sampling may start from either of two levels: they may be made on the level of the groups to be compared or they may directly focus on specific persons. In both cases, the sampling of concrete individuals, groups, or fields is not based on the usual criteria and techniques of statistical sampling. You would employ neither

random sampling nor stratification to make a sample representative. Rather, you select individuals, groups, and so on according to their (expected) level of new insights for the developing theory in relation to the state of theory elaboration so far. Sampling decisions aim at that material that promises the greatest insights, viewed in the light of the material already used, and the knowledge drawn from it.

Table 6.3: Theoretical versus Statistical Sampling

Theoretical sampling	Statistical sampling
Extension of the basic population is not known in advance	Extension of the basic population is known in advance
Features of the basic population are not known in advance	Distribution of features in the basic population can be estimated
Repeated drawing of sampling elements with criteria to be defined again in each step	One-shot drawing of a sample following a plan defined in advance
Sample size is not defined in advance	Sample size is defined in advance
Sampling is finished when theoretical saturation has been reached	Sampling is finished when the whole sample has been studied

Sampling is finished when theoretical saturation has been reached Sampling is finished when the whole sample has been studied.

6.6.3 Sampling Strategies in Qualitative Research are: Sampling strategy involves a priori determination; complete collection; theoretical sampling; extreme case sampling; typical case sampling; maximal variation sampling; intensity sampling; critical case sampling; sensitive case sampling and convenience sampling.

6.7 Selection of Locale and Entering into the Field

In a qualitative research, the researcher and the respondent (participant/actor) and communicative competencies are the main "instruments" of collecting data and of recognition. Attitudinal gap between the researcher and the actor needs to be minimal. Integrity, capability, confidentiality, and participation are to be maintained and sustained throughout the field study. The researcher has to develop his or her skill as how to inspire, inform and involve actor to get the clear picture of reality or truth.

6.7.1 Access to Institutions: The locale is the place in which the study can be undertaken. Group comprises of individuals members to be studied. These are clearly defined by the research problem to be addressed. First, there is a level of the persons responsible for authorising the research. In case of difficulties, they are held responsible for this authorisation by external authorities. Second, there is a level of those to be interviewed or observed, who will be investing their time and willingness. For an institution, research is a disturbance, and it disrupts routines, with no perceptible immediate or long-term payoff for the institution and its members. Therefore, the researcher has to make his or her request in formal terms. In the end, the researcher's request can be fitted into administrative routines and treated using institutionally familiar procedures.

6.7.2 Access to Individuals: Once you have gained access to the field or the institution in general, you will face the problem of how to reach those persons within it who are the most interesting participants. Here again, processes of negotiation, strategies of reference in the sense of snowballing, and, above all, competencies in establishing relationships play a major part.

6.7.3 Strangeness and Familiarity: Qualitative research is normally not simply interested in the exterior presentation of social groups. Rather, it is an involvement in a different world or subculture. It is essential to understand it as far as possible from inside and from its own logic. A source of knowledge in this context is to gradually take an insider's perspective – to understand the individual's view-point. Take organisational view from a member's perspective. The mediation is a key factor. The researcher has to design strategy. For example, Whyte gives detailed description of how he negotiated his access to the area he studied, and how he used his key person to find access and to get accepted by the social group. He also describes the need to keep a distance from the field to avoid becoming a member of the group and going native in the group and the field. Deviant behaviour, even as far as criminality, may be seen as a transient faulty adaptation that bears within itself both the options of adaptation and of permanent non-adaptation. (Atteslander 1996, p. XIII).

6.8 Tools for the Collection of Data

Qualitative Research cannot be conducted through static tools and techniques, because very often the researcher employing qualitative research methodology does not have a sound theoretical base related to the reality. Theory in fact is the product of enquiry. Data are created by human efforts; put more prosaically, the way in which information is collected affects the content of the data themselves; scholar who 'produce data' are complex creatures whose perceptions and communications are shaped at every turn by the context in which they find themselves; and both the content and the quality of data are prime concerns. It is in-depth analysis of contextually–bound data. It involves the subjectivity of the researcher. All qualitative research methods adhere to certain themes such as qualitative data, content sensitivity, emphatic neutrality, inductive analysis and naturalistic inquiry.

6.8.1 Tools and techniques of qualitative research are such as, Observation (participants or non-participants), Interview (focused interview, semi-standardised interview, problem-centred interview, expert interview, ethnographic interview) Triangulation, Focus Group Discussion, Reflective Dialogue, Case-diary, and Documents (primary or secondary).

6.9 Establishing Reliability and Validity: A number of leading qualitative researchers argued that reliability and validity were terms pertaining to the quantitative paradigm and were not pertinent to qualitative inquiry (Altheide and Johnson, 1998; Leininger, 1994). Some suggested adopting new criteria for determining reliability and validity, and hence ensuring rigour, in qualitative inquiry (Lincoln and Guba, 1985; Leininger, 1994; Rubin and Rubin, 1995). In seminal work in the 1980s, Guba and Lincoln substituted reliability and validity with the parallel concept of "*trustworthiness*," containing four aspects: *credibility, transferability, dependability, and confirmability*. Within these were specific methodological strategies for demonstrating qualitative rigour, such as the audit trail, member checks when coding, categorising, or confirming results with participants, peer debriefing, negative case analysis, structural corroboration, and referential material adequacy (Guba and Lincoln, 1981; Lincoln and Guba, 1985; Guba and Lincoln, 1982). Later, Guba and Lincoln developed authenticity criteria.

Thus, over the past two decades, reliability and validity have been subtly replaced by criteria and standards for evaluation of the overall significance, relevance, impact, and utility of completed research. Guba and Lincoln (1981) stated that while all research must have "truth value", "applicability", "consistency", and "neutrality" in order to be considered worthwhile. The nature of knowledge within the rationalistic (or quantitative) paradigm is different from the knowledge in naturalistic (qualitative) paradigm. Consequently, each paradigm requires paradigm-specific criteria for addressing "rigour". Accordingly, specific strategies be used to attain trustworthiness such as negative cases, peer debriefing, prolonged engagement and persistent observation, audit trails and member checks. Also important were characteristics of the investigator, who must be responsive and adaptable to changing circumstances, holistic, having processional immediacy, sensitivity, and ability for clarification and summarisation (Guba and Lincoln, 1981).

6.10 Criteria for Evaluating the Building of Theories

For evaluating the research seven criteria are suggested namely, (i) Are concepts generated? (ii) Are the concepts systematically related? (iii) Are there many conceptual linkages and are the categories well developed? (iv) Do the categories have conceptual density? (v) Is there much variation built into the theory? (vi) Are broader conditions that affect the phenomenon under study built into its explanation? Has "process" been taken into account? and (vi) Do the theoretical findings seem significant and to what extent?

6.11 Analysis of Qualitative Data

Research design should specify the nature of data and techniques for its analysis. Data analysis is most comprehensive, and the main components are: **Data reduction; Data display**; **Comparing.** It involves triangulation and Drawing and verifying conclusions. The whole phenomenon under study is understood as a complex system that is more than sum of its parts; focus on complex interdependencies and system dynamics that cannot meaningfully be reduced to a few discrete and linear, cause-effect relationships.

Further Readings

Bailey, K.D. (1987). *Methods of Social Research.* 3rd.edn.New York: Free Press.

Cozby, P. (2009). *Methods in Behavioural Research.* 10th edition, Bemont: Wadsworth.

Festinger, L. and Katz, D. (1976) (eds.). *Research Methods in the Behavioral Sciences.* New Delhi: Amerind Publishing Co.

Good, Carter V. (1966). *Essentials of Educational Research: Methodology and Design.* New York: Applleton-Century Crofts.

Goode, W.J., and Hatt, P.K. (1990). *Methods in Social Research.* New Delhi: McGraw-Hill.

Guthrie, G. (2010). *Basic Research Methods.* New Delhi: Sage.

Robert, C.B., and Sari, K.B. (2011). *Qualitative Research for Education: An Introduction to Theories and Methods.* New Delhi: PHI Learning.

Uwe Flick. (2009). *An Introduction to Qualitative Research.*

7

Hypotheses/Research Questions

7.1 Hypothesis

The hypothesis is derived from the ancient Greek term, 'hypotithenai' which means "to put under" or "to suppose".

NULL HYPOTHESIS (HO)

Null Hypothesis – the hypothesis of "no relationship or difference" is the one actually tested statistically

- Any relation or difference in the findings is due to chance or sampling error
- this supposition is put to a probability test

Stating the null hypothesis (four alternatives)

(a) There is no difference between the means of two populations from which the two samples were drawn at random;

(b) The two means in the two populations from which the samples were respectively drawn at random are equal;

(c) The mean of the sampling distribution of differences between an infinite number of pairs of means of randomly drawn samples equals zero;

(d) Any difference between two samples means drawn randomly from the respective populations is due to sampling error- i.e. such differences can readily be attributed to chance

Accepting or Rejecting the Null Hypothesis

(a) Accepting (failing to reject) the null hypothesis as true, in which case it is concluded that any difference in the results are;
   (1) not statistically significant, therefore are probably
   (2) due to sampling error or chance.

(b) Rejecting the null hypothesis as false, in which case it is concluded that the differences in the results are:
   (1) statistically significant, therefore, are probably
   (2) due to some determining factor or condition, other than chance.

Two Types of Errors

(a) Type I (Alpha) Error- to reject the null hypothesis of no difference when it is true

(b) Type II (Beta) Error- to accept the null hypothesis of no differences when it is false.

One-tailed and Two-tailed tests of the Null Hypothesis

Hypothesis is, however, a combination of two words: Hypo: means less and Thesis: means statement. 'It is a proposition which can be put to a test to determine its validity' (Goode and Hatt, 1952). 'It is shrewd guess or influence that is formulated and provisionally adopted to explain observed facts or conditions' (John W. Best, 2005).

A hypothesis is an informed or shrewd guess or inference, with a reasonable chance of being right, formulated and tentatively adopted to explain observed facts or conditions and to guide in further investigation, in other words, to serve as the investigator's "eyes" in seeking answers to questions. (Good, 2008).

Hypothesis is a tentative explanation that accounts for facts and can be tested by further investigation. A hypothesis may be precisely defined as a tentative proposition suggested as a solution to a problem or an explanation of some phenomenon (Ary, Jacobs and Razavich, 1984). Hypothesis relates theory to observation and observation to theory. A hypothesis is a conjectural statement of the relation between two or more variables. (Kerlinger, 1956). Hypothesis is a formal statement that presents the expected relationship between an independent and dependent variable (Creswell, 1994).

7.2 Hypotheses / Research Questions

Research question states what we are trying to find out answer. The hypothesis predicts, a priori, the answer to that question.

Hypothesis is used when we do have an explanation (a theory) in mind behind our hypothesis. If this is the case, we should by all means formulate hypothesis as predicted answer to research questions and test them, if not, we can ignore hypotheses and proceed with research questions, if we can not predict with any confidence, we need go no further into the matter of hypotheses.

The researcher needs to understand the differences between hypotheses, assumptions and postulates. Differences have been shown in Table 7.1.

Table 7.1: Differences between Hypotheses, Assumptions and Postulates

Hypotheses	***Assumptions***	***Postulates***
Hypotheses are tentative statements or a proposed explanation of any observable phenomenon.	Assumptions are statements of what the researcher believes to be facts but can not verify.	Postulates are propositions that are accepted as true. Postulates are fundamental propositions used to prove other statements.
The experiment will either prove the hypothesis right or wrong.	Assumptions are basically hunches or feelings is anything that is taken for granted.	Postulates are not proven, they are simply accepted at their face values. Hull's Theory of Reinforcement is based on eight postulates of behaviour of an organism.
Hypothesis provides enough evidence, to be regarded a valid theory.	Assumption can be used as premise of a particular argument but may not be otherwise accepted.	Postulate provides basis for logical reasoning. A mathematician begins by postulating a system of numbers which range from 0 to 9 and can permute and combine only thereafter.
Parametric and non-parametric tests are used to identify the significance of difference between two or more variables.	Assumption has no evidence or not enough behind it, to be regarded a valid theory.	Postulates are used to for the discovery of other facts of nature.
Hypothesis is goalpost to find answer to research questions.	Formulae of statistics and measurement are based on number of assumptions	(a) Essential to development of any intellectual discipline; (b) Assumptions that do not lend themselves to direct verification; (c) A basis for reference; (d) A foundation for erection of any theoretical structure; provide the framework for developing and testing theory; (e) Susceptible to challenge in the light of later advancement of knowledge. (Robert k. Mautz,

(Contd...)

A hypothesis is (a) a very useful aid to organising the research effort. (b) It specifically limits the enquiry to the interaction of certain variables. (c) It suggests the methods appropriate for collection, analysing and interpreting the data, and the (d) resultant confirmation or rejection of the hypothesis through empirical or experimental testing; and (e) it gives a clear indication of the extent of knowledge gained. (Walliman, 2001).	Assumption is used to simplify the Situation for logical procedure. How researchers approach research has a great deal to do with: (a) Ontological assumptions concerning the nature of social reality. (A person see social reality- as external, independent, given and objectively real, or, in stead, as socially constructed, subjectively experienced and the result of human thoughts as expressed through language (b) Assumptions concerning epistemological bases of knowledge. (knowledge is real, objective and out there in the world to be captured, researcher can observe, measure and quantify it). (c) Assumptions concerning human nature and agency..(Do people respond in mechanistic way to their environment and the things that happen to them or do they initiate action and make choices? Is their behaviour determined by innate instinctual forces or by external conditions and forces, or do they act voluntarily and out of their free will?)	

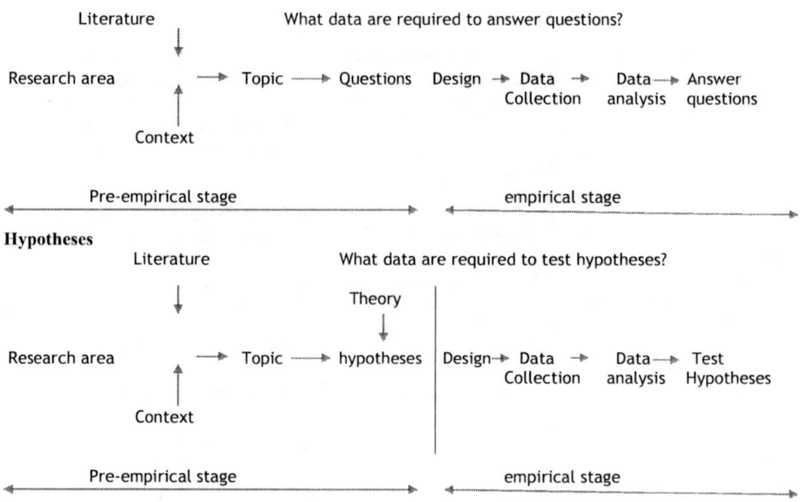

Figure 7.1: Explains difference between Research Question and Hypothesis

7.3 Sources of Hypotheses / Research Questions

Collection of factual information may be useful but alone does not lead to successful formulation of hypothesis. Deep knowledge of the area of investigation is essential for the formulation of hypothesis. Hypotheses are the products of considerable speculation, imagination, creative and divergent thinking. The research has to explore the various sources of knowledge and resort to extensive and intensive study of specific area before formulation of hypotheses for study. If a scholar is interested in theoretical research or testing of theory he should go for deductive reasoning for the formulation of hypothesis. On the other hand if a scholar is interested in field study or developing theory in the field, he should employ inductive reasoning for the formulation of research questions.

7.3.1 Richness of background knowledge of the specific area of investigation which is to be undertaken by the researcher is essential for the formulation of hypothesis. One finds limitless knowledge in almost any area of human pursuit which has accumulated in the form of literature as a result of painstaking efforts of past generations. Treasure of past researches, thus, needs to be explored to get knowledge of the specific area. The researcher should encapsulate, modify and develop hypothesis through interaction with the world of knowledge in area of his or her study. It would help the researcher to get insight into the matrix of relationships already established and what other relational variables are needed to be explored.

7.3.2 Interaction with Experts: We may find that there are specialists or experts who have already conducted researches on the specific areas of your choice. They have rich and varied experience. The researcher may approach the experts to seek their advice for the formulation of specific and researchable hypotheses/research questions. Researchers try outing different ideas and linguistic formulations- all entailing a question and discussing them with experts as a means of clarifying their thoughts and identifying weaknesses in their formulations. A well designed specific hypothesis / research question can be carved out in consultation with expert that may be helpful in the conduct of study.

7.3.3 Personal Field Experience: Formulation of hypothesis/ research questions is experiential and a creative process. Rich and varied experience enables researcher to formulate adequate and researchable hypothesis. The researcher has to invent new ideas, arguments, and conjectures. Weak and ill-conceived hypotheses can be subsequently reframed through critical and creative thinking to suit the purpose of the study. Researcher seeks to challenge expectation through the formulation and testing of hypothesis. Being critical about ideas in which we have a vested interest is not always easy. But, in wider sense, researchers have the responsibility to search for error, to find out where theories are false, where arguments are invalid, and in what respects policies and practices have undesirable consequences. This would provide rich materials for the formulation of good and testable hypothesis. For example, a classroom teacher observes unrecognised mismatch between expectation and experience (actual or anticipated) that has far reaching practical or theoretical implications. On the basis of his experience and his knowledge, the researcher may inductively formulate hypotheses that attempt to explore the field for improving the learning outcomes.

7.3.4 Versatility of intellect: Hypotheses are also derived through deductive reasoning from a theory. A researcher may begin a study by selecting one of the theories in his own area of interest. After selecting the particular theory, the researcher proceeds to deduce a hypothesis from the theory through symbolic logic or mathematics. This is possible only when the researcher has a versatile intellect and can make use of it for restructuring his experiences. Considerable time and efforts are needed in formulation and refining of hypothesis. In addition to a versatile intellect, researcher should also be analytical so as to formulate adequate hypothesis.

7.3.5 Analogy and other practices: Reasoning by analogy generally is considered unacceptable as a source of proof, but it is a very fertile source of hypothesis. The premise is that if two situations are alike in certain aspects relevant from the standpoint of the problem under consideration, they are probably similar in other relevant aspects. It is assumed that the existence of similarities between two situations is not accidental, that it is the result of the operation of some law common to the two situations. The insights that analogy provide are useful as much as they lead to their own refinement and verification through the acquisition of relevant data and the formulation of more adequate hypothesis.

7.4 Importance of Hypothesis / Research Question

- It has become an important tool for working out the plan of action to achieve the objectives of the study. With increasing use, the strengths of hypothesis have become more apparent. A well thought out set of hypotheses place clear and specific goals before the researcher. Researcher can not build his research thesis on a weak foundation of hypotheses.
- Hypothesis activates or stimulates exploration. Karl Popper (1992) argued, "We have inborn expectations; we have latent inborn knowledge, in the form of latent expectations, to be activated by the stimuli to which we react as a rule while engaged in active exploration."
- Hypotheses provide direction to research. A hypothesis serves as powerful beacon those lights the way for the research work. It provides the roadmap that expedites the exploration of the phenomena under consideration.
- Hypotheses sensitise the investigation to certain aspects i.e. what is fruitful? What is fruitless? A hypothesis, therefore, provides criteria for evaluating research techniques, and organising principles.
- Hypotheses are means by which investigator can understand with greater clarity his problem, and its ramifications. It provides him sources of research methodology and procedures to meet the goals.
- Hypothesis enables the researcher to relate logically known facts to intelligent guesses about unknown conditions. It explains what is needed to be done? How is to be done? and what are expected outcomes of research study?
- Hypotheses are framework for the conclusions of the study. Hypotheses, thus, formulated before the conduct of study are tested one by one on the bases of data evidences (quantitative or qualitative) to arrive at logical conclusions whether they are confirmed or rejected

Further Reading

Campbell, J.P., Daft, R.L., and Hulin, C.L.(1982). *What to Study: Generating and Developing Research Questions.* Beverly Hills, CA: Sage.

Charters, W.W.jr. (1967). Hypothesis in scientific research. Unpublished paper. University of Oregon, Eugene, OR.

Chaters, W.M.(1997). Hypothesis in scientific research. Unpublished paper. University of Oregon, Eugene, OR.

Good, Carter V.(2008). *Introduction to Educational Research.* Second Edition. Surjeet publications, Delhi -7.

Charters, W.W.jr. (1967). Hypothesis in scientific research. Unpublished paper. University of Oregon, Eugene, OR.

Goethals, George W.(1958). A Framework for educational Research. Harvard Educational Review 28, 29-43.

Kothari, C.R.(2011). *Research Methodology: Methods and Techniques.* New Delhi: New Age International Publishers.

Koul, L. (2009). *Methodology of Educational Research.* New Delhi: Vikas Publications.

Travers, R.M.W.(1958). *An Introduction to Educational Research.* New York: The Mcmillan Co.

Van Dalen, Deobold B. (1962*). Understanding Educational Research.* An Introduction. New York: McGraw-Hill Book Co.

8

Sampling Procedures

8.1 What is Sampling?

It is not possible to gather information from everyone or everything of a population. The primary purpose of research is to discover principles that have universal application. But study of whole population would be impracticable if not impossible. Some populations are so large that their characteristics cannot be measured, before the measurement could be completed, the population would have changed. For example, it is very difficult to conduct a reading experiment of fifth grade students in English subject of private and government schools in India. In this study, a large number of manpower would be required. A lot of cost would be involved. Researchers and students working hours would also be required in the conduct of such a huge experiment. Time, money manpower involved in complete enumeration is very, very high. The goal of finding a representative sample (or subset) of population, therefore, becomes necessity. Hence, a small proportion of a population called sample is selected for observation and analysis. In other words, a finite part of a statistical population is selected whose properties are studied to gain information about the whole (Webster, 1085).

Sampling is, therefore, is a process concerned with the selection of a relatively small portion of population to draw valid inferences or generalisation on the basis of careful observation and analysis. However, a measured value based upon sample is a ***statistic.*** A population value inferred from a statistic is a ***parameter.***

8.2 Sampling Methods in Qualitative Research

8.2.1 Non-probability Sampling

Non-probability sampling is any sampling method where some elements of the population have *no* chance of selection (these are sometimes referred to as 'out of coverage'/'under covered'), or where the probability of selection can't be accurately determined. It involves the selection of elements based on assumptions regarding the population of interest, which forms the criteria for selection. Hence, because the selection of elements is non-random, non-probability sampling does not allow the estimation of sampling errors. These conditions place limits on how much information a sample can provide about the population. Information about the relationship between sample and population is limited, making it difficult to extrapolate from the sample to the population. In non-probability sampling the units of population are selected at the discretion of the researcher.

Key points

In qualitative research, sampling is a very important step:

- Sampling decisions (who or which group next?) are often taken during and as a result of data collection and analysis.
- Sampling decisions in qualitative research are often taken on a substantial, concrete level rather than on an abstract and formal level: they may be based on purposeful decisions for a specific case rather than random sampling.
- In sampling, you will construct the cases you study in your research.

Non-probability Sampling includes: Convenience Sampling, Quota Sampling, Purposive Sampling, Judgment Sampling, and Snowball Sampling.

8.2.2 Purposive Sampling: Purposive sampling targets a particular group of people. When the desired population for the study is rare or very difficult to locate, purposive sampling may be the only option. For example, you are interested in studying cognitive processing speed of young adults who have suffered head injury in automobile accidents. This would be a difficult to find out such population. The major problem with purposive sampling is that the type of people required for study may be different from those in the population who can't be located easily and this might introduce a source of bias. Similarly, purposive sampling technique is used in the study of mentally retarded children.

Patton (2002) contrasts random sampling in general with purposive sampling and makes some concrete suggestions:

- One is to integrate purposively extreme or deviant cases. In order to study the functioning of a reform programme, particularly successful examples of realising it are chosen and analysed.
- Another suggestion is to select particularly typical cases (i.e., those cases in which success and failure are particularly typical for the average or the majority of the cases). Here the field is disclosed from inside and from its centre.
- A further suggestion aims at the maximal variation in the sample-to integrate only a few cases, but those which are as different as possible, to disclose the range of variation and differentiation in the field.
- Additionally, cases may be selected according to the intensity with which the interesting features, processes, experiences, and so on are given or assumed in them. Either cases with the greatest intensity are chosen or cases with different intensities are systematically integrated and compared.
- The selection of critical cases aims at those cases in which the relations to be studied become especially clear (e.g., in the opinion of experts in the field) or which are particularly important for the functioning of a programme to be evaluated.
- It may be appropriate to select a politically important or sensitive case in order to present positive findings in evaluation most effectively, which is an argument for integrating them. However, where these may endanger the programme as a whole, due to their explosive force, they should rather be excluded.

- Finally, Patton mentions the criterion of convenience, which refers to the selection of those cases that are the easiest to access under given conditions. This may simply be to reduce the effort. However, from time to time it may be the only way to do an evaluation with limited resources of time and people.

Morse (1998, p.73) defines several general criteria for a "good informant." These may serve more generally as criteria for selecting meaningful cases. They should have the necessary knowledge and experience of the issue or object at their disposal for answering the questions in the interview or –in observational studies-for performing the actions of interest. They should also have the capability to reflect and articulate, should have time to be asked, and should be ready to participate in the study. If all these conditions are fulfilled, this case is most likely to be integrated into the study.

8.2.3 Convenience sampling. It is also known as **grab** or **opportunity sampling**. Convenience sampling is a type of non-probability sampling which involves thc sample being drawn from that part of the population which is close to hand or it is readily available and convenient. The researcher using such a sample cannot scientifically make generalisations about the total population from this sample because it would not be representative enough. For example, if the interviewer is suppose s to conduct such a survey at a shopping centre early in the morning on a given day, the people that he/she could interview would be limited to those available at that given time. However, this would not represent the views of other non-available members. This type of sampling is most useful for pilot testing.

Several important considerations for researchers using convenience samples include:

- Variables of controls are to be within the research design. Convenience sample is to be made more representative of the population through cross-checks and comparison.
- The researcher should have good reasons or evidences to believe that a particular convenience sample would respond or behave differently than a random sample from the same population.

- The researcher needs to ensure that the research questions being asked are to be answered appropriately and adequately using a convenience sample.

Quota sampling: In quota sampling, the population is first segmented into mutually exclusive sub-groups, just as in stratified sampling. Then judgment is used to select the subjects or units from each segment based on a specified proportion. For example, an interviewer may be told to sample 200 females and 300 males between the age of 45 and 60. Let percentage of males and females between the age of 45 and 60 is 25 per cent and 20 per cent respectively. The sample size of males will be 50 and 60 for females. (i.e. 0.25n for males and 0.20n for females).

In quota sampling the selection of the sample is non-random. For example, interviewers might be tempted to interview those who look most helpful. The problem is that these samples may be biased because not everyone gets a chance of selection. This random element is its greatest weakness and quota versus probability has been a matter of controversy for many years.

8.2.4 Judgment Sampling: The judgment sampling is non-probability sampling in which the sampling units are selected on the advice of some experts or by the institution or opinion of the researcher himself. Steps involved in the selection of sampling units are:

- In the first case, an expert who is familiar with the sampling frame guides the researcher in selecting the sampling units from the sampling frame.
- In the second case, researcher applies his or her intuitive judgment and previous experience in selecting the sampling units.

In this sampling method, there is more chance of biases. If the exercise is done more seriously, it would lead to better results. This sampling is also called purposive sampling when sampling units are identified from the population selectively. This sampling technique is applied for sampling the population related to the events in which the members of the population are not equally qualified to become the member of the sampling frame and hence the members of the sample. For instance, people living below poverty line and their educational problems. It may be the sampling of the visually impaired children.

8.2.5 Snowball Sampling: The snowball sampling is a restrictive multi-stage sampling in which initially certain numbers of sampling units (respondents) are randomly selected. Later, additional sampling units are selected based on referral process. This means that the initially selected respondents provide addresses of additional respondents for the interviewers.

Initial respondents may be randomly selected, for example, from the information contained in telephone directories. Similarly, students are identified randomly from the classroom attendance register, and additional students are included on the basis of information from the already selected sample. This is an inexpensive and convenient non-probability sampling method which suits the situations where the development of sampling frame is difficult and time-consuming task.

8.2.6 Complete Collection: The sampling is limited in the advance by certain criteria: for instance, a specific disease, a specific age, a specific case. These criteria delimit the totality of possible case in such a way that all the case may be integrated in thc study. But here, as, well, sampling is carried out because virtual cases which do not meet one or more of these criteria are excluded in advance. It is possible to use such method of sampling mainly in regional studies. In research designs using a prior definition of the sample structure, you take sampling decision with a view to selecting case or group of case.

8.2.7 Case Constitution in the Sample

What is the case that is to be considered in a sample and, more concretely, what this case represents? The case is treated as a case. Sampling as well as collecting and interpreting of data proceed as a sequence of case studies. Each case is unique, for instance:

- The case represents itself. According to Hildenbrand, the "single case dialectically can be understood as an individualised universal". This socialisation has led to different, subjective opinions, attitudes, and viewpoints, which can be found in the actual interview situation.
- The case represents a specific institutional context in which the individual acts and which he or she also has to represent to others.
- The case represents a specific professionalisation (as doctor, psychologist, social worker, information engineer, etc.), which

he or she has attained and which is represented in his/her concepts and ways of acting.

- The case represents a developed subjectivity as a result of acquiring certain stocks of knowledge and of evolving specific ways of acting and perceiving.
- The case represents an interactively made and make-able context of activity (e.g., counseling, developing technology).

8.3 Gradual Definition of the Sample Structure: Theoretical Sampling

Gradual strategies of sampling are mostly based on theoretical sampling developed by Glaser and Strauss (1967). Decisions about choosing and putting together empirical material (cases, groups, institutions, etc.) are made in the process of collecting and interpreting data. Glaser and Strauss describe this strategy as follows:

Theoretical sampling is the process of data collection for generating theory whereby the analyst jointly collects, codes, and analyses his data and decides what data to collect next and where to find them, in order to develop his theory as it emerges. This process of data collection is controlled by the emerging theory.

Table 8.1: Theoretical Sampling verses Statistical Sampling

Theoretical sampling	Statistical sampling
Extension of the basic population is not known in advance	Extension of the basic population is known in advance
Features of the basic population are not known in advance	Distribution of features in the basic population can be estimated
Repeated drawing of sampling elements with criteria to be defined again in each step	One-shot drawing of a sample following a plan defined in advance
Sample size is not defined in advance	Sample size is defined in advance
Sampling is finished when theoretical saturation has been reached	Sampling is finished when the whole sample has been studied

Sampling decisions in theoretical sampling may start from either of two levels: they may be made on the level of the groups to be compared or they may directly focus on specific persons. In both cases, the sampling of concrete individuals, groups, or fields is not based on the usual criteria and techniques of statistical sampling. You would employ neither random sampling nor stratification to make a sample representative. Rather, you select individuals, groups, and so on according to their (expected) level of new insights for the developing theory in relation to the state of theory elaboration so far. Sampling decisions aim at that material that promises the greatest insights, viewed in the light of the material already used, and the knowledge drawn from it.

References

Aggarwal, Y.P. (1988). Better sampling- concepts, techniques and Evaluation. New Delhi: Sterling Publications.

Best, J. and Kahn, J. (2009). *Research in Education.* 10th edition, Needham Heights: Allyn and Bacon.

Chaudary, A. and Stenger, H. (1992). Survey Sampling: Theory and Methods. New York: Marcel Dekker.

Cochran, WG. (1984). Sampling Techniques. New Delhi: Wiley Eastern.

Deming, W. E. (1960). Sample Design in Business Research. New York: John Wiley and Sons.

Hennerson, M.E., Morris, E.E. and Fitz-Gubbon, C.T.(1988). How to Measure Attitudes. New Delhi: Sage.

Kothari, C.R. (2004). Research Methodology: Methods and Techniques. New Delhi: New Age International Publishers.

Koul, L. (2009). *Methodology of Educational Research.* Vikas Publishing House, New Delhi-14.

Panneersevam, R. (2004). Research Methodology. New Delhi: Prentice-Hall of India.

Plutchik, R. (1968). Foundations of Experimental Research. New York: Harper and Row.

UNIT - 3

QUALITATIVE TECHNIQUES

9

Qualitative Tools and Techniques

"Unless you gather the right data, there is no way you can fully answer your research problem and objectives" (Polonsky and Waller, 2010).

Tools for Data Gathering

Data gathering is an indispensable part of research process. The choice of tool affects the research activities. Appropriate tool for the gathering of data puts the researcher on right track to get answer to research questions. Research analysis, results or evidence, prediction and conclusions are based on data. Therefore, good data produces good results. Need arises that the tools for the collection of data should be reliable, valid, appropriate, substantial (error free), flexible, cost effective, time bond, and simplified (understandable to participants). Main tools for gathering data are discussed herein - Focus Group Discussion, 0bservation (participant and non-participant), Interview, Documents, Diary and Audio-Visual (films, video, and photograph).

Focus Group Discussion

9.1 What is Focus Group Discussion?

A small number of individuals, brought together for discussion and acts as resource group to probe and provide insight into seeking answer to research question. Unlike group interview, the group discussion stimulates a discussion and uses its dynamics of developing conversation in the discussion as the central source of knowledge. Group discussion corresponds to the way in which opinions are produced, expressed and exchanged in everyday life (Flick, 2010). Group discussion is the analysis of common processes of problem solving in the group. Therefore, a concrete problem is introduced and alternatives are explored or discovered through discussion. Through group discussion, the best strategy is evolved for solving the problem. Mangold (1973) takes the group opinion as an empirical issue, which is expressed in the discussion but exists independently of the situation and applies for the group outside the situation. The hallmark of focus group is the explicit use of group interaction to produce data and insights that would be less accessible without the interaction found in a group (Morgan, 1988, p. 12).

A small number of individuals, brought together as a discussion or resource group, is more valuable many times over than any representative sample. Such a group, discussing collectively their sphere of life and probing into it as they meet one another's disagreements, will do more to lift the veils covering the sphere of life than any other device that I know of. (1969, p. 41). Focus group is useful for: (a) orientating oneself to a new field; (b) generating hypotheses based on informants' insights; (c) evaluating different research sites or study populations; (d) developing interview schedules and questionnaires; (e) identifying indicators of achievement/ development; and (f) getting participants' interpretations of results from earlier studies.

First, members of the focus group generate discussion on the specific topic or theme. In the free, fair and natural setting meaningful data is produced. Second, focus groups generate diversity and difference, either within or between groups. What Billig (1987) has called the dilemmatic nature of everyday arguments.(Lunt and Livingstone, 1996, p. 96).

9.2 Selection of Group

Group is a unit of members for the collection and analysis of data. Group may comprise of members of Gram-Panchayat or Village Welfare Committee or Members of an organisation, or a group of stakeholders. Group may be homogenous or heterogeneous.

Homogeneous Group members are comparable in the essential dimensions related to research question and have a similar background. For instance, a group of women of same age in relation to research question 'empowerment', or a group of students having same age and class in relation to research question 'learning mathematics'. In heterogeneous group, members should be different in the characteristics that are relevant for research question. For instance, a group of boys and girls of seventh class related to research question 'learning difficulty in mathematics' or empowerment of various marginalised sections of society or a group of stakeholders in relation to research question 'welfare of SC/ST/OBC'.

Selection of Groups is based upon purposive or incidental sampling technique. Random Sampling Technique can be used in case the members of a group are fifteen or more than fifteen or unmanageable. Make group integrated by giving representation specifically to the marginalised section of the society.

9.3 Processes of Focus Group Discussions

The following processes are involved in the Focus Group Discussion (FGD)

- The first step in FGD generally involves introducing members and fostering interest and commitment to participate.
- At the beginning, an explanation of the (formal) procedure is given. Here the expectations of the participants are formulated. Participants are to be involved in the discussion, perhaps to argue certain topics, to manage a common task or to solve a problem together.
- Identification of domains by the Group for discussion and laying down the procedures for free and frank discussions are to be chalked out.
- Actual discussion starts with 'discussion stimulus' i.e., providing space for the exchange of past and present experiences by the members of the group so as to get expected answers to research questions. This may consist of a provocative thesis, a short film, a lecture on a text, or the unfolding of a concrete problem for which a solution is to be found.
- Provide opportunity to participant group and individual members to make choice regarding: Selection of Locale;

Selection of Problem; Identification of Research Questions; Selection of Social Setting and Selection of methodology.

- Comparison and Control are fundamental in the process of Focus Group Discussions. Formal direction is limited to control of the agenda of the speakers. Natural setting for discussion at the beginning and logical end of the discussion need to be ensured. The choices of individuals within those collectivities need to be picked up for implicit and explicit comparisons. At the same time, control is very important that the participants do not drift into just chatting or presenting endless anecdotes with little reference to the issue of the focus group and the study.
- Another possibility is the use of texts, images, and so on to further stimulate the discussion or topics dealt with during the discussion. However, these interventions should only support the dynamics and the functioning of the group.
- Parameters of evaluation of development programme, welfare schemes, and socio-economic-political empowerment need to be discussed and identified by the participants group.
- Procedures for identification of significant change have to be defined by the group. Moreover, the group has to decide the Most Significant Change.

9.4 Limitations

It is hardly possible to design relatively common conditions for the collection of data in different groups involved in a study. The researcher cannot predict sudden turn of the discussion into inappropriate narrations. Thus, it remains difficult to handle the problem because of the dynamics of the situation and the group; individual members may dominate while others may refrain from entering into the discussion. Sometimes the participants do drift into just chatting or presenting endless anecdotes with little reference to the issue of the focus group and the study.

9.5 Selection of Locale

The locale is the place in which the study can be undertaken. Group comprises of individuals members to be studied. These are clearly defined by the research problem to be addressed. For instance, to identify people below poverty line, the researcher has to identify the specific place and specific group where he can get response to research questions. A particular intervention, the researcher intends to introduce to empower them, applies to specific people in specific a place. However, questions may arise about the best comparator groups or exactly how to design the work, but the people and the place are determined from the start.

9.6 Selection of Techniques

9.6.1 Technique-1: Developing a Story through Play

The participants, for instance, are asked to develop a story of their social mobility or empowerment. Each group is asked to prepare three scenes: the first illustrating life before association with the regards to the theme/themes; the scene second illustrating the current situation, and the third one depicting their aspirations for the near future. Apart from this framework, the groups are given no other guidance, hints, or input: anything from investigator. The intention is to enable the groups to express themselves freely and spontaneously. Data generated through this process is analysed by the participants to identify the change and to evolve future strategy.

9.6.2 Technique-2: Open House Focus Group Discussion

Two or more themes specific to the phenomenon under study are identified by the members of the group. Research questions on the specific theme/ themes are designed by the participants (members) of the group. These questions are discussed by the participants. It is to be ensured that each participant must take part in the group discussion. At the same time, control is very important that the participants do not drift into just chatting or presenting endless anecdotes with little reference to the issue of the focus group and the study. They are free to speak out from their mind.

- The group members present their real observation before joining the movement. Research questions are: gender discrimination, confinement of girl child to home, to help the mother with the chores, or does work in the house of the rich in order to be fed, preferential treatment to male child, domestic violence or do tender children engaged in unorganised sector to supplement their family income, taboo on girl child education.

- The group members discuss the present scenario. Research questions are discussed to identify changes in relation to near past- gender equality and empowerment, education of girl child, , treatment to girl via-à-vis male child, domestic violence on women, preferential treatment to male child, opportunities for girls and boys to shape their future.
- The group members chalk out the future plan of action regarding Research questions are: gender equality and empowerment, education of girl child, equal treatment to girl and male child, family cohesiveness and reduction of domestic violence, preferential treatment to girl child, open opportunities for girl shape their future.

Group views as a unit and as well social negotiations of individual views have been essential element of the social constructionist theoretical approach to reality.

9.6.3 Technique-3: Online Focus Group Discussion

There are two types of group namely, synchronous (real-time) and asynchronous (non-real-time). The first type of online focus group requires that all participants are online at the same time and may take part in a chat room or by using specific conferencing software. The number of participants in real-time focus groups should be limited because too many participants might make the discussion in the group too fast and superficial, whereas you can manage this problem more easily in asynchronous groups. In second type, participants are not online at the same time. All participants need to have software on their computers to load it onto their computers. As in an e-mail interview; people can take their time to respond to entries by the other participants (or to your questions or stimulus). The interventions by every participant will be addressed to a conference site and stored in a folder to which all participants have access. This type of focus group has its advantages when people from different time zones participate or when people vary in their speed of typing or responding, which might produce differences in the chance to articulate in the group. For example, it is important that the participants can take part in the discussions from their computers at home or at their workplace and not from a special research site.

It is important that you choose a topic for the discussion that is relevant for the group and participants in your study, so that it is attractive for them to join the group and the discussion. Or, the other way around, it is important that you find groups for whom your topic is relevant in order to have fruitful discussions and interesting data. Sampling will be purposive sampling. Online focus groups can be analysed quite easily by coding and categorisation, whereas hermeneutic approaches have to be adapted to these sorts of data.

9.7 Analysis of Data

9.7.1 Qualitative Analysis: Groups data are compiled. The results derived from the discussions/data are compared between the groups. Similarity and differences of the groups are identified, aggregated, processed and analysed to get the pattern and evidence of change or empowerment. The data are categorised and weighted to enable trends.

9.7.2 Quantitative Analysis: Qualitative information is quantified by assigning numerical values based on the number of fully realised empowerment statements. An overall Group Development Index (GDI) is calculated that combines information from the individuals and their groups on specific phenomenon (social mobility or empowerment). This is a composite numerical score which usefully accommodates multiple largely qualitative indicators. Thus, GDIs are calculated for each group, and in several successive years. Group GDIs are also aggregated by age of group, geographic area, gender, or other variables. This information provides insights into the effectiveness of different elements of the support programme. Not only do the GDI provide information about the pace and quality of development of groups (process), but is also provided a means of continuous impact.

9.8 Criteria for Selecting Significant Change

There are several ways of reaching a decision about the Most Significant Change (MSC).

- **Majority rules**: A simple way of coming to a decision is to read the stories, make sure everyone understands them, and then vote by show of hands.
- **Iterative Voting**: In iterative voting, after the first vote, people discuss why they voted as they did. This is followed by a

second and then a third vote, ideally with some movement towards consensus.

- **Scoring:** Instead of voting, participants can rate the value of a SC story. The ratings for each of the stories are then aggregated and the story with the highest rating is selected as the most significant.
- **Pre-scoring then a group vote**: This method is suitable for groups who are short of meeting time. Prior to the meeting, participants are asked to read SC stories and rate their significance. These ratings are summarised in a table and presented to the participants when they meet face-to-face. Participants discuss the scores and cast their votes.
- **Secret ballot:** Each person writes his/her choice of SC story on a slip of paper, and then the total votes are presented. This should be followed by an open discussion of the reasons for the choices.

References

Barbour, R.(2007). *Doing Focus Groups*. London: Sage.

Lunt, P. and Livingstone, S. (1990). Rethinking the Focus Group in Media and Communications Research. *Journal of Communication*, 46: 79-98.

Morgan, D.L.(1988). Focus group as qualitative research.Newbury Park, CA: Sage.

Morgan, D.L. and Krueger, R.A. (eds.) (1998). *The Focus Group Kit* (6 vols.). Thousand Oaks, CA: Sage.

Ponosky, M.J., and Waller, D.S. (2010). *Designing and Managing a Research Project: A Business Student's Guide*. New Delhi (India): SAGE publications.

Puchta, C. and Potter, J.(2004). *Focus Group Practice*. London: Sage.

Stewart, D.W., and Shamdasani, P.N. (1990). *Focus groups: Theory and practice*. Newbury Park, CA: Sage.

Waller, S.C., and Romney, A.K. (1988). Systematic data collection. Newbury Park, CA: Sage.

10

Observation as a Research Tool

10.1 Observation

From the earliest history of scientific activity, observation has generally been used a method of inquiry. The accumulated knowledge of biologists, physicists, astronomers and other natural scientists is built upon centuries of systematic observation. Most of such studies were conducted in their natural surrounding rather than in the laboratory. Observation as a research tool in the psychology and the social areas came into prominence during the last century. Marked progress has been observed in educational studies during the second quarter of the century. However, observation continues to characterise all research: experimental, descriptive and qualitative. Among the factors favourable to the wider use of observation as an investigational tool has been the demand of the newer and progressive researchers. Purpose has been to probe deeply the various aspects of learner's behaviour not accessible to the conventional paper-pencil-test, interview or laboratory technique. Establishment of centres for research in child development gave rise to studying children in their natural situation.

In experimental or laboratory research, systematic observations are made. In order to get precise results of the observation, the investigation is done under carefully arranged and controlled conditions. But many important aspects of human behaviours cannot be observed under controlled conditions. Researches in social sciences and education are conducted under less rigid control and more under natural conditions to understand the behaviour of the learner.

In descriptive research, direct observation is used as a data gathering device. Certain information can best be obtained through direct observation by the researcher. For instance, observation of infrastructure- classroom, seating capacity, ventilation, furniture, teaching and learning aids is relatively easy classify, measure. or count. But when the process involves the study of a human subject in action, it is much more complex.

In qualitative research, social scientists are literally surrounded by their subject matter. They have to open their eyes and observe their fellow men and women, and the institutions and societies they have created, in action (Kalton, 1977). Besides subject matter, method must be suitable for investigating the problem in which the social scientist is interested; it must be appropriate to the population and samples he wishes to study; and it should be reasonably reliable and authentic. However, observation needs to be 'accurate watching and noting of phenomena as they occur in nature with regard to cause and effect or mutual relations.

Observation as a research technique, in order to be most reliable and valid tool for data gathering, must be systematic, directed by a specific purpose, carefully focused, and thoroughly recorded. Because human behaviour is complex and many important traits and characteristics are difficult or impossible to observe directly, they must be carefully defined in precise operational form. Operational definition helps in measuring those traits and characteristics objectively. Instruments such as stopwatches, mechanical counters, audio and videotape recorders, note-book computers and other devices make possible observations that are more precise and meaningful. In brief:

- Information required is obtained directly, rather than through the reports of others; in the case of behaviour one finds out what the individual does, rather than what he says he does.
- Observation as a research tool is used in understanding, prediction, and modification of human behaviour. If future conditions can be simulated on a sample basis, the behaviour

of the sample may provide a good indicator of understanding learner's behaviour.

- It is to observe the behaviour of person in appropriate natural situations.
- Observation is conducted purposively, systematically, carefully focused and thoroughly recorded to get reliable and valid results.
- For accuracy in measuring and recording, variables are operationally defined. Tools such as check-list, score-card or some other inquiry forms are utilised along with cameras and tape-recorder.

10.2 Issues Regarding Observations

- **Deciding who is to be studied and in what situations:** The researcher first has to decide on the type of individual to study, for instant, special children, adolescents, or children at different levels of education, or children with different socio-economic status, etc. If school children are selected, then the observations might occur inside a classroom, or on playing field. They are needed to be observed in their natural settings.
- **Formal Groups, Informal Groups or Occasional Groups:** There are different kinds of group one can study. A formal group is stable, with the same people serving as nucleus, such as a class, a family, a team, etc. Formal Groups are aware about the rules, procedures, boundaries and limitations. Informal group do not meet regularly. An occasional group consists of who might come together on certain specific function. All types of groups have their specific objectives, problems, and mode of operation. The researcher might look for different things in each.
- **Gaining Access:** If studies are conducted in schools, gaining access is often difficult. In the current scenario, many schools officials are reluctant to let outsiders enter the schools. The researcher has to submit detail plans outlining what he wants to do and how much time he will take doing it. The researcher has to seek prior permission for the classroom observations.
- **What to study:** There are numerous aspects, traits, characteristics which can be observed, but it is not desirable

to study each and every aspects. Identify the most significant and meaningful variables specific to your study.

- **Frequency and length of time:** Frequency and length of observation depends upon the nature of the study. Time involved in observation should be reasonable and may not tantamount to undue interference in the regular class-work. If the research study is of intensive nature and requires more than one sitting, it is suggested that each session should not be more than 30 minutes duration.

Researcher has to decide as per prevailing situation whether to go for participant or non-participant observation in order to get more reliable and valid results.

10.3. Participant Observation

In participant observation, the observer becomes a member of the group which is to be observed. In this process, he has to be an attentive listener, and an eager learner. He has to spin and reel at the same time i.e., simultaneously interacting, registering, observing, recording and interpreting behaviour of the group. The observer gets the feel of what the various activities of a group mean to the members. Researcher tries to understand the frame of reference of the group he is investigating, primarily, by joining the members in their daily activities in order to experience things as they do. The observer does not rely on intuition. This process of observation has built-in validity.

The social scientist observes the life of community as a whole, the relationship between its members and its activities and institutions. The community may be as small as family or as large as a city. It may be a 'closed' community, like a family or a tribe, or an 'open' one, such as a factory, a town or a village. An important difference between the two is that in the 'open' community, observation can sometimes remain unnoticed, while in 'closed' this is not possible.

The observer's task is to place himself in the best position for getting complete and unbiased picture of the life of the community, and this at once raises the question; what is the best role for the observer to adopt in the community. The successful utilisation of observation method calls for:

- The observer should be skilled and experienced and be fully aware of the risks of getting a biased and unrepresentative picture.

- The observer should ensure that the behaviour of the participant may not become self-conscious and untypical.
- The observer should have prolonged stay in the community to have authentic and trustworthy inquiry.
- Lastly, the materials obtained by observation should be supported wherever necessary by other methods.

Participation observation is commonly used in an exploratory way, at least in the initial stage. Becker (1958) distinguished three stages in the field work:

- The first being the selection and definition of problems, concepts, and indices. The participant observer's early observations help to develop his ideas on these subjects.
- The second stage involves checking of the numerous preliminary ideas which are worth pursuing. This is done by collecting further data to check on the frequency and distribution of phenomena in the community.
- The third stage of fieldwork consists of attempting to incorporate the individual findings into a model of the social system under study.
- After the fieldwork, the final systematic analysis, checking the models and rebuilding them if necessary, is conducted.
- An important feature of the procedure is its sequential nature, the observer beginning with speculations suggested by observation and developing his ideas until he can try to build a general model.

Participant observation is a somewhat individual method. One cannot expect it to yield a completely faithful and objective picture, nor suppose that several observers studying the same situation would bring back identical pictures. (Paddock, 1961).

Participant observation will be defined as a field strategy that simultaneously combines document analysis, interviewing of respondents and informants, direct participation and observation, and introspection.

- Seven features of participant observation listed by Jorgensen (1989): a special interest is evoked in human interaction. Especially as viewed from the perspective of people who are insiders or members of particular situations and settings;
- location in the here and now of everyday life situations and settings as the foundation of inquiry and method;
- a form of theory and theorising stressing interpretation and understanding of human existence;
- a logic and process of inquiry that is open-ended, flexible, opportunistic, and requires constant redefinition of what is problematic, based on facts gathered in concrete settings of human existence;
- an in-depth, qualitative, case study approach and design;
- the performance of a participant role or roles that involves establishing and maintaining relationships with natives in the field; and
- the use of direct observation along with other methods of gathering information.

10.4.1 What are the Phases of Participant Observation?

Participant observation should be understood as a process in two respects. First, the researcher should increasingly become a participant and gain access to the field and to persons. Second, the observation should also move through a process of becoming increasingly concrete and concentrate on the aspects that are essential for the research questions. Thus, Spradley (1980, p. 34) distinguishes three phases of participant observation:

- descriptive observation, at the beginning, serves to provide the researcher with an orientation to the field under study. It provides nonspecific descriptions and is used to grasp the complexity of the field as far as possible and to develop (at the same time) more concrete research questions and lines of vision;
- focused observation narrows your perspective on those processes and problems, which are most essential for your research question;

- selective observations, towards the end of the data collection, is focused on finding further evidence and examples for the types of practices and processes found in the second step.

10.4.2 What are the Problems in Conducting the Method?

One problem is how to delimit or select observational situations in which the problem under study becomes really "visible." According to Spradley (1980) social situations generally may be described along nine dimensions for observational purposes:

- **space:** the physical place or places
- **actor:** the people involved
- **activity:** a set of related acts people do
- **object:** the physical things that are present
- **act:** single actions that people do
- **event:** a set of related activities that people carry out
- **time:** the sequencing that takes place over time
- **goal:** the things people are trying to accomplish
- **feeling:** the emotions felt and expressed.

10.5 Non-Participant Observation

In process of observation, researcher or observer is not a part of the group under study. Observer takes position outside where his or her presence is least observed. He is surreptitious or unobtrusive observer. If one observes in cyberspace, the observer is completely unknown or unnoticed. This method is mostly used in observing infants, children and abnormal persons. Validity increases by keeping the setting as natural as possible and not letting the subjects be unduly influenced by the presence of the observer or by his measuring or recording devices.

Besides the competencies of speaking and listening used in interviews, observing is another everyday skill, which is methodologically systematised and applied in qualitative research. Practically all the senses—seeing, hearing, feeling, and smelling—are integrated into observations. According to different authors, we generally classify observational methods along five dimensions:

- **Covert versus overt observation:** how far is the observation revealed to those who are observed?

- **Non-participant versus participant observation:** how far does the observer have to go to become an active part of the observed field?
- **Systematic versus unsystematic observation:** is a more or less standardised observation scheme applied or does the observation remain flexible and responsive to the processes themselves?
- **Observation in natural versus artificial situations:** are observations done in the field of interest or are interactions "moved" to a special place (e.g., a laboratory) to make them observable more systematically?
- **Self-observation versus observing others:** mostly other people are observed, so how much attention is paid to the researcher's reflexive self-observation for further grounding the interpretation of the observed?

The observer maintains distance from the observed events in order to avoid influencing them. You may partly accomplish this by replacing the actual observation in the situation by videotaping. Alternatively, attempts may be made to distract the attention of those under observation from the researcher so that they become oblivious to the process of observation. In this context, covert observation is applied, in which observed persons are not informed that they are being observed.

10.5 Phases of Observation (Non-Participant)?

Adler and Adler (1998), Denzin (1989b), and Spradley (1980) name the following phases of such an observation:

- The selection of a setting (i.e., where and when the interesting processes and persons can be observed);
- The definition of what is to be documented in the observation and in every case;
- The training of the observers in order to standardise such focuses;
- Descriptive observations that provide an initial, general presentation of the field;
- Focused observations that concentrate on aspects that are relevant to the research question;

- Selective observations that are intended to purposively grasp central aspects;
- The end of the observation, when theoretical saturation has been reached, which means that further observations do not provide any further knowledge.

10.6 Steps of Observation

10.6.1 Planning

Mechanisms involved in observation

- Identify and define specifically the activities or aspects of behaviour to be observed.
- Realistically consider access/acceptance to the group/situation/activities you wish to observe.
- Familiarise yourself and plan for any potential language and/or cultural issues likely to affect the process.
- Consider the presentation of self, including what role you will take and how involved you will be.
- Decide about the process of observation whether it is participant or non-participant.

10.6.2 Temporal course of observation

- Decide approximately how long you think you will be observing and whether the process will be covert or candid.
- Fix time, date and number of observations to be undertaken.
- Identify the conditions of observation, variations in subjects, and variations in apparatus.

10.6.3 Consider strategies for ensuring credibility

- Replication of observations to achieve repetitiveness.
- Designing the study in order to increase the number of observations.
- Identify statistical techniques to be used.

10.6.4 Tools for recording

- Prepare an observation schedule/checklist based on relevant themes which are to be explored.
- Identify apparatus to be used for recording and its limitations.

10.6.5 Seek ethics approval

- Freedom, and dignity of the subjects should be kept in mind.

10.6.6 Conducting the Observations

- Ease into the observation situation. If structured and candid, this will be similar to the opening stages of an interview where you need to be on time, set up and check any equipment, introduce the study, and establish rapport. If your study involves greater immersion into a culture, early stages will require you to sit back, listen, attempt to gain trust, and then establish rapport.
- Use all your senses, and possibly your intuition, to gather data.
- Because you will not be directing the process, you need to be prepared to invest significant time in your observations.
- The observer has to decide what to focus on. In some settings, there may be several different things happening at the same time, and you will need to set some priorities. There is no right thing to look at. One has to decide what is challenging or interesting to study.
- Look for saturation (your observations no longer yield new knowledge) before ending the process.

10.6.7 Recordings

- Observations need to be recorded in a timely manner. If using schedules, they should be filled in concurrently along with observation. If you are more immersed in your research context, you may want to record your observations when removed from the situation either on data sheets or in a journal. Your record may also include photographs and video/audio recordings. Checklists, rating scales, scorecards, and scaled specimens provide systematic means of summarising or quantifying data collected by observation. Attempt to record your data in a systematic fashion that will ease future analysis.

10.6.8 Reviewing

- Review the process and note any difficulties encountered, i.e. access, time taken, engagement, cultural 'ignorance', comfort zones, recording/note-taking, roles, objectivity, etc.

- Review your observation records and note any difficulties you might encounter in making sense of your record.
- See if you can confirm your record by checking with an insider, asking another observer to compare notes, or triangulating your observational data with other data types.

10.6.9 Refining

- Make modifications based on your own review of the process and the quality of the data generated.
- Keep reviewing and refining your observation until you are comfortable with the process and data collected.

10.6.10 Other Issues

- Observer should know, what is his/her role? Does he/she want to participate in the interaction? Does he/she want to remain aloof? Can he/she behave one way one time and another way another time? It is up to the observer to choose what he/she wants to do.
- There are two options before the observer, either one should have narrow focus or look at every things. Better way is to strike balance. Basic purpose is to uncover deep meaning rather than surface bumbling.
- Exercises that involve observing the same phenomenon, for example, looking at films, videos, Discus with others, what you have observed with, and then looking again at the same videos- will heighten your power of observation. In this process one is trained to focus on details or look at the whole.

10.6.11 Analysing Data

- Work through data management and analysis. Treatment of data is according to the nature of research problem-qualitative, quantitative. Use appropriate techniques for the analysis of data.

10.7 Characteristics of Good Observation

- Observation as a research data gathering process, demands rigorous adherence to the spirit of scientific inquiry. The following standards should be observed in the process of observation.

- Observation is carefully planned specifying who is to be studied, what is to be studied and in what situation, where, and frequency and length.
- Observation is based upon the nature of study- whether it is qualitative or quantitative, or participative or non-participative.
- Temporal course of observation is planned in advance specifying time, date and venue.
- Strategies for ensuring creditability, reliability and validity are chalked out.
- Tools of observation such as camera, videos, tape-recorder, audio-meter (recording instruments) as well as Checklists, rating scales, scorecards, and scaled specimens are selected carefully and used appropriately.
- Observation is conducted as per objectives, hypotheses and design of the study.
- Observation is checked and verified whenever possible by repetition or by comparison with those of other competent observers. The process of observation is, therefore, continuously revised and refined.
- Observation should be objective, free from biases and based upon the principle of neutrality.
- Observations are carefully and expertly recorded. Information gathered is systematised, quantified and analysed to arrive at logical conclusions.
- Good observation presents the holistic view of the phenomenon.
- Good observation is based upon the foundations of freedom, liberty, and dignity of the subject (individual who is to be observed).

10.8 Reliability of Observation

There are some points to be kept in mind:

- Sample should be adequate and well defined.
- Variables of observation should be objective, specific and properly defined.
- Methods of recording appropriate to the situation should be predetermined.

- There should be a simple and understandable interaction.
- The observer should follow the principle of neutrality (unbiased).
- Anxiety is a source of distortion and its adequate handling is a major problem in refining the human instrument for gathering reliable data.
- Manageable time-schedule should be designed.
- Impact of the observer should be minimised.
- Observer should be trained as how to observe as well as how to handle apparatus.

10.8.3 Validity of Observation

- The truly significant incidents of behaviour must be identified and sampled.
- Seek the help of experts in identifying significant incidents of behaviour which are based on sound, established theories.
- Criterion-related and construct validity may also be necessary, depending on the purpose of study and inferences made regarding behaviours.
- Contextual content of the observation is validated through internal validity criterion.

10.9 Implications

- Observation is an appropriate research instrument in qualitative, experimental and descriptive research.
- Significant aspects of personality which express themselves in behaviour can be best studied directly through observation rather than indirectly through questionnaire and interview.
- Physical aspects can be measured and compared with standard norms.
- Processes and procedures can be assessed and compared with quality norms.
- Impacts of various programmes can be assessed through research tool of observation.
- Observation in the classroom is made to analyse learning behaviour which is a more complex phenomenon, to improve

classroom performance. Most of the classroom interactions are observed through observations.

- Longitudinal studies are conducted on the basis of continuous periodical observation of specific phenomenon.
- It is more reliable, very flexible and extremely searching.
- It discloses the minute, delicate and hidden facts, usually at lesser expense.
- For accuracy in measuring and recording, tools such as check-list, and score-card or some other inquiry form are utilised along with camera and tape-recorder and measuring instruments like thermo-meter, audio-meter, stop-watch, binocular, etc.
- Observation is repeated by the same individual or by simultaneous observation done by many individuals.

References

Adler, P.A. and Adler, P. (1998). "Observation Techniques, " in N. Denzin and Y.S. Lincoln (eds.), Collecting and Interpreting Qualitative Materials. London: SAGE. pp. 79-110.

Angrosumo, M.V. and May-de-Perez, K.A. (2000). 'Rethinking observation' in N.K. Denzin and Y.S. Lincoln (eds), *Handbook of Qualitative Research*, 2nd edn., Thousand Oaks, CA & London : Sage, pp. 673-702.

Crol, P. (1986). *Systematic Classroom observation.* London & Philadelphia: Falmer Press.

Jorgensen, D.L. (1989). Participant Observation: A Methodology for Human Studies. London: SAGE.

Jackson, P.W. (1968). *Life in Classrooms,* New York : Holt, Rinechart and Winston.

Rolfe, S.A. (2001). 'Direct observation' in G. Macnavigaton, S.A. Rolfe and I. Siraj – Blatechford (eds), *Doing early childhood research: International perspective on Theory and practice,* Buckinghan: OVP. pp. 224-39.

Sanger, Jl(1996). *The complete Observer: A Field Guide to Observation*, London: Falmer Press.

Spradley, J.P. (1980). Participant Observation. New York: Holt, Rinehart and Winston.

11

Interview as a Research Tool

Interview as a research tool is an oral type of questionnaire or schedule to gather information in a face to face relationship. It is an intimate contact between interviewee and interviewer to get information for the solution of the problem. It is a causal interaction between expert and interviewee where interviewee is willing to get interviewed. It is also an in-depth contextual understanding of the problem through interaction with the interviewee. Interview is, therefore, a two person conversation initiated by the researcher on content specified by research objectives and to get reliable and valid answers to research questions. The data from in-depth or open-ended interviews consist of direct questions from people, their experiences, opinions, feelings and knowledge.

The dynamics of interviewing, however, involves much more than an oral questionnaire. Interview is relatively more flexible tool than any written inquiry form. It provides ample scope for explanation, adjustment and variation according to the situation. In order to make it more reliable, authentic and trustworthy, it is essential that physical, cultural and communication barriers are to be narrowed down. The interviewee and the interviewer should come on the same waive-length so that more authentic and more trustworthy information may come forth spontaneously.

Interview as a research tool is used both in quantitative and qualitative research. In case of quantitative approach, interview is used when sample size is large, interview schedule is structured, and statistical techniques are used to draw inferences. It is also used as a research tool where it is not possible to get requisite information through questionnaire, for example, from illiterate or who cannot write or understand written words, small children who have not gone through formal education. Most data-collection methods in behavioural research are moderately indirect. The indirect approach is more useful where anxiety or conformity pressures are apt to conceal true response tendencies.

Therefore, interview occupies a very significant place in the conduct of qualitative research. This tool is invariably used in ethnographic, phenomenological, case studies and grounded theory. It gives large margin to 'in-depth analyses of the problem. Interview technique as a research tool produces spectacular results in terms of depth. It allows the reader to gain deeper understanding of, and empathy for, lives lived and values held in a very different fashion from one's own eyes (Lareau and Shultz, 1996). Being an exploratory device and contextual, it helps in understanding numerous variables and their relationships having impact on the phenomenon.

11.1 Interview Schedule

11.1.1 Unstructured Interview Schedule

The client-centred counselling technique of Carl Rogers illustrates the unstructured approach, giving the respondent broad freedom to express himself in his own way and in his own time. The interviewer may have a general or specific objective which he feels can best be met without imposing a structure on the respondent. Usually the information involved is of a highly personal and potentially threatening nature. Unstructured interview is one of the most vulnerable to subjective bias or errors of inexperience. The researcher has to labour hard to sift grains from the chaff.

11.1.2 Semi-structured interview

These are built around a core of structured questions from which the interviewer branches off to explore in depth. Again, accurate and complete information is desired with additional opportunity to probe for underlying factors or relationships which are too complex or elusive to encompass in more straight-forward questions. Semi-structured interviews require more training and skill both to probe at significant points and to avoid biasing tendencies. It is partially structured interview which helps the researcher to focus on specific and significant themes.

11.1.3 Structured Interviews

The interviewers follow a well-defined structure resembling the format of an objective questionnaire, allowing clarification and elaboration within narrow limits. These tend to be factually oriented, aimed at specific information, and relatively brief. Structured interviews are suitable when accurate and complete information from all respondents is important and when the type of information sought fits readily into a structured inquiry.

11.2 Types of Interview

11.2.1 The Clinical Interview

In clinical work some form of the interview or personal contact has been used in many kinds of situations to secure information about the client and to understand his problems. The two major purposes of the interview in clinical work are diagnosis and treatment. Social workers employ the interview to secure information about the client's problem, his past history, family relations, and social and emotional adjustment. Other persons than the client frequently are interviewed when the client is a child, a mentally challenged, or a psychotic, or when there are unusual discrepancies in the client's presentation of data about himself. The psychiatric examination and even the standardised individual psychological examination are essential.

Types of interview are given in Figure-11.1.

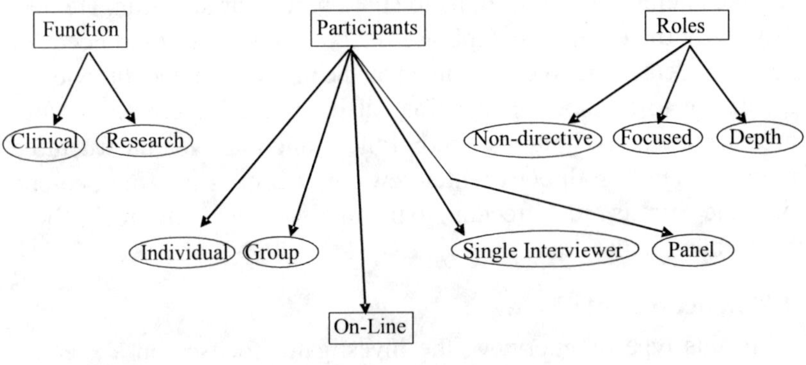

Figure 11.1: Types of Interview.

During the clinical interview, certain nonverbal behaviour on the part of the patient has useful diagnostic value, including gait, expression posture, rate of speech, topics avoided, digressions, and word choice. In addition to the general techniques that apply to any interview situation, special procedures may be needed to deal effectively with the problems that arise in the several types of clinical interviews: the intake or admission interview, concerned chiefly with the patient's complaint's the personal and social-history interview, to gather background data with a bearing on the complaints; the screening or diagnostic interview, to arrive at a judgment concerning the patient's condition; interviews before and after psychological test administration, and as a means of introducing the patient to therapy; the interview to assist friends and relatives in their dealings with the patient; and the exit or termination interview to facilitate the patient's discharge or transition from hospital to home.

11.2.2 Research Interview

Research interview is used both in quantitative and qualitative research. In quantitative research, structured interview schedule is used to gather certain facts about large number of persons. Data thus collected is put to statistical analysis so as to derive inferences. In qualitative research, in-depth open interview schedule is used in case studies, ethnographic and phenomenological studies. Data thus collected are interpreted by the investigator to identify pattern and draw conclusions.

11.2.3 Non-Directive Interview

In non-directive interview, the interviewer has full freedom to make suitable alterations in questions to suit a particular situation. He may also revise the order or paraphrase the questions to suit the needs of the respondents. The role is assumed by the interviewer and interviewee in relation to the socio-psychological process of interaction. Non-directive interview implies uncontrolled, unguided, or unstructured interview. The non-directive interview includes questions of open-end form and permits much freedom to the interviewee to talk freely about the problem under study.

11.2.4 Focused Interview

In this type of interview, the investigator focuses on a specific problem or event or experience rather than on general lines of inquiry about it. The interviewer presents a set of well defined questions, pictures, or video to get response from the interviewee on specific experience and records the answers of the respondents in logical way. In general the focused interview employs nondirective procedures in encouraging the respondent to structure the stimulus situation by indicating aspects of the situation most significant and by progressively exploring his responses. Non-direction in the focused interview means reliance on unstructured questions, but varying degrees of structure may be present. Interviewee is placed in concrete situation, field of inquiry and hypotheses are clearly stated, and the inner feelings and emotional attitudes of the interviewee vis-à-vis given problem or situation are given particular attention.

Rolf Oerter (1995) developed the "adulthood interview" for studying concepts of human nature and adulthood in different cultures (United States, West Germany, Indonesia, Japan and Korea). The interview was divided into four main parts. In the first part, general questions about adulthood were asked. The second part dealt with the three main roles of adulthood: family, occupational and political. The third part drew attention to the past of the interviewee, asking for developmental changes during previous two or three years. The last part dealt with the near future of the interviewee, asking for his or her goals in life and his or her development.

11.2.5 Criteria of Focus Interview

In the focused interview, significant information is gathered from participant (interviewee) on specific event, programme, and themes of the study. Its impact on the interviewee is studied using an interview guide. The original aim of the interview is to provide a basis for interpreting statistically significant findings. The stimulus presented is content analysed beforehand. This enables a distinction to be made between the "objective" facts of the situation and the interviewees' subjective definitions of the situation with a view to comparing them. The interview guide contains criteria namely,

- **Non-direction:** that is, flexible use of the interview schedule;
- **Specificity:** it implies bringing out the specific elements which determine the impact or meaning of an event for the interviewees;

- **Range:** contains all aspects and topics relevant to the research questions are mentioned during the interview;
- **Depth:** Personal Context that is shown by the interviewee. "a maximum of self-revelatory comments concerning how the stimulus material is experienced" by the interviewee (Merton and Kendall, 1946).

The successful carrying out of such interview depends on:

- The interviewer's situational competence which can be increased by practical experience of making decisions necessary in interview situation, in rehearsal interviews, and interview training.
- Specific, reliable, authentic and trustworthy information may be obtained by more depth (deep probing) and guaranteeing the range (by introducing new topics or the next question of the interview guide) and with the different solutions at each point.

11.3 In-depth Interview

In-depth interview is an intensive and searching type of interview with emphasis on such psychological and social factors as attitudes, emotions or convictions. It determines the respondent's degree of attachment or detachment towards an experience or an activity. It usually involves flexibility of interview situation, focus on feelings and restatement of implied or expressed feelings. It helps in understanding the behaviour of an individual which is otherwise not possible through questionnaire. The procedures of such depth interviewing are as follows:

(a) **Interview Situation:** Flexible interviews encourage orientation to stimulus situation, rather than to interviewer, thus facilitating depth and curbing stereotyped reports.

(b) **Retrospective Focus:** Focus is on past experience, through reinstatement of stimulus situation, promotes elaboration of reported responses.

(c) **Focus on Feelings:** Questions explicitly referring to affective aspects (e.g., "How did you feel when . . . ?" encourage reports of in-depth responses.

(d) Restatement of Implied or Expressed Feelings.

Occasional restatements of implied or expressed feelings prove effective (1) inviting progressive elaboration of response, and (2) establishing common ground for understanding.

11.4 Group and Individual Interviews

Individual interview is when interviewer and interviewee meet to together to find out the solution of a problem. It is used in clinical, counselling, or criminal investigation. Group interview is used to identify leader or the leadership qualities, consensus on particular issue/theme or most significant change. The size of the group should not be so large to conduct the interview in effective way. It generally observed that the large group becomes unwieldy or inhibits participation by most members. Moreover, it should not be very small. Small group lacks substantially greater coverage. The optimum size is approximately six to eight persons. Social, intellectual, and educational homogeneity are important for effective participation of all group members. A circular seating arrangement, with the interviewer as one of the group, is conducive to full and spontaneous reporting and participation.

11.5 Single Interviewer or Panel

Both individual and group interviews may be conducted by a single interviewer or panel of interviewers, according to the design and purpose of the interview. For instance, interviews for selection and treatment purposes are held by the panel of experts in different and related fields. Interview for research purposes are usually held by a single investigator.

11.6 The Ethnographic Interview

Participant observation is mainly used in ethnographic field research. However, interview is also used in the ethnographic study. A particular problem is how to shape conversations arising in the field into interview. Specific experiences of others are gathered and aligned with the issue of the research in a systematic way. In such interview, the flexible local and temporal framework is used. Opportunities for an interview often arise spontaneously and surprisingly from regular field contacts. According to Spradley (1979), ethnographic interviews as a series of friendly conversations into which the researcher slowly introduces new elements to assist informants to respond as informants. The ethnographic interviews include the following elements:

- Ethnographic interview demands for co-creation of a situation where respondent can answer questions freely. Second, rich and varied experience should be used to get most trustworthy interview questions and guide before conducting interviews. Focus should not be to discover theoretical concepts but to capture the life lived experience.

- Ethnographic explanations: the interviewer explains the project and the noting of certain statements. Local language in which respondent is well versed is used for explanations with the aim that the informant gets involved. Explanations for certain questions, and the way of asking explicitly are worked out.
- Ethnographic questions: these are, descriptive and structural questions (answering them should show how informants organise their knowledge about the issue), and contrast questions (they should provide information about the meaning dimensions used by informants to differentiate objects and events in their world).
- In these explanations and questions, some of the clarifications may be made outside the actual interview situation.
- The ethnographic interview needs to used in combination with field research and observational strategies.

11.7 Conducting Interviews: Problems of Mediation and Steering

One of the problems is how to secure topically, (i) relevant subjective perspectives in an interview; (ii) mediate between the input of the interview guide and the aims of the research question, and (iii) the interviewee's style of presentation. These decisions, which can only be taken in the interview situation itself, require a high degree of sensitivity to the concrete course of the interview and the interviewee. Additionally, they require a great deal of overview of what has already been said and its relevance for the research question in the study.

11.8 Narrative Interview

Narrative interview refers to the course of a single case, and the context of experiences is the central aim of research. First the initial situation is outlined ("how everything started"), then the events relevant to the narrative are selected from the whole host of experiences and presented as a coherent progression of events ("how things developed"), and finally the situation at the end of the development is presented ("what became"). (Hermanns 1995, p. 183). The narrative interview is mainly used in the context of biographical research (Bertaux, 1981; Rosenthal, 2004). The method was developed in the context of a project on local power structures and decision processes. Its basic principle of collecting data is described as follows:

In the narrative interview, the informant is asked to present the history of an area of interest, in which the interviewee participated, in an extempore narrative.... The interviewer's task is to make the informant tell the story of the area of interest in question as a consistent story of all relevant events from its beginning to its end. (Hermanns, 1995, p. 183)

11.8.1 Conduct of the Narrative Interview

The narrative interview begins using a "generative narrative question" (Riemann and Schütze, 1987, p. 353), on the topic of the study with intension to stimulate the interviewee. It is followed by the stage of narrative probing in which narrative fragments that were not exhaustively detailed before are completed. The last stage of the interview is the "balancing phase, in which the interviewee may also be asked questions that aim at theoretical accounts of what happened and at balancing the story, reducing the 'meaning' of the whole to its common denominator" (Hermanns, 1995, p. 184). At this stage, the interviewees are taken as experts and theoreticians of themselves. The narration is not interrupted or obstructed by the interviewer.

11.8.2 What are the Problems in Conducting the Narrative Interview?

One problem in conducting narrative interviews is the systematic violation of the role expectations of both participants. First, expectations relating to the situation of an "interview" are violated, because (at least for the most part) questions in the usual sense of the word are not asked. Second, rarely is an interviewee's narrative of everyday life given. These violations of situational expectations often produce irritations in both parties, which prevent them from settling down into the interview situation.

"We must assume that not all interviewees are capable of giving narrative presentations of their lives. We meet reticent, shy, uncommunicative, or excessively reserved people not only in everyday social life but also in biographical interviews" (Fuchs, 1984, p. 249).

Additionally, some authors see problems in applying this method in foreign cultures, because the validity of the narrative schema dominant in Western culture cannot simply be presumed for other, non-Western cultures.

This solution includes three elements: (i) the primary orientation is to provide the interviewees with the scope to tell their story; (ii) proceed from simple narration to complex thematically deepening interventions, and (iii) focus the narrative on the topical area and the period of the biography with which the interview is concerned.

11.9 The Episodic Interview

Episodic interview refers to subjects' experiences of a certain domain; these experiences are stored and remembered in forms of narrative-episodic and semantic knowledge. It starts from episodic-situational forms of experiential knowledge. Special attention is paid in the interview to situations or episodes in which the interviewee has had experiences that seem to be relevant to the question of the study. Both the form of the presentation (description or narrative) of the situation and the selection of other situations can be chosen by the interviewee according to aspects of subjective relevance.

11.9.1 Problems in Conducting the Episodic Interview

The general problem of interviews generating narratives—that some people have greater problems with narrating. There are several delimited narratives. The problem is how to focus situation and establish rapport with the interviewee. As in other forms of interviews, it is an essential precondition that you as the interviewer have really internalised the principle of the interview. In episodic interviews, you try to employ the advantages of both the narrative interview and the semi-structured interview. These interviews use the interviewee's competence to present experiences in their 'course' and 'context' as narratives.

11.10 On-Line Interview

The purpose of on-line interview is to gather information from a participant on a particular topic. On-line interview is considered to be cost effective and dominant data collection method. On-line interview is without face to face experience; therefore, an on-line interviewer might need to develop a new set of techniques or skills. On-line sampling provides some interesting challenges. If e-mail is used as a means of interviewing, there is there are no issues regarding travelling, recording or transcribing. On-line sampling also makes possible interviewing people who are geographically dispersed. Telephones, mobiles, teleconferencing, and web-based on-line can be used for conducting interviews.

Usually, on-line interview is pre-planned. A participant is selected who agrees to be interviewed at a particular time and with the use of a particular technology. Both interviewer and participant agree to be online at the same time, and the interview questions are posed by the interviewer and responded to be the participant.

E-mail, Instant Messenger, Online chat, Face Book or Social Networking can be used. This type of interview is most feasible. Because it provides freedom to interviewee to post his/her views. In this process, huge information can be gathered and analysed to find solution of the specific problem. It is necessary in online interviewing to build up a temporal relationship (rapport) with the interviewees, even if the communication may be asynchronous and responses come with some delay (even days). Face-to-face communication (and interviewing) may be more spontaneous than online communication, but the latter allows the participants to reflect on their answers more than the former. Mann and Stewart (2000, p. 129) have identified five factorse influencing computer-mediated interaction in interview:

- What is the purpose of the interaction/interview? This will influence the interest of possible participants of whether or not to become involved in the study.
- What is the temporal structure of the research? Are synchronous or asynchronous methods used and will there be a series of interactions in the research or not?
- What are the possibilities and limitations coming from the software influencing the interaction?
- What are the characteristics of the interviewer and the participants? What about the experience of and attitude to using technology? What about their knowledge of the topics, writing skills, insights, etc.? Is one-to-one interaction or researcher group interaction planned? Has there been any interaction between researcher and participant before? How is the

structure of the group addressed by the research (hierarchies, gender, age, ethnicity, social status, etc.)?

- What is the external context of the research—inter/national culture and/or communities of meaning that are involved? How do their communicative practices outside the research influence the latter?

When running the interview itself, you can send one question or a couple of questions, wait for the answers, and then probe (as in a face-to-face interview) or go on with sending the next questions. If there is a longer delay before answers come, you can send a reminder.

11.11 Steps for Conducting an Interview

Interviewing is an art which requires appropriate training, skills and guided experience as essential background. Careful preparation of questions for the interview is fully as important as has been emphasised in preparing the questionnaire. A well-conducted interview is not just a haphazard series of questions and answers of a pleasant conversation. The interviewer has a set of carefully prepared questions to serve as a thread conversation, although he may vary the order of the questions to adapt to special circumstances. These characterisations apply especially to data gathering studies; nondirective or client-centered counselling permits greater freedom by way of an unstructured interview.

11.11.1 Planning an Interview

- Define the purpose of the study—its background, theoretical basis, general goals, possible applications of results, and reasons for using the interview method.
- Translate the general goals into detailed and specific objectives which can be fitted to the particular interview pattern you plan to follow, constructing questions yielding useful information.
- Develop a tentative guide to be used during the interview, exploiting the advantages of the interview technique.
- Develop a satisfactory method of coding and / or recording responses. General responses can be pre-categorised in a pilot study to anticipate the most frequent response patterns. Only responses falling outside these general categories would need to be written out.

- Tape recording of the interview may offer advantages, unless the nature of the interview is highly personal and produces guarded responses.
- A generally poor technique is a written summary of information recorded during or following the interview. Because of the pace of an interview, the act of writing either slows the interview unnecessarily or causes the interviewer to be selective in the kind and amount of information he records, at the risk of introducing bias.
- Develop a contingency plan in case key interviews fall through. Familiarise yourself with, and plan for, any potential language and / or cultural issues likely to affect the process.
- Engage a good translator if necessary. Consider the presentation of self, including what role you will take and how involved you will be in conversations.
- Decide approximately how long you think the interviews should take. Make and confirm appointments in advance. Plan travel time, interview time, and wait around time.

11.11.2 Framing Questions for the Interview

- Questions must be framed in language that ensures effective communication between the interviewer and the respondent. Omit all ambiguous vocabulary.
- Make certain respondent appreciates the purpose of each questions he is asked. Avoid arousing any suspicion or resistance.
- Ascertain whether the population from which the respondents have been selected actually has the information sought by the interview and that the questions permit the reasonable recovery of this information.
- Avoid leading questions (questions which suggest a desirable or preferred answer).
- Ensure that the frame of reference surrounding each question is clear so that each respondent hears the question in the same way, avoiding misinterpretations.
- Pretest the interview in a pilot study to eliminate weaknesses and experiment with alternative items or techniques.

- Carefully read questions and consider whether they might be considered confusing, leading, or problematic in any way for the interviewee.
- Rewrite the questions in relation to considerations above and run them past a few peers/supervisor for their assessment. Repeat this step as many times as necessary to get each question as right as possible.
- Attempt to put your questions into an order that is logical and will ease respondents into the interview.

11.11.3 Pilot Study

- Attempt a pilot interview with a couple of respondents whose background is similar to those in your 'sample'.
- Note any difficulties encountered, i.e. access, time taken, pacing, comfort zones, recording/note-taking, roles, objectivity, conversational flow, ambiguities, etc.
- Get feedback from the interviewees on the above and anything else they wish to discuss.
- Attempt to make sense of your notes and / or transcribe your data.

11.11.4 Modification and Revision

- Make modifications based on your own reflections, the feedback from the interviewees, and the quality of the data generated.
- If modifications are substantial, start again from step one.
- Get ethical clearance for the final interview schedule/question/ theme.

11.11.5 Executing the Interview

- The initial task of the interview is securing the confidence of the interviewee through establishing rapport with him. This process involves expertise of interviewer and art of communication.
- Interviewer should secure desired information through asking the planned sequence of questions. It should not be conducted in a rigid manner. Interviewer should give simulating and encouragement and necessary explanation wherever required.

- The recording devices selected should be used without distracting the interviewee.

11.11.6 A check list for Conducting the Interview

- Open an interview by asking factual non-threatening questions.
- Locate the major data by unstructured head questions.
- Make an effort to pick up the lead.
- Cut through generalities with well-formulated probes.
- Stick with the fruitful areas once they open up.
- Reflect on the meaning of emerging data and ask questions that clarify or amplify their meaning for the research problem.
- Follow up only areas where the respondents show emotional involvement.
- Redirect the interview to more faithful topics when useful data are not emerging.
- The interviewer should try to turn back respondent's direct questions.
- Wind up the interview before the respondent becomes tired.
- Whether an interviewer should take notes depends on the situation.

Inadequate responses which call for probing or secondary questions may be partial response, nonresponse, irrelevant response, inaccurate response, or verbalised response. In addition to problems of motivation and conflict of motives, the following things are to be sorted out and be given due consideration by the interviewer.

- The respondent may fail to understand the purpose of the question or the kind of answer needed.
- The language or concepts may go beyond the respondent's comprehension.
- The respondent may lack the information or background necessary to answer the question.
- The respondent may not remember the information requested.
- The respondent may not be able to verbalise his feelings, as in the case of intimate "depth" questions or materials.
- The respondent may feel that the question does not fit the purpose of the interview.

- The respondent may regard a question as going beyond the limits of what he is willing to confide in the interviewer.
- The respondent may feel that the interviewer is unable to understand his true feelings.

11.11.7 Recording and interpretation of the responses

- It is best to employ, if possible, a device of recording which would retain the actual wording of the responses. Tape-recording is convenient but ensures that it may not be nuisance. More sophisticated and high frequency gadgets are now available for recording which could be used for recording the interview.
- The responses to the questions in the interview have to be noted down on a diary. In case it is not recorded on spot, then should be noted down immediately after the interview. The former is often found to be of a distracting nature while the latter often fails in being complete in detail. For using either of these devices successfully a skillful and experienced hand is necessary.
- Sometimes, instead of recording responses, the interviewer tend to record his evaluation of them as the interview goes on it is, however, advisable to interpret and evaluate the responses later on the basis of the recording of responses rather than simultaneously.
- In order to ensure the validity of the interview, it is essential that apparent and hidden biases should be identified and eliminated.
- Authenticity of interview is about conversation between researcher and participants, and the situations and emotional compassion that arise during the investigation (Ellis and Bochner, 2000). The authenticity criteria contain: ontological authenticity (understanding social milieu), educative authenticity (appreciating others' perspectives), catalytic authenticity (acting for change), and tactical authenticity (empowering members for action) (Bryman, 2008).
- The recordings of the interview should be interpreted in such a way that the whole phenomenon under study is understood as a complex system that is more than sum of its parts; focus

on complex interdependencies and system dynamics that cannot meaningfully be reduced to a few discrete and linear, cause-effect relationships.

Further Reading

Atkinsons, J.A.(1968). A Handbook for Interviewers. HMSO, London.

Bertaux, D. (ed.) (1981). Biography and History: The Life History Approach to Social Sciences. Beverly Hills, CA: Sage.

Bruner, J. (1987). "Life as Narrative, " Social Research, 54:11-32.

Bruner, J. (1991). "The Narrative Construction of Reality, " Critical Inquiry, 18:1-21.

Denzin, N.K. (1988). Interpretive Biography. London: Sage.

Flick, U. (2000a). "Episodic Interviewing, " in M. Bauer and G. Gaskell (eds.), Qualitative Researching with Text, Image and Sound: A Practical Handbook. London: SAGE. pp. 75-92.

Gillham, B. (2005). Research Interviewing: The Range of Techniques. Maidenhead: Open University Press.

Gubrium, J.F. and Hostein, J.A. (2003). Postmodern Interviewing, London: Thousand Oaks, CA: Sage.

Hyman, H.H.(1954). *Interviewing in Social Research.*Chicago; University of Chicago Press.

Kahn, R. L., and Cannel, C.F. (1957). *The dynamics of interviewing : Theory, techniques, and cases.* New York: John Wiley and Sons.

Kreuger, R., and Casey, M. (2009). Focus Group: A practical Guide for Appplied research. 4th edition, Thousand Oaks: Sage.

Kvale, S. (2008). Doing Interviews. London: Sage.

Merton, R.K., Fiske, M., and Kendall, P.L.(1956). The focused interview: A manual problems and procedures. Glencoe: Free Press.

Mishler, E. (1986). Research Interviewing. Cambridge, MA: HarvardUniversity Press.

Oppenheim, A.N. (1992). Questionnaire Design, Interviewing and Attitude Measurement. London: Pinter.

Rosenthal, G. (2004). "Biographical Research," in C. Seale, G. Gobo, J. Gubrium, and D. Silverman (eds.), Qualitative Research Practice. London: SAGE. pp. 48-65.

Schostak, J.F. (2010). Interviewing and Representation in Qualitative Research Projects, Buckingham and Philadelphia: University Open Press.

12

Documents

12.1 What are Documents?

Documents are standardised artefacts, in so far as they typically occur in particular formats- as notes, case reports, contracts, drafts, death certificates, remarks, diaries, statistics, annual reports, certificates, judgments, and letters or expert opinions. (Wolff 2004b, p. 284). Term document refers to material such as photographs, videos, films, memos, letters, diaries clinical case records, and memorabilia of all sorts that can be used as supplementary information as a part of study.

Prior (2003, p. 2) gives a more dynamic, use-oriented definition: 'If we are to get to grip with the nature of documents then we have to move away from consideration of them as stable, static and pre-defined artefacts. Instead we must consider them in terms of fields, frames and networks of action. In fact, the status of things as "documents" depends precisely on the ways which such objects are integrated into fields of action, and documents can only be defined in terms of such fields'.

12.2 Types of Documents

Solicited and Unsolicited: Solicited documents are used for research purposes (e.g., ask people to write diaries for the next

12 months and then analyse and compare these documents), or unsolicited documents can also be used (e.g., the diaries people have written as part of an everyday routine). Documents are most often available as texts (in a printed form), but they can also have the form of an electronic file (a database). Scott (1990, p. 14) distinguishes 12 types of documents, which are constituted by a combination of two dimensions: the authorship (who produced the document) and the access to the documents. The authorship can be divided into personal and official documents and the latter again into private and state documents. Scott distinguishes four alternatives. The access can be closed (e.g., the medical records of a general practitioner are not accessible to third persons). The access can be restricted (e.g., juridical records are only accessible to specific professional groups like lawyers in a trial). The access can be open archival, which means that everyone can access the documents but (only) in a specific archive. And the access can be open published; then the documents are published and accessible to any interested party. Besides, personal and official documents, there are popular culture documents. These are commercial and non-commercial documentaries, videos and photographs. Their purpose is to entertain, persuade, educate and enlighten the public. Researchers interested in critical theory, culture and media generally make use of documents as main source.

12.3 Sources of Documents

12.3.1 A primary source is an original or firsthand account of the event or experience. These are documents or remains, the first witness to the event, with only the mind of the observer or eye witness coming between the original event and the user of the source. They are available in written, pictorial and mechanical forms as under:

12.3.2 Personal Documents: in qualitative research, the personal documents are used as any first person narrative that describes an individual life lived experiences, actions and beliefs, for instance, diaries, autobiographies, notes, original drafts of speeches, articles, books and pamphlets. However, certificates, affidavits, declarations, personal letters, will, deeds, contracts notes are also personal documents. The aim of collecting such materials is to "obtain detailed evidence as to how social situations appear to actors in them and what meaning various factors have for participants" (Angell, 1945, p. 178).

12.3.3 Official Documents: Legislative, judicial or executive documents such as constitutions, laws, charters, court proceedings and decisions; data preserved by missionaries, and other religious organisations; the information compiled by central or state government or planning departments; records of various commissions and committees, socio-economic surveys, annual reports, interlocutors reports and other records maintained by organisations of learning or socio-economic-cultural development.

12.3.4 Cultural Documents: Post-modernism researchers have been found using these methods to study culture. Popular culture documents include videos, documentary films, and television, fictions. For instance:

- **Oral testimony of traditions and events:** Such as folklore, legends, ballads, tales, anecdotes, sagas, traditions, customs, manners, burials, ceremonials, social institutions, and language.
- **Pictorial records:** photographs, movies, micro-films, drawings, paintings, coins and sculpture.
- **Mechanical records:** tape recordings of interviews, meetings and speeches.
- **Remains or relics:** Fossils, skeletons, tools, clothing, historical sites, furniture, utensils, art objects, and museum pieces.

These documents are used in two ways –first as a 'text' where the transcripts of the shows, lyrics, and films are treated as footnotes; and second as interpretations of the viewers as a central part of the study.

12.4 Secondary Sources

All indirect sources or second hand information i.e. the accounts of an event provided by a person who did not directly observe the event, object, or condition. It may be record of the statements of contemporaries. Information thus gathered is subject to an inherent danger of inaccuracy and distortion. Most history textbooks and encyclopaedias are examples of secondary sources.

A newspaper editorial concerning the problem would be a secondary source. In a study including, among other things, the relationships between teachers and community members in nineteenth-century America, Clifford (1978) used teachers' written accounts of living with community families. These accounts were primary sources.

A report on the same topic by another author would be a secondary source. The writings of John Dewey are primary sources of his views, whereas an interpretation by his students would be considered a secondary source.

Example: Some researchers sit and watch videos of films and then do an analysis of the content. This may involve elaborate coding and a great deal of systematic work and may present important and interesting findings about the depiction of violence, sexuality, gender and racial stereotypes, and other issues of broad concern.

The Library of Congress (USA), or National Achieves or Google Search Engines are treasure troves of documents of all kinds. Other documents can be found in the files of organisations, the desk drawers of principles, the attics of buildings, and in the archives of historical and cultural societies.

Before researchers get seriously involved in the study, they need to assess the internal and external validity of the documents. Moreover, a researcher should find out more about how it was produced, for what purpose and under what circumstances, what other supportive documents are available to serve the purpose of study undertaken. Analysis of documents is given below in Box 12.1.

Box 12.1 Analysis of Documents

Plan

1. Create a list of documents you wish to explore.
2. If any documents are considered 'sensitive', seek ethics approval.
3. Do preliminary groundwork to determine whether they will be accessible.
4. Consider and plan for any translation needs.
5. If there are too many documents for analysis, develop an appropriate Sampling Strategy.
6. Consider what types of data you wish to gather from the documents.

Gather

7. Gather relevant documents – be prepared for hiccups.

(Contd...)

8. Develop and employ a scheme for organising and managing the documents.
9. Make copies of original documents that can be annotated.

Review

10. Assess the authenticity and credibility of the 'text'.
11. Explore the 'agenda' of the document and look for any biases.

Interrogate

12. Extract background information on author, audience, purpose, style.
13. Explore content – this can be done by occurrence, or by themes and issues.
14. Look for 'writing evidence' (what the document was meant to impart) and 'unwitting evidence' (everything else you can glean from the documents).

Reflect/Refine

15. View document analysis as an iterative and ongoing process.
16. Reflect on any difficulties associated with gathering the data, reviewing the sources, and exploring the content.
17. Modify the plan based on your reflections.
18. Gather, review, and interrogate additional documents as needed.

12.5 Selecting Documents

For assessing the quality of documents, Scott (1990) suggests four criteria, which you can use for deciding whether or not to employ a specific document (or set of documents) for your research: authenticity. Is the evidence genuine and of unquestionable origin? Credibility. Is the evidence free from error and distortion? Representative: Is the evidence typical of its kind, and, if not, is the extent of its untypically known? Meaning. Is the evidence clear and comprehensible?

The first criterion addresses the question of whether the document is a primary or secondary document: Is it the original report of an accident, for instance, or is it a summary of this original report by someone who did not witness the accident itself? Credibility refers to the accuracy of the documentation, the reliability of the producer of the document, the freedom from errors. Representativeness is linked to typicality. It may be helpful to know of a specific record and whether it is a typical record. Meaning can be distinguished by the intended meaning for the author of the document, the meaning for the reader of it.

12.6 The Practicalities of Using Documents

Document should be seen as a way of contextualising information. Rather than using them as "information containers." These should be seen and analysed as methodologically created communicative turns in constructing versions of events. Examine these parts of documents more clearly, so that it may be helpful to compare documents from different contexts—a record from juridical processes to a record from the health system, referring to the same issue or even case. Other practical problems may be that you have problems of understanding the content of the documents, because you cannot decipher the words, abbreviations, codes, or references that are used or because they are difficult to read (e.g., handwritten documents) or are damaged. Who has produced this document and for what purpose? What has been left out in producing the record, by whom, and why? What are the social circumstances which may have influenced the production of the record?

References

Allport, G. (1942). *The use of personal documents in psychological science*. New York: Social Science Research Council.

Bodgam, C. Robert and Biklen, S. Knopp ((2011).*Qualitative Research for Education: An Introduction to Theory and Methods*. PHI Learning: New Delhi.

Flick, Uwe (2009). *An Introduction to Qualitative Research*. New Delhi: SAGE-SA.

Prior, L. (2003*).Using Documents in Social Research*. London: SAGE.

Rapley, T. (2007). *Doing Conversation, Discourse and Document Analysis*. London: SAGE.

Schoonmaker, M.(1994). *Videoasis: The character of viewing in a video community*. Unpublished doctoral dissertation, Syracuse University.

Scott, J. (1990). *A Matter of Record: Documentary Sources in Social Research*. Cambridge: Polity Press.

Wolff, S. (2004b). "Analysis of Documents and Records, " in U. Flick, E.V. Kardorff, and I. Steinke (eds.), *A Companion to Qualitative Research*. London: SAGE. pp. 284-290.

13

Diary as a Tool or Document

Sociology, medical research, and psychology have used diaries as authentic and trustworthy research data. As a research tool, diaries have often been employed to provide insight into personal phenomena that are difficult to access through other methods (Zimmerman and Wielder, 1977). Research diary refers to the researcher's notes as "the vehicle for ordered creativity" (Schatzman and Strauss 1973: 105). The diary is employed as a log of researcher's activities during the research process. The diary used to provide a chronology of the researcher's thinking and experiences. It is a detailed record of the research process, research design, data collection and analysis to writing up and presenting the study (Robson, 2011). This is also true of experimental and scientific research, as Faraday's diary is primarily a detailed daily log of scientific experiments. Diary can also be used in the context of 'the diary as a document' (Bryman, 2004:141).

Diary is personal notes describing an event or events. Diary often provides more information than an interview or observation. The diaries are meaningful units that organise and structure reflections and experiences of the participants in narrations. Diaries can potentially complement and in some cases replace more traditional techniques of data collection. In some key areas of social life, diaries have been shown to be most effective in providing insight into various processes such as the unfolding of adaptation processes. One of the major strengths of diary is easier to write about certain things than to speak about them (Bedrwel, MacGowan and Lavender, 2012). Observational research is confined to what is visible. In process of interview, the respondent may have poor sources of information.

Larson *et al.* (1983) called this methodology 'experience sampling methods' or 'ecological momentary assessment' (EMA).This method revolutionised modern psychological research by allowing investigators to capture daily experiences in participants' own, natural environment. However, open-ended, or solicited diaries can be of great use in capturing truth and perceptions of participants.

As a research technique, the investigator focuses on; (a) what are the average experiences of an individual, how much do the experiences vary over time? (b) Is there systematic (e.g., linear, exponential) change across days, and do such trajectories differ across persons? (c) What processes underlie a person's changes, and how do people differ in this process? Diary generally generates high quality data relating to health or person with disability. It is not distorted by the retrospective views of the informant. Longitudinal data gathered through diaries can be used fruitfully in phenomenological research. It provides ample space for the reflection on the changes taking place in his or her life. A good sense of coherence helps in understanding the behaviour of an individual.

Proactive interaction between the researcher and the informant is followed (i.e. hermeneutic traditional way to the development of new understanding). It has the potential to give participants much more space for reasoning and reflection to build authentic story. At the same time, participants can develop an individual relationship with the diary and the imagined readership. To grasp the phenomena of everyday life, a method is appropriate if it gets close to participants but leaves them enough space for personal reflections. Diaries as a source of data give researchers the ability to apply narrations as a method to grasp forms of identity and meaningful construction. Confidentiality is guaranteed throughout the whole project. Double structured format connecting time and themes will aid the researcher's data analysis. When the same theme is arranged in table of contents, patterns of behaviour and patterns of the informant reaction to conditions and to the changes in those conditions will change. The researchers can imagine and potentially understand the everyday lives of our participants. Diaries kept over a longer period also allow for development of a triangular relationship between the diarist, the diary, and the researcher.

Diary studies have become increasingly common in variety of fields of psychology, personality, clinical and socio and emotional development. It is made more systematic through structured reporting forms and response intervals. Biographers, historians and professionals have used diary as an important document. The sociologists have also taken seriously the idea of using personal documents to construct pictures of social reality from the actors' perspective. Diaries are being used as research instruments to collect detailed information about behaviour, events and other aspects of individuals' daily lives. Areas covered using diary methods are social networks, health, illness and associated behaviour, diet and nutrition, social work and other areas of social policy, clinical psychology and family therapy, crime behaviour, alcohol consumption and drug usage, and sexual behaviour. Diaries are also increasingly being used in market research. In development research, particular areas: (1) projects requiring information relating to bodily health practices and attitudes; (2) research in the aftermath of war, conflict and violence; and (3) research with marginalised social groups. Diaries have been used as a 'Tool' or 'Document' or 'Case Study'. In some cases, diary has been preferred over other methods. First, diaries can provide a reliable alternative to the traditional interview method for events that are difficult to recall accurately. Second, diaries can help in collecting sensitive information. Finally, diaries provide a rich source of information on respondents' behaviour and experiences on a daily basis.

13.1 Diary Design

13.1.1 Open-ended design: In open design, focus is on subjective states and perception of social phenomena (Gershuny and Sullivan, 1998). Activities and events, whatsoever, are recorded freely in his or her own words. The data provided in open-ended diaries are investigated as narratives constructing the participant's identity. Centrality is on certain topics or events in everyday life. Diaries give the researcher the possibility of "getting close" to the participants (Burgess, 1999). At the same time, room is left to the diarists, who are not constrained by a certain interview situation, focus group discussions, or participatory observation, by the researcher. Unstructured diaries are used to elicit data as a personal response to change, upheaval and exploration. They provide information about everyday life and trivia. They are particularly useful when exploring cultural phenomena, providing valuable insights into spiritual, interpersonal and emotional domains.

13.1.2 Device-Contingent Design-The diary makes use of cell phones and other electronic devices. These devices often come with a set of inputs and outputs of sensory information, such as camera on devices on cell phones, micro-phones, bluetooth, accelerometer, and global positioning system (GPS). These capabilities allow researchers to collect collateral information. Intille *et al.* (2003) developed a programme called 'context-aware experience sampling (CAES)'. It allows researchers to acquire feedback from participants only in particular situations detected by sensors attached to the mobile devices.

Research online is a flourishing topic within empirical and theoretical research. Within the realm of online research, one can identify a strand of research focusing on weblogs and life journals. They are popular forms of self-reporting and self-reflection (e.g., Macdonald and Ounis, 2006; Marwick, 2008; Serfaty, 2004). Sudweeks and Simoff (1999), therefore, stressed that "a modern Internet research methodology should take into account rapidly changing technology, social norms and communication behaviour". The online environment offers the potential to observe new social phenomena, such as the behaviour of very large groups (e.g., Facebook users). In addition, the researcher is provided with a widespread geographical access to participants. Furthermore, online research has rather low monetary costs and a low time investment compared to traditional forms of data collection like large-scale transnational surveys using paper-and-pencil questionnaires, telephone interviews, face-to-face interviews, or focus groups (Kraut, Olson, Banaji, Bruckmann, Cohen, and Couper, 2004).

In highly structured diaries all activities are pre-categorised. Structured diaries are constrained to quantitative and strongly structured documentation or recollections of certain behaviours, habits, or feelings under particular conditions (Bolger, Davis, and Rafaeli, 2003). Structured or solicited diaries provide space for participants to log the events and experiences of daily life. They reflect on significant predetermined events or experiences. They have the potential to capture rich, chronological data on feelings, beliefs, motives and desires in an unobtrusive manner. Therefore, these are popular in research associated with sensitive matters and as well the marginalised groups in society.

Diary designs can also be classified into two broad categories: time-based and event-based protocols. In the first data collection is scheduled or sampled according to the passage of time, and in the second, data collection is triggered by some focal experience of the participant. Time-based diaries follow fixed or variable or random schedules defined by the researcher on the basis of research questions and aims. Event-based diaries are kept after or during certain instances take place; for example, after a great loss of close relatives. They are especially appropriate for capturing rare and/or isolated processes.

13.1.3 Time-Based Design: Time-based design serves the purpose of investigating experiences as they unfolded over time. These designs include fixed-interval schedules, where participants report on their experiences or events at predetermined intervals, and variable interval schedules, the participants report at random intervals or temporal-based pattern. In fixed interval schedule it is important to consider the prototypic pattern of change over time and to identify which components of the change are significant or of most interest. Researchers use online assessment in variable time schedule. This type of design minimise retrospective recall bias. It allows for random sampling of events, experiences, and behaviour throughout the day.

Example-1: one might be interested in how a student makes sense of and negotiates a particular learning environment. Besides the collection of subjective data, the participant can also record- the number of times engaged in an activity and the duration of the activity. In organisational and industrial research, diaries have been used as record-keeping devices and as aids for promoting awareness and understanding of day-to-day work processes.

Example-2: doctor can record and monitor the progrees of patient recovery over a long period. (case study). Diary has also been used to record and study the profile of 'Aging with Cerebral Palsy'.

13.1.4 Event-Based Design: When researcher is interested in rare event such as learning disabilities or seizures among epileptic patients who are generally under controlled conditions. Event-based designs are also known as event- contingent designs. Participants in this type of design will report every time an event. An event or events should be as per investigator prescribed criterion. Event-based design requires investigators to give a clear definition of the event in which they are interested. Although the time and event-based designs have been given two separate categories, some recent studies have combined these two designs. Time of occuring and description of events are recorded simultaneously. Five steps are involved in this process:

- Description of event i.e., restructuring the data set. In cross-sectional study, data set is structured in such a way that each participant responses are entered in a single row.
- Description of thoughts and feelings about the incident.
- Evolution of the event.
- Evaluation of the event, and
- Analysis of the event, conclusion and plan of action.

Focus is on theme or themes already decided. Some time, new theme can emerge during writing diary and will become the essential part of the research.

13.1.5 Case Diary is generally used in health studies to monitor the development of disease or to explore the experiences of those who are ill (Richardson, 1994). Diaries have frequently been used in health research during the course of time of studies. In these studies, informants are often encouraged to make use of structured diaries to register their use of time daily, weekly, or over the course of months. Diaries have been used to gain information from informants about subjects such as their social networks, health, illnesses, use of drugs, and patterns of waking and sleeping (Furness and Garrud, 2010; Lawrence and Shank, 1995; Ross, Rideout and Carson, 1994; Rogers, Caruso and Aldrich, 1993; Temple and Walkley, 2003).

Box 15.1: Instructions for the Researcher regarding the Maintenance of diary

- An A4 booklet of about 5 to 20 pages is desirable.
- The inside cover page should contain a clear set of instructions on how to complete the diary.
- A model example of a correctly completed diary should feature on the second page.

(Contd...)

- Depending on how long a period the diary will cover, each page denoting either a week, a day of the week or a 24 hour period or less.
- Pages should be clearly ruled up as a calendar with prominent heading and enough space to enter all the desired information.
- Checklists of the items, events or behaviour to help jog the diary keeper's memory should be printed somewhere fairly prominent.
- All possible relevant activities should be listed together with the appropriate codes.
- Different versions of the diary should be used for different groups.
- Include a simple set of questions for the respondent to complete.

13.2 Data Quality and Response Rates

- Diaries are needed to be free from errors arising from respondent conditioning, incomplete recording of information and under-reporting, inadequate recall, insufficient cooperation and sample selection bias.
- The period over which a diary is to be kept needs to be long enough to capture the behaviour or events of interest without jeopardising successful completion by imposing an overly burdensome task.
- Reporting errors are to be eliminated. They may be due to respondents changing their behaviour as a result of keeping the diary (conditioning), or becoming less conscientious than when they started the diary.
- The respondent should have a reasonable standard of literacy to provide reliable and valid data/ information.
- Participants need to be inspired, informed and involved to get the requisite information. Appeal to respondents' altruistic nature, and reassure them of confidentiality.

13.3 Collection of Data

Diary is an appropriate tool to grasp the phenomena of everyday life. It helps get close to participants. It allows the participant enough space for personal reflections. Diaries as a source of data give researchers the ability to apply narrations as a method to grasp forms of identity and meaning construction. The participants are asked to elaborate on issues and topics. All participants were informed about the purpose of the study. Confidentiality of the participant needs to be ensured. The participant consent is to be got confirmed. First, information on 'Personal Data' is recorded. Diarist has the opportunity to create content pages and to edit them, as well as the option to share files with the researcher. The participants are free to write on their everyday lives: topics they discuss with their friends and family, those that appear in the media, or those about which they actively search for information.

Researcher should keep in mind while recording diary

Ensure that diary is an appropriate tool for the intended research. Call for diligent planning, preparation, construction and deconstruction. Ensure potential effects (social/economic/cultural/health) on participants. Have a critical reflection on ethical dilemmas and conflicts. Have a clear cut reflection on the observer's frame of mind.

13.4 Analysis of Data

Coding, Editing and Processing

The amount of work required to process a diary depends largely on how structured it is. For many large scale diary surveys, part of the editing and coding process is done by the interviewer while still in the field. Following this is an intensive editing procedure which includes checking entries against information collected in the personal interview. For unstructured diaries, involving coding of verbatim entries, the processing can be very labour intensive, in much the same way as it is for processing qualitative interview transcripts. Using highly trained coders and a rigorous unambiguous coding scheme is very important particularly where there is no clear demarcation of events or behaviour in the diary entries. Clearly, a well designed diary with a coherent pre-coding system should cut down on the degree of editing and coding.

Data is analysed in light of the research questions. These research questions are: (a) What are the lived experiences of an individual, and how much do experiences vary from day-to-day? (b) What is the individual trajectory of experiences across days, and how do trajectories differ by person? (c) What process underlies a person's changes, and how do people differ? Before addressing these questions, reliability and validity of measurement are established.

Methods of Analysis

Grounded theory: The process of discovering theory from systematically collected data and analysis.

Content analysis: An objective process of determining the occurrence and presence of keywords or phrases in a document.

Thematic analysis: A systematic process, in which key themes and ideas are identified, organised and interpreted.

Focused is on three main underpinnings of narratives as research methods. First, all experiences are organised within narratives. Those narratives are told by individuals, but they are also produced as introspective. Through diary, one assigns meaning to certain experiences or aspects of experiences. Second, narratives being told depend on the social past and present of the informant as well as the themes of the narrations. The narrations are not isolatable single structures but identity constructions that are continuously negotiated and revised. Third, narratives are multivoiced; namely, they are shaped by the individual experiences, knowledge, values, and feelings. These are influenced by "cultural, historical and institutional settings in which they occur" (Moen, 2006, p. 61).

First diary data is structured, the patterns of data are established and next a Grounded Theory analysis is carried out. Finally, multilevel models are applied to describe between person differences in context of the diary experience. A consensus is emerging among diary researchers that multilevel models (also called hierarchical linear models, general mixed models, and random regression models), modified to handle repeated-measures data, and is appropriate for diary data analysis. Although these models are complex, we believe they are in important. Widely used models such as structural equation modelling (SEM) or meta-analysis are used to get the authentic and trustworthy picture because. They provide a way to explore truth; an understanding of data set, how the informant understands; transforming the expression given by the informant into research language; and a consistent description of essential features of the specific phenomena.

13.5 Computer Software for Processing and Analysis

Diary data is accessed, stored and processed in the computer. Software is used for the analysis of data. One of the problems of developing software for processing and manipulating diary data is the complex and bulk of the information collected. Although computer assisted methods may help to reduce the amount of manual preparatory work, there are few packages and most of them are custom built to suit the specifics of a particular project. Time-budget- researchers are probably the most advanced group of users of machine. Readable diary data and the structure of these data allow them to use traditional statistical packages for analysis. More recently, methods of analysis based on algorithms for searching for patterns of behaviour in diary data are being used (Coxon, 1991). Software development is certainly an area which merits future attention. For textual diaries, qualitative software packages such as The ETHNOGRAPH can be used to code them in the same way as interview transcripts (Fielding and Lee, 1991).

Interpretation of Narrative Data

In interpreting the 'data', the researcher constantly asks how good the evidence is for the interference which he or she is drawing. The data comes from what people say and feel, how they interact with others and what they do in different situations, and these data are constantly cross-checked as fieldwork proceeds. As the researcher develops an understanding of what is going on, or an explanation for something, alternative understandings and explanations are considered, modified, incorporated or cast aside. The researcher always has to maintain some degree of distance and detachment in order to continually evaluate what is going on, fitting it into the analytic frame provided by their professional knowledge and training.

In interpreting the 'case diary' the researcher should:

- Explore *significant* features of the case;
- Create plausible interpretations of what is found;
- Test for the trustworthiness of these interpretations;
- Construct a worthwhile argument or story recorded in diary;
- Relate the argument or story to any relevant research in the literature;
- Convey convincingly to an audience these arguments of the diarist;

- Provide an audit trail by which other researchers may validate or challenge the findings, or construct alternative arguments.

13.6 Limitations of Use of Diary as a Research Tool

The diary method is not a 'quick fix' solution for the rapid collection of data. Considerable investment of time, resources and effort is required by participants and researcher to ensure that a diary is developed that is fit for purpose and the aims of the research, and that the diarists are prepared appropriately. Similar time and effort is required to develop a diary as to develop a questionnaire. The associated costs should be offset against the benefits of acquiring rich and balanced data, especially in areas where greater reliance on recall may provide less favourable results. Diary research is more labour intensive than a simple interview. It is costly in terms of data collection and analysis. Maintaining the interest of the diarist may be problematic if the process is arduous or complex.

Similarly, recruitment of suitable diarists may be problematic. The diarist must know what to include in the diary and how it should be recorded; the chosen device or form should be easy to use and the diarist should be competent with its use. Both paper diaries and e-diaries are not suitable for everyone. The researcher should pay attention to the times-scale and frequency of the diary entries; diarists may, sometime become fatigued with the process. Moreover, as the process goes on, participants may become tired of keeping records and less thorough in their reporting. Missing, incomplete or unclear data may be difficult to resolve. Training and ongoing support for the diarist are required (Alaszewski, 2006).

References

Alaszewski, A. (2006). *Using Diaries for Social Research*. London: Sage Publications.

Gershuny, J.I. et al. (1986). 'Time Budgets: A preliminary analysis of a national survey' *Quarterly Journal of Social Research*, 2, 1.

Harvey, A.S. (1990). Guidelines for Time Use Data Collection, Working paper No. 5, General Social Survey, *Statistics,* Canada.

Juster, T. and Stafford, F.P. (eds) (1985). *Time, Goods and Well-being*, Ann Arbor: Institute for Social Research, University of Michigan.

Szalai, A. et al. (eds) (1972). *The Use of Time,* The Hague, Netherlands: Mouton.

Sorokin, P.A. and Berger, C.Q. (1938). *Time Budgets of Human Behaviour*, Cambridge Massachusetts: Harvard University Press.

Redpath, R. (1991). "Memory problems in Family Budget Surveys: I. Diaries", *Survey Methodology Bulletin, OPCS,* July 1990, London: HMSO.

Robson, C (2011). *Real World Research*. Third edition. Wiley: Chichester.

Silberstein, A.R. and Scott, S. (1991). "Expenditure Diary Surveys and their Associated errors", in P. Biemer, R.M. Groves, L.E. Lyberg, N.A. Mathiowetz and S. Sudman (eds) (1991) *Measurement Errors in Surveys*, New York: Wiley.

Verbrugge, L.M. (1980). "Health diaries", Medical Care, 18:73-95.*Child Psychology*: Douglas, J.W.B., Lawson, A., Cooper, J.E & Cooper, J. (1968)."Family interaction and the activities of young children", *Journal of Child Psychology and Psychiatry, 9:157-71.*

Travel Diaries: Butcher, R. and Eldridge, J.(1990). "The Use of Diaries in Data collection", *The Statistician*, 1990, : 25-41.

Gregory, J. (1990). "The Adult Dietary Survey", *Survey Methodology Bulletin, OPCS,* July 1990, London: HMSO; OPCS, The National Food Survey.

Coxon, A.P.M., Davies, P.M. and T.J. McManus (1990). Project Sigma, *Longitudinal Study of the Sexual Behaviour of Homosexual males under the impact of AIDS: A Final Report to the Department of Health,* Project Sigma Working Papers, Southbank Polytechnic, London: Project Sigma.

Hilton, M.E. (1989). "A comparison of a prospective diary and two summary recall techniques for recording alcohol consumption", *British Journal of Addiction,* 1989, 84: 1085-1092.

Plummer, K. (1983). *Documents of Life*, Allen &Unwin: London.

Fothergill, R.A. (9174). Private Chronicles: A Study of English Diaries, London: Oxford University Press.

Fielding, N. and Lee, R.M. (eds) (1991). *Using Computers in Qualitative Research*, Sage.

Coxon, A.P.M. (1991). *"The structure of sexual behaviour",* Research paper, ESRC Research Centre, University of Essex.

14

Electronic Tools for the Collection of Data

14.1 Video and Film

Video and film provide detailed recordings of facts. Comprehensive data on lifestyle and its holistic presentation can be captured. Process of capturing video is too fast or too complex for the human eye to record for further for deep analysis. Cameras also allow non-reactive recordings of observations, and, finally, they are less selective than observations. Researchers have used video (and before that film) for many years particularly in workplace studies (Heath, Luff, Hindmarsh, 2010), the learning sciences (Goldman *et al,* 2009), and the significant events in home (Norris, 2004; Goodwin, 2000). Studies have used video to ask questions in a variety of sites including how social class and race are articulated in the school classroom (e.g. Mehan, 1979); how museum visitors interact with one another and exhibits (Heath and vom Lehn, 2004); how patients and General Practitioners manage consultations, including how digital resources, such as the Electronic Patient Record (EPR) shape these interactions (Swinglehurst, 2015). Video has also been used to examine cultural aspects of everyday life, for example, Pink (2003) has used video tours to explore the aesthetics of home décor in relation to social identities, others have explored how families use video recording in the home to construct their domestic narratives (Willet and Buckingham, 2009). Video has been employed to explore children and young people's identities, media practices and digital cultural production (Marsh, 2004; Domingo, 2011; Gilje, 2009). Others have approached videos made by others, for instance exploring how people produce, share and comment on videos. The films based on the caste conflict have altered the way the audience perceives the caste theme. This shift has also led to a greater understanding of caste reality (Shukla, 2016).

Video and film have penetrated significantly in the field of social science, including anthropology, education, psychology, geopolitics and economics. In the past the cost of film and video equipment and production placed it out of the hands of most researchers. Now, video is increasingly a significant resource for many contemporary social researchers. The increased presence of video in the people's everyday lives as well as institutional practices and public environments means researchers often have access to 'naturally occurring' video data. Video is increasingly the data collection tool of choice for researchers interested in the multimodal character of social interaction. The use of video has also been expanded by increased access through the low cost of video cameras high quality video facilities on mobile phones, cheap webcams and easy to use computer applications for editing.

Denzin (1989b, pp. 213-214) referred the plus points of video and film as a research tool.

- Theoretical presumptions that determine what are photographed and when? Which features are selected from the photograph for analysis? How photographs are used as data or for the documentation of relations?
- Cameras are incorruptible in terms of their perception and documentation of the world: they do not forget, do not get tired, and do not make mistakes. However, photographs also transform the world, which they present in a specific shape.
- However, photos are also marked by the interpretation and ascription of meaning by those who take them.
- Photos (and films) reveal an approach to the symbolic world of the subjects and their views.

- Photos are only expressive when they are taken at the right moment—when the interesting action occurs and the relevant persons step into the camera's field of vision.

14.1 Video can be used in a number of ways for research including participatory ideography, the use of existing video data, video interviews and elicitation and video based fieldwork. Video data specifically in history, sociology, psychology, politics and education provide evidence about the reality. Participatory video approach has grown up since the late 1990's in the context of action research and practice based interventions. Generally, participatory video is used to explore people's experiences and it produces three kinds of data: (1) the video 'as product', (2) the process of its production – which itself is often video recorded and (3) the process of video editing.

14.2 Knoblauch (2004b, p. 126) lists several data sorts which are used in video research: scientific recording of natural social situations; scientific recording of experimental social situations; interviews; natural social situations recorded by the actors (surveillance, audio recording); posed situations recorded by actors (video diaries); situations recorded and edited by actors (wedding videos); and also by professionals (wedding videos, documentations).

14.3 Video elicitation can be used alongside interviews or focus groups to prompt discussion stimulate recall or provide a basis for reflection (Roth, 2009). Tochon (2009) suggests that video based reflections can be focused on three distinct ways: (i) reconstructing past-thinking, (ii) post-activity narratives, or (iii) the construction of reflections on present and future actions. Video elicitation interviews are particularly useful in helping to generate accounts of the characteristics of 'invisible' phenomena. Video elicitation can also be used to provide a basis for reflection on practice and continuing professional development. The use of video to collect 'naturally occurring data' in these different contexts involves decisions that shape the production of data and its interpretation.

14.4 It has been observed that video recording can lead to overwhelming amounts of rich video data. It is for this reason that the collection of video data needs to be *planned and managed* with analysis in mind, and to avoid the collection of video data that is not necessary and that the researcher will not have time to analyse. Video data required needs to be determined by the research approach, aim and questions of a study. Using visual technologies to collect data can give new insights into classroom interaction and established methodological practices (Flewitt, 2006).

14.5 There are three ways of thinking about video selection, (i) inductive, (ii) deductive and (iii) narrative-evolving. Inductive approaches are considered most apt for sampling when working with 'raw' video data sets that have been collected with broad questions in mind but without a strong orienting theory. A deductive approach to video data is appropriate for sampling when the researcher has a strong theory and clear research questions. Narrative approaches focus on communication, discourse analysis, and genre analysis. The study is adapted reflectively in which participants are observed and consulted. (Goldman *et al,* 2007: 26).

14.6 In a mixed method (quantitative and qualitative) data is collected at the macro level for quantitative analysis, whereas extreme segments or case studies are put to micro analysis. Therefore, video data analysis can tend to focus on short segments or typical cases.

Example: Extreme cases of learning disability can be analysed at the micro level. However, it is through this micro-analysis that they can also explore larger societal issues.

Example: Some researchers sit and watch videos of films and then do an analysis of the content. This may involve elaborate coding and a great deal of systematic work and may present important and interesting findings about the depiction of violence, sexuality, gender and racial stereotypes, and other issues of broad concern.

14.7 Knoblauch (2004b) develops a video interaction analysis as a method from using these sorts of video data, which he characterises by three features: **methodicity (**presentations of situations and actors in video material), **order** (ways of producing and interpreting the performed activities), and **reflexivity** reflect what they do in their presentations). Video recordings in naturally occurring activities are the primary data. For example: using video recordings of doctor-patient interactions.

14.8 Transcribing video data: Multimodal transcripts are produced in conversation analysis, discourse analysis, social semiotics and micro-ethnography. Focus is on the meaning-making principles.

14.8.1 Coding Video: One way to look across a set of video data is to code it. Some researchers undertake systematic coding using pre-established coding schemes drawn from theoretical approaches and disciplines; others build codes from their data and or the literature on a specific area, while some researchers remain at the case level and descriptive analysis without the use of coding.

14.8.2 Qualitative Data Analysis Packages: Most Computer Assisted Qualitative Data Analysis packages can be used with video files although they vary in the types of features they offer. There are a range of digital applications such as Interact, Transana, DRS, Hypermedia, ATLAS.ti, and NVivo.

14.9 Films as a Research Instrument

Film is a powerful tool for bringing the voices of communities and individuals in lime light. Social structure, social facts, order, action, social can be studied. It is an instrument for critical evaluation of our socio-economic-political and cultural scenarios. It provides substantial live data on violence, exploitation, gender discrimination, and disruption. Films provide a rich and impactful portrait of the textures of participants' daily lives - revealing influences, causes, cultural contexts and ideas in places that might otherwise remain hidden. They can also be shared time and again with relevant stakeholders. One of the strengths of film is that it can be repeatedly viewed, shared and discussed at events or with teams to focus on facts to develop just and equitable social order.

Film is a powerful tool for both the process of understanding and exploration in fieldwork and for the representation of sensorial aspects of social life. Films capture the observable and manifest expression of culture. The camera is a neutral tool for the collection of "objective" data. Social scientists later concentrated on the more abstract aspects of life such as social structures, social order and its stratification, psychological traits, cultural ethos, and the threads that held a society together to form a coherent whole. After many decades of technological improvements in film cameras and recording equipment, social scientists continue to use the medium as a tool for documentation, and to illustrate their arguments.

Visual social scientists have recently begun using the camera not so much as an objective recording devise, but as an instrument of discovery and exploration within ethnographic research. Cameras can be employed to elicit discussions, provoke meaningful performances and to reveal what Margaret Mead referred to as the intangibles of social life. Such intangibles may be better represented through the observation of body gestures, facial expressions, nuanced glances, tone of voice, and pauses in speech, which usually escape the written ethnomethodology.

Movies are seismographs of socio-economic- political and cultural trends. They reflect the status of society in its genesis and complexity. They provide information about class, caste, ethnic groups, and their interaction, social facts, social order; economic status and standard, occupations and professions, accountability, equity and equality, justice, rights and duties, ethical values, political activities and public action and reaction, etc. they make in-depth descriptions of the audience in order to reconstruct the latent "Komplexentwicklung," the development of psychological lines. Suspense and spellbound is based on activating a meaningful transformational experience—only movies stimulate such a process which touch the heart of the viewers. The psychological analysis works out the morphological dramaturgy of the film -experience, which is shaped into a specific dynamic figure.

Cinematography has been found of great value in many fields of human endeavour. Cinematography is systematic research for new knowledge, new practices and new models. Cinematography is used as an instrument of observation, description or explanation as well as for the provisions of data observation, description, or classification or the formulation and testing of hypotheses. Scientific cinematography denotes the techniques of production, analysis and usage of research fills in the sciences.

The fairer sex alone is not the marginalised community that needs a voice. There are Dalits and other caste based issues all of which are, interestingly, finding greater representation in regional cinema. GinniMahi takes Dalits ideology to another level in her robust songs.

Marathi superhit Sairat, a love story of a low caste boy and a rich upper caste girl sets new trend. Films in this technological age direct the course and content of new narratives.

Television and films influence everyday life. Qualitative research uses these to tell us about the social construction of reality. Denzin (1989b) analyses Hollywood movies that contain social reflections on social experiences (such as alcoholism, corruption, and so on). Such films reflect also on key moments of history (World Wars; the Vietnam War; ISIS Conflict Zones), on certain institutions (hospitals), on social values (such as marriage and family) and relations, on domains of everyday life, and on emotions.

Fifty film experts were asked to remember specific film scenes that elicited fear, anger, sadness, disgust, amusement, tenderness, as well as emotionally neutral scenes. For each emotion, the 10 most frequently mentioned scenes were selected and cut into film clips. Next, 364 participants viewed the film clips in individual laboratory sessions and rated each film on multiple dimensions. Results showed that the film clips were effective with regard to several criteria such as emotional discreteness, arousal, positive and negative effect (Schaefer, *et al.,* 2010)

A film is a truthful description of a phenomenon. Socio-ethnic-cultural meaning can be derived through a detailed analysis of the contents. The interpretation serves to validate the truth claims. The film provided ample evidence about reality. Subversive readings take into account that the author's ideas of reality influence the film. The interpreter will influence its interpretation.

A 13-episode TV serial followed by a two-hour film Aashiq-e-Vatan: Maulana Azad made in the document-drama format, the film that took more than three years to be made juxtaposes live footage with enactment of scenes highlighting the turning point in India's history. This would leave a greater impact on the viewers.

Bollywood films have taken up themes of social justice (Samajko Badaldalo); Political corruption (Nayak, Ardh Satya); Communal riots (Tamas) and (Pinger) and Capability development of special child (Tare Zami Par) etc. Do Bigha Zamin talks of the struggle of farmers, Sujata, Biraj Bahu, Bandini and Parineeta reveal social injustices against women, prisoners, and immigrants. Dangal has captured the real story of women excelling in a space traditionally marked for men.

Film 'No Man Land' gives the narration of two soldiers facing each other in the war.

14.10 Key Questions

- It might be used at the beginning of a project to learn about a community, or to help define an area of enquiry and focus on a set of research questions;
- Later, it can respond to already-established research objectives through "deep-dive" filmed fieldwork. Edits can be used at interim workshops to include the voice of participants in insight and design sessions;
- Towards the end of a process, films can be used to present key findings or to act as an evaluative tool, testing service design in context and engaging community members for their feedback.

14.11 Film Data: Ethnography, photography, films and videos are observational and mediated data. In social science researches, photos, recordings, and video clips can provide a more comprehensive and holistic presentation of lifestyle and situation. During interviews, one can take help from photographer or videographer for photo and recording (Dabbs, 1982). Genuine analytical procedures that directly relate to image or photos still remain to be developed (Flick, 2009).We know about research instruments used in educational and behavioural researches. Researcher can collect information or data from sample through research instrument. Like that, the analysis of film can give proper data; some time other instruments can be helpful in film analysis (Flik, 2010). Photos are not a clinical task, picking these images; they are documents of a time (Nair, 2016).

14.12 Methodologies

- **Observational ethnography**: Filming events unfold in context can be more informative than solely relying on interview.
- **Co-direction and collaborative filmmaking**: Filmmaking involves engaging participants in a dialogue, sharing aims and questions as part of a collaborative and organic process. Participants tell us about themselves in their own words and in their own way, in the environments where they feel most comfortable.

- **Documentation and Communication:** Conduct and edit on-camera interviews to support research projects, manage 'video diary' creation, document workshops and focus groups, and create films that illustrate the key findings of a wider project – all to a high professional standard. We recognise the power of film to provide concise, engaging storytelling that communicates the findings of a project for an audience beyond the core team or stakeholder group. Film offers an accessible alternative or complement to the written word. Filmmaking and visual ethnography use research design, investigate organisations, academic institutions and community groups to understand and to make others to understand the reality.

Case studies: The Film designers and directors collaborate with each other's to create a short film. They seek help of a group of service users. They run a series of workshops with service users and staff, drawing on their experiences to explore how best to express complex cultural aspects of the society. They then worked with one service user to tell their personal story through observational film and interview. The film is being used to provoke discussion and reflection for individuals and organisations.

14.13 Steps of Film Analysis

To analyse the film, the analyser has to see the film more than once then he or she can follow the following five steps of film analysis for data collection.

- **Effectiveness of the Dialogue and Storyline:** During analysing film, examine that the dialogue give true and authentic picture. Ensure that the scenes flow in a logical progression and stay with the storyline.
- **Cinematography:** When you watch a film for analysis, pay attention to the background information. Analyse scenes having appropriate background information or cinematography.
- **Actors:** Performance of Hero of the film as well the supporting actor is to be analysed Analyser must focus his or her attention on supportive actors' efforts. Supporting characters may not have much dialogue, but their presence can still be felt by the audience.

- **Editing of the Film:** The film critics say the real movie or film begins in the editing room. Sometimes a potentially good film is less successful because of poor editing. To analyse the editing of film is difficult task. Action scenes should maintain a steady, exciting pace that builds to a climax. At the time of analysis analyser should through light on flow of scene to scene going without denying the audience enough information to follow the arc of the story. Analyser must think about scrip writer's ideas, vision and reality reflect in whole film, also think about the message of writer and film reach to the people who see the film. The film has a huge and long materials and contents, so it is difficult for researcher to analyse it. Here some problems are discussed.

Denzin (2004a, pp. 241-242) suggests four phases for film analyses

- "Looking and feeling": the films are regarded as a whole, and impressions, questions, and patterns of meaning which are conspicuous are noted.
- What research question are you asking? Formulate the questions to pursue. Therefore, note key scenes.
- Structured microanalysis is conducted of individual scenes and sequences, which should lead to detailed descriptions and patterns in the display (of conflicts and so on) in these excerpts.
- When answering the research question, search for patterns in the entire film. Searching for patterns extends to the whole film in order to answer the research question. The film's realistic and subversive readings are contrasted and a final interpretation is written.

Bergmann (2006, p. 496) outlines several alternatives of how to make mediated documents (images, photos, films, Internet documents) undergo a "data-transformation":

- Descriptions in the form of text (which involve a high degree of interpretation by the researcher and of data reduction from image to text) may help to represent visual information in publications.
- Transcription and notation: Images—similar to spoken texts—are transcribed according to certain rules and excerpts are integrated in publications.

- Photo inserts: Images or drawings are exemplarily integrated in a published text.
- Photo series: a series of images are integrated in the text or complement it in order to document processes.
- Ethnographic films are an alternative to a textual representation for presenting processes and results drawn from them.

14.14 Problems in Analysis of Films

Selection: There are many dialogues and scenes in a film. Deep knowledge and visual expertise are required to identify scenes or dialogue attuned to the purposes of study and appropriate for analysis.

Formulation of Research Questions is difficult and strenuous exercise. The researcher needs to be familiar with theoretical backgrounds, field experiences of the experts. Carefully construction of research questions and documentation of the film materials can make easy the analysis and interpretation.

Content: The description is made on the basis of 'content' of films shots or scenes. Content analysis is complex and meticulous exercise. The researcher has to keep in mind the objectives, research themes, methodology and expected outcomes or logical conclusions.

Film analysis is useful and effective method and tool for research. Consistency, conviction, focus, minute and continuous observation, and specific skills of microanalysis are required to get to the solution of problem or to get answers to the research questions.

Interpretation is complex because it is carried out using sequential procedures. Researcher needs to be systemic in his or her approach i.e. establishing cyclic relation between objectives, themes and interpretation.

14.15 Limitations of Film Analysis

Films are visual texts and there is no direct method of interpretation for visual data (Denzin). So film is transformed into text by transcription. Script writer's ideas and views and views of film observer are different, so it is difficult to find out about the message of writer is passed through the film observer. Therefore, film analysis is rarely used as a genuine strategy but rather as an addition to or a part of other methods aimed at analysing verbal data (Flick, 2010). So film analysis is best used in combination with other methods.

14.16 Photography as a Research Tool

Since photography has always "served as an instrument of communication and as a means of sharing experience" (Pink, 2011, p. 95). It has gained much currency as a research tool. Three concurrent trends in social research have been observed namely, first, a re-emergence of the visual within social science research, and the increasing attention given to the role of all of the senses in the construction and representation of experience (the so-called *sensory turn*) (Pink *et al.,* 2011); second, a focus on memory and imagination in research practice (Clover, 2006; Hogan, 2012); and finally, the emergence of the participation paradigm. These developments have influenced ethnographic practices. New methodologies have come up to redesign the production of scholarly knowledge (Pink *et al.,* 2011).

Photography is seen to be closely aligned with lived experience, and consequently more representative of how participants themselves interpret their context, relationships, decisions and realities (Castleden *et al.,* 2008; Liebenberg, 2009; Murray, 2009; Svensson *et al.,* 2009), allowing people to tell their stories and realities in new ways (Bolton *et al.,* 2001; Clover 2006; Croghan *et al.,* 2008; Morrow and Richards, 1996; Newman *et al.,* 2006; Singhal *et al.,* 2007), letting us tap into the complexities of social relationships in ways that include more conventional means of investigation (Mizen, 2005; Luttrell, 2010), and perhaps even bridging the different worlds of the researcher and the researched (Croghan *et al.,* 2008). It does not offer some single lens authority, but affords multiple perspectives and interpretations" (Parker, 2005) Photography is a means of directly engaging with people's socio-spatial lives, and thus of enhancing our understandings of the constitution of people's lived space (Anderson and Jones, 2009; Pink, 2011). Clover (2006): "our understandings of learning, knowledge, meaning-making, and empowerment would only be enriched if we included imagination and its ability to invent new lives, new spirits, new spaces, and new forms of social engagement". Photograph encapsulates the soul, culture and community (Krabbe, 2016). Photograph can illustrate a grand idea on a minimal and intimate scale, coupled with adventurous and perpetually self-critical nature (Shadbolt, 2016).

Photography allows detailed recordings of facts as well as provides a more comprehensive and holistic presentation of lifestyles and conditions (Mead, 1963). Fantastical photographs across the world have deliberated on terrorism, power, Islamophobia and other modern malaises. The photograph of five years old Syrian refugee Galip Kurdi whose body was washed ashore at Turkish beach (2015) has attracted the attention of whole world. They allow the transportation of artefacts and the presentation of them as pictures and also the transgression of borders of time and space. They can catch facts and processes that are too fast or too complex for the human eye. Cameras also allow non-reactive recordings of observations, and, finally, they are less selective than observations:

- Photographs are used as data or for the documentation of relations or case study and serve as an instrument of communication and as a means of sharing experience.
- Photos are also marked by the interpretation and ascription of meaning by those who take or regard them.
- Photos (and films) reveal an approach to the symbolic world of the subjects and their views.
- It is detailed recordings of facts as well as provides a more comprehensive and holistic presentation of lifestyles and conditions.
- They can catch facts and processes that are too fast or too complex for the human eye.

14.17 Methodology

14.17.1 Communication and Documentation

Photographic diary is used to capture aspects and events of daily lives. The subject decides the events or aspects worthy of photographing. Researcher analyses the data captured through photographic diary and draws conclusions. Data and features captured through photographs could be compared to arrive at the reality.

14.17.2 Case Study Analysis

Photos are produced for research purposes. But sometimes, the existing photos are used as material for research. Haupert (1994) analysed soldiers' photos using the method of objective hermeneutics in order to reconstruct biographical processes. In general, photos have a high iconic quality, which may help to activate people's memories or to stimulate or encourage them to make statements about complex processes and situations. Case studies of learner, special child, and patient can be projected and analysed though sequence of data derived from video, film and sequence of photographs.

14.18 Application of the Method in the Field

The choice of film, development and paper, of lens and camera, of exposures and framing, of moment and relations with subjects—all of these, directly under the photographer's control, shape the end product...A second influence on the image the photographer produces, is his theory about what he is looking at, his understanding of what he is investigating. (Denzin, 1986a, pp. 241-242)

Photographer has niche and skills as how to use camera for research purpose. He focuses on research questions to get descriptions of aspects of reality through photographs. Material is selected in a step-by-step manner. Sequential procedures are used for interpretation. The analysis of visual material is mostly triangulated with other methods and data.

14.19 Consent, Ethics and Data Release

The agreement to protect the participant's privacy and anonymity needs to be adhered. They are to share their insights and interpretations without fear of outsiders judging their work. Increase the participant's sense of ownership and mastery over the job of interpreting the image. The researcher has to establish an acceptable balance between protection and empowerment. Researcher needs to get consent of participant, institution, and the competent authority. An agreement has to be signed in advance for not releasing the images and 'context' (data) to anybody.

14.20 Data Construction

The participants or actors are allowed without interruption to construct and analyse their own images. Allow them to set the research agenda i.e. location and situation. The interview of the participant is to be held prior to photography. Interview should be brief, precise, and theme oriented.

Data are created by participant efforts to understand complex change processes and their contribution to (predicted and unpredicted) outcomes. It comprises complex, interrelated elements embracing values, knowledge, behaviour, and relationships. Both the content and the quality of data are prime concerns. Scoring of qualitative changes in behaviour and relationships is generated through photographic processes. It involves objectivity in the subjectivity of the researcher. All qualitative research methods adhere to certain themes such as qualitative data, content sensitivity, emphatic neutrality, inductive analysis and naturalistic inquiry. Empower participants to feel in control of the research process and to elicit meaningful data.

14.21 Data Analysis

The significance of the images lay solely in the interpretations given to them by the actors/participants. These interpretations and insights, shared at interview, formed the basis for analysis. The photographs also lend themselves to analysis following the interviews. Initially, this required 'macro-analysis', first mooted by Collier (1979), in which the photographs are categorised according to their 'holistic content', rather than their more micro-analytical cultural or theoretical significance (Helen C., 2005).

In macro-analysis, the focus is on 'special' events. Interface between participants on the research themes or research questions would provide cues and insight for the analysis of data. A comparison between participants is to be undertaken to identify the significant difference or change. It is useful to examine photography not simply as a research method, but also as a visual language.

References

Film

Denzin, N.K. (2004a). "Reading Film, " in U. Flick, E.v. Kardorff, and I. Steinke (eds.), A Companion to Qualitative Research. London: SAGE. pp. 237-242.

Dodia, D.R.(2012). Film Analysis: A Research Instrument. *Indian Streams Research Journal*, Vol. 1, Issue.V/June; 12pp.1-4.

Gloria Dahl.(2016). Qualitative Analysis of Films: Cultural Processes in the Mirror of Film.

Schaefer, A., Niles, F., Sanchez, X. and Philipoot, P. (2010). Assessing the effectiveness of a large database of emotion eliciting films: Tool for emotion researchers. *Cognition and emotion.* Vol. 24, Issue 7.

Video

Banks, M. (2001). Visual Methods in Social Research. London: Sage.

Barron, B. and ENGLE, R. (2007). Analysing Data Derived From Video Records in Derry, S. (ed) Guidelines For Video Research In Education: Recommendations From An Expert Panel, Data Research and Development Center (NORC at the University of Chicago) http://drdc.uchicago.edu/what/video-research.html: 28-37

Bezemer, J. and Mavers, D. (2011). 'Multimodal transcription as academic practice: a social semiotic perspective', International Journal of Social Research Methodology, 14: 3, 191-206.

Goldman, R. (2009). Video representations and the perspectivity framework, in Goldman, R., Pea, R, Barron and Derry Video Research in the learning sciences, Routledge: New York: 3-38.

Hall, R. (2007). Strategies For Video Recording: in Derry, S. (ed) (2007) Guidelines For Video Research In Education: Recommendations From An Expert Panel, Data Research and Development Center (NORC at the University of Chicago) http://drdc.uchicago.edu/what/video-research.html: 8-18

Heath, C. and Hindmarsh, J. (2002). "Analysing Interaction: Video, Ethnography and Situated Conduct, " in T. May (cd.), Qualitative Research in Action. London: SAGE, pp. 99-120.

Knoblauch, H., SchnettLer, B., Raab, J., and Soeffiier, H.-G. (eds.) (2006b). Video Analysis: Methodology and Methods. Frankfurt: Peter Lang.

Photography

Anderson, J., and Jones, K. (2009). The difference that place makes to methodology: Uncovering the lived space of young people's spatial practices. *Children's Geographies,* 7(3), 291-303.

Becker, H.S. (1986a). Doing Things Together: Selected Papers. Evanston, IL: Northwestern University Press.

Close, H. (2005). Roles and responsibilities in understanding, accepting and adapting in the chronic illness trajectory. Unpublished PhD thesis. Northumbria University.

Clover, D. E. (2006). Out of the dark room: Participatory photography as a critical, imaginative, and public aesthetic practice of transformative education. *Journal of Transformative Education, 4*(3), 275-290.

Croghan, R., Griffin, C., Hunter, J., and Phoenix, A. (2008). Young people's constructions of self: Notes on the use and analysis of the photoelicitation methods. *International Journal of Social Research Methodology, 11*(4), 345–356.

Denzin, N.K. (1989b). The Research Act (3rd edn). Englewood Cliffs, NJ: Prentice Hall.

Harper, D. (2004). "Photography as Social Science Data, " in U. Flick, E.v. Kardorff, and Rudkin, J. K., and Davis, A. (2007). *Photography as a tool for understanding youth connections to their neighborhood.Children, Youth and Environments, 17*(4), 107-123.

Pink, S. (2011). Amateur photographic practice, collective representation and the constitution of place. *Visual Studies, 26*(2), 92-101.

Steinke (eds.). A Companion to Qualitative Research. London: SAGE. pp. 231-236.

Van House, N. A. (2011). Personal photography, digital technologies and the uses of the visual. *Visual Studies, 26*(2), 125-134.

Winton, A. (2016). Using Photography as a Creative, Collaborative Research Tool. *The Qualitative Report,* Volume 21, No. 2.

15

Reliability and Validity in Qualitative Research

Research is based on scientific inquiry which calls for rigour. Without rigour, research is worthless, becomes fiction, and loses its utility. At technical level, rigour means being methodical, using appropriate techniques and attending to detail. At another-logical-level, it is expressed as a concern for the reliability and the validity of argument, and the soundness of evidence. In quantitative research, statistical packages and computing systems are invariably used to derive the reliability and validity. Qualitative research lacks the certainty of hard numbers and p-values with levels of confidence (0.01 and 0.05).

A number of leading qualitative researchers argued that reliability and validity were terms pertaining to the quantitative paradigm and were not pertinent to qualitative inquiry (Altheide and Johnson, 1998; Leininger, 1994). Some suggested adopting new criteria for determining reliability and validity, and hence ensuring rigour, in qualitative inquiry (Lincoln and Guba, 1985; Leininger, 1994; Rubin and Rubin, 1995). In seminal work in the 1980s, Guba and Lincoln substituted reliability and validity with the parallel concept of "*trustworthiness*," containing four aspects: *credibility, transferability, dependability and confirm ability*. Within these are specific methodological strategies for demonstrating qualitative rigour, such as the audit trail, member checks when coding, categorising, or confirming results with participants, peer debriefing, negative case analysis, structural corroboration, and referential material adequacy (Guba and Lincoln, 1981; Lincoln and Guba, 1985; Guba and Lincoln, 1982). Later, Guba and Lincoln developed authenticity criteria.

Thus, over the past two decades, reliability and validity have been subtly replaced by criteria and standards for evaluation of the overall significance, relevance, impact, and utility of completed research. Guba and Lincoln (1981) stated that while all research must have "truth value", "applicability", "consistency", and "neutrality" in order to be considered worthwhile. The nature of knowledge within the rationalistic (or quantitative) paradigm is different from the knowledge in naturalistic (qualitative) paradigm. Consequently, each paradigm requires paradigm-specific criteria for addressing "rigour". Accordingly, specific strategies are used to attain trustworthiness such as negative cases, peer debriefing, prolonged engagement and persistent observation, audit trails and member checks. Also important were characteristics of the investigator, who must be responsive and adaptable to changing circumstances, holistic, having processional immediacy, sensitivity, and ability for clarification and summarisation (Guba and Lincoln, 1981).

Most of the researchers argue that strategies for ensuring rigour must be built into the qualitative research process per se. These strategies include investigator responsiveness, methodological coherence, theoretical sampling and sampling adequacy, an active analytic stance, and saturation. These strategies, when used appropriately, force the researcher to correct both the direction of the analysis and the development of the study as necessary, thus ensuring reliability and validity of the completed project (Creswell, 1997; Kvale, 1989).

Qualitative research is iterative rather than linear, so that a good qualitative researcher moves back and forth between design and implementation to ensure congruence among question formulation, literature, recruitment, data collection strategies, and analysis. Data are systematically checked, focus is maintained, and the fit of data and the conceptual work of analysis and interpretation are monitored and confirmed constantly.

Reliability and validity of data could be ensured through methodological coherence, sampling sufficiency, developing a dynamic relationship between sampling, data collection and analysis, thinking theoretically, and theory development.

First, the aim of *methodological coherence* is to ensure congruence between the research question and the components of the method. Second, the *sample must be appropriate*, consisting of participants who best represent. Sampling adequacy, evidenced by saturation and replication (Morse, 1991), means that sufficient data to account for all aspects of the phenomenon have to be obtained. *Seeking negative cases is essential for ensuring validity. Third, collecting and analysing data concurrently* forms a mutual interaction between what is known and what one needs to know. This pacing and the iterative interaction between data and analysis (as discussed earlier) is the essence of attaining reliability and validity. The fourth aspect is *thinking theoretically*. Ideas emerging from data are reconfirmed in new data; this gives rise to new ideas that, in turn, must be verified in data already collected. Thinking theoretically requires macro-micro perspectives.

15.1 Reliability

In order to specify the sense of reliability as a criterion for assessing qualitative research, Kirk and Miller (1986) identified three forms namely;

- Quixotic reliability as the attempt to specify how far a particular method can continuously lead to the same measurements or results.
- Diachronic reliability as the stability of measurements or observations in their temporal course.
- Synchronic reliability is the constancy or consistency of results obtained at the same moment but by using different instruments. Thus, the criterion of reliability is reformulated in the direction of checking the dependability of data and procedures, which can be grounded in the specificity of the various qualitative methods.

15.2 Validity

In quantitative research, validity refers to a judgment concerning how well a test does in fact measure what it purports to measure. More specifically, it is a judgment based on evidence about the appropriateness of inferences drawn from test scores. An inference is a logical or deduction in reasoning process. In other words, does the test serve specific purpose for which it is designed.

In qualitative research, it refers to whether the researchers see what they think they see. Basically, three errors may occur: to see a relation, a principle, and so on where they are not correct (type 1 error); to reject them when they are indeed correct (type 2 error); and finally to ask the wrong questions (type 3 error) (Kirk and Miller, 1986, pp. 29-30). And is the researcher's version grounded in the versions in the field.

Hammersley (1992, pp. 50-52) mentioned that (1) the validity of knowledge cannot be assessed with certainty. It is to Judge assumptions based on their plausibility and credibility. (2) Phenomena also exist independently of our claims concerning them. Our assumptions about them can only more or less approximate these phenomena. (3) Reality becomes accessible, across the (different) perspectives on phenomena. Research aims at presenting reality, not reproducing it.

Mishler (1990) defines "validation as the social construction of knowledge" by which we "evaluate the 'trustworthiness' of reported observations, interpretations, and generalisations" Finally, "reformulating validation as the social discourse through which trustworthiness is established elides such familiar shibboleths as reliability, falsifiability, and objectivity". As an empirical basis for this discourse and the construction of credibility, Mishler (1990) discusses the use of examples from narrative studies.

- From Baudrillard she derives the idea of an "ironic validity." The background assumption is that more and more simulacra, as copies without originals, have replaced representations as copies of real objects (1993, p. 677).
- From Lyotard (1984) she derives the idea of "paralogic/neo-pragmatic validity": scientific knowledge does not aim at corresponding to reality, but aims at discovering differences and at leaving contradictions in their tension. You can specify the validity of knowledge by answering the question of how far these goals have been reached.
- From Deleuze and Guattari (1976) and Derrida (1990), Lather takes the idea of rhizomatic validity.

- Sensual validity or situated validity, the question of the centeredness of knowledge and in looking at scientific knowledge is asked.

15.3 Procedural Validity

(1) The researcher should refrain from talking in the field but rather should listen as much as possible. He or she should (2) produce notes that are as exact as possible, (3) begin to write early, and in a way (4) which allows readers of his or her notes and reports to see for themselves. This means providing enough data for readers to make their own inferences and follow those of the researcher. The report should be as complete (5) and candid (6) as possible. The researcher should seek feedback on his or her findings and presentations in the field or from his or her colleagues (7). Presentations should be characterised by a balance (8) between the various aspects and (9) by accuracy in writing. (1990a, pp. 127-128)

15.4 Trustworthiness, Credibility, Dependability

Lincoln and Guba (1985) outlined five strategies for increasing the credibility of qualitative research:

- Credible results will be produced by a "prolonged engagement" and "persistent observation" in the field and the triangulation of different methods, researchers, and data;
- "Peer debriefing": regular meetings with other people who are not involved in the research in order to disclose one's own blind spots and to discuss working hypotheses and results with them;
- The analysis of negative cases in the sense of analytic induction;
- Appropriateness of the terms of reference of interpretations and their assessment;
- "Member Checks" : communicative validation of data and interpretations with members of the fields under study.

15.5 Procedural Dependability (Auditing)

Dependability is checked through a process of auditing. Schwandt and Halpern 1988) have outlined the procedures as mentioned below.

- Review and reflexion of the raw data, their collection and recording; data reduction and results of syntheses by summarising, theoretical notes, memos, and so on, summaries, short descriptions of cases, etc.;

- reconstruction of data and results of syntheses according to the structure of developed and used categories (themes, definitions, relationships), findings (interpretations and inferences), and the reports produced with their integration of concepts and links to the existing literature;
- auditing of process notes (i.e., methodological notes and decisions concerning the production of trustworthiness and credibility of findings);
- materials concerning intentions and dispositions like the concepts of research, personal notes, and expectations of the participants;
- information about the development of the instruments including the pilot version and preliminary plan. (Lincoln and Guba, 1985).

15.6 Procedure

- *Reflection on analysis:* The investigator speculate what the participants and the researcher are learning, the themes that are emerging, patterns that are present, connections between pieces of data, additional ideas, and thoughts that pop up in the active action of the participants.
- *Reflection on method:* Materials contain procedures and strategies employed.
- *Reflection on ethical dilemmas and conflicts.* There are two sets of behaviour- subject's ideology, values, moral, and ethic on one hand and observer's comment on the other.
- *Reflection on the observer's frame of mind:* These preconceptions relate to religious beliefs, political ideology, and cultural background, position in society, race and gender.

15.7 Criteria for Evaluating the Building of Theories

Corbin and Strauss (1990, p. 16) have mentioned four points of departure for judging empirically grounded theories namely, (i) the validity, reliability, and credibility of the data, (ii) the plausibility, and the value of the theory itself, (iii) the adequacy of the research process which has generated, elaborated, or tested the theory, and (iv) the empirical grounding of the research findings.

For evaluating the research process itself, they suggest seven criteria namely, (i) Are concepts generated? (ii) Are the concepts systematically related? (iii) Are there many conceptual linkages and are the categories well developed? (iv) Do the categories have conceptual density? (v) Is there much variation built into the theory? (vi) Are broader conditions that affect the phenomenon under study built into its explanation? Has "process" been taken into account? and (Vii) Do the theoretical findings seem significant and to what extent?

References

Altheide, D., Johnson, J. M. C. (1998). Criteria for assessing interpretive validity in qualitative research. In Denzin N. K., Lincoln Y. S. (Eds.), *Collecting and interpreting qualitative materials.* (pp. 283-312). Thousand Oaks, CA: Sage.

Guba, E. G. (1981). Criteria for assessing the trustworthiness of naturalistic inquiries, *Educational Communication and Technology Journal,* 29 (2), 75-91.

Kuzel, A., Engel, J. (2001). Some pragmatic thought on evaluating qualitative health research. In Morse J., Swanson J., Kuzel A. (Eds.), *The Nature of Qualitative Evidence* (pp. 114-138). Thousand Oaks, CA: Sage.

Kvale, S. (1989). *Issues of validity in qualitative research.* Lund, Sweden: Chartwell Bratt.

Morse, J. M. (2001). Constructing evidence within the qualitative project. In Morse J. M., Swanson J., Kuzel A., (Eds.). *The nature of evidence in qualitative inquiry.* (pp. 187-202), Thousand Oaks, CA: Sage.

Morse, J. M. (1998). Validity by committee. [Editorial] Qualitative Health Research, 8, 443-445.

UNIT - 4

PUBLIC POLICY

16

Ethics in Research

'Ethics' is a set of 'moral prisms' through which researchers are observed. It enables them to determine the right things for themselves. A set of 'prisms' includes: - virtue ethic, result ethic, universal ethic, public exposure ethic, and caring ethic. (David, A. Sharpiro, 1999)

16. Ethics and Research

Research involving human subjects raises unique and complex ethical, legal, social and political issues. Question arises what they (researchers) do and why they do (research). An easy and short cut method to get degree for eligibility to the profession of teaching has given rise to many scandals. Dr Rais Ahmed and Madulka, studied 9000 theses (ICSSR-Sponsored Study) and found that 78 per cent of the theses failed to make any intellectual contribution, 60 per cent of the research studies were found repetitive, and 80 per cent studies in applied research were found trivial, mediocre, and without any intellectual input. Most incompetent and inaptitude persons made way to teaching profession. Quality of teaching and learning has been diluted. Question arises how to check these incriminatory elements in research. The need has propped up to evolve ethical codes and ethical committee to check mal-practices in research. The growing sensitivity for ethical issues in research over the years has also drawn the attention of academia.

Despite methodological and ideological differences, the researchers have something common. None of them is motivated purely by self-interest. Nor are they motivated solely by the pursuit of knowledge for own sake. Some are attempting to improve class-room practice, learning outcomes, and value addition; some are concerned with new ideas and policy planning. Others look to the wider socio-economic and political issues. It is fact that the formulation of research problem is both expectation-laden and value- impregnated. The first and broadest objective is to protect participants who are to be researched. The second objective is to ensure that research is conducted in a way that serves interests of individuals, groups and/or society as a whole. Finally, the third objective is to examine specific research activities and projects for their ethical soundness, looking at issues such as the management of risk, protection of confidentiality and the process of informed consent.

Nonetheless, codes of ethics are formulated to regulate the relations between researcher and who is researched (participant). It is based upon three principles; (i) ensuring the welfare of the participants and avoid harming participants involved in the process; (ii) taking into account their needs and interests; (iii) recognising their capacities and potentials.

Murphy and Ding Hall (2001, p. 339) speak of "ethical theory" in this context, which they see linked to four issues:

- *Non-maleficence*- researcher should avoid harming participants.
- *Beneficence*- research on human subjects should produce more positive and identifiable benefit rather than simply carried out for its own sake.
- *Autonomy or self-determination*- research participants' values and decisions should be respected.
- *Justice*- all people should be treated equally.

For example, persons, who are observed, questioned or who are involved in some other way in investigation in connection with the analysis of personal documents, shall not be subjected to any disadvantages or dangers as a result of research. All risks that exceed what is normal in everyday life must be explained to the parties concerned. The autonomy of interviewees or informants must be protected. (Ethik-Kodex, 1993: I B5).

The principles of informed consent and of voluntary participation in studies are basic. Participation in investigation is voluntary. It takes place on the basis of fullest possible information about the goals and methods of the particular piece of research. The principle of informed consent cannot be applied in practice, for instance if comprehensive pre-information would distort the results of the research in an unjustifiable way. In such cases an attempt must be made to use other possible modes of informed content. (Ehik-Kodes, 1993: I B2). Unselfish, altruistic, and principled researcher is obviously set to do better than others who have none of these traits.

16.1 Building Blocks of Ethics in Research

Six elements have been identified to build blocks of ethics in research. These are given below:

- **Rigour** – at technical level it implies being methodical, using appropriate techniques and attending to detail. At logical level, it is expressed as a concern for validity of argument, and the soundness of evidence, and reporting findings precisely and taking care to avoid errors.
- **Accountability** - conveying information truthfully and honouring commitments, it involves openness of mind, persistence, and courage and, in particular, imaginative criticism.
- **Economy-** using resources wisely and avoiding waste, and
- **Impartiality-** letting the facts speak for themselves and avoiding improper bias.
- **Care for others** – it is the moral duty of the researchers to follow the principle of care for others in the provision of a public service or service to children in education.
- **Participatory**- participants (stakeholders or actors) should be inspired, informed and involved in the choice of locale, design of research, and methods to be employed. Both their dignity and capacity need to be recognised.

16.2 Monitoring: Roles and Responsibility of Ethics Research Committee

Every society that is recognisably human will need some institution of proprieties, some norms governing truth-telling, some conception of promise-giving, and some standards restraining malfeasance. (Blackburn, 2003). Therefore, Ethics Research Committee has been constituted to ensure ethical standards. Ethics Committee of the respective area of research examines the research design and methods before they can be applied. Researchers have to fulfill two conditions: They will conduct research in accordance with ethical codes and research proposals have to be vetted by the Ethics Research Committees for their ethical soundness. Reviews will focus on: scientific quality, the welfare of participants, and respect for the dignity and rights of participants. Research Recognition Committee examines the following issues:

16.2.1 Approval of a Problem: In most of the Indian universities a Research Recognition Committee evaluates the research topics. Two or more experts are to examine the work of various fields of studies. Purpose and usefulness of the research are evaluated critically (what? and why? and how?). The convener of the board should invite experts after considering the nature of the topics or these can be sent to the expert concerned for obtaining their opinions.

16.2.2 Methodology: It is concerned with how the research is to be conducted. Method, selection of sample, tools for the collection of data, analysis of data are taken into consideration. Reliability and validity or trustworthiness and authenticity of the instruments are examined.

16.2.3 Evaluation of Ph.D. Thesis: The Research Committee evaluates research thesis or project. There is a standardised criterion for evaluating Ph.D. thesis. A Performa for evaluating thesis is designed by expert in the respective discipline. The recommendations for specific point must be given. The thesis is referred to at least three experts of the field. There should be at least ***two open viva-voce*** examination.

The following questions need to be answered.

- Is present study a continuous process of rigorous reasoning supported by a dynamic interplay among methods, theories, and findings?
- Is it descriptively oriented, dependent on context, and intuitive? Does it recognise the importance of philosophical, historical, social and cultural context, participant involvement, political considerations, and ethical requirements as inherent features of the study of social and educational phenomenon?
- How is it convincing, logical, relevant, authentic, trustworthy, connected, supported by evidence, practical, meaningful, humane or fit a bigger picture?
- How does it have greater explanatory or predictive power compared to other models? How does it have more elegance, simplicity, order or symmetry? How does it fit into other ways of explaining the world? How does it uplift, inspire or contribute to new ideas or innovations? In what ways can it be ethically applied? Does it produce more positive and identifiable benefit or tangible rather than simply carried out for its own sake?
- What are my underlying beliefs and values about the world and how does this idea interact with these? How much of this idea am I willing to take on board and with what provisos? In what ways have the audience been convinced to accept this idea. Are the internal and external validity claims appropriate?
- The formulation of research problem in social sciences is both expectation-laden and value-impregnated. Research in social sciences is based on the principle of caring others i.e. how to protect the subjects of research from the breach of confidence, undue pressure, and stress. The researcher is responsible for ensuring the integrity of the research. If we accept that social sciences research should speak about those things where we cannot pronounce with certainty and scientific detachment, we must accept that other intellectual virtues, specifically, practical wisdom – "a true and practical state involving reason, concerned with what is good and bad for a human being." (Aristotle, 2000). Fundamental principles of ethics could be seen to be true by the 'natural light of reason'. Table 16.1 reveals the ethical issues in research and needed interventions.

Table 16.1: Ethical Issues in Research and Compensation*

Ethical Issues	***Right Violated***	***Compensation***
Preserving participants' anonymity	Right to privacy	
Exposing participants to mental stress	Right to safety	Right to be heard Right to redress
Involving participants in research without their knowledge	Right to be informed Right to privacy	Right to redress
Involving participants in research without their knowledge	Right to be informed Right to privacy	Right to redress
Use of deception	Right to be informed	Right to be heard
Use of coercion	Right to choose	
Selling under the guise of research	Right to be informed	
Causing embarrassment, hindrance, or offense	Right to respect	Right to redress
Ethical Issues	Right Violated	Compensation
Preserving participants' anonymity	Right to privacy	
Exposing participants to mental stress	Right to safety	Right to be heard Right to redress
Involving participants in research without their knowledge	Right to be informed Right to privacy	Right to redress
Involving participants in research without their knowledge	Right to be informed Right to privacy	Right to redress
Use of deception	Right to be informed	Right to be heard
Use of coercion	Right to choose	
Selling under the guise of research	Right to be informed	
Causing embarrassment, hindrance, or offense	Right to respect	Right to redress

* (Smith and Quelch, 1992, p. 162)

Table 16.1 focuses on the following points

- Participants' anonymity, freedom from coercion, stress, and pressure are to be followed in letter and spirit. Anonymity should extend not only to writing but also to the verbal reporting of information that you have learned through observation.

- The researcher should not relate specific information about individuals to other and should be particularly watchful of sharing information with people at the research site who could choose to use the information in political or personal ways.
- Participants are to be inspired, informed and involved in the processes in the conduct of research. Selling under the guise of research is unethical and not to be adhered.
- Capability and capacity of the participants are to be honoured and explored.
- The researcher should not see only his or her own opinions, unworthy to be foisted on others. Cynicism and self-consciousness may not come in the way of contextual narratives.

There should be no discrimination between the researcher (empowered) and who are to be researched (participants). For researcher, an action that might be thought wrong, or undutiful, or unjust, or trespass against participant's rights, might apparently be whitewashed or justified by its consequences, if it can be shown to be conducive to the general good. It is point of view that treats everyone equally: every person has equal weight. Dignity of the participants needs to be ensured through recognising their potentials and capacities. Their right to participate in the research activities is voluntary and not mandatory. Participants opinions or decisions are to be acknowledged and given due consideration. It is true "Fiat justitia et ruant coeli"- let justice be done though the heavens fall. Rules concerning rights in general are justified by their impact on the general welfare of the participants. Everyone has a right to realisation of the 'economic, social and cultural rights indispensable for his dignity and the development of his personality'.

- **For example-1**: Avoid research sites where teachers or student (or student's parents) or actors may feel coerced to participate in your research. Often when teacher or principals work toward their doctorate and keep their jobs, they look for convenient ways to collect data in the field. This often includes collection of data in their classrooms or schools.
- **Example-2**: If you are interested in studying the perspective of parents of children with learning disabilities, ask teachers or the school psychologist or the special service coordinator

in the schools to send a letter to parents describing your research study. The letter can include an envelope addressed to you (researcher) and a form agreeing to participate. This way, the parents get to choose what they reveal to you.

Welfare of the participant is based on weighing risks against the benefits accruing in terms of addition to knowledge or finding a new solution to existing problem. Research in social sciences is intellectually stimulating and its outcomes may be good for one's career. The intellectual stimulation comes from experimenting with ideas, and, more importantly, because it is a means by which human experience may be improved. (Swann, 2005). Research in social sciences is not be purely motivated by self-interest. Nor it is motivated solely by the pursuit of knowledge for its own sake. Rather, it is concerned that research should be of benefit to participants.

The consequences of a piece of research, including the effects on the participants and the social consequences of its publication and application must enhance the general welfare. Researchers should be aware of the variety of human goods and the variety of views on the good life, and the complex relation of education with these. They should recognise that research is an ethical matter, and that its purpose is the development of human good.

Example: In social science research**, t**he actors in the research process make common effort to inform, perform and transform their situation. In this research process their level of confidence is increased; awareness, capacity and knowledge levels are enhanced and collective involvement pave way for their empowerment and self-sustainability.

16.3 Ethical Issues in Research Focus on

(i) Design of Research, (ii) Applying Standards, (iii) Implementing the Research and (iv) Reporting the Research.

16.3.1 Design of Research: Have a clear design and strategies explaining what? why? how? of research study and there systemic relationship to achieve the objectives of the study observing ethical codes. Construct operational definition based on the critically examined pre-existing definitions of a topic. No compromise on the validity (internal and external) or authenticity and trustworthiness of the data. Inadequate definitional scoping of the boundaries of a project can be regarded as disguising preconceived assumptions which inherently bias the results.

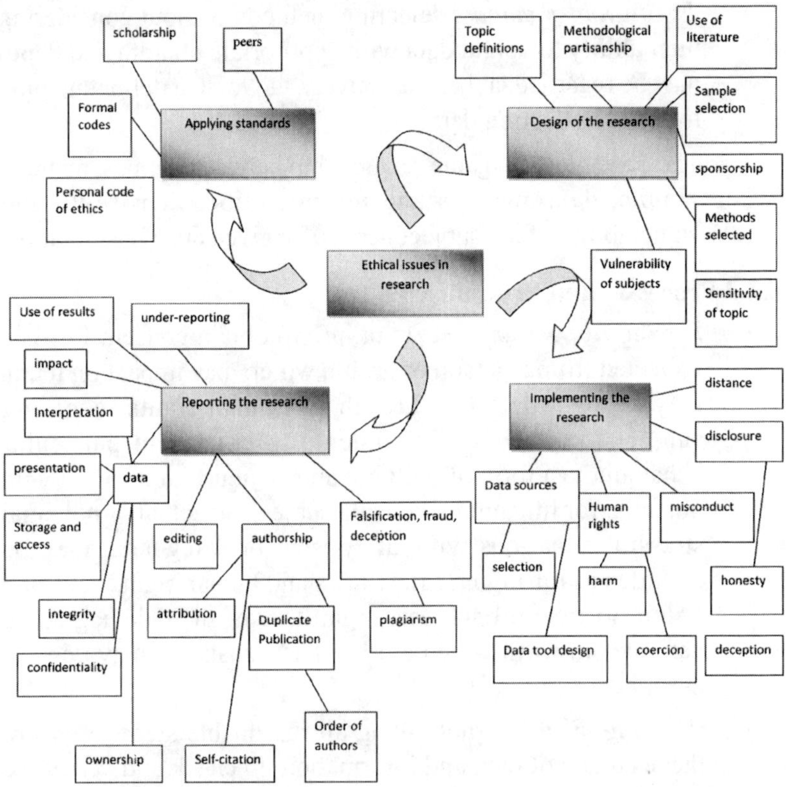

Figure 16.1: Ethical Issues in Research (Chris Hart, 2005).

- *Be open to all methodologies:* failure to consider and evaluate alternative methodologies and tools for the collection of data may be regarded as partisanship resulting in a biased study.
- *Employ all of the literature:* an inadequate search and review of the topic and methodological literature is bad practice; and not giving fair and balanced assessments of other people's ideas and arguments amounts to bad scholarship.
- *Ensure a sound sample:* selection of a biased sample will invalidate the findings and be regarded as deliberate tampering with the design to achieve a predetermined result.
- *Be independent:* failure to demonstrate a non-partisan and detached standpoint from the topic and subjects may be a cause to question the findings and methods of a piece of research.

- *Justify your methods:* selecting methods without considering their ability to obtain data with appropriate breadth and depth may be regarded, at best, as naivety, at worst, a deliberate ploy to avoid collecting data.
- There should be organic relationship between themes, method, sample, data analysis and interpretation. Sensitivity and vulnerability of the subject need to be given due consideration.

16.2.2 Processes and Procedures

- *Having respect for others:* failure to obtain consent for data collected from a person or group, which may impact on them, may be regarded as a breach of human rights; coercing subjects, colleagues or students to engage in particular behaviour is a form of bullying and an abuse of position with potential for litigation; exposing subjects to actual or potential stressful situations without consent or safeguards may be regarded as infringing safety laws and human rights acts; and failure to treat all subjects regardless of their demographic variables in ways which are fair and consistent may be seen as an act of prejudice.
- *Avoiding mistakes:* not taking all reasonable steps to ensure the accuracy of data and information, to check and verify the proper use of statistical calculations and the presentation of data may be regarded either as incompetence or as a deliberate act to allow unchecked sources to be included in the results; presenting incomplete data, either quantitative or qualitative, as if adequate, amounts to deception; and having no means to verify data because no detailed records exist may invalidate the value of a piece of research or be regarded as a deliberate act to hide the source of, or lack of, data.
- *Being self-reflective:* failure to reflect upon your role and status as a researcher, including your own choice of affiliations to a methodological position, may be regarded as a form of methodological myopia; and omitting to articulate your own methodological assumptions and beliefs while using them as the basis for interpretation might be regarded as a deliberate ploy to present an interpretation as based only in the data and this amounts to deception.

16.2.3 Applying Standards

The most effective method for ensuring the integrity of research data is to ensure high standards for openness and transparency.

- To the extent that data and other information integral to research results are provided to other experts, errors in data collection, analysis, and interpretation (intentional or unintentional) can be discovered and corrected.
- This requires that the methods and tools used to generate and manipulate the data be available to peers who have the background to understand that information.

Trustworthiness is the fundamental criteria because it is deliberated parallel to the positivist criteria that are internal validity, external validity, reliability and objectivity (Guba and Lincoln, 1989). The trustworthiness criteria comprise four quality standards: the credibility (via member checking), transferability (via thick description), dependability (via outside reviewer), and conformability (conformability data audit).

Authenticity is about conversation between researcher and participants, and the situations and emotional compassion that arise during the investigation (Ellis and Bochner, 2000). The authenticity criteria contain: ontological authenticity (understanding social milieu), educative authenticity (appreciating others' perspectives), catalytic authenticity (acting for change), and tactical authenticity (empowering members for action) (Bryman, 2008). Findings are qualitative, valuable and idiographic or transferable.

16.2.4 Implementing the Research

- One way to ensure that you are getting informed consent from people you will interview is to tell them when you are getting permission from people, then how long the interview will take. Some universities insist that you put this information in the letter of consent that your informant signs, for example, "This interview would take an hour or hour and half of your time. Researcher may ask participants for another interview if it seems necessary."
- Implementing the research demands use of appropriate methods and techniques. Reliability and validity of arguments, and the soundness of evidence are to be ensured.

- Researcher has to convey the information truthfully and honour the commitments; it involves openness of mind, persistence, courage and, in particular, imaginative criticism.
- Economic resources should be used wisely and judicially.
- The facts should speak for themselves. Impartiality and objectivity need to be followed.
- It is the moral duty of the researchers to follow the principle of care for others in the provision of a public service or service to children in education. Participant's dignity, potential and capacity should be honoured.
- Participants (stakeholders or actors) should be inspired, informed and involved in the choice of locale, design of research, and methods to be employed.
- Treat information with respect and seek their cooperation in the research. While some advocate covert research, there is general consensus that under usual circumstances the subject should be told of your research interests and should give you permission to precede. Get written consent. Be particularly sensitive and diligent in explaining yourself and getting consent when studying people who are vulnerable to manipulation, such as people labeled mentally disabled or people who very young or very old or who lack formal education. Research should neither lie to subject nor record conversations on hidden mechanical devices.

16.3 Reporting Your Research

The following guidelines are to observed for reporting your research.

- *Take note of:* scientific vigour, the welfare of participants, and respect for the dignity and rights of participants.
- *Full and proper attribution of ideas:* presenting the words, data or ideas of another person as your own without properly citing them, and thereby showing the attribution amounts in varying degrees to plagiarism. This is not only misconduct, but can also be an infringement of Copyright and therefore, is a criminal act.
- *Ensuring the integrity of your data:* falsifying, fabricating or omitting data constitute misconduct - any of these acts is

unacceptable because to varying degrees they are either lies or distortions of the truth; using some techniques of presentation which give a biased impression about the significance of the data constitutes misconduct; ownership of and access to data and knowledge generated by a research project done in a public institution needs to be clarified before the beginning of a project; and destroying data generated by a project within five years of the completion of a project is bad practice as it prevents any subsequent interpretation or challenge.

- *Safeguarding confidential information:* use of information about a person or group without their permission may violate laws covering data protection and be regarded as a breach of trust; revealing or selling confidential data to a third party will violate data protection laws; and making known the identities of participant/respondent.
- Tell the truth when you write up and report your findings. Although for ideological reason you may not like the conclusions you reach, and although other may put pressure on you to show certain results that your data do not reveal. The most important trademark of a researcher should be his or her devotion to reporting what the data reveal. Compromising with report writing as per convenience ultimately tantamount to unethical practice.

Figure 16.2 reveals the variables of ethical integrity.

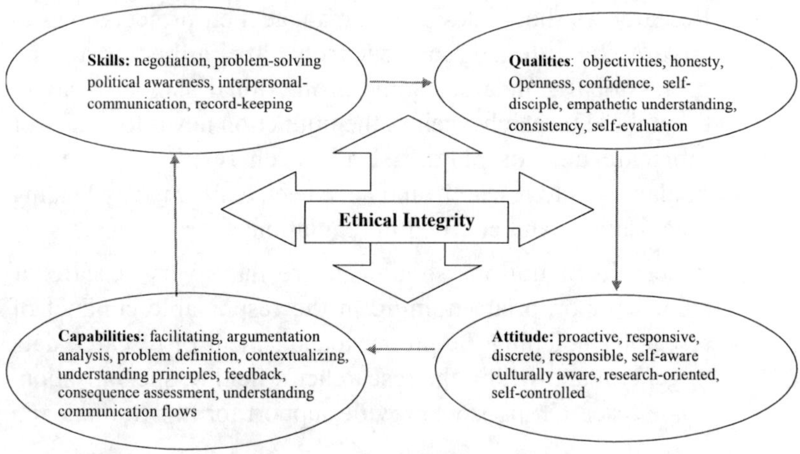

Figure 16.2: Variables of Ethical Integrity (Kapoor, D.R., 2014).

Research and ethical integrity of researcher are covariance of professional sustainability. Ethical integrity has four significant dimensions namely, qualities, skills, capabilities, and attitude as mentioned in Figure 16.2. There is systemic rational and relationship between these dimensions. Ethic in research directs, motivates and supports professionals at the deepest level. A professional vision would inspire, inform and involve them in research investigation.. Provide them a realistic and justifiable pride in them and in their work. These ethical values are reflected in their logical, psychological, and moral acts. These may be love, ecstasy, mutual communication, respect, fun, growth, support, challenge, creativity, freedom, honesty and spiritual unity. Perseverance, integrity, maturity, commitment, involvement, and accountability are the essential ingredients to achieve the ends with appropriate means. It means ability to walk the talk and integrating professional acts, matured ways of thinking and doing job purposefully, sharing ideas, knowledge, and skills with others, positive mindset and alignment with organisational mission and vision. It is application of skills, capabilities, and variables of attitude to achieve ethical integrity. It is a ability to observe, examine assumptions, hypothesis, conduct empirical investigation, and the ability to interact effectively with others, ability to listen, communicate and work toward synergistic solutions, the ability to see and operate effectively and cooperatively.

16.4 Recommendation of Committee on Ensuring the Utility and Integrity of Research Data in a Digital Age; National Academy of Sciences (2009)

- Researchers should design and manage their projects so as to ensure the integrity of research data, adhering to the professional standards. Some professional standards apply throughout research, such as the injunction never to falsify or fabricate data or plagiarise research results. These are fundamental to research, and have been confirmed by leading organisations and codified in regulations.
- Research institutions should ensure that every researcher receives appropriate training in the responsible conduct of research, including the proper management of research data in general and within the researcher's field of specialisation. Some research sponsors provide support for this training and

for the development of training programmes. Researchers, research institutions, research sponsors, professional societies, and journals all are responsible for creating and sustaining an environment that supports the efforts of researchers to ensure the integrity of research data.

- The research enterprise and its stakeholders—research institutions, research sponsors, professional societies, journals, and individual researchers—should develop and disseminate professional standards for ensuring the integrity of research data and for ensuring adherence to these standards. In areas where standards differ between fields, it is important that differences be clearly defined and explained. Specific guidelines for data management may require re-examination and updating as technologies and research practices evolve.
- Research institutions, professional societies, and journals should ensure that the contributions of data professionals to research are appropriately recognised. In addition, research sponsors should acknowledge that financial support for data professionals is an appropriate component of research support in an increasing number of fields.

References

Bechhofer, F., and Pterson, L. (2000). *Principles of Research design in the Social Sciences.* London:Routledge.

Bulmer.(ed) (1982). *Social Research ethics: An examination of the merits of covert participant observation.* London: MacMillan.

Chris Hart (2005). *Doing your master Dissertation*. New Delhi : Vistaar Publications.

Kapoor, D.R. (2009). *Dynamics of Learning Organisations.* New Delhi: Regal Publications.

Kapoor, D.R. (2014). Research Methodology: Methods and Techniques. New Delhi: Regal Publications.

Ethics in Educational Research, www.aare.edu.au/ethics/ethcfull.htm

Flick Uwe. (2009). *An Introduction to Qualitative Research.* New Delhi: SAGE

Hopf, C. (2004b). Research Ethics and Qualitative Research. In U. Flick, E.V. Kardorff, and Steinke (eds), *A Companion to Qualitative Research.* London: SAGE, pp. 334-339.

Homan, R. (1991). *The ethics of social research.* London: Longman House.

Israel, A.M. and Hay, I.(2006). *Research Ethics for Social Scientists*. London: Sage.

Kapoor, D.R. (2014). *Research Methodology: Methods and Techniques.* New Delhi: Regal Publications.

Polonsky, M.J., and Waller, D.S. (2010). *Designing and Managing a Research Project.* New Delhi: SAGE.

Research Ethics, en.wikipedia.org/wiki/Research_ethics

Simon Blackburn. (2003). *Ethics: A Very Short Introduction,* New York: Oxford University Press.

Srivastava, P. and Srivastava, Savita.(2008). *A Call for Ethics in Educational Research.* Researchers Meet at M.S. University, Vadodra.

What is Research Ethics, www.researchethics.ca/what-is-research-ethics.htm

What is Research Ethics, www.researchethics.ca/what-is-research-ethics.htm

Asociations/ Society/Institution

The American Sociological Association (ASA). *Code of Ethics* (SRA). www.the.sra.org.uk).

The British Psychological Society (BPS). *A Code of Conduct, Ethical Principles, and Guidelines* (www.bps.uk/the society/ethics-rules-charter-code)

The British Sociological Association (BSA). *A Statement of Ethical Practice.* (Error! Hyperlink reference not valid.).

National Academy of Sciences (2009). Ensuring the Utility and Integrity of Research Data in a Digital Age (http://www.nap.edu/catalog).

Press at http://www.nap.edu/catalog.php?record_id=12615 The National Academies Press at http://www.nap.edu/catalog.php?record_id=12615 National Academies Press at http://www.nap.edu/catalog.php?record_id=12615

17

Research and Policy Planning

17. Research and Policy

Research is viewed as a professionally oriented activity- to improve practice, aspects of human experience and/ or contribute to the sum total of human knowledge. Experts agree that it is a "critical, scientific and systemic enquiry" aimed at informing judgments and decisions in order to improve action. Every year new facts, new concepts, innovative practices, new methods, new models, new processes and new ways of doing things come into our lives due to ever-increasing significant research in the physical, the biological, as well as in the social and psychological fields. In this technological age, it is now possible and easy to gain access to research findings that can possibly make a difference to human capital, institutions and outcomes. Research is recognised as the basis of our personal, social, cultural, economic and political development. Therefore, need for research is to improve our practices, re-design programmes and evolve new policies.

There is an 'assumptive world' of the policy makers. It refers that policy-makers drive their ideas from common sense, from unsystematic observation, and from thoughtful speculation (Lindblom, 1988: 224).

As a result, research can make on the policy process through stimulating what Weiss (1977b; 1982; 1986) calls 'enlightenment'. It refers how does a particular policy is actively accomplishing what is set out to accomplish? Terms such as "informed choice", "considered decision", "rational policy", "evidence-based policy", "strategic research", and "essential national research" have been used to express the belief in the need to build a "bridge" between research and policy.

Trostle *et al.* (2006) summarise these models in three basic approaches: (1) the *rational approach* includes the models that Weiss calls "*knowledge-driven*" and "*problem-solving*", representing the conventional manner of thinking about this relationship: the policy process is inherently rational, with research results being used when they exist and decision-makers calling for research when it is needed; (2) the *strategic approach* groups the models Weiss calls "*political*" and "*tactical*" and views research as a kind of ammunition in support or critical of certain positions, prompting or delaying policy action; and (3) the *enlightenment* or *diffusion approach*, comprising Weiss' three remaining models – "*interactive*", "*enlightenment*", and "*intellectual enterprise*" – and stressing that both the research and decision-making processes take place in parallel with a number of other social processes and thus play several different roles.

Researchers have three options for the formulation of policy namely, positivist policy analysis or post-positivist policy analysis or mixed approach. Positivist policy analysis focuses on scientific inquiry, statistics, and rationality in identifying problems and designing strategies for its solution. Post-positivist policy analysis, on the other hand, is inductive, participatory, and go for qualitative analysis of data, for substantial evidence for the formulation of policy. A key concern of post-positivist policy analysis involves increasing meaningful participation of citizens in the formation of problem definitions, the generation of policy alternatives, and the determination of policy. In the mixed methodology, the researcher proceeds from qualitative to quantitative analysis of data to get substantial evidence for the formulation or modification of existing public policy.

The importance of using qualitative methods of data analysis for applied policy research is to "understand complex behaviours, needs, systems and cultures, " (Ritchie and Spencer, 2002, p. 2) further argue that policy research needs "to be appropriately targeted towards providing 'answers, '" and at the same time, "making its methods more explicit" (Schon and Rein, 1994). The decision-makers, planners, and policy executioners in the government, private sector, and even community leaders are induced to make use of research findings.

Policy is one of the most important ways of achieving change. For instance, how best to teach children of different abilities, how to prepare and motivate teachers to deliver the best, how to deal with the disparities of opportunity arising from class, sex or race. The object of research into policy is to find out how to change things. Research is, therefore, research into policy. In policy, this is crucial; we should have some grounds for believing that the outcomes of policy will be what we hope. Policy is based on theories which are not only testable but also tested.

New approaches to policy research are linked to complex problems, issues and challenges. These have given rise to new methods of inquiry which allow deep-level interpretations beyond the surface-level reception of policy positions and statements. This involves the "inherent" purposes of texts or data sets on one hand, and on the other of relevant problem solving and focused inquiry. For instance, Grounded Theory provides in-depth analysis of policy at the ground level. Figure 17.1 reveals an "optimal" GT framework for the knowledge-building process.

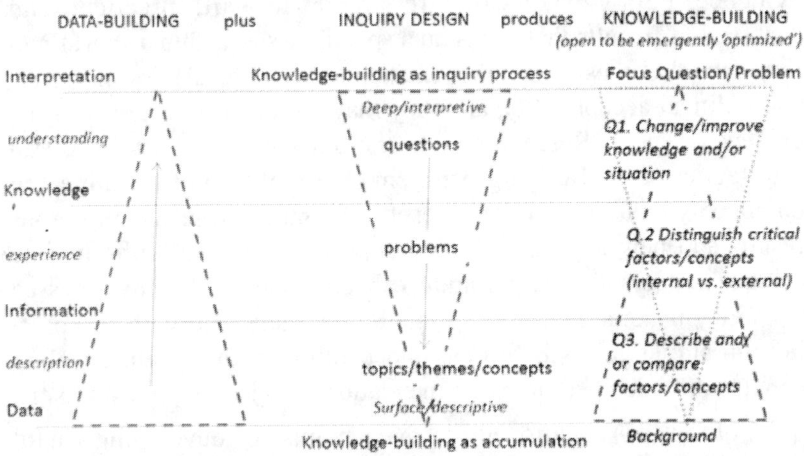

Figure 17.1: An "optimal" framework for the knowledge-building process. (Richards, 2011).

An "optimal" framework for the knowledge-building process starts at the ground level. Data is generated by the men in the field. Data building involves description of data, relevant and specific information, experience, knowledge, and its interpretation. Knowledge building as inquiry process proceeds from deep understanding of problems, research questions and themes/concepts. Data building plus inquiry process leads to knowledge building. The initial foundations of any inquiry framed as an optimal knowledge-building process thus lie in the posing of a relevant central research question which can provide a "thread of inquiry" to link all the related aspects and subsequent stages of the process. As a means of also linking words and ideas in an act of predication—as well as the knowledge-building models of description and interpretation—an effective central research question should basically link some particular problem or issue emphasis to a general concept, theme, or topic area (Richards *et al,* 2011). Inquiry design seeks to effectively connect the macro-level inquiry purposes and the micro-level data-building aspects. Knowledge thus gained or gathered would be helpful in the formulation of public policy.

Policy-makers function in a complex environment in which decisions are based on many factors including political and pragmatic pressures, competing priorities, prior commitments to stakeholders, ideologies, values, and economics in addition to the best objective evidence. Policy-makers require straight-forward, practical, and "actionable" results that focus on a specific issue within a short time-frame and that consider contextual factors such as local relevance, cost, and political acceptability, and they may be forced to act even if the evidence is poor. Researchers, on the other hand, seek to study an intellectually challenging problem thoroughly and examine the complexity of issues without preset time frames to provide rigorous results and new approaches to solving problems that withstand the critique of peers. Research findings are commonly not easily accessed by policy-makers and, when available, are suffused with technical jargon, statistical estimations, and cautions rather than the clear conclusions and specific recommendations needed by policy makers.

Gold (1997) mentioned six main points for developing useful research in policy:

- First, fact-based/scientific knowledge is only one type of "knowing".

- Second, there are many pathways to translating research into policy.
- Third, relationships and trust matter and they make researchers more effective.
- Fourth, researchers do not have to do it alone and the use of information intermediaries is highly encouraged.
- Fifth, findings have to be salient at the time.
- Finally, researchers must distil the bottom-line message.

17.2 Policy planning demands sustained contact between researchers and policy-makers through a series of forums. A comprehensive media strategy needs to be designed to engage researchers, the public, legislators and policymakers. But it has been generally alleged that the decision-makers typically take action only in response to a crisis or some other political opportunity (Clemons and McBeth, 2009). Policy planning is not incidental or crisis but a perpetual search or in-depth analysis of data or wide range of data to get substantial evidence in order to devise actions for better results. It is identifying problems or strategies and mechanism for its implementation within the given time framework. In this context, the researcher needs to pick a technically appropriate and feasible solution from an array of policy options, understand social relationships, anticipate and response to questions extemporaneously, handle emotionally challenging situations with ease, and interpret issues that are just appearing on the agency's radar screen. (Clemons *et al,* 2009). Figure 17.2 reveals the paradigms of influences.

Policy-makers choose policy that is likely to be practical and attuned to public welfare. Merely to experiment is dangerous, and in this context, even immoral. The policy planners generally opt for evidence-based policy. Research can also contribute to policy change. Policy research is, therefore, 'contested terrain' (Jenny Ozga, 2000, p.1). In government and administration decisions are taken and implemented, needs are met and obstacles surmounted, the new circumstances arise and new pressures impinge, other policies are evolved, new decisions are taken (Burgess and Pratt, 1970, p.168). Therefore, all government policies, indeed all executive and administrative decisions, involve empirical predictions (Bryan Magee, 1973).

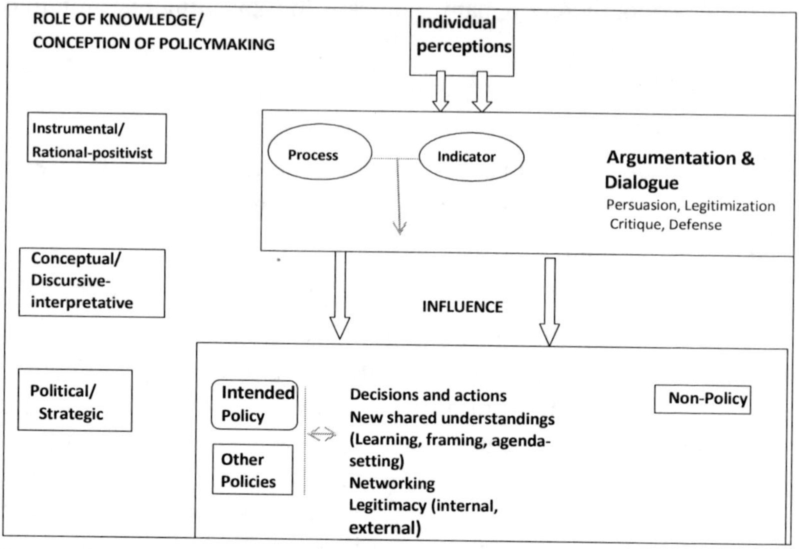

Figure 17.2: Paradigms of Influence (Lehtonen, 2013).

Research for policy formulation is based upon the relationship between policy research and the policy process, the extent to which the knowledge that is relevant to policy is distinctive, and loaded with substantial evidence of change, a change for the betterment of the society. Schon (1977:235) describes this as the 'problem solving' approach. It is an applied research to inform policy making. Weiss (1977b: 13) suggests that it is knowledge created through research. It can stimulate policy-makers into taking action.

Knowledge is 'iterative' – not the rational analysis, but a much more diffuse process. For instance, the reform of education in the India has been going on since time immemorial. Educational policy (1984) and Plan of Action (1992) have contributed significantly in Educational Development. Research formulates hypotheses/research questions on the basis of field data, and uses appropriate methodology to get response or substantial evidence which can be used in designing the public policy.

The research findings are used selectively on deriving substantial evidence. The findings are put to debate in practitioners' domain. Sometimes the research questions which have been addressed by social scientists are not those in which the policy-makers are interested, but mostly because important social issues rarely admit of easy resolution.

Sometimes research evidences are not substantial. Some important issues are under public debate such as under performance of government schools, education and employability, or midday meal and learning outcomes, quality vs quantity question in education. In development research, question arises what necessary changes are required in policy in order to make it more effective or tool for economic growth and poverty reduction.

More precisely, centrality of focus in public policy is on growth, social change and justice. It is micro and macro; inclusive and comprehensive; quintessentially practical and epistemic, technological and economic (cost effectiveness); participatory, capability development and value for people; and mechanism of execution and evaluation within the given timeframe.

In brief:

- Policy research generates knowledge for action,
- Policy research is integral to change and provides substantial evidence for change,
- Policy research is more interested in the multiple consequences of particular policy innovations,
- Scientific objectivity can be described as the inter-subjectivity of scientific method (Popper, 1966),
- Policy research is 'contested terrain' (Jenny Ozga, 2000, p.1),
- Policy is based on theories which are not only testable but also tested,
- There is inescapably political character of policy research.

The policies are being redesigned and reframed in light of new emerging priorities. Question is how can the governmental programmes and schemes be made more effective on the evidence of researches? Government policy and commitment under 'Right to Education Act', that 'No Child is Left Uneducated' has attracted the attention of researchers as how to make it successful through the participation of stakeholders.

17.3 Characteristics of Policy Research

- Policy research is persuasive to diverse audiences. Its results have to be quite substantial to convince the social groups and the policy-planners to accept them. A piece of policy research has also substantial ground to convince government.

- Policy research works in a world that is structured by the immediate demands of policy making. Policy research has to work to a strict timetable which has been set by the policy-makers.
- The results of policy research are published. They enter the realm of politics and ideology. The researchers can, of course, and then join the debate, but they do so as citizens, not as researchers.
- Policy research is not only about working out the best means to given ends. It can also be about questioning/sharing these ends professionals, by interest groups, and by the society.
- Policy research is a partnership between government, researchers and users of the research. This extends to the choice of problems, the framing of the questions to be put to respondents or beneficiaries. It also involves the choice of method (standardised questionnaire or some other technique), the analysis of the data, and the dissemination of the results.
- Comparison is crucial, that is, comparing some policy options with others. The policy agenda always contains more than the government admits. All new ideas, conflicting views and experiences are analysed. Control is exercised through inter-subjectivity of scientific method (Popper, 1966).

17.4 Methodological Issues

Source: Logical reasoning, common sense and argument suggest that some practices may be better than others, and we can develop a policy on empirical foundation which challenge existing expectations about what works and why, and produce new theories which conjecturally are better. (Swann, 2000). Role of theories in policy is very significant especially those which offer courses of action rather than simply explanation. Policy needs to be based on not only testable but also tested theories. Theories need to explore and explain the relationship between social background and attainment or develop the idea of human capital as an explanation of differential outputs.

All government policies, indeed all executive and administrative decisions, involve empirical predictions. At best, it identifies what works and what does not, and it can offer explanation and understanding of why things work. For instance, how can the use and application of ICT in educational institutions increase learning outcomes? To create policy or to change policy, we need to know how and why some things work and why others do not, and to what extent they work under different circumstances. We need both explanatory and predictive knowledge. What kinds of evidence are needed to test if it is working or not? What is the best way of collecting that evidence?

A substantial literature on policy offers 'rational models' (Simon, 1947; Lindblom, 1959). A few researches reveal the various ways in which this ideal eludes human endeavour, by flawed decision-making and imperfect implementation. (Barrett and Fudge, 1981). Further analysis has added wider social, organisational, political and economic factors to explain the failings (Shore and Wright, 1997). Situational logic helps to avoid such errors and blunders. The conjectures resulting from situational analysis form testable hypotheses (Popper, 1992). It is a mark of intelligence in policy-making, as in other forms of human endeavour, to learn from experiences of others. We learn from mistakes without making them (Magee, 1973).

Doing Policy Research

- Values, goals, and objectives are set out;
- A problem requiring action is identified;
- Social norms, mindsets, and institutions are examined critically;
- All important strategies for solving the problem are chalked out;
- The tangible and non-tangible outcomes which would follow from these are predicted;
- A policy is chosen in which the outcomes most closely match the values, goals and objectives.

17.5 Policy Formulation, Execution and Impact Assessment

Vision, mission, values and goals of policy are essences of public policy. These provide direction and motivation. People are empowered and equipped with knowledge and skills to act consciously in the backdrop of reality, in a dynamic environment, and motivated to provide inputs for policy formulation. One of the basic and fundamental elements of the policy is 'ethics' a set of 'moral prisms' through which it has to pass through. A set of 'prisms' includes: - virtue ethic, result ethic, universal ethic, public exposure ethic, and caring ethic (David, A. Sharpiro, 1999).

Designing and formulation of policy is a complex activity which involves defining and weighing the merits and risks of various alternatives. It generally involves formal policy analysis, that is, policy work specifically undertaken to generate and evaluate policy options or alternative course of actions to address problems or issues on a policy agenda ((Howlett *et al.,* 2009). Policy formulation involves the use of analytical methods (i.e., either formal or informal) to appraise policy on the parameters of epistemology, ontology and ethno-methodology. Policy appraisal is concerned with "how evidence is collected, marshaled, communicated, digested and used." (Turnpenny *et al.,* 2013). Public policy is anchored on expectations of analysts and policy-makers with respect to the roles of expert knowledge in decision-making, which are enumerated by Lehtonen (2009) as threefold:

- **Instrumental role** –information put to use for specific decisions or requested by decision-makers for specific projects;
- **Conceptual or "enlightenment" role** –knowledge provides broad information base for decisions, by providing conceptual frameworks and fostering different types of learning; and
- **Political role** –justifying or legitimising policies, decisions and actions, or postponing actual decisions are to be examined critically.

Policy, however, involves resources, people as agents and moreover, it is implemented through institutions. It also identifies and earmarks processes, procedures and mechanisms of governance. In order to achieve the desired goals of policy, it is essential that institutions should work effectively and efficiently. The focus is on encouraging commitment and involvement of all in the process of change as well acknowledging individually the contribution made towards achieving excellence in the execution. Team configuration, skill-development, reduced structure, and defining new roles, prompt feedback and time bond action are very necessary in the execution of policy programmes. The bureaucratic rigmaroles need to be removed. Metrics and non-metrics techniques are used to assess the impact of policy implementation. Therefore, pre- and post-period analysis of data is done. Metric results reveal whether the change is statistical significant or insignificant. Non-metric (narrative) outcomes show what change people have experienced.

17.6 Public Policy Framework

Policy formulation is the first step in any planning cycle. Planners must appreciate the dynamics of policy formulation before they can design implementation and evaluation processes. Policies, however, differ in terms of their scope, complexity, decision environment, range of choices, and decision criteria. Methodological and political issues become more pronounced such as, definition of the problem in conflictive societies; use of analytical techniques and optimisation; questions of proper theoretical base, measurement, valuation and aggregation; hard objective data vs. soft subjective data; and technical analysis vs. public participation.

The term 'policy making' implies plan of action for addressing the array of issues within the ambit of policy framework. It is analysis of competing conceptions and assumptions to find practical solution of problems. A study of the theoretical and empirical work of social scientists reveals the two essential dimensions of policy-making: who does it (the actors) and how (the processes). Historically, the actor in

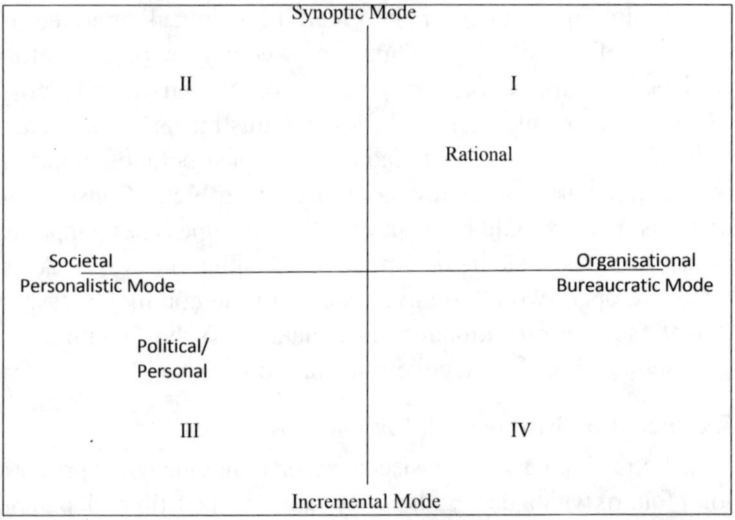

Figure 17.3: Dimensions of Policy Framework (Lindblom, 1959).

policy-making has been considered unitary and rational; more recently policy analysts have introduced the organisational (public interest) model and the personalistic (self-interest) model. The process element has fluctuated between a synoptic (comprehensive) approach and an incremental approach. Lindblom and Cohen (1979) laid out the differences between the synoptic and incremental methods of policy-making. Figure 17.3 reveals dimensions of policy making.

According to him, the synoptic method entails, in its extreme form, one single central planning authority for the whole of society, combining economic, political, and social control into one integrated planning process that makes interaction unnecessary. It assumes: (a) that the problem at hand does not go beyond man's cognitive capacities and (b) there exist agreed criteria (rather than social conflict on values) by which solutions can be judged and (c) that the problem-solvers have adequate incentives to stay with synoptic analysis until it is completed (rather than 'regress' to using incremental planning). Incremental policy-making, on the other hand, relies on interaction rather than on a complete analysis of the situation to develop a blueprint for solving problems. The incremental approach to policy-making is built on the following assumptions: (a) Policy options are based on highly uncertain and fluid knowledge, and are in response to a dynamic situation (ever changing problems, and evolving contexts); (b) No 'correct' solution can therefore be found, or technically derived from a diagnosis of the situation. Thus, no sweeping or drastic reforms should be attempted; (c) Only incremental and limited policy adjustments can be made; and (d) Policy adjustments are expected to remedy an experienced dissatisfaction with past policies, improving the existing situation or relieving an urgent problem. Consequently, these adjustments should be tentative - and in some cases temporary - and must be revised as the dynamics of the situation evolve. Allison (1971) developed two alternative models to the commonly assumed model of the unitary rational policy-maker: (a) the Organisational process model, and (b) the governmental politics model.

17.7 Conceptual Framework for Policy Analysis

The Policy Framework consists of seven policy-planning processes, the first four of which deal with policy-making, the fifth with planning and sixth and seventh with policy adjustment:

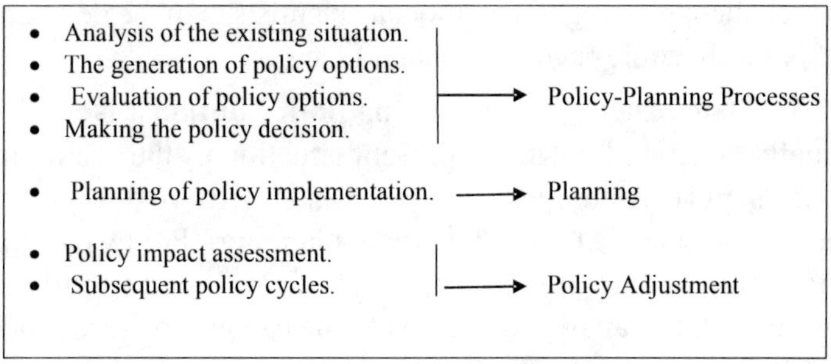

Figure 17.4: Policy Planning Processes.

Policy Adjustment

17.7.1 Policy analysis should consider a number of aspects of the social context, including political, economic, demographic, cultural, and social issues which are likely to affect the decision-making and even implementation processes. This may include:

- **Background Data:** The general character of a country (location, geography, population, culture, and social stratification patterns) has obvious implications for policy analysis.
- **Political context:** The preceding observation emphasises that an analysis of the political environment is necessary for an understanding of the national decision-making process.
- **Economic context:** In this area, the analyst wants to understand the present macro-economic situation in general and the human resources situation in particular. It is, however, more important to estimate the likely trends in the various sectors in the future and the financial resources of the country in order to assess what the economy requires from the intended policy and what the sector expects to face from the rest of the economy, particularly in terms of general infrastructure and financial resources.
- **Dynamics of change:** An assessment of the present situation cannot be complete without evaluating the forces for or against change in the event that policy changes need to be made. Such an assessment has implications for the chances of success of different types of policies and for strategies that must be employed to promote and implement such policies. Nobel laureate North (1994) confesses that "there is no greater

challenge facing today's social scientists than the development of a dynamic theory of social change".

17.7.2. The process of generating policy options: New policies are usually generated when the present situation of the sector and its context is perturbed by a problem, a political decision or a reorganisation scheme (overall national planning). Policy options can be generated in several different ways to accommodate the disequilibrium. For analytical purposes one can group these processes under the following four modes: systemic, incremental, ad hoc and importation. In concrete situations, though, several of these modes may be combined.

17.7.3 Evaluation of policy options: Policy options can be evaluated only if alternative scenarios are developed to allow estimations of the likely implications of the options considered. The 'imaginary' situation that would be created if a policy option implemented is compared with the present situation, and the scenario of transition from the existing to the imaginary case is evaluated in terms of desirability, affordability, and feasibility.

17.7.4 Making the policy decision: The role of Policy planners, academia, participants and NGOs is crucial. Good policy decision depends on coordinated efforts. Each option is examined and evaluated on prior designed criteria or grounded research evidence. Policy decision is, therefore, made on the basis of substantial evidence. Figure 17.5 shows policy formulation and adoption.

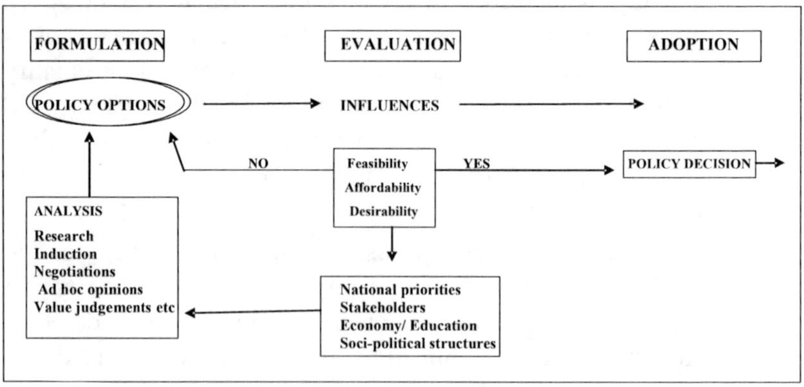

Figure 17.5: Policy Formulation and Adoption.

17.7.5 Planning policy implementation: After scientific analysis of policy options, feasibility, affordability, and desirability of the policy are evaluated along with national priorities, and socio-political structures to arrive at logical policy decision. Once a policy has been chosen, planning for policy implementation begins. What is abstract during the evaluation stage begins to become concrete during planning. A temporal schedule for execution, physical targets and financial implications are drawn up. Details about who will do what, when and how are earmarked. Physical and financial resources are identified to be used judicially. The technical knowledge is needed to guide the policy implementation. The administrative systems within which the policy will be directed must be clearly structured and firmly in place. Political support, public participation, and tenets of good governance – transparency, accountability, and responsiveness are essential ingredients for effect policy implementation. Impact of policy is reflected in Figure 17.6.

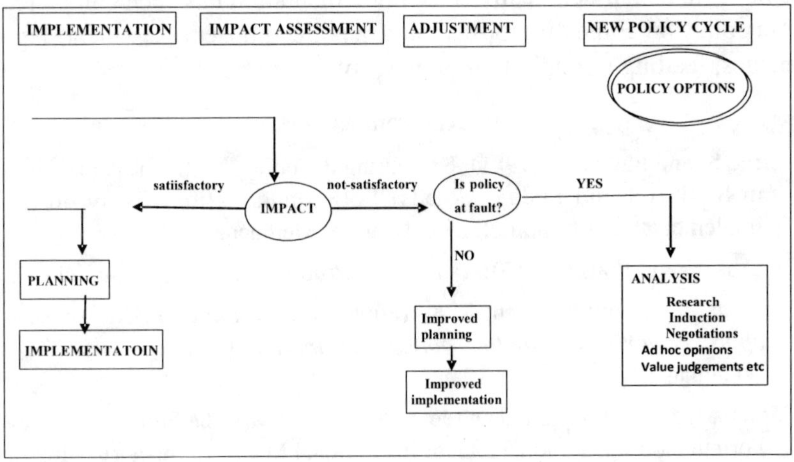

Figure 17.6: Impact Assessment and New Policy Cycle.

17.7.6 Policy impact assessment is a linear process. Policy output measurement is carried out on a continual basis. Metric and non-metric techniques can be used to identify the impact. Pre- and post-period analysis of data is done. Metric results reveal whether the change is statistical significant or insignificant. Non-metric (narrative) outcomes show what change people have experienced. If assessment reveals that the policy outcome is lacking, it is necessary to determine whether the policy itself is inadequate, or whether poor implementation is at fault.

Human capital inadequacies, under-funding, or inadequate economic stimulus during the implementation stage are among the many possible causes of failure of a well-designed policy. On the other hand, if assessment reveals deficiencies in outcomes and if implementation can be shown to have been well done, then it is necessary to re-examine the policy decision and to determine what adjustments or what new policy is to be substituted to get good results.

17.7.7 Subsequent policy cycles: Often the results of verification are not ploughed back into policy. Instead, verification is often seen as a stock-taking exercise needed in order to close the books on a policy initiative. When policy change is once again needed in the policy under discussion, a policy process often begins de novo and may duplicate much of the analysis, derivation of alternative options, evaluation, and planning carried out earlier. The conclusion, then, of policy analysis is never to conclude. Ideally, once implementation has been completed and policy outcomes are forthcoming, a policy impact assessment stage ensues, leading potentially to a new policy cycle.

References

Barret, S. and Fudge, C. (1981). Examining the policy –action relationship – in S. Barret and Fudge, C (eds) Policy and Action: Essay on the Implementation of Public Policy, London: Methuen.

Burgess, T. and Prat, J. (1970). *Policy and Practice.* London: Penguin Press.

Clemons, R.S., and McBeth, M.K. (2009). *Public policy praxis: A case approach for understanding policy and analysis* (2nd ed.). New York: Longman.

Corkery, Joan, Anthony Land and Jean Bossuyt. (1995).The Process of Policy Formulation: Institutional Path or Institutional Maze? European Centre for Development Policy Management.

Greenberg JN, Choi T. The role of the social sciences in the health services research: an overview. In: Choi T, Greenberg JN, editors. Social science approaches to health services research. Ann Arbor: Health Administration Press; 1982. pp. 2-20.

Howlett, Michael, M. Ramesh, and A. Perl. (2009). *Studying Public Policy.* Toronto: Oxford University Press.

Lehtonen, Markku. 2013. Indicators as a Tool for Policy Formulation. Paper prepared for the workshop on the role of analytical tools within the Policy Formulation Process, London, April 18-19, 2013.

Lindblom, C.E.(!959). The science of 'muddling through', *Public Administration Review,* 19(2), 79-88.

Miller, H.T. (2002). *Postmodren public policy*. Albany: State University of New York Press.

Pawson, R. (2002). Evidence-Based Policy: In Search of a Method? *Evaluation* 8, no. 2 157–81.

Popper, K.R. (1979). *Objective Knowledge: An Evolutionary Approach.* UK: Oxford University Press.

Pratt, J. (1999). Testing Policy, in J. Swann and J. Pratt (eds) *Improving evaluation: Realist Approaches to Method and Research.* London: Cassell.

Richards, C., and Farrokhnia, F. (2013). Optimising Grounded Theory for Policy *International Journal of qualitative Methods*, Vol.15, Issue 1, pp. 12-22.

Rich, R.F. (1997). Measuring knowledge utilisation: processes and outcomes. Knowledge and Policy: *The International Journal of Knowledge Transfer and Utilisation*; 10:11-24.

Shore, C. and Wright, S. ((eds) (1997). *The Anthropology of Public Policy: Critical Perspectives on Governance and Power.* London: Routledge.

Trostle, J, Bronfman, M, Langer, A. (1999). How do researchers influence decision-makers? Case studies of Mexican policies. *Health Policy Plan*; 14:103-14.

Turnpenny, John et al. (2013). Policy Appraisal. *In Routledge Handbook of Public Policy,* edited by E. Araral, S. Fritzen, M. Howlett, M. Ramesh, and X. Wu, 244-254. New York: Routledge.

Wadi, D. Haddad.(1995). Education policy planning process: an applied framework. UNESCO: International Institute for Educational Planning, Paris.

Weimer, D.L., and Vining, A.R. (2004). *Policy analysis: Concepts and practice* (4th ed.). Upper Saddle River, NJ: Prentice Hall.

18

Policy Planning and Good Governance

18. Goals of Policy

Major goals of public policy are growth, social change and justice. First, growth implies equity and equality. It needs to be inclusive but should not be skewed. Sanders (2016) mentions, "a nation will not survive morally or economically when so few have so much, while so many have so little." Study conducted by Pickett and Wilkinsons (2014) demonstrates the strong correlation between higher level of economic inequality and a wide range of health and social problems. For instance, one per cent in India owned nearly 60 per cent of the country's total wealth. Nearly half of Indians 1.30 billion can be classified as "excluded, " "deprived, " or "vulnerable." The goal of inclusive growth is to fill the gap between haves and have-nots. The poor need basic services that ensure a decent standard of living and a modest sense of security. "Put simply, a severely skewed income distribution harms the pace and sustainability of growth over the longer term. It leads to an economy of exclusion and a wasteland of discarded potential (Lagarde, 2014).

Policy is one of the most important ways of achieving change, a change for the betterment of the society. Policy is quintessentially concerned with finding practical ways of solving the problems. For instance, how best to teach children of different abilities, how to prepare and motivate teachers to deliver the best, how to deal with the disparities of opportunity arising from class, sex or race. The object of research in policy is not only to identify the opportunities but to evolve strategies for change and transformation of society. It is crucial that we should have some grounds for believing that the outcomes of policy will be what we hope.

Policy calls for actions to ensure justice for all. Questions arise how can the rights of deprived be protected? How can persons with disability get their rights to education and employment? How can the government ensure the right to education for all between 6 to 14 years ages? How can we bridge socio-economic-political and cultural gaps between the rich and the poor? How can we safeguard the child right to development, education, participation and protection from exploitation? and so on.

We have a comprehensive written constitution of India. The constitution rests on three pillars- the Legislature, the Judiciary, and the Executive. Apart from these, the constitution has also created a number of agencies to assist in the process of governance; this is in addition to the large number of implementing agencies and institutions, created as part of the executive. The role of government and governance is frequently projected in terms of people versus government. The government, created by the people, is designed to help manage the problem of the people. Each organ of the constitution is an independent entity guided by the Constitution in the discharge of its responsibility. Moreover, the Legislature, the Judiciary, and the executive have to work in tandem to ensure good governance. But facts speak out something else that they have not discharged the onerous responsibilities cast on them by the Constitution to the full extent. Indeed, there have been large gaps and critical failures. The current theory is that the law cannot make a distinction between a common citizen and a 'privileged' person; and therefore, the same processes are applied. The reality is that the privileged in our society, i.e. the politicians, the businessmen, government servants, are able to circumvent the law through money power and other means.

Public policy is designed by the specialised and experienced professionals. It is collaborative effort in gathering and analysing research evidence in order to make the policy more inclusive and comprehensive; quintessentially practical and epistemic, technological fit and cost effectiveness, participatory, and value for people. Processes, procedures, rules are simplified and clearly defined. Sector-wise temporal framework and financial plan are prepared in advance. Implementation and governance is entrusted to generalists- bureaucrats and government servants. Therefore, all government policies, indeed all executive and administrative decisions, involve empirical predictions.

18.1 Good Governance: Issues and Strategies

18.1.1 What is good governance? Generally speaking it implies a system which is effective and efficient, inclusive, participatory, transparent, accountable, and responsive to deliver the best to the expectations of the people. It is benchmarked as SMART- Simple, Moral, Accountable, Responsive and Transparent. Therefore, good governance demands honest, mature, and committed bureaucracy, inspired political leadership and also a healthy social and cultural environment in order to ensure inclusive growth, social change, and justice.

The World Bank defines governance as "the manner in which power is exercised in the management of a country's economic and social resources." The UNDP puts it as "the complex mechanisms, processes, relationships and institutions through which citizens and groups articulate their interests, exercise their rights and obligations and mediate their differences" . The concept evolved by the Tokyo Institute of Technology refers to Governance as a complex set of values, norms, processes and institutions by which society manages its development and resolves its conflicts, formally or informally; it not only involves the state but also the civil society-economic and social actors, community-based institutions and unstructured groups- at the local, national, regional and global levels.

UNDP (1997) recognises the nine indicators of good governance namely, (i) Participation, (ii) Rule of law, (iii) Transparency, (iv) Responsiveness, (v) Consensus oriented, (vi) Equity, (vii) Effectiveness and Efficiency, (viii) Accountability, and (ix) Strategic vision. In fact, all these variables of good governance have been incorporated in the evaluation of good governance across the national, state, regional, and local levels.

18.2 Issues

The profound questions involved in bringing about a humane, enlightened and dynamic system of governance have generally been ignored. The need to upgrade the total capacity of the state and society has not been considered (Jagmohan. 2008). The strategic issues need to be explored as such mentioned below.

18.2.1.Mindset- It has been generally observed in all democracies that the Executive develops a mind, spirit, and attitude of its own over time, which need not always be pro-people or pro-citizen In India, with large segments of the electorate being poor and powerless, illiterate, ill informed. And in an ill organised environment, the Executive silences the voice of the people through subtle means and treats itself as being beyond accountability. These signals clearly point towards a very dangerous situation this is why correctives become called for.

18.2.2 Good governance rests on the edifice of Legislative, Executive and Judiciary. Questions arise, are these apex organs of constitution functioning well to the expectation and aspiration of the people? Are these bodies pursue and share common goals of freedom, development, and justice? or is each following its own agenda of non-accountability as being independent entity? Are these working to serve the vested interest or common citizens? For instance, land meant for infrastructure, essential services, forest, was legally passed on to the unscrupulous politicians, bureaucrats, the police officers and land mafia. which negates the basic concept of good governance. Question arises as how to break obnoxious nexus?

18.2.3 Rules and Regulations, Processes and Procedures are clearly defined. There is no scope for by-passing them. But dare devils politicians, bureaucrats, and criminals are above laws, rules and norms. For instance, as reported in media, numbers of fake bills have been found drawn without execution of the work. Such cases have been pending disposal by the court for pretty long period. Who suffered most, the poor people? Why our enforcement agencies are ineffective at the implementation level and it needs to be examined critically.

18.2.4 Issue of People Participation is crucial in democratic set up. Over the past decades, citizens have become more assertive about their right to participate, be informed and to influence governments' decision-making processes. Governments, especially those that came to power with a strong commitment to introduce policy reform to address social problems, are looking for new ways to evaluate their performance, and in turn strengthen their legitimacy and political capital. In many regions, citizens have not acquired new capacities to evaluate and monitor their governments and are not engaged in some form of social audit activity at the local, provincial and/or national level.

18.2.5 Role of Civil Society, NGOs and Media: Good governance can be ensured through civil society and non-governmental organisations, as well as an independent media, watchdog organisations and influential think-tanks and/or research organisations. As such, initiatives to enhance the ability of citizens and stakeholders to engage with public officials and policymakers in a more informed, direct and constructive manner have not been getting more attention and support.

18.2.6 Ethical Issues: Accountability, transparency, and responsiveness are the primary variables of good governance. Participation of public in democratic setup is prerequisite of governance. Traditionally, efforts to address issues of accountability have focused on improving and/or strengthening the "supply-side" of democratic governance. Right to information is to key to ensuring transparency in the system. Similarly, administrative procedures and internal controls, auditing requirements (both internal and external), and law enforcement (through comptrollers, courts and the police) have been there in the system. Are we free from the rigmoles of administrative machinery? Transparency implies publication and display of development works under various schemes, its progress, and impact. Moreover, processes are to be hassle free and access to data should be on demand. Transparency, in fact, generates greater confidence between citizens and public officials. Responsiveness calls for commitment at the highest level, and beneficiary-centric intervention. Role of technology is significant. Use of technology for obtaining and generating useful information in timely manner are to be given top priority. However, the above mentioned issues of ethics are rarely found in actual practice.

18.3 Strategies

Like any strategic plan, government strategy seeks to answer three questions:

- Where are we now? (i.e. how are systems working now, and what external factors affect them).
- Where do we want to get to? (i.e. in future, how should the government systems be or work differently from at present).
- How do we get there? What actions need to be undertaken to achieve the outcome identified in answering the second question).

1. *Pre-Post Period Analysis:* It involves comparison of base-line data and Present data (after the execution of policy or specific project).
2. *Strategic Audit Analysis:* Government specific answer to the question "where are we now" requires a comprehensive understanding of present status. Information may include systems perspective, issues perspective, Stakeholder perspective, and contextual perspective.

18.3.1 Data Base: good governance is built on comprehensive data base. Number of questions may arise. Is data official? Is data adequate? Is data generated by the stakeholders at the field level? Are grounded data and official data compared? Is data reliable and valid? or is data trustworthy and authentic? Is data accessible and available on demand? Has data been put on public domain? Again there is question of methodology- is it survey (ex-post facto) or ethnomethodolgy (Narrative and Visual), or both? With good data base, one can capture the real picture of good governance. We should define data quality in terms of five "CARTA" i.e. completeness, accuracy, relevance, timeliness, appropriateness of presentation.

18.3.2 Institutions: 1. Democratic-it refers to- for the people, of the people, by the people. There should be ample space for multi-voices to be heard, 2. Participatory: stakeholders have rights to project their demands, right to be informed, right to participate in processes of governance, and evaluation. Their ideas, capacity and potentials need to be recognised. 3. Effective and Efficient Management: imply best inputs to get good results, regular monitoring, evaluation and accreditation. 4. Execution: refers to get job done within time-frame and at low cost. All ethical norms are to be followed. Our institutions at all levels are to be strengthened to meet the perceived needs of the people.

18.3.3 Participation of stakeholders (actors) is very much essential for the implementation and good governance where they are inspired, informed, and involved to achieve the stipulated goals within the timeframe and at low cost. In this process, the public should get comprehensive information on equality and equity in system. Regular feedback from stakeholders should be the basis for further improvement. The participants should establish a systemic relationship between goals, execution and evaluation and help in identifying meaningfully change or most significant change experienced. Active participation should be ensured through focus group discussions, focus interview, and ehnomethodology (i.e. conversation, discourse and genre analysis).

18.3.4 Human Resource Development: 1. Attitude: Only the committed, informed and inspired field functionaries can deliver the best. Deadwoods need to be weeded out. Aptitude: their potentials and Knowledge-base need to be enhanced. 2. Ethics: it is essential each should go through the acid test of transparency, accountability and responsiveness; 3. Assessment is to be done on the basis of value-addition.

18.3.5 Delivery System: Governance should ensure effective planning, implementation and delivery system. Effective implementation involves well defined coordination and flow of communication and participation at all levels: centre, state and local. State, region and local should get due consideration and space to adopt innovative practices of good governance. Policy-making needs to (a) be aligned to its governance structure and (b) take into account the respective responsibilities of different actors (Fazekas and Burns, 2012). Institutions need to be strengthened to work effectively and efficiently. The context should be a key to the process of policy design and implementation. Therefore, the degree of decentralisation in decision-making across systems and the greater simplicity in the policy making process should be given top priority in governance. Delivery system should meet the perceived needs of the stakeholders, Questions arise: is work executed within the given timeframe? If not what are the reasons? Are all stakeholders satisfied with the quality of work? Are the processes and procedures simple and to the understanding level of stakeholders (participants)?

Furthermore, adequate infrastructure (ergonomics), simple procedures (smart card), quick processing (single window delivery and adequate number of counters) are the hallmarks of good governance. Introduction of new technologies in delivery system or governance is meant to make the system more effective (accessibility and availability of information through electronic media), transparent, accountable, and economical (in terms of time and energy saving). The citizen demands better services even at a little higher cost. It should also be proactive and responsive to the needs of deprived and marginalised section of the society and to empower them to lead an enriched quality of life. Delivery system needs to be got evaluated by the stakeholders

The United Nations Handbook of Public Administration mentions "Political neutrality is an essential compliment to the merit system, for it guarantees that the career officials will give the government, whatever its political make-up, absolutely impartial advice, criticism and assistance in any manner which concerns it." The political leadership has become more challenging on account of public expression and participation. Citizens around the country would demand that the government deliver public services in time frames, of consistent quality, and often at lower cost. In this context, policy-makers need to use what McKinsey calls a Delivery 2.0 approach – a well-designed programme with appropriate metrics, experimental "delivery labs" small and high powered execution teams, visible support from leaders, a culture of performance and accountability.

18.4 Evaluation

1. Summation techniques can be used for outcomes evaluation, impact evaluation, cost-benefit analysis, or meta-analysis. 2. Formative techniques can be used for need assessment, feasibility assessment and process assessment. 3. Most Significant Change: Stakeholders experience of empowerment-social, economic, political can be identified. 4. Social Audit: Should be used as a mechanism of accountability.

Funding is only one way to measure what a government actually does. Broadly, policy actions geared at achieving desired outcomes tend to fall under three categories: incentives, regulation, and information and government should employ all three approaches to navigate the changing landscape with agility, innovation, and best-in-class implementation.

System evaluation requires policy coherence, credibility of execution, high technical and analytical capacity, a strategic approach, transparent reporting, and a valuable use of results. This involves a strategic approach to research, analysis and evaluation, and information management activities to support the provision of evidence-based policy advice. Credibility of system evaluation activities facilitates good governance. Great care is needed in ensuring adequate accessibility of system evaluation results, clarifying the interpretability of the results, establishing protocols to share data among stakeholders, providing clear and timely reporting of results to different audiences, articulating key messages on the major results, and offering opportunities for discussion.

References

Abdul Kalam, A.P.J. (2014). *Governance for Growth in India.* New Delhi: Rupa Publications.

Ashkenas, R. (2010). *Simply Effective.* Boston: Harward Business Press.

Bossidy, L., and Ram, C. (2011). *Execution: The Discipline of Getting Things Done.* London: Random House.

Chandler, C., and Zainulbhai. (2013). *Reimagining India*. New York: Simon & Schuster.

Dobbs, R., Manyika, J., and Woetzel, J. (2015). *No Ordinary Disruption*. New York: Public Affairs.

Heeks, R. (2006). *Implementing and Managing e-Government: An International Text*. New Delhi: Vistaar Publications.

Jagmohan (2008). *Shaping India's New Destiny.* New Delhi: Allied Publishers.

Largarde, C.(2014). A new multilateralism for the 21st century: Richard Dimbleby Lecture. International Monetary Fund (IMF).

19

Participatory Research Approach

19 What is Participatory Approach?

Participatory research can be viewed as a relatively pure form of research in practice. It privileges the experience and needs of project participants. One of the basic principles of the approach is that ordinary men and women have the capacity to name their own reality. Actors (participants) are co-investigators in seeking solutions to the problems that they encounter in their everyday lives. The investigative process is collective, dialogical, educative, and emancipator. Expertise, whether from within the community or brought in from outside, does not direct procedures. The power of decision-making is vested with the participants.

In participatory research, data are generated by human efforts to understand complex change processes and their contribution to (predicted and unpredicted) the society. It comprises complex, interrelated elements embracing values, knowledge, behaviour, and relationships. Both the content and the quality of data are prime concerns. Scoring of qualitative changes in behaviour and relationships is done through participatory processes. It creates space and legitimacy in project monitoring framework and paves way for 'in-depth participatory diagnostic analyses". It is in-depth analysis of contextually–bound data. It involves objectivity in the subjectivity of the researcher. All qualitative research methods lay emphasis on qualitative data, content sensitivity, emphatic neutrality, inductive analysis and naturalistic inquiry.

Main concerns of participatory research are to: (a) provide adequate understanding of complexity of reality; (b) derive substantial evidence for policy planning and programme redesigning; (c) set individuals as active agent in their environment (contextual) rather than passive objects to be researched; (d) analyse impact on the participants; (e) view and analyse the problem in a holistic perspective.

Participatory research explicitly requires clients participation "in the control of entire process" and defines all participants as "researchers" (Hall, 1981, pp. 7-8). Participatory researchers use collaborative data collection and analysis strategies with participants, much like action researchers. They develop "education for critical consciousness" (Freire, 1974) and method of "collective analysis" (Barndt, 1981). The participatory research tradition uses "militant observers" (Darcy de Oliverira, 1975), investigative and advocacy research (Laue, 1978) and "conflict methodologies" of various kind (Lehmann and Young, 1975) to extract information from un-cooperative adversaries.

In participatory research it is alleged that the process of empowerment of 'marginalised' is non-linear. It depends largely on experience gained from opportunities to exercise rights which are inherently context specific. So, for example, people may become socially empowered but have limited political empowerment in one context, but may become relatively politically empowered with limited social empowerment in another. The non-linear and context-specific nature of empowerment poses a challenge for conventional monitoring, which generally assumes a linear progression and defines normative milestones to be attained. The approach presented here embraces the idea that different aspects of empowerment may be achieved asymmetrically and at a different pace in different contexts, by recognising and quantifying all positive changes. It implies 'participatory grass-roots review'. Participatory research focuses on actors (e.g. oppressed groups), issues (e.g. conflicts with power holders), and values and ideologies (e.g. empowerment, equity and self-reliance) that put it in opposition to dominant forces in society (Brown and Tandon, 1981). However, emphasis is on human development, equitable distribution of resources, and ecological and temporal sustainability as central concerns of development strategy (Korten and Klauss, 1984). It has implications for inquiry, education, and organised intervention to transform local patterns of awareness, distribution of power and resources and participation in development activity.

19.1 Research Design

Research Design involves three processes namely:

WHY: What motivations have they to go for research? Why are the participants interested in the problem to be researched? What is the importance of the problem? Will it bring about substantial change in their lives? Will it empower them to be proactive in socio-economic, educational and political environment?

WHAT: The participant will decide what problem is to be undertaken for research. Professional researcher may facilitate them in identifying the problem. Two or more themes are to be identified by the participants in the consultation with the professional researcher.

HOW: This comprises: (a) sampling for the research; (b) approach- qualitative or from qualitative to quantification; (c) tools and procedures for data collection. How data will be analysed? The main components are: (a) contextual content analysis; (b) data reduction- without loss of significant information; (c) data display-the process to organise, compress and assemble information (graphs, charts, and Venn diagrams, causal models etc.) and (d) drawing and verifying conclusions.

Broad Features of Participatory Research

- The researcher must have sensitivity and democratic identification with the people.
- There is close involvement of the researcher with the researched community. The participatory research is undertaken in a manner that the distinction between subject and object is eliminated and power equalisation takes place.
- People are the critical resource. People can contribute ideas, information, and insight. Conceived as an empowerment process for the people with whom the research is conducted.

(*Contd...*)

- The participatory research entails a framework that is evolved from the local context. It uses technology that is small and appropriate. Methods of data collection and analysis are such that they contribute towards an understanding of micro situation and their micro contexts.
- Understand the conditions underlying a problem in order to resolve the problem by transforming those conditions (Socio-Cultural-Economic-Political-Psychological).
- Recognise the people's own capability and potential to produce knowledge base. Knowledge and learning outcomes are not confined to the researcher alone but shared by the people.

Outcomes: The focus is on the assessment (value added) of (a) most significant changes in the situation; (b) increased knowledge base; (c) increased capacity among actors to inquire into and change their situation. Different levels of outcomes of participatory research to be assessed are; (i) the actors in the research process engage in a common effort to transform their situation because they become aware of the causes of the present state and their own potential to be agents of change, (ii) the actors are empowered (increased in their capacity and knowledge base) to participate in decision-making process. In this research process their level of confidence is increased, (iii) awareness, increased in capacity and knowledge base, and collective involvement pave way for their growth and sustainability.

19.2 Processes of Participatory Research

- Processes are simplified to the understanding levels of the participants. Participants are informed, inspired and involved in the selection of locale, focus group, temporal plan and decision-making process. Free, frank and fearless environment is developed to provide space for dissension, disagreement, discourse and consensus.
- Processes for monitoring are streamlined which require no special professional skills. Communicative processes are made easy across cultures. Indicators are identified by the participants. Everyone can tell story about event he/she thinks is important.

- People have to explain why they believe one change is more important than another.

Motivation involvement of the actors in the problem situation.	→	**Consensus** between actors and researcher on theme/ themes	→	**Identification** of small group responsible for research cycle	→	**Formulation**of Research Design by the actors and researcher
						↓
Outcomes Most Significant Change Significant Change, or no change	←	**Analysis**of data jointly by actors and researcher	←	**Identification** and weight-age of indicators of change	←	**From Qualitative** understanding to quantification

Figure 19.1: Processes in a Participatory Research Approach.

- Processes lay focus on building staff capacity through analysing data and conceptualising impact.
- Systemic relationship between objectives, methods, data analysis and its interpretation is established through participatory approach in order to capture the real picture of phenomena and to get answers of research questions.
- Participatory processes are designed and followed to identify the Most Significant Change.

Participatory Research Design is shown in Table 19.1

- Participatory approach is based on flexible research design wherein participants are informed and involved to make choices regarding selection of problem, themes, social setting and group formation.
- Purposive or incidental sampling technique is used. It involves the selection of elements based on assumptions regarding the population of interest, which forms the criteria for selection. Hence, because the selection of elements is non-random, non-probability sampling does not allow the estimation of sampling errors. These conditions place limits on how much information a sample can provide about the population. Information about the relationship between sample and population is limited, making it difficult to extrapolate from the sample to the population.

Table 19.1: Participatory Research Design

Design	Flexible design: Must provide opportunity to participant group and individual members to make choice regarding; • Selection of Problem • Research questions • Selection of Social Setting • Selection of Methodology • Mixed Method (Quantitative and Qualitative) (Researcher as Facilitator)
Sampling design	Non-probability sampling design (purposive or judgment sampling) Choice of Locale and Groups for collection of data
Tools	• Focus Group Discussion • Semi-structured-Interview Schedule • Dialogue • Story telling • Observation
Operational Design	Of the participants, by the participants and for the participants focusing on: • Theme/Themes • Research Questions • Generation of Data • Outcomes Decision
Statistical design	No pre-planned design for analysis • Comparison and Control • Development of Understanding and Meaning • Qualitative understanding to quantification • Graphs/ Statistical Matrix
Outcomes	Most Significant Change/Changes affecting their lives

- Instruments for collection of data may include-Focus Group Discussion, Semi-structured-Interview Schedule or Focus Interview, Diary, Dialogue, Conversation, Story Telling, Observation, Films, Video, and Photographs.
- In operational design research questions are evolved in cooperation with participants. Data is generated at the field level through active involvement of the participants in order to get answers to research questions (outcomes).
- There is no pre-plan for the analysis of data. No pre-planned design for analysis. It comprises of control, comparison, understanding, meaning and conceptualisation. Descriptive data may contain-graphs, diagrams, and statistical matrix etc.

Findings from the focus groups help to contextualise those numbers, providing diagnostic solutions and highlighting which of the 'areas of dissatisfaction,' are most pressing and crucial.

- Most Significant Changes are identified by the participants on basis of (i) majority rule, or (ii) Voting by Group, or (iii) Secret Ballot or (iv) Scoring by Individual Members.

19.3 The Choice of Locale and Group

The locale is the place in which the study can be undertaken. Group comprises of individuals members to be studied. These are clearly defined by the research problem to be addressed. For instance, to identify people below poverty line, the researcher has to identify the specific place and specific group where he can get response to research questions. A particular intervention, the researcher intends to introduce to empower them, applies to specific people in specific a place. However, questions may arise about the best comparator groups or exactly how to design the work, but the people and the place are determined from the start. Research design focuses on sample selection and control, the research instruments and comparisons. All good designs are compromises, and in this process the problem is refined, the group(s) and locale(s) reconsidered, alternative methods evaluated, some are adopted and some rejected, and the whole process continues until a satisfactory overall design emerges (Bechhhofer and Paterson, 2000).

19.4 Participants Own Analysis

The participants are asked to share their experiences of their social change. Each group is asked to prepare notes: the first illustrating life before association with the movement, the second illustrating the current situation, and the third depicting their aspirations for the near future (around 2-3 years). Apart from this framework, the groups are given no other guidance, hints, or input from researchers/investigators. The intention is to enable the groups to express themselves freely and spontaneously. The narration is to be based on real experiences on specific theme or themes.

- The group members are asked to present their past experiences before joining the present research project. Research questions are: gender discrimination (i.e. social, economic, cultural and political).

- The group members discuss the present scenario. Research questions are: (i.e., Research questions are: gender discrimination (i.e. social, economic, cultural and political).
- The group members present their views on future plan of action regarding research questions (i.e., social, economic, cultural and political).

19.5 From Qualitative Understanding to Quantification of Results

The process of translating this complex qualitative understanding of change into quantified indicators is done by the participants. This process is entirely driven by the research project participants. The self-assessment is done in a trusted space. Purpose is benefiting the future of the group and shaping its future plan and what they demand from service providers. There is no sense of competition between groups. Each group undertakes the reflection exercise for themselves. The process of evaluation is in itself empowering. Thus, the data generated in the field by the participants are put for analysis to identify the significant change. The data are categorised and weighted to identify change, and trends towards sustainability.

Empowerment of women (Most Significant Change) fall naturally into four categories: (i) Enhanced power expressed and experienced by the participants through their ability to present their own views and negotiate for their own ends in formal and informal decision making (political empowerment); (ii) Those to do with mutual support, trust, respect, and equality (social empowerment); (iii) Those to do with access to and use of resources (economic empowerment), and (iv) Those to do with access, availability and affordability of education). These variables are further assessed to identify the level of (i) awareness, (ii) capability building, and (iii) sustainability.

19.6 Analysis of data should take note of the following processes

The researcher has to undertake ***'Review and Reflection Exercise'*** in order to get appropriate answer to research questions. The exercise includes 'Reflection on analyses', 'Reflection on method', 'Reflection on ethical dilemmas and conflicts' and 'Reflection on observer's frame of mind'.

19.7 Most Significant Change (MSC)

There are several ways of reaching a decision about Significant Change in people's lives. These can be identified through majority rule, or individual scoring, securing by a group vote and secret ballot.

The broad domains of Significant Changes identified by the actors (actual users) are given below:

- Significant changes in the quality of social life of people (mutual support, trust, respect, and equality, interaction and participation, and social mobility) have been observed.
- Changes in income of people and sharing of economic resources (equity in income and resource sharing, and upward shift from below poverty line) have been observed.
- Significant changes in formal and informal decision-making and participation in political activities have been observed.
- Changes in the sustainability of people's organisations and activities have been observed.

17.8 Findings of Study of Women Empowerment of Block Vijaypur-District Samba (J and K State) (Kapoor and Sharma, 2016)

Qualitative information is quantified by assigning numerical values based on the number of fully realised empowerment statements. Indicators of awareness were weighted with score 1, whereas indicators for capability were weighted with 2 and indicators for self-sustaining with a score of 3. Data comprise of analysis of (i) Individuals scores (N=36) and (ii) Focus Groups Scores (N=9). Results of Individual scores were presented in a matrix as shown in Table 19.2.

Table 19.2: Scores of Individuals on the Indicators and Levels of Change

	Awareness	**Capability**	**Self-Sustainability**
Political Empowerment	**16**	**10**	**5**
Social Empowerment	**25**	**20**	**8**
Economic Empowerment	**15**	**9**	**4**

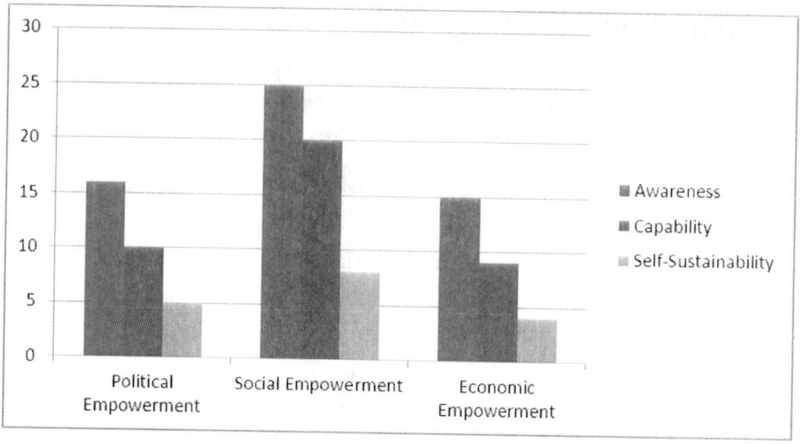

Figure 19.2: Bar Diagram Showing Levels of Change.

Figure 19.2 Analysis of data reveals that political, social and economic empowerment had increased which is reflected in their levels of awareness, capability and sustainability in the process of development. It had also been established non-linearity of empowerment of women. Their social empowerment had been found higher in terms of levels of awareness, capability and sustainability as compared to political and economic empowerment. Economic empowerment had been fond the lowest. Reasons reported by the people reveal that economic programmes initiated by the various agencies had not produced substantial results over the time (i.e. Level of sustainability of marginalised women).

Results of Focus Groups has been shown in Table 19.3.

Table 19.3: Table Showing Levels of Change (Group Development Index)

Variable	Awareness	Capacity	Sustainability
Social Empowerment	9	8	7
Political Empowerment	7	6	5
Economic Empowerment	6	5	4

Figure 19.3 Analysis of data reveals that the Group Development Index had been found higher in social empowerment which is reflected in their levels of awareness, capacity and sustainability as compared to political and economic empowerment. Economic empowerment had

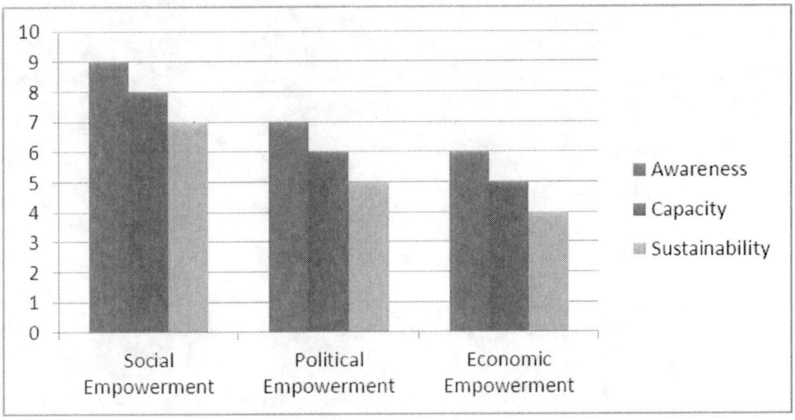

Figure 19.3: Bar Diagram Showing Levels of Change (Group Development Index).

been found low as compared to social and political empowerment. The graph of social, political and economic empowerment had been founds non-linear over the period of development. Group Development Index had also validated the outcomes of individual's scores on the Indicators of Levels of Change regarding socio-economic and political empowerment.

The comparison of group-based and 'individual-based scorecard had been found useful to strengthen the insights and credibility of qualitative and quantitative results. It had also captured the real picture through participatory approach in a timely, efficient, and effective way. Results obtained through comparison validated that the process of socio-economic and political empowerment is non-linear.

References

Fernandes, W., and Tandon, R. (1981). *Participatory Research and Evaluation: Experiments in Research as a Process of Liberation.* New Delhi: Indian Social Institute.

Freire, P. (1970). *Pedagogy of the Oppressed.* New York: Herder and Herder.

Gayfer, M.(1981). Participatory Research, Development and Issues. *Convergence,* 14 (3) 5.

Hall, B.L. (1981). Participatory research: Popular Knowledge and Power: A personal reflection. 14 (3), 47 *Convergence.*

Korten, D. and Klauss, R. (eds) (1984). *People Centered Development: Contributions Toward Theory and Planning Frameworks*. West Hertford, CT: Kumarian.

20

Social Audit: A Mechanism of Accountability

Huge investment is being made by the state, central and international agencies in various development programmes in India. It becomes necessary to assess the impacts of the various development programmes on the socio-economic level of the people, especially below the poverty line. Numbers of questions have come into discussion in public parley as who are accountable for lapses? Are programmes executed within time-frame? Are people quarries or grievances get redressed? Are people involved in decision making? Are people engaged in the implementation of programmes? Whether Gram Panchayats are being run by coterie of vested interest? or under the control of departmental officials?. Whether programme are being planned and executed whimsically or need based as per the requirement of the public? Whether beneficiaries are being empowered (i.e. capacity building) to demand their rightful benefits? Whether internal social audits allow people to enforce accountability and transparency? Whether it provides the ultimate users an opportunity to scrutinise development initiatives? Is there a need for creating a culture of social audits? What is the level of (i) transparency; (ii) accountability; (iii) participation; and (iv) good governance in the execution of development programmes?

20. What is Social Audit?

Traditionally, efforts to address issues of accountability have focused on improving and/or strengthening the "supply-side" of democratic governance. As such, the different branches and levels of government play a role in ensuring political checks and balances. Similarly, administrative procedures and internal controls, auditing requirements (both internal and external), and law enforcement (through comptrollers, courts and the police) have been used as top-down means and approaches to improve accountability.

A social audit is a mechanism through which transparency, participation, responsiveness and accountability of the system can be ensured. In this process public (beneficiaries/stakeholders) are mobilised to evaluate or audit government's performance and policy decisions. It is an instrument by which public resources are optimally and judiciously utilised, government officials are watched and monitored as not to abuse their power. Therefore, from the perspective of social audit the critical questions and premise are whether citizens have the skills, capacity and tools to effectively monitor and evaluate their governments and decision-makers. It relies on engagement from citizens and/or Civil Society Organisations (CSOs) to directly and/or indirectly demand accountability and transparency in the public policy and budget cycles. Social audit is participatory and empowering mechanism for social change. Observations reveal that:

1. Social audit has become a key component of any democratic governance. It provides space and credence to public voices. It can provide answers to the key questions of the public resources being managed by governments.
2. Social audit provides substantial evidences to government, institutions and decision-makers to review their programmes, management practices, and monitoring strategies for the welfare of the people with social justice.
3. Social audits can greatly enhance the legitimacy and credibility of democratic institutions and generate greater confidence among citizens and public officials.

'Social Audit' is, therefore, "a public assembly where all the details of the project are scrutinised". It is "a way of measuring, understanding, reporting and ultimately improving an organisation's social and ethical performance." It provides critical inputs to correctly assess the impact of government activities on the social well being of citizens. It determines the social cost and gauges the benefit to the society (MoRD, 2013).

20.1 Scope of Social Audit: The scope of social audit activities can be broad and cover a number of areas and sectors. Berthin, G. (2011) mentions that social audit can be used to:

- Assess the physical and financial gaps between needs and resources available for public policies.
- Create awareness among beneficiaries and providers of social and productive services.
- Increase efficacy and effectiveness of public policy/ programmes.
- Analyse various policy decisions, keeping in view stakeholder needs and priorities, particularly of those historically excluded (rural poor, minorities).
- Estimate the opportunity cost for stakeholders of not getting timely access to public services.
- Strengthen integrated management systems and strategies.
- Facilitate organisational learning on how to improve public policy performance.
- Identify areas for institutional and bureaucratic reforms of institutions.
- Promote dialogue and deliberation to promote effective public-private partnerships.
- Ensure that implementation of a policy/programme is transparent, comes to completion and known to everyone.
- Increase public participation at all stages of the public policy and budget cycle.
- Increasing accountability and transparency.
- Identify, control and report irregularities and prevent abuse of funds and power.
- Measure the impact of policies/programmes.
- Enable citizens to exercise their rights.

20.3 Main Objectives

- To assess the status of Social Audit.
- To recommend measures for ensuring social justice and public involvement, quality deliverance of services for sustainable socio-economic development.

20.3.1 Specific Objectives

- To assess the status of Social Audit at the gross-root level.
- To assess the people participation in the development programmes.
- To study the level of transparency, accountability and responsiveness in the execution of development programmes.
- To enable citizens to exercise their rights to information.
- To provide feedback to government and public about strengths and weaknesses of the functioning of democratic system.
- To measure the impacts of policies and programmes on the lives of people especially marginalised section of the society.

20.4 Design of Social Audit

Focus:- Democratic Institutions Participation in Planning, and Implementation and Evaluation Processes of Development Programmes.

Purpose:- To Identify Transparency, Accountability and Responsiveness of Various Agencies Involved in Planning, Implementation and Monitoring of Development Programmes.

20.5 Outcomes

20.5.1 Enhance Governance: Accountability and transparency of public officials is the cornerstone of democratic governance. A social audit, therefore, is expected to enhance accountability by allowing ordinary citizens to access information, voice their needs, evaluate performance, and demand greater accountability and transparency.

20.5.2 Increase Public Policy Effectiveness: By enhancing the availability of information, strengthening citizen voice, promoting dialogue and consultation between stakeholders and creating incentives for improved public policy performance, social audits can go a long way toward improving the effectiveness of service delivery and making public decision-making more transparent and participatory. It leads to efficient resource utilisation.

20.5.3 Increase citizen participation: Social audit is a source of policy dialogue and conflict resolution. By providing critical information on policies and rights and soliciting systematic feedback from constituencies, social audit can provide a means to increase and aggregate the voice of excluded and vulnerable groups. In turn, this can enhance voice and increase the chance of greater policy responsiveness on the part of government. Thus, social audits also become a confidence building measure.

20.6 Methodology

Producing relevant information and building credible evidence that will serve to hold public officials accountable, is a critical aspect of social audit. There are a number of tools that can be selected to collect and analyse data for social audit. Nonetheless, generally all aim at obtaining "supply-side" data/information (from government and service providers) and "demand-side" data/information (from users of government services, communities and citizens).

20.6.1 Service Delivery Surveys: Quantitative Service Delivery Surveys focus on public service providers and on factors that may affect the quality of service delivery. In such surveys, the frontline service facility or service provider is typically the main unit of analysis.

20.6.2 Household Surveys of Social Audit: The audit covered the "social needs" cluster of services: health, welfare, education and sports, arts and culture. The audit collected information from households in representative communities about people's use, experience and perceptions of service delivery in these four sectors, focusing on quality of service delivery and efforts to improve this.

20.6.3 Tools for Collection of Data: Use of Primary and Secondary Data; Scrutiny of Records; Field Work: Purposively Selected Sample is to be put to Qualitative Research Analysis. Focus Group Discussions, In-depth Interviews techniques are to be used for the collection of data. Benchmarks are to be laid-down on the parameters of (a) Responsiveness, (b) Transparency, (c) Participation and (d) Accountability. For instance, detail of each is given below:

20.6.4 Participation refers to democratic governance of elected representatives of the Gram Panchayat, participation in demand assessment, planning, decision-making. Specifically the participation of scheduled caste, scheduled tribes and people living BPL.

20.6.5 Transparency implies publication and display of development works under various schemes, its progress, and expenditure incurred, and sign-post in the place of work. Access to data from the Department of Rural Development at Panchayat and block level (data of development open to public for examination).

20.6.6 Accountability refers to gaps between sanction and release of funds for the development programmes, assessment of quality of works, action taken report against defaulters and processes and frequency of internal social audits.

20.6.7 Governance implies processes of governance, devolution powers to Panchayats, internal and external communication, time framework schedule, and grievance redressal forum and disposal of complaints.

20.7 Processes of Focus Group Discussions

- The first step in FGD generally involves introducing members and fostering interest and commitment to participate.
- Actual discussion starts with 'discussion stimulus' i.e., providing space for the exchange of past and present experiences by the members of the group so as to get expected answers to questions.

  (a) Must provide opportunity to participant group and individual members to raise their voice regarding; Identification of domains; (b) Selection of Social Setting and

  (b) Proactive Participation of each member.
- Comparison and Control are fundamental in the process of Focus Group Discussions. The choices of individuals need to be picked up for implicit and explicit comparisons. At the same time, control is very important that the participants do not drift into just chatting or presenting endless anecdotes with little reference to the issue of the focus group and the study.

20.8 Analysis of Data: All information collected from secondary and primary sources was collated and put into order to provide a logical form for analysis. Quantitative and Qualitative analyses of data are undertaken, As the data is primarily of qualitative nature, extra care has been taken to ensure that the authenticity and meaning of the same is presented in undiluted form.

Individuals' assessment and groups' assessment data are compiled and analysed. Shifting through data, similar and related ideas and patterns emerged are identified. It reveals the groups and individual group members' (1) feelings of enhanced power expressed through their ability to present their own views and negotiate for their own ends in formal and informal decision making. (political empowerment); (2) those to do with mutual support, trust, respect, and equality (social empowerment); (3) those to do with access to and use of resources); and (4) those to do with the groups own capability and independence (capability and self-empowerment). Indicators are further categorised by three levels of developmental progression: (1) awareness, (2) confidence and capability and (3) effectiveness and self-sustaining.

References

Barbour, R. (2007). *Doing Focus Groups*. London: Sage Publications.

Gahlot Sushmita (2013). Social Audits in India. *International Research Journal of Social Sciences,* ISSN 2319–3565 Vol. 2(11), 41-45.

Gayfer, M.(1981).Participatory Research, Development and issues. *Convergence, 14 (3) 5.*

Gerardo Berthin (2011). A practical Guide to Social Audit as a Participatory Tool to Strengthen Democratic Governance, Transparency, and Accountability. United Nations Development Programme (UNDP).

Kapoor, D.R. (2000). *Hand-Book of Audit.* New Delhi: Anmol Publications.

Kapoor, D.R., and Saigal, P. (2013). *Research Methodology: Methods & Techniques.* New Delhi: Regal Publications.

Korten, D. and Klauss, R. (eds) (1984). *People Centered Development: Contributions Toward Theory and Planning Frameworks*. West Hertford, CT: Kumarian.

Malena, C., Reiner, F, and Janmejay, S. (2004). "Social Accountability: An Introduction to the Concept and Emerging Practices, " *Social Development Papers*, No. 76, Washington, DC: The World Bank, December.

Nidhi Vij. (2011). "Social Protection for Social Justice" *Institute of Development Studies,* UK 13–15 April 2011 B.

Pyun, Ho-Bum (2006). "Audit and Civil Society: The Korean Experience, " in the *International Journal of Government Auditing*. Washington D.C.: International Budget Project, Center on Budget and Policy Priorities, April.

Ramkumar, V. (2007), "Expanding Collaboration between Public Audit Institutions and Civil Society." Washington, D.C.: International Budget Project.

Ramkumar, V., and Warren K. (2006). "The Role of Civil Society Organisations in Auditing and Public Finance Management, " Washington D.C.: The International Budget Project.

Ravindra, Adikeshavalu (2004). *An Assessment of the Impact of Bangalore Citizen Report Cards on the Performance of Public Agencies.* Washington D.C., World Bank.

Ritva Reinikka and Jakob Svensson. "Explaining Leakage of Public Funds, " (2001). Policy Research Working Paper 2709, World Bank, Washington, D.C. November.

Roberts, Alasdair (2006). *Blacked Out: Government Secrecy in the Information Age.* Cambridge University Press: Cambridge.

Roy, S.K., Social Audit in India – An overview, *International Journal of Scientific Research,* 1(5), 16-18 (2012).

Sampford, Charles J. G. (2006). *Measuring Corruption.* Burlington, VT: Ashgate Publishing.

Schedler, Andreas Schedler, Andreas, Diamond, Larry and Plattner, Marc F. (eds) (1999). Conceptualising accountability. *The Self-Restraining State: Power and Accountability in New Democracies,* pp. 13-28. Lynne Reinner, Boulder, CO.

Spink, Peter K., et al (2008). "Government and Citizens: The Changing Nature of Civil Society." in Wilson, Robert, *et. al., Governance in the Americas: Decentralisation, Democracy, and Sub-national Government in Brazil, Mexico, and the USA.* Notre Dame, In: University of Notre Dame Press.

Sullivan, J, D. (2006). "Corruption, Economic Development, and Governance: Private Sector Perspectives from Developing Countries," *Private Sector Opinion,* No. 2.

Transparency International (2002). *Corruption Fighters' Tool Kit,* Berlin: Transparency International.

UNDP (2008). Anti-Corruption Practice Note. Mainstreaming Corruption in Development. New York. DGG/BDP.

UNDP (2011). A Practical Guide to Social Audit as a Participatory Tool to Strengthen Democratic Governance, Transparency, and Accountability.

Yadav, S., and Bhilwara, B. (2009). For Social Audit: Civil Society.

Unit - 5

Qualitative Methods

21

Ethnographic Research Method

21.1 Nature of Ethnographic Research

Ethnography has it roots planted in the fields of anthropology and sociology. The Random House Dictionary of the English Language defines ethnography "A branch of anthropology dealing with the scientific description of individual culture." An ethnography is a written description of a particular culture - the customs, beliefs, and behaviour - based on information collected through fieldwork. (Harris, M., and Johnson, O. (2000). Ethnography in educational research implies a process of providing scientific descriptions of educational systems, processes, and phenomena within their specific contexts. Psychological and social elements are also embedded in ethnographical studies. The emphasis in ethnographic research is on describing the context in qualitative terms without superimposing the researcher's (observer's) own value system on the situation. Thus, ethnographic research takes a qualitative – phenomenological approach.

In its most characteristic form, it involves the ethnographer participating, overtly or covertly, in people's daily lives for an extended period of time, watching what happens, listening to what is said, asking questions – in fact, collecting whatever data are available to throw light on the issues that are the focus of the research. (Hammersley and Atkinson, 1995, p. 1)

Some of the features of ethnographic studies are:

- A tendency to work primarily with "unstructured" data: that is, data that have not been coded at the point of data collection in terms of a closed set of analytic categories.
- Investigation of a small number of cases, perhaps just one case, in detail.
- Analysis of data that involves explicit interpretation of the meanings and functions of human actions, the product of which mainly takes the form of verbal descriptions and explanations, with quantification and statistical analysis playing a subordinate at the most. (Atkinson and Hammersley, (1998, pp. 110-111)
- Ethnographic research involves field research and hypotheses are more likely to emerge from the data than to be formulated prior to the research.
- Ethnographic research is the contextualisation, which requires that all data be interpreted only in the context of the situation or environment in which they were collected.
- Ethnographic research is often not concerned about generalisation. Of course, generalisation of results depends on the correspondence between the context under study and other situations.

Experimentation and survey research traditionally have involved a priori hypothesis formation, followed by specific procedures designed to test hypotheses. In contrast, ethnographic research proceeds from the position that hypotheses may emerge as the data collection occurs or ethnographic research does not begin from specified, preconceived hypotheses; it relies heavily upon description as the research proceeds. The observer attempts to suspend any preconceived ideas or notions that might undesirably influence the interpretation of what is being observed. The observer wishes to concentrate on the entire context and thus maintains a holistic view, rather than focusing on bits and pieces. The ethnographic researcher attempts to maintain a perspective on the totality of the situation. Theory is considered only as it appears relevant.

- Ethnographic research is conducted in the field setting, based on the premise that the situation influences people's interpretations, thoughts, and actions. The researcher attempts to interpret the situation from the perspective of the individuals being studied, and the researcher is involved in the situation as a participant-observer. (Geertz, 1973).
- The methodology of ethnographic research is different from that of experimental research. For example, statistical procedures for analysis are usually not so complex, nor are they so clearly specified beforehand as they are in experimental and survey research. Some of the key elements in ethnographical research are:

Key Elements of Ethnographical studies

- The shared cultural meanings of the group are crucial to understanding its behaviour.
- Insider's perspective on those events, actions and contexts are essential.
- The group will be studied in its natural setting.
- It is an unfolding and evolving sort of study rather than pre-structured.
- Ethnography is eclectic not restricted.
- Relies on the field of anthropology for its theoretical base.
- Addresses issues of gaining access, role of observer, power crisis; and
- Often uses words of participants in written presentations.

Ethnographic studies also focus on organisations, which consist of defined groups of people who interact in regular and structured ways. An organisation can be viewed as consisting of cultures. For example, a school has a student culture (possibly more than one student culture), a faculty culture, an administrative culture (assuming that the school is large enough), and possibly a teacher aid culture and a maintenance personnel culture. A culture consists of the collective understandings among the members of a group that are related to their particular role. Whatever makes up the parts of a culture, there is coherence and consistency among these parts. We will call the makeup culture perspectives. In a nutshell, Organisations are considered to be composed of cultures, and cultures are made up of perspectives. Ethnography is based on the apparently simple idea that in order to understand what people are up to, it is best to observe them by interacting with them intimately and over an extended period (Monaghan *et al.,* 2000).

21.2 The Process of Ethnographic Research

The process of ethnographic research is an integrated process in which procedures are conducted concurrently.

21.2.1 Identification of the Phenomenon to be studied

Some of the statements identifying the phenomenon to be studied as social interaction of high school students are:

(A) 1. Interaction among the students across races.

2. Interaction among the students across the sexes.

3. Faculty social systems.

4. Role of thc faculty in the social interaction of students.

Typical ethnographic studies in education might have the following research statements.

(B) 1. A study of life in an urban classroom.

2. A study of decision-making in an inner-city high school.

3. A study of peer interactions in racially mixed classrooms of a suburban high school.

4. A study of interaction patterns among faculty in a private pre-primary schools.

5. A study of socialisation within a rural high school.

21.2.2 Identification of Subjects

Subjects to be studied must be identified; this often includes specifying conditions so that the study may become feasible. For example, a study of interaction patterns among faculty (subjects) in private colleges.

21.2.3 Hypothesis Generation/ Research Question

As the data collection proceeds in an ethnographic study, hypotheses/research questions may be formulated and modified. A study may begin with few participants. However, the researcher is very amenable to introducing new hypotheses and discarding hypotheses that are not supportive. There is no a priori limit on the number or nature of hypotheses. Hypothesis generation is continuing activity throughout an ethnographic study. Unlike survey research or experimentation, for which hypotheses are initially specified and then tested, ethnographic research may begin with no hypotheses, and hypotheses may be formulated and modified along the way.

21.2.4 Data Collection

Typical ethnographic research employs three kinds of data collection: interviews, observation, and documents. This in turn produces three kinds of data: quotations, descriptions, and excerpts of documents, are resulting in one product: narrative description. This narrative often includes charts, diagrams, photos and additional artifacts that help to tell "the story" (Hammersley, 1990). The use of questionnaires or the collection of quantitative behavioural data is likely to produce an incomplete-even misleading- understanding of the people studied, especially when those people are members of foreign or unfamiliar societies (Monaghan, 2000).

21.2.5 Observation

Observation in ethnographic research is comprehensive – that is, continued and total. The observer attempts to record all relevant information in an unobtrusive way. Consequently, observation is quite unstructured. The emphasis is on capturing the perspective of the individuals being observed, which requires careful listening to pick up subtle cues and nuances. Observation is a continuing process; it is not limited to one or two sessions. The recordings made by the observer while actually conducting the observations are recorded in the field notes/ diary. An observer may be identified openly as a researcher or may be in a disguised role. Whatever the case, observers try to be as unobtrusive as possible so that they do not interfere with normal activities. An important part of observation relates to the idea of contextualisation; that is, to understand behaviour, the observer must understand the context in which individuals are thinking and reacting. The observer must have the option of interpreting events. Thus, observation extends beyond objective recording of what happens. The participant–observer attempts to assume the role of the individuals under study and experience their thoughts, feelings, and actions.

21.2.6 Interviewing

Interviewing might be quite casual and informal, or it might be structured. Questions might be asked of those being observed in an attempt to clarify what is happening or in an attempt to capture the feelings of those observed. However, the formal structured interview may be conducted with a predefined set of questions. In the social interaction, for example, number of students might be interviewed. Faculty and administrators might also be interviewed. Other people, such as cooks lunchroom and attendants might be interviewed to obtain their perceptions of the student's social interaction. Such interviews would be helpful in determining the tone of the social interaction, which might not be entirely apparent from observing behaviour. Interviewing may be used, and supportive quantitative data may be brought to bear from internal or external sources. Whatever the source, however, the data should reflect the perspectives of the subjects under study.

21.2.7 Other Sources

In addition to participant observation and interviews, ethnographers may also make use of various documents in answering guiding questions. When available, these documents can add additional insight or information to projects. Because ethnographic attention has been and continues to be focused on both literate and non-literate peoples, not all research projects will have site documents available. It is also possible that even research among a literate group will not have relevant site documents to consider; this could vary depending on the focus of the research. Thinking carefully about your participants and how they function and asking questions of your informants helps to decide what kinds of documents might be available.

Possible documents include: budgets, advertisements, work descriptions, annual reports, memos, school records, correspondence, informational brochures, teaching materials, newsletters, websites, recruitment or orientation packets, contracts, records of court proceedings, posters, minutes of meetings, menus, and many other kinds of written items. It may be story telling. The story is an account of a real event in the real world, as witnessed by the ethnographer. Dialogue is the backbone of ethnography. Ethnographers also employ a variety of more specialised techniques. Audio recording of speech and music, photography, film, drawing, genealogy, mapping, census-taking, archival research, all have their ethnographic uses, depending on the ethnographer's specific research project.

21.2.8 Analysis

Analysis in ethnographic research consists of synthesising the information from the observations, interviews, and other data sources. The analysis of the data involves interpretation of the meanings and functions of human actions and mainly takes the form of verbal descriptions and explanations, with quantification and statistical analysis playing a subordinate role at the most. However, there are proportions and percentages that can be computed, based on classifications of items from interviews or types of activities and events observed.

21.2.9 Interpreting and Reporting Findings

Remember that the researcher is the detective looking for trends and patterns that occur across the various groups or within individuals (Krueger, 1994). The process of analysis and interpretation involve disciplined examination, creative insight, and careful attention to the purposes of the research study. Analysis and interpretation are conceptually separate processes. The analysis process begins with assembling the raw materials and getting an overview or total picture of the entire process. The researcher's role in analysis covers a continuum with assembly of raw data on one extreme and interpretative comment on the other. Analysis is the process of bringing order to the data, organising what is there into patterns, categories, and basic descriptive units. The analysis process involves consideration of words, tone, context, non-verbal, internal consistency, frequency, extensiveness, intensity, specificity of responses and big ideas. Data reduction strategies are essential in the analysis (Krueger, 1994). Interpretation involves attaching meaning and significance to the analysis, explaining descriptive patterns, and looking for relationships and linkages among descriptive dimensions. Once these processes have been completed the researcher must report his or her interpretations and conclusions.

21.2.10 Reliability and Validity

In a specific study, internal reliability would depend on the extent to which two or more observers agree on what they saw and how they interpret what they saw. External validity can be strengthened by multisite studies. If a phenomenon seems to be consistent across a number of studies, its generalisability is increased. Even if there is inconsistency in the phenomenon, a study of the differences between the sites may reveal the limitations or special conditions of generalisation. The use of multiple data collection procedures, along with triangulation, tends to enhance reliability.

21.3 Triangulation

"By combining multiple observers, theories, methods, and empirical materials, researchers can hope to overcome the weakness or intrinsic biases and the problems that come from single-method, single-observer, single-theory studies. Often the purpose of triangulation in specific contexts is to obtain confirmation of findings through convergence of different perspectives. The point at which the perspectives converge is seen to represent reality." —Alexander Jakob (2001).

Triangulation refers to the use of multiple methods or data sources in qualitative research to develop a comprehensive understanding of phenomena (Patton, 1999). Triangulation also has been viewed as a qualitative research strategy to test validity through the convergence of information from different sources; "attempt to map out, or explain more fully, the richness and complexity of human behaviour by studying it from more than one standpoint (Cohen and Manion, 2000); "gives a more detailed and balanced picture of the situation." (Altrichter *et al.* 2008); "method of cross-checking data from multiple sources to search for regularities in the research data (O'Donoghue and Punch, 2003), and "Triangulation also crosschecks information to produce accurate results for certainty in data collection." (Erina Audrey, 2013).

As Fielding and Fielding (1986) stated, "Triangulation puts the researcher in a frame of mind to regard his or her own material critically, to test it, to identify its weaknesses, to identify where to test further doing something different." Creswell (2002) added, triangulation is the process of corroborating evidence from different individuals, of methods of data collection... This ensures that the study will be accurate because the information is not drawn from single source, individual, of process of data collection. In this way, it encourages the researcher to develop a report that is both accurate and credible.

Triangulation method is used in combination with different methods, study groups, local and temporal settings, and different theoretical perspectives in dealing with a phenomenon. It can be used to describe and formalise the relation between qualitative and quantitative research and as a strategy for promoting the quality of qualitative research. Triangulation means that researchers take different perspectives on an issue under study for getting answering to research questions.

Triangulation is used in a cross-sectional study. Triangulation can also be used in a longitudinal study. It can be very fruitful to use different methodological approaches in a case study, although mostly the focus is comparative. In this process, the researcher need more time for a triangulation study, for example, collecting data with different methods produces methodological problems and affects the time frames of each of the methods. Interviews need some time for arranging a date and travelling to meet the interviewee. Observation in most cases means coming back to the field several times over a longer period.

Triangulation is also used as a strategy for improving the quality of qualitative research by extending the approach to the issue under study. This can be done in four ways.

(1) The first way is to use additional methods (e.g. two qualitative methods of by adding a quantitative approach) or using two methodological approaches in one method;

(2) The second way is to include different sorts of data in your project;

(3) The third way is to take a different theoretical perspective-studying the issue under study with more than one research perspective in qualitative research; and

(4) The fourth way is to involve two or more researchers in the project with different theoretical-methodological background. (Denzin, 1986b)

21.3.1 Types of Triangulation

Denzin (1978) and Patton (1999) identified four types of triangulation: (a) method triangulation, (b) investigator triangulation, (c) theory triangulation, and (d) data source triangulation. Denzin took up this concept in the 1970s and developed a more systematic approach of triangulation for social research. He distinguishes four types of triangulation (1989b, pp. 237-241).

21.3.2 Method Triangulation: Denzin mentions methodological triangulation wherein two sub-types should be differentiated: within-method and between-method triangulation.

1. **Investigator Triangulation:** As the second type of triangulation, Denzin names investigator triangulation. Different observers or interviewers are employed to detect or minimise biases resulting from the researcher as a person.
2. **Theory Triangulation:** It is the third type in Denzin's systematology. The starting point is "approaching data with multiple perspectives and hypotheses in mind ....Various theoretical points of view could be placed side by side to assess their utility and power" (1989b, pp. 239-240).
3. **Data Source Triangulation:** In this context, triangulation refers to the use of different data sources, which should be distinguished from the use of different methods for producing data. As "sub-types of data triangulation, " Denzin makes a distinction between time, space, and persons and suggests studying phenomena at different dates and places and from different persons. Thus, he comes close to Glaser and Strauss's strategy of theoretical sampling. In both cases, the starting point is to involve purposively and systematically, persons, study groups, and local and temporal settings in the study.

21.3.3 Sampling in Triangulation

Sampling in ethnographic studies using triangulation should be considered from three angles: (1) How can we guarantee that a sampling strategy fitting each single method can also be put into practice in the context of triangulation? (2) Which options of an interlaced sampling make sense? (3) How can we take into account or bring together the different logics of sampling of different methods or approaches? Purpose sampling is a part of study.

21.3.4 Triangulation in Collecting Data: Different Sorts of Data

If researchers apply methodological triangulation, in most cases they refer to different ways of collecting data. For example, it does not make much sense to interview the same people twice with different methods of interviewing. Rather you should seek approaches on different levels. For example, combining interviews with observation focuses on subjective knowledge and experience and allows issues of the past to be introduced in the first approach. If you combine a semi-structured interview based on an interview schedule of questions with a narrative interview focusing on the life history of the participant you will not obtain data on different levels, but rather similar data in different shapes. For instance. interactions among the adolescents talking about their own problems or those of fellows from the scene. The second approach in this study was to run episodic interviews with the adolescents. A third approach was to do expert interviews with health and social work professionals, in order to obtain an external perspective complementing the subjective experiences reported by the adolescents themselves. Thus, the three ways of collecting data addressed different levels of the "same" problem—subjective knowledge, practices/interactions, and professional expert knowledge of health problems and help-seeking behaviour of homeless adolescents with chronic illness. It is to examine data from different respondents but collected using the same method. If we consider that each participant has a unique and valid world view, the researcher's job is often to try and look for a pattern or contradictions beyond the individual experience. You might also consider the need to triangulate between data collected at different times, to show changes in lived experience.

In 'theoretical triangulation', a variety of different theories are used to interpret the data, such as discourse, narrative and context analysis, and these different ways of dissecting and illuminating the data are compared.

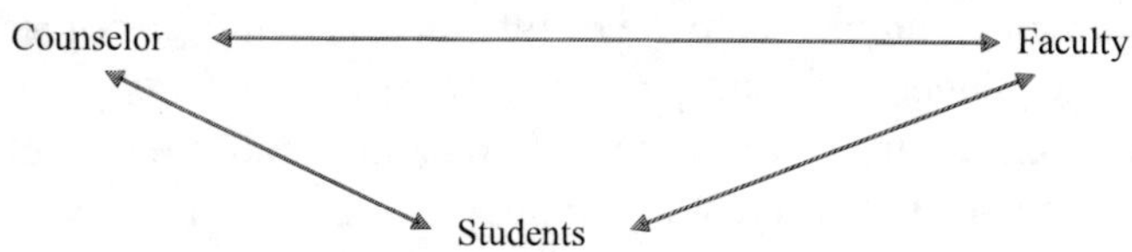

Figure 21.1: Triangulation (the process of Qualitative Cross –Validation) for the Social Interaction.

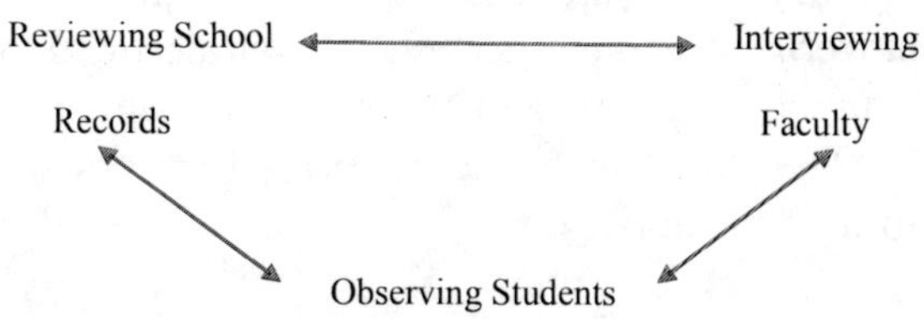

Figure 21.2: Triangulation Involving Multiple Data Sources.

Triangulation is qualitative cross-validation. It can be conducted among different data sources or different data collection methods. Basically, triangulation is comparison – Comparison of information to determine whether or not there is corroboration. It is a search for convergence of the information on a common finding or concept. To a large extent, the triangulation process assesses the sufficiency of the data. If the data are inconsistent or do not converge, they are insufficient. The researcher is then faced with a dilemma regarding what to believe. Denzin (1978, p. 308). Triangulation is qualitative cross-validation. It assesses the sufficiency of the data according to the convergence of multiple data sources or multiple data collection procedures.

There is 'investigator triangulation', where different researchers each conduct separate analysis of the data, and their different interpretations are reconciled or compared. In participatory analysis it's also possible to have a kind of respondent triangulation, where a researcher is trying to compare their own interpretations of data with that of their respondents. Figure 21.1 shows the process of cross-validation.

Figure 21.1 and 21.2 reveals convergence of multiple data sources or multiple data collection procedures for cross-validation. For example, students are examined by the counselor and faculty to know their level of participation in extracurricular activities.

Figure 21.2 other multiple data sources and procedures such as school records, faculty interview and field observation, are used to cross validate or authenticate the results. In reviewing school records, caste-wise, gender-wise and performance of the students –academic and extracurricular are to be considered. Substantial evidences are gathered to confirm or reject the hypotheses/ research questions.

Figure 21.3 'Group-based and 'Individual-based scorecard vis-à-vis and records of women empowerment have to be triangulated through convergence of multi data resources to get real picture of women empowerment. It also generates accurate the generalisable statistics in a timely, efficient, and effective way. Similar and related ideas are clustered to identify the patterns. Benefits seem to fall naturally into four categories:

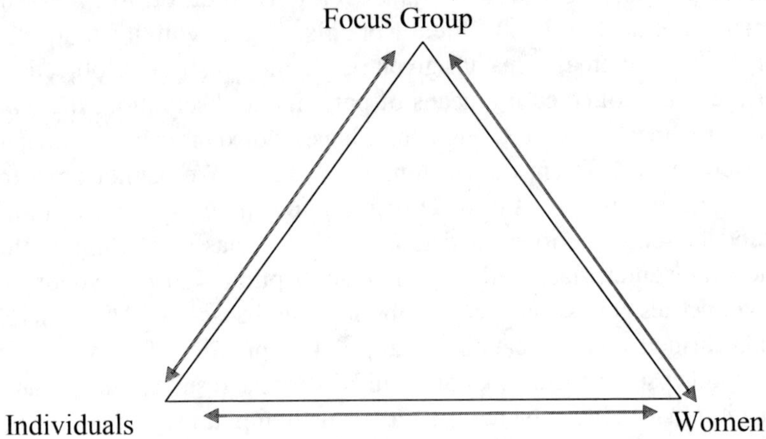

Figure 21.3: Triangulation of Multi-Data Sources.

(1) Those to do with the groups and individual group members feelings of enhanced power expressed through their ability to present their own views and negotiate for their own ends in formal and informal decision making (political empowerment);

(2) Those to do with mutual support, trust, respect, and equality (social empowerment);

(3) Those to do with access to and use of economic resources (economic empowerment);

(4) Those to do with availability, accessibility and affordability of education.

The three categories of indicators can further be categorised by three levels of developmental progression: (1) Awareness, (2) Capability, and (3) Sustainability. There are several ways of reaching a decision about Significant Changes in people's lives namely, Majority rules, Scoring (rating); Scoring by a group vote, and Secret ballot (each person writes their choice of Significant Changes on a slip of paper, and then the total votes are presented).

Limitations

For all its virtues, researchers cannot claim that ethnographic field work is the best method of all kinds of social science research, nor that participant observation is the only method employed by ethnographers. Field work is beset with methodological and epistemological problems. Field work also carries with it a unique set of ethical dilemmas. This has given rise to the question of 'objectivity of the data' collected by means of participant observation; there are instances in which two ethnographers have studied the same community but come to different conclusions about them. We cannot deny the problems of observer's bias. This problem can be overcome through standardised categories for data collection. It has also admitted that the whole enterprise of ethnographic description is suspect so long as asymmetries persist between the observers and observed. The principle of informed consent cannot be applied in practice, for instance if comprehensive pre-information would distort the results of the research in an unjustifiable way. In such cases an attempt must be made to use other possible modes of informed content. (Ehik-Kodes, 1993: I B2). Unselfish, altruistic, and principled researcher is obviously set to do better than others who have none of these traits.

References

Altrichter, H., Feldman, A., Posch, P. and Somekh, B. (2008). *Teachers investigate their work; An introduction to action research across the professions.* Routledge. p. 147. (2nd edition).

Agar, M. (1996). *Professional Stranger: An Informal Introduction to Ethnography*, (2nd ed.). New Delhi: Academic Press.

Angrosino, M. (2007). Doing Ethnographic and Observational Research. London: SAGE.

Atkinson, P, Coffey, A, Delamont, S. Lofland, J and Lofland, L. (eds) (2001). *Handbook of Ethnography*. London: Sage.

Cohen, L., and Manion, L. (2000). *Research methods in education.* Routledge. p. 254. (5th edition).

Denzin, N. (2006). *Sociological Methods: A Sourcebook.* Aldine Transaction. (5th edition).

Fetterman, D.M. (1989). *Ethnography step by step*. Newbury Park, CA: Sage.

Hammersley, M. and Atkinson, P. (1995). *Ethnography: Principles in Practice.* 2nd edn. London: Routledge.

Harris, M. and Johnson, O. (2000). *Cultural Anthropology*, (5th ed.), Needham Heights, MA: Allyn and Bacon.

Jakob, K. (2001).Triangulation of Quantitative and Qualitative Data. *Typological Social Research,* Volume 2, No. 1.

John. and Peter, J. (2000). *Social and Cultural Anthropology: A Very Short Introduction.* Oxford University Press: New York.

Krueger, A. R. (1994). *Focus Groups: A Practical guide for Applied Research*, Thousand Oaks, CA: Sage Publications.

O'Donoghue, T., Punch K. (2003). *Qualitative Educational Research in Action: Doing and Reflecting*. Routledge. p. 78.

Woods, P. (1986*). Inside Schools: Ethnography in Educational Research.* London: Routledge & Kegan Paul.

22

Phenomenological Method

The phenomenological movement was initiated by Husserl (1936/1970) based upon philosophical discipline. Later theorists, such as Heidegger (1927) and Merleau-Ponty M (1962), have recast the phenomenological project, moving away from a philosophical discipline. They focused on consciousness and hermeneutic (interpretive) dimensions. Social scientists have observed that methods and assumptions of the natural sciences are inappropriate to the study of man. The natural sciences deal with matter whereas phenomenology deals with phenomena. For example, atoms and molecules do not have consciousness. Matter simply reacts 'unconsciously' to external stimuli. Unlike matter, man has consciousness-thoughts, feelings, meanings, intentions, and an awareness of being. Man reacts 'consciously' to internal stimuli. Phenomenological approach, therefore, offers a better alternative to the study of man.

Applied to research, phenomenology is the study of phenomena: their nature and meanings. The focus is on lived experience. The phenomenological researcher aims to provide a rich textured description of lived experience. The lived experience comprises the world of objects around us as we perceive them. It is an experience of our self, body and relationships. It is the "locus of interaction between ourselves and our perceptual environments and the world of experienced horizons within which we meaningfully dwell together" (von Eckartsberg, 1998). It can be defined as the world that is lived and experienced - a world "that appears meaningfully to consciousness in its qualitative, flowing given-ness; not an objective world 'out there', but a humanly relational world" (Todres *et al,* 2006, p.55). Merleau-Ponty explained, "man is in the world, and only in the world does he know himself." (1962).

There are certain essential features of the life world, such as a person's sense of selfhood, embodiment, sociality, spatiality, temporality, project, discourse and mood-as-atmosphere (Ashworth, 2003, 2006). These interlinked 'fractions' (Ashworth, 2003) act as a lens through which to view the data. The task of the researcher is to bring out these dimensions and show the structural whole that is socially shared while also experienced in individual and particular ways. "The overall aim of life world research", says Dahlberg *et al* (2008, p.37) is "to describe and elucidate the lived world in a way that expands our understanding of human being and human experience."

The important phenomenological concept is intentionality: relationship between the person and the meanings of the things they're focusing on and experiencing. For example, one woman's lived experience of divorce and its impact on her relationship with her children were studied. The intentional, embodied relationship between a mother and her children was highlighted. The challenge for phenomenological researchers is twofold: how to help participants express their world as directly as possible; and how to explicate these dimensions such that they lived world – the life world - is revealed.

22.1 Approaches

Different schools have emerged which focus more explicitly on the life world (Ashworth, 2003; Dahlberg *et al*, 2008) and lived experience (van Manen, 1991). **Hermeneutic** variants highlight the researcher's role and horizons of interpretation such as in the Reflective Life world approach (Dalhlberg *et al* (2008), Interpretative Phenomenological Analysis (IPA) (Smith and Osborne, 2003), Embodied Enquiry (Todres, 2007), Critical Narrative Analysis (CNA)(Langdridge, 2007) and in the Dallas' approach to phenomenological research (Garza, 2007). For example, a *life world researcher* would ask 'What is the life world of one who feels lost?'

Collecting and analysing interview data, they would focus on existential themes such as the person's sense of self-identity and embodied relations with others when experiencing a feeling of being lost.

With the **heuristic approach** adopted by Moustakas (1990), the researcher's role in self-reflection towards producing a creative synthesis to explicate lived experience is brought to the fore. For example, the *heuristic researcher* could well focus more intensely on the question: 'What is my experience of feeling lost?' While they might draw on a range of data from stories, poems, artwork, literature, journals, they would also look inward, attending to their own feelings/experiences by using a reflective diary. They would aim to produce a composite description and creative synthesis of the experience.

In **relational research** approaches (Finlay and Evans, 2009), attention is paid to the researcher's journey and the research process focusing on how data emerges out of embodied dialogical encounters between researchers and co-researchers. One variant of such relational research is the dialogue research approach (described by Halling and Leifer, 1991 and Rowe *et al.,* 1989) where groups of phenomenologists investigate a phenomenon, dwelling in and negotiating layered meanings together. For example, the r*elational researcher* might similarly interview just one person asking ask 'What is it like to feel lost?'. They might focus on the co-researchers' self-identity and 'creative adjustment' (their sense of self, their being-in-the-world and the defensive way they've learned to cope). The research data would be seen to be co-created in the dialogical research encounter and the relational dynamics between researcher and co-researchers would be reflexively explored.

A *descriptive empirical phenomenologist* might well ask: 'What is the lived experience of feeling lost?' They might compare the protocols (written descriptions) offered by participants about one instance of feeling lost and attempt to identify the essential or general structures underlying the phenomenon of feeling lost.

A *life world researcher* would ask 'What is the life world of one who feels lost?' Collecting and analysing interview data, they would focus on existential themes such as the person's sense of self-identity and embodied relations with others when experiencing a feeling of being lost.

The *IPA researcher* would focus on 'What is the individual experience of feeling lost?' They would aim to capture individual variations between co-researchers. Thematic analysis would involve some explicit interpretation on the part of both co-researcher and researcher.

The *Critical Narrative Approach researcher* would ask 'What story or stories does a person tell of their experience of feeling lost?' having interviewed perhaps just one person. The analysis would be focused on the narrative produced and how it was co-created in the research context.

All the variants of phenomenology above share a similar focus on describing lived experience and recognising the significance of our embodied, inter-subjective lifeworld. Giorgi (1989) indicates certain core characteristics hold across the variations, namely that the research is *descriptive*, explores the *intentional relationship* between persons and situations, uses *phenomenological reductions* and provides knowledge of psychological *essences* or structures of meanings immanent in human experience through imaginative variation (Wertz, 2005). Other phenomenologists argue that the project to identify essences and to use phenomenological reductions may be less central. Some methodologies, for example the explicitly hermeneutic and idiographic approach of IPA, downplays (or even rejects) these features.

22.2 Gathering and Analysing Phenomenological Data

22.2.1 Method

Inductive- Research questions are formulated and modified in the process of observations in the field. Hypotheses are more likely to emerge from the data than to be formulated prior to the research.

22.2.2 Sampling

Purposeful Sampling: Purpose is to get insight about phenomenon, not empirical generalisation from a sample to a population. Qualitative research cannot be conducted through a-priori samples only. Sampling goes on throughout research, through various sampling techniques, such as, typical case sampling, intensity sampling, critical case sampling, sensitive case sampling, convenience sampling, primary selection and secondary selection.

22.2.3 Tools and Data Collection

The most common tools used include the use of: narratives in interviews, diaries and protocols; participant observation; questionnaires; and reflective diaries or researcher's own introspective accounts. Supplementary techniques such as repertory grids, artwork or use of external literary or documentary sources may also be used to explore meanings.

Phenomenologist doing interviews, for example, will tend to ask participants to describe their experience concretely by posing such questions as: 'Could you describe a typical day?' or 'Can you describe that particular incident in more detail?'. This way of opening a dialogue is valued over and above asking more general abstract questions such as 'what is your role?' or 'What is depression?'

Participant observations need to be conducted in a natural setting and with openness. "Openness is the mark of a true willingness to listen, see, and understand. It involves respect, and certain humility toward the phenomenon, as well as sensitivity and flexibility." Dahlberg *et al.,* (2001, p. 97). The aim is to allow the phenomenon to present itself to us instead of us imposing preconceived ideas on it. This openness needs to be maintained throughout the entire research process, not just at the start.

A questionnaire consists of a list of preset questions to which respondents asked to supply answers. Questions should be open ended. Open ended questions allow the respondent to compose his own answer rather than choosing between a number of given answers. This may provide more valid data since he can say what he means in his own words. However, this kind of response may be difficult to classify and quantify.

22.2.4 Analysis

The analytical method suggested by Wertz (1983) and Giorgi (1985) is used i.e. (1) systematic readings of the transcript are undertaken by first dwelling on the phenomenon (through empathetic immersion and reflection), (2) then describing emergent psychological structures (i.e., constituents and recurrent themes).

In contrast, with dialogic analysis (Rowe *et al*, 1989), researchers prefer to use open, spontaneous, fluid dialogue in a group context rather than adhering to any explicit procedures. Whichever the approach, researchers are involved in "an extreme form of care that saves the situations described in a slow, meditative way and attends to, even magnifies, all the details" Wertz (2005, p.172).

Significant themes or narratives emerging from the data are identified. Each type of analysis and way of presenting the data simultaneously reveals and conceals. Different analyses highlight particular nuances and indicate various immanent possibilities of meaning as *figural* against a *ground* of othcr possiblc mcanings. Thc analytical process invariably involves a process of reflective writing and rewriting. This process aims to create depth: multiple layers of meaning are crafted to lay bare certain truths while retaining the ambiguity of experience. Methods of interpretation involve Grounded Theory coding, content analysis, narrative analysis, and hermeneutic methods. Biographical research analysis of everyday knowledge is field of application.

22.3 Reliability and Validity of Phenomenological Studies

Trustworthiness is the fundamental criteria because it is deliberated parallel to the positivist criteria that are internal validity, external validity, reliability and objectivity (Guba and Lincoln, 1989). The trustworthiness criteria comprise four quality standards: the credibility (via member checking), transferability (via thick description), dependability (via outside reviewer), and conformability (conformability data audit). ***Trustworthiness of phenomenological accounts rests on vividness, accuracy, richness and elegance of evidence of life lived and experience*** (Polkinghorne, 1983). Many qualitative researchers embrace the use of ***participant validation*** as a way to 'prove' the validity of their research. When the participant agrees with the researcher's assessment, it is seen as strengthening the researcher's argument. As Dahlberg *et al* (2008, p. 94) warn, researchers need to be "careful not to make definite what is indefinite". Lifeworld research is characterised by its capacity to present the paradoxes and integrate opposites demonstrating holism (Dahlberg *et al,* 2008). Sources of error, bias, and invalidity need to be identified in order to make the study most trustworthy and authentic.

Authenticity is about conversation between researcher and participants, and the situations and emotional compassion that arise during the investigation (Ellis and Bochner, 2000). The authenticity criteria contain: ontological authenticity (understanding social milieu), educative authenticity (appreciating others' perspectives), catalytic authenticity (acting for change), and tactical authenticity (empowering members for action) (Bryman, 2008).

References

Ashworth, P D (1993). Participant agreement in the justification of qualitative findings. *Journal of Phenomenological Psychology* 24: 3-16.

Ashworth, P D (2003). An approach to phenomenological psychology: the contingencies of the lifeworld. *Journal of Phenomenological Psychology* 34 (6):145-156.

Dahlberg, K, Dahlberg, H and Nystrom, M (2008) (eds.). *Reflective Lifeworld Research*. 2nd edition. Lund, Sweden: Student Literature.

Feldman, N. (ed.) (2001). *Strategies for Interpreting Qualitative Data*. Thousand Oaks, CA: Sage.

Finlay, L (2003a). The intertwining of body, self and world: a phenomenological study of living with recently-diagnosed multiple sclerosis, *Journal of Phenomenological Psychology,* 34(2), 157-178.

Finlay, L (2003b). Through the looking glass: inter subjectivity and hermeneutic reflection. In L Finlay and B Gough (eds) *Reflexivity: a Practical Guide for Researchers in Health and Social Sciences*. Oxford: Blackwell Publishing.

Finlay, L (2005). Reflexive embodied empathy: a phenomenology of participant-researcher inters subjectivity, *Methods Issue: The Humanistic Psychologist,* 33(4), 271-92.

Garza, G (2007). Varieties of Phenomenological Research at the University of Dallas, *Qualitative Research in Psychology*, 4(4), 313-342.

Giorgi, A (1985). Sketch of a psychological phenomenological method. In A Giorgi (ed) *Phenomenology and Psychological Research*. Pittsburgh, PA: Duquesne University Press.

Giorgi, A (1994). A phenomenological perspective on certain qualitative research methods. *Journal of Phenomenological Psychology*, 25:190-220.

Giorgi, A and Giorgi, B (2003). Phenomenology. In J A Smith (ed.) *Qualitative psychology: a practical guide to research methods*. London: Sage.

Halling, S., and Leifer, M. (1991). The theory and practice of dialogic research. *Journal of Phenomenological Psychology*, 22(1), 1-15.

Heidegger, M (1962). *Being and Time*. New York: Harper and Row.

Hertz, R (1997). Introduction: reflexivity and voice. In R Hertz (ed) *Reflexivity and voice*. Thousand Oaks, CA: Sage.

Husserl, E (1931). *Ideas: general introduction to pure phenomenology*. (Boyce Gibson, W.R. Trans.). London: George Allen and Unwin. (Originally published 1913).

Langdridge, D. (2007). *Phenomenological psychology: theory, research and method*. Harlow, England: Pearson Prentice Hall.

Linda Finlay (2007). Introducing phenomenolodgical research (DOC) retrieved from Google.com under heading phenmenological research method.

Moran, D (2000). *Introduction to phenomenology*. London: Routledge.

Smith, JA and Osborn, M (2003). Interpretative phenomenological analysis. In J A Smith (ed) *Qualitative psychology: a practical guide to research methods*. London: Sage Publications.

Todres, L (2007) *Embodied enquiry: phenomenological touchstones for research, psychotherapy and spirituality*. Palgrave: Macmillan.

Van Manen, M. (1990). *Researching Lived Experience: Human Science for an Action Sensitive Pedagogy*. New York: State University of New York Press.

Vedder, B. (2002). On the Meaning of Metaphor in Gadamer's Hermeneutics, *Research in Phenomenology*, 32(1): 196-209.

Wertz, F. J. (2005). Phenomenological research methods for counseling psychology, *Journal of Counseling Psychology*, 52(2), 167-177.

23

Field Studies

Field studies involve collecting data outside of an experimental or lab setting. This type of data collection is most often done in natural settings or environments and can be done in a variety of ways for various disciplines. Field studies employ participatory approach. One of the basic principles in participatory approach is that ordinary men and women have the capacity to name their own reality. Actors (participants) are co-investigators in seeking solutions to the problems that they encounter in their everyday lives. Fieldwork describes and analyses the activities that have taken place in a particular research locale over the medium to long period. Field studies start with the task of obtaining access to people. Objectives of the field studies are to (a) provide adequate understanding of complexity of reality; (b) derive substantial evidence for policy planning and programme redesigning; (c) set individuals as active agent in their environment (contextual) rather than passive objects to be researched; (d) analyse impact on the participants; (e) view and analyse the problem in a holistic perspective.

In field studies, data is generated by men. People are inspired, involved and informed to gather good data. The researcher then studies the locale by living or working there for a period of time, or by making repeated visits. At the end of field work, the process is bought to a close by a planned and carefully managed departure. Field study involves the efforts to gain understanding by observing naturally-occurring events. Field study is based on **three cardinal principles** of social research:

- Each research question is uniquely defined by a specific set of circumstances.
- There can be no attempt to answer a question without deep knowledge of the specific contextual parameters defining those circumstances.
- Such deep knowledge comes only to those who have paid their dues.

23.1 Focus is on

- **Detached observation or principle of neutrality:** The roles of researchers carrying out empirical research could be seen as ranging along a continuum. Continuum runs from participation at one end through to observation at the other, via two intermediate points: the participant-as-observer and the observer-as-participant (Gold, 1958). The researcher always has to maintain some degree of distance and detachment in order to continually evaluate what is going on, fitting it into the analytic frame provided by their professional knowledge and training. Researchers doing fieldwork always have to strike a careful balance, something which is closely connected to achieving a degree of control.
- **Getting on 'insider's view of reality':** Study of social life is more effectively carried out by research procedures which more closely mirror life itself. If we are all expert of everyday analysis of social life, yet we achieve this by living in the situation rather than asking questions about it.
- **Striving to maintain unobtrusiveness:** The gap between the empowered (Researcher) and yet to be empowered (respondents) needs to be brought down to minimal level. The researcher would have not influenced events in any way. Observation can be carried out in ways which to all intents and purposes have no effect at all on those observed.

23.2 Areas of Field Studies

- Field studies may include ethnographical or phenomenological, grounded theory and case studies of institutions, communities and individuals. Longitudinal field studies are undertaken to assess the trends, and impact of policy or programmes on the lives of people. Socio-economic-educational-political and cultural studies are also undertaken to identify and assess the reality at the ground level.

23.3 Need and Importance of Field Study

- Field study is quite useful when one immerse oneself in a situation to get the holistic view of the 'event or theme'. The researcher in the fieldwork situation will inevitably become well known in the research locale, and will become extremely well acquainted with some people. It is experiential knowledge which researcher tries to access in fieldwork. Certainly, it enables to generate data more directly, more naturally and in a less mediated way.
- When subjects are unable/ unwilling to participate in the surveys: Participatory approach is followed to motivate the participants. Face to face intimacy is built through regular interaction with participants. Gap between the researcher and participants has to be bridged in order to get reliable and valid data. The power of decision-making is vested with the participants. Observation in the natural setting also stimulates them to participate proactively in the research processes.
- Fieldwork gives access to the details of everyday life. In this process, researcher gains close, sometimes intimate, acquaintance with those with whom they interact. The researcher can obtain the more intimate details of social life. In the field study, the actors can experience their strengths, weaknesses, opportunities and challenges.
- The participants (actors) are engaged in the research processes in order to get the truth and make common effort to transform their situation. In this process, they are empowered (capacity building) to participate in decision-making process. In this research process, participant level of confidence is increased. People knowledge base is enhanced. Collectively informed and

involved community becomes driving force for sustainable development.

23.4 Research Design

The choice of the locale where field research is to be carried out and identification of participants for the generation data and its analysis to get answers of research questions form the core of the research design. The process of making these decisions depends largely on imagination, ingenuity and a capacity for lateral thinking than straightforward application of scientific principle (Bechhofer and Paterson, 2000). Research Design involves three processes namely, **WHY**? Have the participants been properly motivated to go for field study? Why are the participants interested in the problem to be researched? What is the relevance of the themes or issues to be undertaken for the field study? Will it bring about substantial change in their lives? Will it empower them to be proactive in socio-economic, educational and political environment? **WHAT?** Who will decide what problem is to be undertaken for research? Who will make them understand the problem? **HOW?** to get representative sample for comparison and control? What are the tools (interview, observation, diary, note taking, and focus group discussions) and techniques (how participants are inspired, informed and involved to generate good data) to be used in the field study? How will the data be analysed (contextual content analysis for comparison, identification of pattern and most significant change)?

23.5 Conducting Field Study

Review of theoretical literature about the topic under study will help in understanding:

- What is already known about the issue?
- Which theories are used and discussed in this area?
- What concepts are used or disputed about?
- What are methodological controversies in this field?
- What has not yet been exploded in this field?
- Is research explicitly guided by some kind of theoretical or conceptual framework which seeks to explain the phenomena they are observing?
- Is research undertaken for generation of Grounded Theory?

Use of the Empirical literature about earlier research in the same or similar field Strauss and Corbin (1998, pp. 49-52) had listed 9-way of using literature.

- Concepts from the literature can be a source of making comparisons in data you have collected;
- To be familiar with the relevant literature can enhance sensitivity to subtle nuances in data;
- Published descriptive materials can give accurate description of reality helpful for understanding your own material or problem;
- Existing philosophical and theoretical knowledge can inspire you and give you an orientation in the field and material;
- The literature can be a secondary source of data – for example, quotations from interview in articles may complement your own materials;
- The literature can be used beforehand to formulate questions that help you as a springboard in early interviews and observations;
- The literature may stimulate questions while you analyse your material;
- Areas for theoretical sampling can be suggested by the literature;
- The literature can be used for confirming/disconfirming findings.

Review of Methodological Literature

- Review of methodological literature will help the researcher in understanding the methods used. Is there any possibility or scope to modify or refine the methods?
- It will facilitate the researcher in understanding the procedures and techniques used in the selection of sample. What controls were applied to get accurate information?
- To see the distinctions, alternatives, and strengths or weaknesses of one technique over the other.
- What criteria were used for establishing reliability and validity of the tools?

Study of Theoretical and Empirical literature for contextualising, comparison and generalisation of your findings

- How the existing literature is relevant for grounding the present researcher argumentation, or findings of the present study are in concordance with the existing research or the present findings contradict existing research.
- Comparison of outcomes of earlier research findings with findings of the present study will help us to identify the most significant changes over the time.
- The review of earlier researches will help the researcher in writing his /her research report.
- The literature can be used for confirming findings or can be overcome by your findings.

Research Questions

Research question states what we are trying to find out. The hypothesis predicts, a priori, the answer to that question. Hypothesis is used when we do have an explanation (a theory) in mind behind our hypothesis. If this is the case, we should by all means formulate hypothesis as predicted answer to research questions and test them, if not, we can ignore hypotheses and proceed with research questions, if we can not predict with any confidence, we need go no further into the matter of hypotheses. Figure 23.1 explains difference between research Question and Hypothesis.

Research question states what we are trying to find out. The hypothesis predicts, a priori, the answer to that question. Hypothesis is used when we do have an explanation (a theory) in mind behind our hypothesis. If this is the case, we should by all means formulate hypothesis as predicted answer to research questions and test them, if not, we can ignore hypotheses and proceed with research questions, if we can not predict with any confidence, we need go no further into the matter of hypotheses. Figure 23.1 explains difference between research Question and Hypothesis.

Research question states what we are trying to find out. The hypothesis predicts, a priori, the answer to that question. Hypothesis is used when we do have an explanation (a theory) in mind behind our hypothesis. If this is the case, we should by all means formulate hypothesis as predicted answer to research questions and test them, if not, we can ignore hypotheses and proceed with research questions, if we can not predict with any confidence, we need go no further into the matter of hypotheses. Figure 23.1 explains difference between research Question and Hypothesis.

Research questions generally emerge in the course of field study. Research Questions must be specific, clear and unambiguous. They are continuously in the process of change and modification. In the course of the project, however, questions become more and more concrete, more focused, and they are also narrowed and revised.

Methodology

Inductive- in this process, the researcher proceeds from bottom to top. Research questions are formulated and modified in the process of observations in the field. Hypotheses are more likely to emerge from the data than to be formulated prior to the research.

Sampling

In qualitative research:

- Features of the basic population are not known.
- Extension of the basic population is not known in advance.
- Repeated drawing of sampling elements with criteria to be defined again in each step.
- Sample size is not defined in advance.
- Sampling is finished when theoretical saturation has been reached.

Therefore, purposive sampling method is generally used in qualitative research. Purpose is to get insight about phenomenon, not empirical generalisation from a sample to a population. Qualitative research cannot be conducted through a-priori samples only. Sampling goes on throughout research, through various sampling techniques, such as, typical case sampling, intensity sampling, critical case sampling, sensitive case sampling, convenience sampling. Primary and Secondary data are used for triangulation.

23.6 Tools and Techniques of Qualitative Research

Tools and techniques of qualitative research are innumerous, such as, observation, interview, triangulation, Focus Group Discussion, Reflective Dialogue.

- **Observation** is a technique of data collection in which one or more persons observe the happenings in a relevant situation on the basis of pre-determined scheme. It could be participant observation in which the observer participates himself in said situation. In non-participant observation the observer observes the behaviour in real life situation. Data from observations consist of detail description of people's activities, actions, and the full range of interpersonal interaction and organisational processes that are part of observable human experience;
- **Interview** is a two-person conversation initiated by the researcher on content specified by research objectives of systematic description, prediction or explanation. The data from in-depth or open-ended interviews consist of direct question from people, their experiences, opinions, feelings and knowledge.
- **Triangulation** uses two or more methods to investigate to get a more complete, accurate picture of human behaviour. This can be done through convergence of data from different sources through different methods.
- **Focus Group Discussions** are organised group discussions which are focused around a single theme. The group is a purposive sample-based on certain pre-determined criteria. Statement(s) of one person initiates a chain reaction of comments/ responses from other respondents. When a group deliberates over a theme/problem, many a time, there is an excitement among participants to put forward their views.
- **Email –Facilitated Reflective Dialogue** may be used to engage human service practitioners as partners in research about sensitive areas of front line work which otherwise can be difficult for a range of reasons, such as, time constraints, geographic limitations, trust in the research relationship, issue of privacy, and fear of professional judgment.
- **Written documents**: document analysis in qualitative inquiry yields excerpts, quotations, or entire passages from organisational clinical or programme records, memoranda and correspondence, official publications and reports, personal diaries, or open-ended written responses to questionnaires and surveys.

Qualitative Research cannot be conducted through static tools and techniques, because very often the researcher employing qualitative research methodology does not have a sound theoretical base related to the reality. Theory in fact is the product of enquiry. Data are created by human efforts; put more prosaically, the way in which information is collected affects the content of the data themselves; scholar who 'produce data' are complex creatures whose perceptions and communications are shaped at every turn by the context in which they find themselves; and both the content and the quality of data are prime concerns. It is in-depth analysis of contextually–bound data. It involves the subjectivity of the researcher.

23.7 The Choice of Locale and Group

The locale is the place in which the study can be undertaken. Group comprises of individuals members to be studied. The researcher has to identify the specific place and specific group where he can get response to research questions. A particular intervention, the researcher intends to introduce to empower them, applies to specific people in specific a place. However, questions may arise about the best comparator groups or exactly how to design the work, but the people and the place are determined from the start. The design research, the focus is on sample selection, the research instruments to be used and the expected comparisons and control. All good designs are compromises, and in this process the problem is refined, the group(s) and locale(s) reconsidered, alternative methods evaluated, some are adopted and some rejected, and the whole process continues until a satisfactory overall design emerges (Bechhhofer and Paterson, 2000).

Field Notes/ Generation of Data

Interview (focused/ethnographic/narrative/episodic), observation (participant/non-participant), diary (process/episode/narrative), and field-notes, tape-recorder, video, film, camera etc. are the tools invariably used for the collection of data.

Analysis of Data

Analysis of data should take note of the following processes:

- ***Reflection on analysis***: The investigator speculate what the participants and the researcher are learning, the themes that are emerging, patterns that are present, connections between pieces of data, additional ideas, and thoughts that pop up in the active action of the participants.

- ***Reflection on method:*** Materials contain procedures and strategies employed.
- ***Reflection on ethical dilemmas and conflicts***. There are two sets of behaviour- subject's ideology, values, moral, and ethic on one hand and observer's comment on the other.
- ***Reflection on the observer's frame of mind:*** These preconceptions relate to religious beliefs, political ideology, and cultural background, position in society, race and gender.

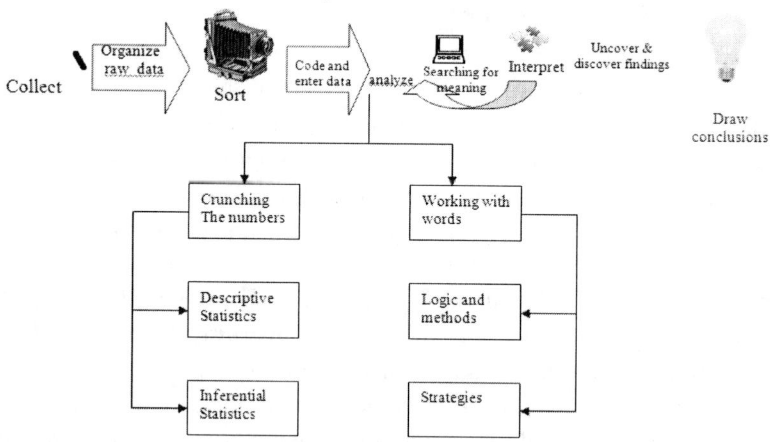

Figure 23.1: Analysis of Data.

Interpretation

The whole phenomenon under study is understood as a complex system that is more than sum of its parts; focus on complex interdependencies and system dynamics that cannot meaningfully be reduced to a few discrete and linear, cause-effect relationships. In interpreting the 'data' the researcher constantly asks how good the evidence is for the interference which they are drawing. The data comes from what people say and feel, how they interact with others and what they do in different situations, and these data are constantly cross-checked as fieldwork proceeds. As the researcher develops an understanding of what is going on, or an explanation for something, alternative understandings and explanations are considered, modified, incorporated or cast aside. For instance-

- Meanings are elicited from the situation by observation, by listening, by interpreting and of course, by the occasional questioning, all backed up by introspection. The researcher starts with some research questions and with some conceptual ideas. Then gather or absorb data, recorded in field notes, on tape recorders, or sometimes as visual images, which are constantly analysed and written. This leads to further research questions and a developing conceptual framework. Of course, this conceptual framework as it develops is tested.
- In interpreting the 'data' the researcher constantly asks how good the evidence is for the inferences which they are drawing. The data comes from what people say and feel, how they interact with others and what they do in different situations, and these data are constantly cross-checked as fieldwork proceeds. As the researcher develops an understanding of what is going on, or an explanation for something, alternative understandings and explanations are considered, modified, incorporated or cast aside.
- It is because the social picture is built up in this painstaking way, because we seek to explain processes, that fieldwork is often said to produce high levels of validity. Control is achieved by these myriad instances of cross-checking, considering alternative explanations, and so on.

Over a long period of time individuals will give various accounts to the fieldworker which can be more effectively cross-checked, compared with and related to what others say, and above all interpreted, than anything that is said in a single interview, be it structured or unstructured. These accounts will inevitably be affected by the relationship which has grown up between the researcher and that individual; because what we say in everyday life to one person we would not say to another. It is again a question of compromise. We have to balance that reactive effect against the control achieved.

Limitations of Field Studies

While field research can be an extremely useful method for gaining first-hand knowledge, but it entails some difficulties:

- It is costly and time consuming (time and money)
- Situation of interest may be fleeting
- It requires excellent observational / interpretive skills
- Risk of 'going native' in participative observation
- Lack of external validity (especially when subjects are selected on the basis of availability or convenience).

Further Reading

Anfara and Mertz. (2006). *Theoretical Frameworks in Qualitative Research.* Thousand Oaks, C A: Sage.

Bailey, K.D. (1987). *Methods of Social Research.* 3rd.edn. New York: Free Press.

Bassey, M.(2001). A solution to the problem of generalisation in educational research: Fuzzy prediction. *Oxford Review of Education*, 27(10), pp. 5-22.

Bechhofer, F. and Pterson, L.(2000). *Principles of Research Design in the Social Sciences.* London:Routledge.

Best, J. and Kahn, J.(2995). *Research in Education.* 10th edition, Needham Heights: Allyn and Bacon.

Cozby, P. (2009). *Methods in Behavioural Research.* 10th edition, Bemont: Wadsworth.

Denzin, N.K., and Lincoln, Y.S.(2000). *Handbook of Qualitative Research,* London: Sage.

Feldman, N. (ed.) (2001). Strategies for Interpreting Qualitative Data. Thousand Oaks, CA: Sage.

Flick, U.(2007c). *Designing Qualitative Research* .Thousand Oaks, CA: SAGE.

Flick, U.(2014). *An Introduction to Qualitative Research.* New Delhi: SAGE.

Goode, W.J., and Hatt, P.K. (1990). *Methods in Social Research.* McGraw-Hill, New Delhi.

Marshall, C., and Rossman, G.B. (2006). *Designing Qualitative Research.* 4th edn., New Delhi: Sage.

Maxwell, J.A. (1996). *Qualitative Research Design: An Interaction Approach.* Thousand Oaks, CA: Sage.

Neuman, W.L (1994). *Social Research Methods: Qualitative and Quantitative Aproaches.* 2nd. Edn. Boston: Allyn and Bacon.

Punch, K. F. (2009). *Introduction to Research Methods in Education.* New Delhi: Sage.

Singh, J. (2008). *Methodology and Techniques of Social Research.* New Delhi: Kanishka Publishers.

Somekh, B., and Lewin, C. (2005). *Research Methods in the Social Sciences.* New Delhi. Vstaar Publications.

Wallen, N.E. and Fraenkel, J.R. (1991). *Educational Research: A Guide to the Process.* New York: McGraw-Hill.

Zeller, R. A. (1996). 'Validity', in J.P. Keeves (ed.), *Educational Research, Methodology, and Measurement: An International Handbook.* 2nd edn. Oxford: Elsevier. pp. 822-9.

24

Mixed Methods Research

24.1 Introduction

Mixed method of research is empirical research that involves the collection and analysis of both quantitative and qualitative data. It has been noted that such terms as 'multi-method', 'integrated', 'blended' and 'combined' methods have been used, along with 'multi- trait' method, 'methodological triangulation', and 'mixed method research' (Creswell amd Clark, 2007, 5-6). It is consistent and systematic use of the term 'mixed method' to describe research. A mixed method of research involves:

- Multi paradigms-qualitative and quantitative.
- Pragmatic approach-methods to be used in research to determine the questions asked.
- Potentially complementary forms of empirical inquiry.
- The investigation of natural versus artificial settings.
- An inductive versus a deductive approach.
- The identification of cultural patterns as against seeking scientific laws.

Creswell and Plano Clark (2007) have identified three main dimensions in analysing data:

1. **The timing dimension:** What will the timing of qualitative and quantitative methods be? In which order will the researcher collect and use the data? Will it be concurrent (both sets of data are collected at the same time or sequential (one set is collected before the other)?
2. **The weighing dimension:** What will be the relative importance and, weight, or priority given to? The general possibilities are equal weighting to both approaches, or unequal weighting, with one approach carrying more weight.
3. **The mixing dimension:** How will qualitative and quantitative methods be mixed, and especially how will the two data sets be mixed? The possibilities are that the two data can be merged, one can be embedded within the other, or they can be connected in some other way.

Mixed Methods Designs

There are four mixed methods designs as such given below:

1. **Triangulation Design:** A triangulation design involves the current but separate collection and analysis the two types of data, which are then merged, perhaps through data transformation, or perhaps at the interpretation –of –result stage. For example, on the general topic of teaching effectiveness, both methods would focus on the different aspects of teaching effectiveness. For instance, 'Group-based and 'Individual-based scorecard vis-à-vis and records of women empowerment have to be triangulated through convergence of multi data resources to get real picture of women empowerment. It also generates accurate the generalisable statistics in a timely, efficient, and effective way.
2. **Embedded Design:** This design takes cognigence that a single data set is not sufficient. Different types of questions require different types of data to answer them. For example, qualitative data is collected as a part of correlational study to trace the relationships between independent variables and teaching effectiveness as the dependent variable. For instance, the Process of translating this complex qualitative understanding

of change into quantified indicators is done by the participants. This process is entirely driven by the research project participants. The self-assessment is done in a trusted space. Purpose is benefiting the group in future. Future plan will be redesigned to meet the perceived demand of the participants.

3. **Explanatory Design:** This is a two-phase mixed method design, where qualitative data are used to help explain, or to built upon, initial quantitative results. Quantitative results guide the selection of subsamples for follow-up in-depth investigation in the second phase. For example, quantitative survey is followed by qualitative in-depth study in order to gain a fuller understanding of both the nature as well as the factors affecting the participants.

4. **Exploratory Design:** In this two-phase mixed method design, qualitative data are collected and followed by quantitative data. For example, a researcher explores some phenomenon of teaching effectiveness in-depth before going for the constructing of tool for the measurement of teaching effectiveness.

24.2 Steps of Mixed Methods Research

Identification of Topic: The researcher may select topic through inductive and deductive seasoning. It should be based on the logic of the research proposed, and ensure that methods chosen are appropriate to the questions asked.

Research Questions: Researcher should check- Is the question right for the researcher?, Is the question right for the mixed methods research ?, Is the question doable? Figure- 24.1 reveals the relationship between objectives of the research study, research questions and theory.

Methodology

Research Design: The researcher has to decide what type of research would be-triangulation, embedded, explanatory or exploratory.

Sampling and Measurement Procedures: Procedures for sampling and collection of data for both quantitative data and qualitative data should be clearly specified, and defined.

Data Analysis: Approaches (soft-wares or manual) to the analysis of both quantitative and qualitative data need to be explained i.e. how data are to be analysed to find meaningful answers to the research questions.

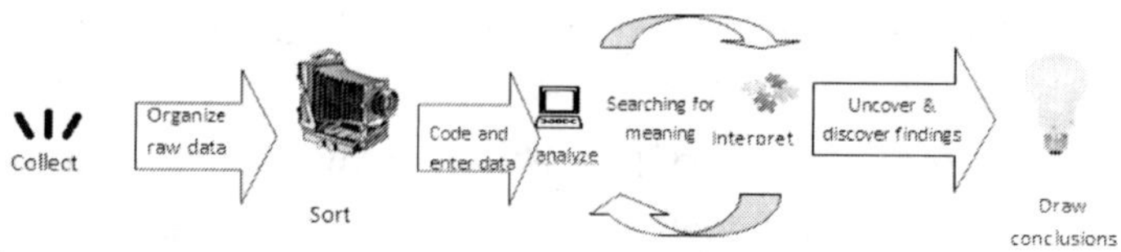

Figure 24.1: Objectives / Research Questions/Theory.

Results and Conclusions

Johnson (2009) proposed a set of guidelines that is more inclusive and might better represent research in education. These guidelines are:

- Identify important problems and pose questions that can be investigated empirically or through other potentially useful approaches. Continuously generate, discover, describe, and construct new knowledge, and test knowledge claims.
- Separately and interconnectively explore, reflect upon, describe, predict, and explain the natural world and meaningful social and personal 'worlds' and experiences.
- Explicate researcher and research values, purposes, commitments, and key background assumptions.
- Use method and strategies that, separately or in combination, can produce warranted investigation of particular research questions.
- Rely on sources of evidences.
- Link exploratory research to relevant theory through theory generation, theory testing, and ongoing theory modification.
- Describe nomological (i.e., general law like) knowledge domain, but also describe ideographic, local and contextual knowledge domains, and interconnect these to continually produce meaningful "practical theory".
- Replicate, document mediating and moderating processes, delineate conditions of generalisation, and identify broad generalisations when possible, but also identify complex contextual interactions to aid in particular understanding and practical application of education/social theory.

- Articulate, explicate, develop, and test "manualised models, practice-based models, middle-level theoretical models, meta-models (i.e., model of models) and trans- theoretical and trans- disciplinary models of educational phenomena, and interconnect these continually for scientific learning."
- Explicate creative and formal reasoning processes (i.e., deductive, inductive, abductive, critical- theory) to help situate and warrant findings and value choices.
- Fully disclose research processes and findings to encourage professional and societal scrutiny.
- Continually encourage self-examination and critique and ongoing improvement of the education scientific enterprise.

Reliability and Validity

Eisenhart and Howe (1992), proposed five criteria namely, (a) ensuring a fit between research questions, data collection, procedures, and analytic techniques, (b) ensuring the effective application of specific data collection and analytic techniques; (c) being alert to and cognizant of prior knowledge; (d) being cognizant of both internal and external value constraints; and (e) assessing a study's comprehensiveness.

Tabe 24.1: Criteria for Mixed Method of Research*

Quantitative Term	*Qualitative Tem*	*Strategy Employed*
Internal validity	Credibility	• Prolonged engagement in field • Use of peer debriefing • Triangulation • Member checks • Time sampling
External validity	Transferability	• Provide thick description • Purposive sampling
Reliability	dependability	• Create an audit trail • Code-recode strategy • Triangulation • Peer examination
Objectivity	Confirmability	• Triangulation • Practice reflexivity

*Educational Researcher, Vol.35, No.9, Page-30.

Further Reading

Best, J. and Kahn, J.(2995). *Research in Education.* 10th edition, Needham Heights: Allyn and Bacon.

Bryant, A. and Charmaz, K. (eds.) (2007a). *The Sage Handbook of Grounded Theory.* London; Sage.

Cozby, P. (2009). *Methods in Behavioural Research.* 10th edition, Bemont: Wadsworth.

Denzin, N.K., and Lincoln, Y.S.(2000). *Handbook of Qualitative Research,* London: Sage.

Feldman, N. (ed.) (2001). Strategies for Interpreting Qualitative Data. Thousand Oaks, CA: Sage.

Flick. U.(2010). *An Introduction to Qualitative Research.* 4th edn., New Delhi: Sage.

Marshall, C., and Rossman, G.B. (2006). *Designing Qualitative Research.* 4th edn. New Delhi: Sage.

Maxwell, J. A. (2002). Literature Review of, and for, Educational Research: A Commentary on Boote and Beile's "Scholars Before Researchers" *Educational Researcher*, Vol. 35, No. 9, pp. 28-31.

Merkens, H. (2004). Selection, Procedures, Sampling, Case Construction. In U.Flick, E.V.Kandroff and I. Steinke (eds), *A Comparison to Qualitative Research.* London: Sage.

Tashakhori, A. and Teddlie, C. (eds.) (2003). *Handbook of Mixed Methods in social and Behavioral Research.* Thousand Oaks, CA: Sage.

25

Grounded Theory

25.1 Introduction

Grounded theory is a qualitative research method. The main purpose is to generate theory from data. The phrase "grounded theory" refers to theory that is developed inductively from a corpus of data. The resulting theory at least needs to fit into data set perfectly. Grounded theory tries to study a phenomenon and a set of data in context. Social patterns and structures of area of interest are conceptualised through the process of control and constant comparison. Only through interaction and discourse can meaning be unlocked and conveyed to the observer. From this perspective, Grounded Theory provides a method which enables a researcher to produce true meaning and understanding. Moreover, the text is read in search of finding answers to the research questions.

Grounded theory methods consist of systematic, yet flexible techniques for collecting and analysing qualitative data and to construct theories. Analytical and interpretive procedures are used for analysing and conceptualising data. The findings of grounded theory are not arrive at by means of statistical procedures or other means of quantification, but are derived from data gathered by a variety of means including 'observation' interview, documents, and videotapes.

Grounded theorists emphasise causal relationships, and fit things into a basic frame of generic relationships. The frame consists of elements, such as, phenomenon, causal conditions, context, intervening conditions, action strategies and consequences. The process of Grounded Theory encompasses an acknowledgment of the researchers' bias, the selection of a data collection site, the data collection process, the process of coding and analysis, and the compilation of results.

Grounded Theory allows the researcher to consider his or her ontological and epistemological position. It also permits the expression of different perspectives. Emphasis can be placed on a particular method or technique to suit one's philosophical viewpoint. It reflects a situation in which its "users" position themselves philosophically to facilitate their interpretation of what is "going on."

25.2 Elements of Grounded Theory

- There is a spiral of cycles of data collection, coding, analysis, writing, design, theoretical, categorisation, and data collection.
- Conduct the constant comparative analysis of cases with each other and to theoretical categories throughout each cycle.
- A theoretical sampling process based upon categories is developed from ongoing data analysis.
- The size of sample is determined by the 'theoretical saturation' of categories rather than by the need for demographic 'representativeness', or simply lack of 'additional information' from new cases.
- The resulting theory is developed inductively from data rather than tested by data, although the developing theory is continuously refined and checked by data.
- Codes 'emerge' from data and are not imposed a priori upon it.
- The substantive and/or formal theory outlined in the final report takes into account all the variations in the data and conditions associated with these variations. The report is an analytical product rather than a purely descriptive account. Theory development is the goal. (Hood, 2007, p. 154)

25.3 Preview

Grounded Theory was initially developed by two researchers – Barney Glaser and Anselm Strauss (1967). However, early in its development the two researchers separated and a bifurcation of the theory enveloped (Glaser, 1992; Strauss and Corbin, 1990). We now have two fundamental schools for Grounded Theory: the Glaserian School and the Straussian School (Stern, 1994). The differences between these are many, and in cases somewhat minor. The major differences, how-ever, can have an important impact in the direction and execution of the primary research. For instance, Glaser takes the stance that researchers should have an empty mind, while Strauss permits a general idea of the area under study. Glaser leads with the principle that theory should emerge, while Strauss uses structured questions to lead a more forced emergence of theory.

A Grounded Theory study which closely follows the guidelines presented by Glaser and Strauss (1967) will transcend thick description to provide substantive theory (Fernández, Martin, Gregor, Stern and Vitale, 2006; Goulding, 2001). This quality of Grounded Theory is further supported by Ellis and Levy (2009) who stated that grounded theory can furnish additional value when literature fails to support the theoretical evolution of phenomena.

Glaser and Strauss are critical realists operating in a post-positivist paradigm (Benoliel, 2001; Chen and Boore, 2009; Mills, Bonner and Francis, 2006a), They focused on objectivity, inductive logic, and the emergence of data. They laid emphasis on the constant comparative method in order to produce grounded theory. (Annells, 1997a; Glaser, 1978; Glaser and Holton, 2007).) Charmaz viewed grounded theory as a constructivist methodology with symbolic interactionist underpinnings. It is reconstruction of events and generation of data (Charmaz, 2001; Mills *et al.,* 2006a).

Holton (2009) explains, "grounded theory adopts an epistemological perspective appropriate to the data and an ontological stance aligned with the researcher. It is in the process of shifting philosophical perspectives over time that we see the *methodological dynamism* of grounded theory. Researchers appear to be responding to social pressures and changes over time and approaching grounded theory with new philosophies to guide how they apply its essential methods.

25.4 Conducting Grounded Theory

25.4.1 Identify your substantive area - your area of interest. Examples of substantive areas included dying (Glaser, 1967)), online learning (Scott, 2007), a cafe (Rosenbaum, 2006), nursing practice (Nathanial, 2007), management studies (Holton, 2007), work processes (Gynnild, 2207), interdisciplinary teams (McCallin, 2007). Your study needs to be about the perspective of one (or more) of the groups of people of the substantive area who will comprise your substantive population e.g. patients, doctors, nurses and social workers (Glaser, 1967), online learners (Scott, 2007), nurses who have practiced in direct contact with patients (Nathanial, 2007), knowledge workers (Holton, 2007) journalists (Gynnild, 2006), health professionals (McCallin, 2007).

The researchers' curiosity, experience, scientific temper, and stimulation can lead them into taking something as a research problem for developing a grounded theory. Second, identifying an issue as a topic for a grounded theory study includes a decision for a research perspective, aiming at developing a new theory, where so far a lack of theoretical knowledge exists.

Any grounded theory study should start with making a research question explicit. A good starting point is to use sensitising concepts. These are concepts which give the researcher a "general sense of references and guidance in approaching empirical instances ... suggest directions along which to look ... and rest on a general sense of what is relevant" (Blumer, 1970, p. 58). They can be helpful as heuristic devices for giving researchers an orientation. Concepts like trust, identity, and the like can be such starting points for identifying relevant problems and first conceptualisations in a field.

25.5 Methodology

25.5.1 Method: Grounded Theory method refers to theory that is developed inductively from a corpus of data. Qualitative researchers tend to analyse their data inductively. They do not search out data or evidence to prove or disprove hypotheses they hold before entering the study; Theory developed this way emerges from the bottom up (rather than from the top down), from many disparate pieces of collected evidence that are interconnected. The theory is grounded in the data. It is constructing a picture that takes shape as you collect and examine the parts.

25.5.2 Purposive Sampling: Sampling goes on throughout research, through various sampling techniques, such as, typical case sampling, intensity sampling, critical case sampling, sensitive case sampling, convenience sampling, primary selection and secondary selection.Theoretical sampling is the process of data collection for generating theory whereby the analyst jointly collects, codes, and analyses his data and decides what data to collect next and where to find them, in order to develop his theory as it emerges. This process of data collection is controlled by the emerging theory.

25.5.3 Instruments for the Collection of Data

Interviews-Open-ended, intermediate, and ending questions should be used for a good interview. The current interview protocol should span the entire range of the sample questions.

Observation-Participant or Non-Participant- Data from observations consist of detail description of people's activities, actions, and the full range of interpersonal interaction and organisational processes that are part of observable human experience.

Triangulation- that is convergence of data gathered from different sources through different methods.

On Online Data- offers endless opportunities for textual analysis and poses methodological issues.

Collecting observations of the substantive area itself and activities occurring within the substantive area;

- Accessing public or private record irrespective of form (e.g. photograph, diary, painting, sculpture, biography, television broadcast, news report, survey, government or organisational document, etc.);
- Conversing with individuals or a group of individuals, face-to-face or remotely [synchronously (e.g. telephone, text chat) or asynchronously (e.g. email or wiki)].

25.6 Producing Relevant Data

A Grounded Theory may use qualitative data, quantitative data (e.g. Glase, 1964 and Glaser, 2008) or a mixture of the two. How researchers use methods matter. Methods *are* merely tools. Some tools are more useful than others. Decisions about methods do have consequences. How you collect data affects which phenomena researcher will see, how, where, and when he will view them, and what sense he will make of them. And the idea that data are constructed or produced by the researcher in the field (see Charmaz, 2006). Beyond the epistemological differences in these notions, it seems obvious that researchers use methods for arriving at data. Grounded theory methodology is not linked to a preferable method for collecting or producing data. Based on participant observation more or less formalised conversations or interviews with members of the field .This research strategy is based on repeated field contacts and allows coming back to the field and participants to collect more data and to adapt data collection to the needs and questions resulting from the analysis of the data so far.

25.7 Analysis of Data

Grounded theory methods consist of systematic, yet flexible techniques for collecting and analysing qualitative data to construct theories. Analytical and interpretive procedures are used for analysing and conceptualising data through coding (open coding, axial coding and selection coding), non-statistical sampling, writing of memos, diagramming of conceptual relationships, written and verbal reports. The findings of grounded theory are not arrive at by means of statistical procedures or other means of quantification, but are derived from data gathered by a variety of means including 'observation' interview, documents, and videotapes. Axial coding is the process of relating codes (categories and properties) to each other, via a combination of inductive and deductive thinking. Grounded theorists emphasise causal relationships, and fit things into a basic frame of generic relationships. The frame consists of elements, such as, phenomenon, causal conditions, context, intervening conditions, action strategies and consequences. In contrast selective coding is the process of choosing one category to be the core category.

25.8 Processes of Grounded Theory

Coding- there are three levels of coding – *open coding, selective coding*, and *theoretical coding*. The coding stages are consecutive and sequential and not iterative. Open Coding-at this stage, the raw data (for example, transcripts) are initially examined and are coded through a process which fractures the interview into discrete threads of datum. Open coding utilises a process of *constant comparison* (Glaser and Strauss, 1967). Charmaz (2006) stresses that initial coding "moves researcher toward fulfilling two criteria for completing a grounded theory analysis: fit and relevance." Selective coding allows the researcher to filter and code data which are deemed to be more relevant to the emerging concepts. Figure 25.2 reveals the processes of grounded theory.

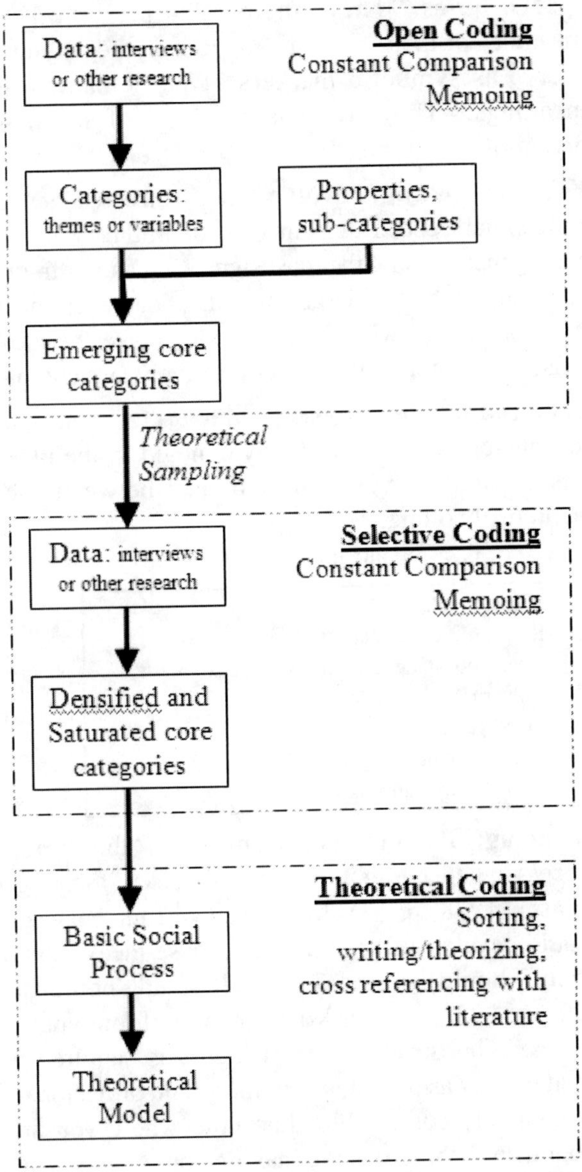

Figure 25.1: Processes of Grounded Theory.

- **Incident-by-incident coding** works well, for example, with observational notes. Following methods may be used:
- **In-vivo codes:** typically, these are "codes of participants' special terms." They: "help us to preserve participants' meanings of their views and actions in the coding itself" and "serve as symbolic markers of participants' speech and meanings." They are "characteristic of social words and organisation settings."
- **Focused Coding:** involve "more directed, selective, and conceptual" codes than in-vivo or initial coding. "Focused coding means using the most significant and/or frequent earlier codes to sift through large amounts of data ... [which] requires decisions about which initial codes make the most analytic sense to categorise your data incisively and completely."
- **Axial coding**: the purpose of which is to "relate categories to subcategories, " is not clearly denoted in the phase flow of this section; however, it is placed between focused and theoretical coding.

In short a code for coding:

- Remain open
- Stay close to the data
- Keep your codes simple and precise
- Construct short codes
- Preserve actions
- Compare data with data
- Move quickly through the data

- **Memoing:** Glaser refers to memoing as "the *core stage* in the process of generating theory, the bedrock of theory generation" (Glaser, 1978, p. 83). Memos have four basic goals: they should develop ideas and codes, these ideas should develop freely, should be stored centrally, and should be sortable (Glaser, 1978, p. 83). Write memos throughout the entire process. The development of theory is captured in memos. Treat memos as partial, preliminary, and provisional. They are immediately correctable. Just note where you are on firm ground and where you are making conjectures. Then go back to the field and check your conjectures. Lempert sees four fundamental principles in memo writing. The intention is the discovery and development of theory rather than application and confirmation. Memos are written, reread, and rewritten in order to advance to more abstract levels of theorising (2007, p. 262).

- **Theoretical coding:** the final stage of coding is known as *theoretical coding*. Theoretical coding occurs when core categories have become saturated. *Saturation* is both a peculiarity and strength of Grounded Theory. Unlike other methods of qualitative analysis which acquire rigour through multiple levels of confirmation or triangulation (Mertens, 1998), Theoretical Coding was introduced by Glaser to conceptualise "how the substantive codes may relate to each other as hypotheses to be integrated into a theory." These not only "specify existing relationships between categories" from focused coding, but, according to Glaser, preclude the need for axial coding.
- **Theoretical Model:** the model is constructed around two axes: one goes from causes to phenomena and to consequences, the other goes from context to intervening conditions and to action and interactional strategies of participants. Strauss's model around two axes led to his step of axial coding, which takes this model as a heuristic device for the further development of a grounded theory.

25.9 Review of the Literature

- Integrate with theory through selective coding.
- Synthesise the literature for making connections between the parts identified, and showing new patterns and arrangements among them. (Hart, 1998, 110).
- Consider the convergence and divergence of the findings, theories, methods, and implications that are found in the literature.
- The dialectical process of thesis-antithesis-synthesis as a framework for developing synthesis in the literature review may be followed. (Burton and Steane, 2004)
- The whole approach is organised around the principle that theory that is developed will be grounded in data.

25.10 Research Ethics in Grounded Theory Research

- **Rigour** – at technical level it implies being methodical, using appropriate techniques and attending to detail. At logical level, it is expressed as a concern for validity of argument, and the soundness of evidence, and reporting findings precisely and taking care to avoid errors.
- **Accountability** - conveying information truthfully and honouring commitments, it involves openness of mind, persistence, courage and, in particular, imaginative criticism.
- **Economy-** using resources wisely and avoiding waste, and
- **Impartiality-** letting the facts speak for themselves and avoiding improper bias.
- **Care for others** – it is the moral duty of the researchers to follow the principle of care for others in the provision of a public service or service to children in education.
- **Participatory-** participants (stakeholders or actors) should be inspired, informed and involved in the choice of locale, design of research, and methods to be employed. Both their dignity and capacity need to be recognised.

25.11 Write up Theory

The quality of that theory will depend upon your skills and the skills you develop as you research. A theory should consist of a set of basic statements called the axioms of theory, which tell us what the theory is all about. Such axiomatic statements or postulates as they are called include primitive terms. These are terms that are intuitively understood and cannot be otherwise completely defined. The criterion by which a theory is judged is not its truth or falsity, but rather its usefulness.

25.11.1 Legitimising Function of Writing

One is made aware that scientific knowledge is always presented scientifically. And the consequence is that "logic of presentation" has to be considered as well as a "logic of research." How researchers' constitution of experiences is linked to the way those experiences are saved in presentations has only begun to become an issue for reflection and research. (1989, p. 527)

The turn towards the text discloses a dimension in the scientific process of knowledge, which remained underexposed up to now. Where knowledge is schematised as the production of text, as the transcription of discourse and practice, the conditions of possibility for discussing ethnographic practices of representation are created. (Fuchs and Berg, 1993, p. 64)

The research report with its presentation of and reflection on the methodological proceedings, with all its narratives about access to and the activities in the field, with its documentation of various materials, with its transcribed observations and conversations, interpretations and theoretical inferences is the only basis for answering the question of the quality of the investigation. (Lüders, 1995, p. 325)

25.11.2 Reflexive Function of Writing

Research, then, includes not only the interaction between the researcher and the issue, but also the interaction between the researchers and their potential readers, for whom they finally write their presentations. This relationship—as well as the text produced for this purpose and the writing linked to it—is determined in multiple ways: "contextually rhetorically institutionally generically politically historically" (Clifford, 1986, p. 6).

Corbin and Strauss (1990, p. 16) mention four points of departure for judging empirically grounded theories and the procedures that led to them. According to their suggestions, researcher should critically assess: (i) the validity, reliability, and credibility of the data, (ii) the plausibility, and the value of the theory itself, (iii) the adequacy of the research process which has generated, elaborated, or tested the theory, and (iv) the empirical grounding of the research findings.

25.12 Importance of Grounded Theory Research

- Theory is generated on the basis of data; the theory will, therefore, be grounded in data. Grounded theory explicitly addresses the question of how to generate theory in research.
- It represents a coordinated, systematic and flexible overall research strategy to generate theory from the corpus of data.
- It brings a disciplined and organised approach to the analysis of qualitative data.
- Its contributions in the area of medical sociology and education have been well recognised.

- Grounded theory is found very useful in the identification of research problems from professonal practice, and from organisational and institutional contexts. In these situations a traditional hypothesis-testing approach is not appropriate.

25.13 Criteria for Grounded Theory Research

Credibility

- Has your research achieved intimate familiarity with the setting or topic?
- Are data sufficient to merit your claims? Consider the range, number and depth of observations contained in the data.
- Have you made systematic comparisons between observations and between categories?
- Do the categories cover a wide range of empirical observations?
- Are there strong logical links between the gathered data and your argument and analysis?
- Has your research provided enough evidence for your claims to allow the reader to form an independent assessment—and agree with your claims?

Originality

- Are your categories fresh? Do they offer new insights?
- Does your analysis provide a new conceptual rendering of the data?
- What is the social and theoretical significance of this work?
- How does your grounded theory challenge, extend, or refine current ideas, concepts, and practices?

Resonance

- Do the categories portray the fullness of the studied experience?
- Have you revealed both liminal and unstable taken-for-granted meanings?
- Have you drawn links between larger collectivities or institutions and individual lives, when the data so indicate?
- Does your grounded theory make sense to your participants or people who share their circumstances? Does your analysis offer them deeper insights about their lives and world?

Usefulness

- Does your analysis offer interpretations that people can use in their everyday worlds?
- Do your analytic categories suggest any generic processes? If so, have you examined these generic processes for tacit implications?
- Can the analysis spark further research in other substantive areas?
- How does your work contribute to knowledge? How does it contribute to making a better world? (Charmaz 2006, pp. 182-183).

References

Annells, M. (1997a). Grounded theory method, Part I: Within the five moments of qualitative research. *Nursing Inquiry,* 4, 120-129.

Annells, M. (1997b). Grounded theory method, Part II: Options for users of the method. *Nursing Inquiry,* 4, 176–180.

Bowers, B., Charmaz, K., Clarke, A.(2009). *Developing grounded theory: The second generation.* Walnut Creek, CA: Left Coast Press.

Bryant, A., and Charmaz, K.(eds) (2007). *The Sage Handbook of Grounded Theory*. Thousand Oaks, CA: Sage.

Charmaz, K. (2006). *Constructing Grounded Theory.* Thousand Oaks, CA: Sage.

Corbin J., Strauss A. (2014). *Basics of qualitative research: Techniques and procedures for developing grounded theory.* Thousand Oaks, CA: Sage.

Feldman, N. (ed.) (2001). Strategies for Interpreting Qualitative Data. Thousand Oaks, CA: Sage.

Glaser, B. (1992). *Basics of Grounded Theory analysis:Emergence vs Forcing.* Mill Valley, CA: Sociology Press.

Glaser, B. G., and Holton, J. (2004). Remodeling grounded theory: Article 4. *Forum: Qualitative Social Re-search,* 5(2), 1-17.

Glaser, B., and Strauss, A.(1967). *The Discovery of Grounded Theory: Strategies for Qualitative Research.* Chicago: Aldine.

Holton J. (2009). Qualitative tussles in undertaking a grounded theory study. *The Grounded Theory Review,* 8, 37-50.

Jones, M., and Alony, I. (2011). Guiding the Use of Grounded Theory in Doctoral Studies – An Example from the Australian Film Industry. *International Journal of Doctoral Studies,* Volume 6, 2011.

Strauss, A., Corbin J. *(1990). Basics of qualitative research: Grounded theory procedures and techniques.* Newbury Park, CA: Sage.

Strauss, A., and Corbib, J. (1994). Grounded Theory Methodology: An overview. In N.K.Denzin and Y.S. Lincoln (eds) *Handbook of Qualitative Research.* Thousand Oaks, CA: Sage, pp. 273-85.

26

Ethnomethodology

26. What is Ethnomethodology?

Ethnomethodology means the study of the methods used by people. It is concerned with examining the methods and procedures employed by the members of the society to construct, account for and give meaning to the social world. With emphasis on members' views of social reality, ethnomethodology is generally regarded as phenomenological approach. Ethnomethodology is a developing prospective which contains a diversity of viewpoints. Garfinkel (1960), for the first time challenged traditional sociological approaches that relied on theoretical constructions to answer the question of how social order is produced. Zimmerman and Wielder state that the ethnomethodologist is concerned with how members of the society go about the task of 'seeing, describing, and explaining order in the world in which they live' and used them as evidence of an underlying pattern. The process is then reversed and particular instances of the underlying pattern are used as evidence for the existence of the pattern. For instance, Documentary Method is seen as reflection of the underlying pattern and vice versa (Garfinkel, 1967). According to Garfinkel (1967) 'Ethnomethodological Studies' analyse everyday activities as members' methods for making those same activities visible-rational-and reportable-for-all-practical-purposes. The reflexivity of that phenomenon is a singular feature of practical action, of practical circumstances, of common sense knowledge of structures, and of practical sociological reasoning.

Ethno-methodologists use careful description of naturally occurring interactions to investigate the interpretive and constitutive practices of members of society. Ethnomethodology is the study of ordinary action by ordinary members of society. The definition of "ordinary" is anything that is regularly and recurrently done by people with such automaticity that it is given very little thought. But this definition is still too simple; ethnomethodology's goal is more complex. Ethnomethodology studies these ordinary practices in order to discover how members of society create a sense of objective reality. That is, what do people do that creates the social facts we take for granted. However, ethnomethodology is the study of ordinary members of society in the everyday situations in which they find themselves and the ways in which they use commonsense knowledge, procedures, and considerations to gain an understanding of, navigate in, and act on those situations.

More precisely, ethnomethodology is the study of methods people use for understanding and producing the social order in which they live. Researchers in this field are often interested in the conventions of society, and the rules which people use to place themselves and others in social contexts. An ethnomethodologist might, for example, look at social cues which people use to determine social class and occupation when interacting with someone for the first time. People in this field are also concerned with general social knowledge and concepts which are widely understood both in larger societies and smaller subsets of society.

Ethnomethodological is a special kind of social inquiry. Members collectively create and maintain a sense of order and intelligibility in social life. This research method has focused more and more on the increasingly formal analysis of conversations. Since the 1980s the second main focus on the "studies of work" has been the analysis of work processes (Bergmann, 2004a; Garfinkel, 1986). Here, processes of work are studied in a broad sense and particularly in the context of scientific work in laboratories or, for example, how mathematicians construct proofs (Livingston, 1986). In general, the sociology of scientific knowledge has been developed from the tradition of ethnomethodology.

Researchers in this field are often interested in the conventions of society, and the rules which people use to place themselves and others in social contexts. An ethnomethodologist might, for example, look at social cues which people use to determine social class and occupation when interacting with someone for the first time. People in this field are also concerned with general social knowledge and concepts which are widely understood both in larger societies and smaller subsets of society. Moreover, it is an empirical research investigation of social interaction. Moreover, it is a continuing process of producing and securing meaningful social order. The elements of social order are present in the local scenes in which interactions take place.

Example-1: In Haryana, people used to gather and discuss social issues in Khap Panchayats. Social issue of 'honour killing' was discussed and confirmed through conversation and interaction. It took the shape of social order even though it has no legal sanction by the competent legal authority.

Example-2: In Kashmir valley on the issue of 'Independence', the youth used to throw stones on security forces. In conversation with them they revealed their ignorance about the meaning of 'Independence'. Throwing stones on security forces has become an activity done automatically by youths, which is bereft of little thought.

Furthermore, the researcher does not need to be concerned about the individual's attitudes, values, beliefs, or experiences in order to understand how order is created. The ordinary actions of society are immortal (a metaphor borrowed from Durkheim), meaning that they occur over and over again regardless of who plays the part of the actor in the scene. In this sense, actors are replaceable; the actors disappear, a new one would step in and produce the same behaviours in the same way.

Ethnomethodological programme seeks to provide a detailed, naturalistic account of competent practice within specific domains of socially organised action. It addresses what Garfinkel and his colleagues refer to as the "quiddity," the "just whatness," of work itself, or the work is said to be "self-explicating." That is: "The activities are reflexive, self-organising, organised entirely in situ, locally" (Livingston, 1987, p. 10)

Garfinkel termed the "formal analytic approach". The formal analytic approach views the populations who make up the scenes of life as the creators of those scenes. Therefore, traditional sociology looked at individuals as being representative of populations defined by socioeconomic status, gender, race, or other demographic variables. In order to determine the behaviour of the populations, researchers make hypotheses about the population's behaviour. Large data sets are studied in order to confirm or disconfirm the shared tendencies that individuals from a specific population exhibit. Examining an individual, or a small number of individuals alone, from this perspective, could not provide an account of social order, because order could only be witnessed when the behaviour of population are examined as a whole. The central goal of conversation analytic research is the description and explication of the competences that ordinary speakers use and rely on in participating in intelligible, socially organised interaction. At its most basic, this objective is one of describing the procedures by which conversationalists produce their own behaviour and understand and deal with the behaviour of others. These activities - producing conduct and understanding and dealing with it -are accomplished as the accountable products of common sets of procedures (Heritage and Atkinson, 1984).

Ethnomethodologists have increasingly contributed to our understanding of social life in institutional settings: legal processes (e. g. Atkinson and Drew, 1979; Lynch, 1982; Maynard, 1984; Pollner, 1974; 1975, 1987); pedagogic encounters (e.g. Cicourel *et al.,* 1974, McHoul, 1978b, Mehan, 1979); medical consultations (e.g. Fisher Todd, 1983; West, 1984; Heath, 1986); scientific work (e.g. Garfinkel *et al.,* 1981, Lynch, 1985; Livingston, 1986); political meetings and confrontations (e.g. J. M. Atkinson, 1984; Molotch and Boden, 1985; Heritage and Greatbatch, 1986). Ethnomethodology has contributed directly to our broader understanding of organisations, diagnoses and assessments, the social production of 'facts' and the construction of written and spoken accounts. They bear directly on the analysis of rationality, practical reasoning, the achievement of everyday reality and normal appearances, moral assessments and categorisations, and inter-subjectivity.

26.1 Basic Methods and Assumptions

Howard Garfinkel began with an assumption that social order exists at a local level in the shared practices that members must use to achieve mutual intelligibility. Garfinkel believes that members of society regularly produce accountable behaviours and practices. Accountable, from his perspective, means being observable and reportable to all who are present; that individuals have to produce accountable behaviours in order to be understood. The elements of social order are present in the local scenes in which interactions occurred. Therefore, one can study social order at the local level. Conversation analysis has helped to map out a distinctive and original field of inquiry. Three basic assumptions given by Heritage (1985, p. 1) are: (1) Interaction is structurally organised; (2) contributions of interaction are both context shaped and context renewing; and (3) thus two properties here in the details of interaction so that no order of detail in conversational interaction can be dismissed *a priori* as disorderly, accidental, or irrelevant.

26.1.1 An Empirical Method: Ethnomethodology is a thoroughly empirical enterprise devoted to the discovery of social order and intelligibility as witnessable collective achievements (Rawls, 1980). For ethnomethodology the topic of study is the social practices of real people in real settings, and the methods by which these people produce and maintain a shared sense of social order. Ethnomethodology treats practical activities, practical circumstances and practical sociological reasoning as topics of empirical studies.

26.1.2 Ethnomethodological indifference: That is the indifference, towards the dictates, prejudices, methods and practices of sociological analysis. It is specifically not to be conceived of as indifference to the problem of social order taken as a group [member's] concern.

26.1.3 Ethnomethodology informs and underlines the complexities of sociological analysis and description. It takes into account particularly the indexical and reflexive properties of the actors', taking place in any given local situation. Such an activity will also reveal the observer's inescapable reliance on the hermeneutic circle as the defining "methodology" of social understanding for both the lay persons and social scientists.

26.1.4 Facts and Social Order: Facts are treated as accomplishments, that is, they are seen as being produced in and through members' practical activities (Melvin Pullner, 1974). It is a method for revealing the common work that is performed by members of particular social groups in maintaining a clearly recognisable and shared social order. For example, driving the wrong way down a busy one-way street can reveal myriads of useful insights into the patterned social practices, and moral order, of the community of road users. The researcher should seek out members of society who, in their daily lives, are responsible for the maintenance of that aspect of the social order. Social orders are embodied in specific accounts, and employed in a particular social setting by the members of the particular group of individuals' party to that setting.

26.1.5 Accounts: Accounts are the ways members signify, describe or explain the properties of a specific social situation. These are consisting of both verbal and non-verbal objectifications and always both indexical to the situation in which they occur and, simultaneously reflexive.

- Focus is on procedural aspects of members' situated practices.
- Account, accountability, reflexity, idexical expression are read within the ethno framework.
- Overt activities or what is 'scenic to participants and their intelligibility and organisation are observed.
- For understanding of social order in its local setting, norms and rules of members are observed or studied.

26.1.6 Documentary method of interpretation: Garfinkel states that the documentary method of interpretation consists of treating an actual appearance as the "document of", "as pointing to", as "standing on behalf of", a presupposed underlying pattern. These "documents" serve to constitute the underlying pattern, but are themselves interpreted on the basis of what is already known about that underlying pattern.

26.1.7 Text and Realities: Texts serve three purposes namely, generating essential data; making interpretations, and presenting and communicating findings. Focus is for objective hermeneutics and textualisation.

26.2 Design of Ethnomethodology

Focus is on the empirical study of mundane practices, through which, interactive order is produced in and outside of institutions. Table 26.1 shows the design of ethnomethodology.

Table 26.1: Design of Ethnomethodology

Methodology	*Description of Making of Social Situation*
Theoretical Position	Ethnomethodology- Constructivism
Methods of Data Collection	Focus Groups Ethnography Participant Observation Recording Interaction Collecting Documents
Methods of Interpretation	Conversation Analysis Discourse Analysis Genre Analysis Analysis of Documents
Fields of Application	Analysis of Life Worlds and Organisations Evaluation Cultural Studies

26.2.1 Theoretical Base: Constructivism

- In the tradition of Piaget, cognition, perception of the world, and knowledge about it are seen as constructs. Radical constructivism (Glasserfeld, 1995) takes this thought to point where every form of cognition-because of the neurobiological processes involved—has direct access only to images of the world and of reality, but not of both.
- Social constructivism in the tradition of Schutz (1962), Berger and Luckmann (1966), and Gergen (1985, 1999) are the social conventions, perception, and knowledge in everyday life.
- The present-day "laboratory-constructivist" (Knorr-Cetina, 1981), seeks to establish how social, historical, local, pragmatic, and other factors influence scientific discovery in such a way that scientific facts may be regarded as social constructs ("local products").

Conversation Analysis; Discourse Analysis; Genre Analysis, and Analysis of Documents are methods of interpretation. A detail of each method is given below.

26.2.2 Conversation Analysis

Conversation analysis focuses more and more on the formal analysis of conversations. It is an empirical research investigation of social interaction. Moreover, it is a continuing process of producing and securing meaningful social order. The elements of social order are present in the local scenes in which interactions take place. Conversation analysis has helped to map out a distinctive and original field of inquiry. Major elements are:

- Conversation Analysis proceeds on the basis of all forms of linguistic and non-linguistic, direct and indirect communication.
- It is based on participatory research approach where actors are inspired, informed and involved. Actors are occupied with the business of analysing the situation and context of their actions, interpreting their utterances of their interlocutors, producing situational appropriateness, intelligibility and effectiveness in their own utterances and coordinating their own dealings with the dealings of others.
- The methodological starting point is to analyse the interpretive repertoires that the participants of certain discourses use to produce a specific version of reality.

Assumptions: First, conversation analysis assumes that interaction proceeds in an orderly way and nothing in it should be random. Second, the context of interaction not only influences the interaction but also is produced and reproduced in it. Third, the decision about what is relevant in social interaction\ and thus for the interpretation can only be made through interpretation and not by *ex-ante* settings. Three basic assumptions given by Heritage (1985, p.1) are: (1) Interaction is structurally organised; (2) contributions of interaction are both context shaped and context renewing; and (3) thus two properties are in the details of interaction so that no order of detail in conversational interaction can be dismissed *a priori* as disorderly, accidental, or irrelevant.

Blumer (1969, p. 2) summarises symbolic interactionism as "three simple premises": The first premise is that human beings act toward things on the basis of the meanings that the things have for them .... The second premise is that the meaning of such things is derived from, or arises out of, the social interaction that one has with one's fellows. The third premise is that these meanings are handled in, and modified through, an interpretative process used by the person in dealing with the things he encounters.

Method involves the richest possible documentation with audio-visual recording and subsequent transcription of real and authentic events. The aim of the study is to see how finely the details of actual, naturally occurring conversation can be subjected to analysis. The idea is to take singular sequences of conversation and tear them apart in such a way as to find rules, techniques, procedures, methods, maxims (a collection of terms that more or less relate to each other) that can be used to generate the orderly features in the conversations. The point is, then, to come back to the singular things we observe in a singular sequence, with some rules that handle those singular features, and also, necessarily, handle lots of other events (Sacks, 1984 b).

Strategies: The following strategies need to be employed in the conduct of conversation analysis:

- The first strategy is the close study of sense-making activities in situations where they are especially prominent (Garfinkel, 1967: 116-85).
- Where one is instructed by a setting's members to see the world in a way that is natural for them but not for oneself. Mehan and Wood (1975) use the expression 'becoming the phenomenon, while Schwartz and Jacobs (1979) recommend strategies of becoming the 'Stranger' or the 'Novice'.
- Third strategy consists of closely observing situated activities in their natural settings and discussing them with the seasoned practitioners, in order to study the competences involved in the routine performance of these activities.
- Fourth strategy involves the study of ordinary practices by first mechanically recording some of their 'products', by the use of audio or video equipment. These recordings are then transcribed in a way that limits the use of common sense procedures to hearing what is being said and noting how it has been said.

The general idea laying behind the use of these strategies is thus to evade as far as possible the unthinking and unnoticed use of common sense that seems to be inherent in empirical research practices in sociology. The episodes to be analysed can be selected from the transcripts on the grounds of a variety of considerations. The researcher, then, tries to make sense of the episode, using mainly his common sense. In a next step, the researcher tries to explicate the interpretation, previously produced on common sense grounds. Reasoning is constructed that arguably leads to the typifications given, specifying its empirical grounds, i.e. the details of the episode under consideration and its analytic resources, the common sense knowledge used. In other words, it is an enterprise of analysing interpretation in interaction.

Conversation Analytic Methodology: Analysing data Conversation analytic methodology is strongly data driven. There are two kinds of studies. In a single case analysis, the researcher develops an analysis of the interaction in a single episode with respect to some interesting or relevant aspect. In multi-cases, the analyst generalises the results of a cumulative series of single case analyses with respect to a specific aspect. All cases are compared with respect to some feature by describing how, and the degrees to which they are the same, similar, or different. Collection studies have two phases (Heritage, 1995). In the first phase, the analyst describes regularities with respect to some particular aspect of the data and develops a description of a candidate pattern by going from case to case in a corpus of transcripts. In a second phase, the analyst attempts to meet the requirement of convergence between the participants' and the analyst's perspective.

Quantification may play a role in determining the distribution of the observed pattern. Quantitative processing of the data, however, is subsidiary to qualitative exploration of the phenomenon in phase 1 and to qualitative validation of the candidate description in phase 2. Distributions that confirm a hypothesis primarily establish regularities.

26.2.3 Discourse Analysis

Discourse analysis is an important qualitative research approach across social science disciplines for analysing (and challenging) how reality in a variety of organisational and institutional arenas is constructed. Discourse Analysis in a general term refers to analysing written, spoken, signed language use or any significant semiotic event. Although conversation analysis is named as a starting point, the empirical focus is more on the "content of talk, its subject matter and with its social rather than linguistic organisation" (Sacks, 1992, p. 28). This allows the analysis of psychological phenomena like memory and cognition as social, and above all, discursive phenomena. A special emphasis is on the construction of versions of the events in reports and presentations. The "interpretative repertoires", which are used in such constructions, are analysed.

In discourse analysis, writing, talk, conversation, communicative event, etc.—are variously defined in terms of coherent sequences of sentences, propositions, speech acts or turns-at-talk. Discourse analysts not only study language use 'beyond the sentence boundary', but also prefer to analyse 'naturally occurring' language use, and not invented examples. Aim of discourse analysis is to reveal socio-psychological characteristics of a person/persons rather than text structure.

Discourse as text refers to the analysis of language use that is confined to the surface level properties of discourse. These include formal, as well as functional aspects of discourse that is phonological, lexico-grammatical, semantic, and organisational. Moreover, these include inter sentential cohesion, and other aspects of text structure such as 'given' and 'new', 'theme' and 'rhyme', or information structures, such as 'general-particular', problem solution, etc., not necessarily having interaction with context in a broad sense. Similarly, the emphasis at this level of analysis is essentially on the properties associated with the construction of the textual product, rather than on the interpretation or use of such a product.

Discourse as genre, in contrast, extends the analysis beyond the textual output to incorporate context in a broader sense to account for not only the way text is constructed, but also for the way it is likely to be interpreted, used and exploited in specific contexts, whether social, institutional, or more narrowly professional, to achieve specific goals. The nature of questions addressed in this kind of analysis may often include not only linguistic, but also socio-cognitive and ethnographic aspects. This kind of grounded analysis of the textual output provides framework for genre-based theory.

Discourse as social practice moves in the direction of social context, where the focus shifts significantly from the textual output to the features of context, such as the changing identities of the participants, the social structures or professional relationships the genres are likely to maintain or change, the benefits or disadvantages such genres are likely to bring to a particular set of readers. These interacting views of discourse are not mutually exclusive, but essentially complementary to each other. It is possible to use the proposed framework in a number of ways, depending upon the objective one may need or decide to pursue. A typical socio-linguist interested in discourse analysis will perhaps begin from the top end, looking deeply and exhaustively into the social context, working his way downward, but rarely getting seriously into the textual space. An applied linguist, on the other hand, would find it more profitable to begin at the bottom end, exploring the textual space exhaustively, working toward social space, often using social context as explanation for the analysis of textualisation of lexico-grammatical and discoursal resources. However, most users of the framework whether interested in socio-cultural issues, or pedagogical ones, at some stage or the other will necessarily pay some attention to the socio-cognitive aspects of genre construction, interpretation, use or exploitation of generic resources.

Procedures: Discourse analytic procedures refer not only to everyday conversations, but also to other sorts of data such as interviews (e.g., in Potter and Wetherell, 1998 on the topic of racism) or media reports (in Potter and Wetherell, 1998 about the construction of versions in the coverage of the Gulf War).

Methodology: First step describes using naturally occurring text and talk. Second is careful reading of the transcripts. Third is coding the material, then analysing it. The analysis focuses on context, variability, and constructions in the text and finally on the interpretative repertoires used in the texts. According to Potter and Wetherell (1987, p. 167), guiding questions are: Why am I reading this passage in this way? What features of the text produce this reading? The analysis focuses on context, variability, and constructions in the text and finally on the interpretative repertoires used in the texts.

Parker (2004) has developed a model of critical discourse analysis, built on the background developed by Michel Foucault (1980) which is why this is also referred to as "Foucauldian Discourse Analysis" (Willig, 2003). Here issues of critique, of ideology, and of power are more in focus than in other versions of discourse analysis. Parker suggests a number of steps in the research process:

- First, the text to be analysed into written form, if it is not already.
- The next step includes free association to varieties of meaning as a way of accessing cultural networks, and these should be noted down.
- The researchers should systematically itemise the objects, usually marked by nouns, in the text or selected portion of text.

- Maintain a distance from the text by treating the text itself as the object of the study rather than what it seems to "refer" to.
- Systematically itemise the "subjects"-characters, persona, and role positions—specified in the text.
- Reconstruct presupposed rights and responsibilities of "subjects" specified in the text.
- Finally, map the networks of relationships into patterns. These patterns in language axe "discourses, " and can then be located in relations of ideology, power, and institutions, (Parker, 2004, p. 310)

Applications

- Discourse analysis has been taken up in a variety of social science disciplines, including linguistics, sociology, anthropology, social work, cognitive psychology, social psychology, international relations, human geography, communication studies and translation studies, each of which is subject to its own assumptions, dimensions of analysis, and methodologies.
- The contribution of the postmodern Discourse Analysis is the application of critical thought to social situations and the unveiling of hidden (or not so hidden) politics within the socially dominant as well as all other discourses (interpretations of the world, belief systems, etc.).
- Discourse Analysis can be applied to any text, that is, to any problem or situation. Since Discourse Analysis is basically an interpretative and deconstructing reading, there are no specific guidelines to follow. One could, however, make use of the theories of Jacques Derrida, Michel Foucault, Julia Kristeva, or Fredric Jameson, as well as of other critical and postmodern thinkers.
- Again, the purpose of Discourse Analysis is not to provide definite answers, but to expand our personal horizons and make us realise our own shortcomings and unacknowledged agendas/ motivations - as well as that of others. In short, critical analysis reveals what is going on behind our backs and those of others and which determines our actions.

- Discourse Analysis applied to the theory of Library Science, would not argue for or against the validity and "truth" of a certain research method (qualitative or quantitative), statement, or value (i.e. the Library Bill of Rights, or policies concerning free speech). Rather, discourse analysis would focus on the existence and message of these texts and locate them within a historical and social context.
- Discourse Analysis aims at revealing the motivation and politics involved in the arguing for or against a specific research method, statement, or value. The concrete result will be the awareness to the qualities and shortcomings of each and the inception of an informed debate. Though this debate will never be settled, it allows for the correction of bias and the inclusion of minorities within the debate and analysed discourse.

Types or theories of Discourse Analysis are:

1. Jacques Derrida's "Deconstruction" is one;
2. Michel Foucault's Genealogy and social criticism and analysis of the uses of discourse to exercise power (such as his analysis of how "Knowledge" is created in our societies and with what purpose or its effect);
3. Fredric Jameson's Marxist analysis of Postmodernism itself would provide another interesting reading on the dominant discourse of our time;
4. Julia Kristeva's 'Feminist interpretations of current social practices.

Issues of Reliability and Validity

A framework developed by Gee (2005, 2011) enables systematic analyses of core discourse building blocks. First, analysis of significance building examines how meanings and significances of certain things, occurrences, institutions, objects, and problems—including their (un)importance or (ir)relevance—are (re)produced, transformed, and/or integrated through discourse. Second, analysis of activity building focuses on how discourses build certain kinds of activities that are being recognised in a social environment, involving main activities and sub-activities composing them. Third, analysis of identity building captures how situated meanings of identities in a discourse are accomplished, including what types of identities are relevant, taken for granted, or under construction. Fourth, analysis of relationship building focuses on how a discourse builds, sustains, takes for granted, transforms, and/or deteriorates the relevance and/or importance of relationships among individuals, groups, institutions, discourses; and/or texts. Fifth, analysis of political building involves analysing how sources of individuals', groups', or institutions' power, status, legitimacy, and worth are built or destroyed, for example, by sustaining (or undermining) connections to entities or concepts that are considered to be normal, important, and/or respected. Sixth, analysis of connection building explores how aspects of reality, such as individuals, themes, institutions, texts, past, present, future, and also discourses are portrayed as connected and relevant (or disconnected and irrelevant) to each other, as well as what connections are taken for granted, transformed, and/or missing. Seventh, analysis of building sign systems and knowledge focuses on how a discourse operates, values, or disvalues certain sign systems (e.g., different forms of written or spoken language) and forms of knowing, thereby making relevant and privileging (or making irrelevant and dis-privileging) certain types of knowledge, or how it uses intertextuality to allude to other forms of knowledge. Discourse or Critical Analysis always remains a matter of interpretation.

As there is no hard data provided through discourse analysis, the reliability and the validity of one's research/findings depends on the force and logic of one's arguments. Even the best constructed arguments are subject to their own deconstructive reading and counter-interpretations. The validity of critical analysis is, therefore, dependent on the quality of the rhetoric. Despite this fact, well-founded arguments remain authoritative over time and have concrete applications.

26.2.4 Genre Analysis

Genre is a term for grouping texts together, representing how writers typically use language to respond to recurring situations (Hyland, 2004). A genre comprises of a set of communicative events, the members of which share some set of communicative purposes (Swales, 1990). For example, a genre exhibits various patterns of similarities in terms of structure, style, content and intended audience. In social science, genre is a social action and a speech event that has communicative goal shared by the members of a particular discourse community. Genre in literary studies for instance includes film, anthropology, folklore and music.

Discourse Community has a broadly agreed set of communicative mechanism for intercommunication. It is participatory. Discourse community provides information and feedback to develop discourse expectations (Swales, 1990). Analysis of discourse as genre often incorporates the use of a range of research methods, some of which are of relatively recent origin in the context of discourse and genre studies. Within each method, the analyst also has a number of rather different frameworks to choose from. Some of the more prominent ones are:

Intuitive description of context: A quick reading of a text makes it possible to make a preliminary analysis of the genre. This is done on the basis of personal experience, world knowledge, knowledge about the field and conventions in the field, and knowledge about language use in specific texts.

Reading relevant literature: In order to support the analysis, it is essential to read various literatures about the genre in question. The researcher needs to go through professionals' experiences and discussions of genre theory. It is also necessary to understand the methods to be used in the analysis of text and image.

Determination of context: An analysis and determination of context includes sender-receiver relationship, situational and intercultural aspects such as national and organisational culture, media, channel, time, place and ideology/orientation.

Corpus studies: The computational analysis of language often enables to reveal patterns. Make its use in particular genres and areas of language that are unsuspected by the researcher and difficult to perceive in other ways. It is necessary to determine criteria for the definition of genre and sub-genres of the text in question. This is done on the basis of context, communicative purpose(s) and distinctive textual characteristics.

Textual analysis: Linguistic descriptions of texts, especially the analysis of lexico-grammatical systems in register analysis, text-linguistics and much of discourse analysis based on systemic functional framework has been extremely influential in the studies of textualisation of a range of professional and institutionalised genres, including those used at school level.

Critical and ethnographic analysis: Interviews and case studies have become increasingly important means of collecting data in academic and educational contexts, particularly for the investigation of developmental aspects of learner language, learning style preferences and writing practices of expert writers, especially in studying some of the following issues. How do members of a particular discourse community see their discipline and its forms of communication? How do they communicate these to novices? How do their understandings influence their own writing practices? All these and other similar questions are little researched and understood as part of academic and professional communication. Swales (1998) work on textography is an excellent example of thick descriptions of texts situated in disciplinary contexts and their typical physical environments.

Genre analysis has always been a multi-disciplinary activity attracting attention not only from linguists (both applied and computational), discourse analysts, communication experts and rhetoricians, but also from sociologists, cognitive scientists, translators, and advertisers. In recent years, it has become multi-faceted too, often prompting varied perspectives on analysing genre

Genre Studies: These incorporate a variety of frameworks used to analyse a range of textual genres constructed, interpreted and used by members of various disciplinary communities in academic, professional, workplace and other institutionalised contexts. Genre studies range from a close linguistic study of texts as product, investigation into a dynamic complexity of communicative practices of professional and workplace communities to a broad understanding of socio-cultural and critical procedures used to interpret these textual genres in real life settings. Understanding the nature of discursive practices of various disciplinary cultures which often give shape to these communicative processes and textual genres is yet another aspect of genre-based investigations. Awareness and understanding of genre knowledge is yet another crucial factor in the understanding of genre-based analysis, which may be understood as situated cognition related to the discursive practices of members of disciplinary cultures. The co-operation and collaboration of such specialists provide an important corrective to purely text based approaches. The analysis of data focuses first on the internal structure of communicative genre including; prosody, language variety, linguistic register, stylistic and rhetorical figures, 'small' and 'minimal' motifs, topoi, and structural markers (Knoblaunch and Luckmann, 2004, p. 305). Finally the external structure of communicative genres and the communicative economy of their use are analysed.

Methodology: Swales (1990) developed CARS (Creating a Research Space) model for genre analysis. Main steps of the CARS Model are given below:

Move-1: Claiming centrality, or Making topic generalisations and Review of items of previous research.

Move-2: Establishing a niche-counter claiming, Indicating a gap. Question raising, and Continuing a tradition.

Move-3: Occupying the niche-outlining purposes, Announcing present research, and Announcing principle findings.

Implications

- Genre Analysis adds to our understanding of how language is used within an important discourse community;
- It provides a model of applied linguistic in its best sense;
- It draws of linguistic and sociolinguistic theory to classify the nature of language use and learning in educational setting
- Genre analysis has always been a multi-disciplinary activity attracting attention not only from linguists (both applied and computational), discourse analysts, communication experts and rhetoricians, but also from sociologists, cognitive scientists, translators, and advertisers. In recent years, it has become multi-faceted too, often prompting varied perspectives on analysing genre.

References

Atkinson, J.M., J. Heritage, eds. (1984). Structures of Social Action: Studies in Conversation Analysis. Cambridge: Cambridge University Press.

Bhatia, V. K., (1998a). "Discourse of Philanthropic Fund-raising", in Working Papers, IU Center for Philanthropy, University of Indiana, Indianapolis.

Bhatia, V. K., (1999a). "Integrating products, processes, purposes and participants in professional writing.

Blommaert, J. (2005). Discourse. Cambridge: Cambridge University Press.

Carter, R. (1997). Investigating English Discourse. London: Routledge.

Christi and Martin (eds) (1997). Genre and Institutions, Social Processes in the Workplace and School. London and Washington: Cassell.

Frandsen, Johansen and Nielsen (1997). International Markedskommunikation I en postmoderne verden. Viborg: Systime.

Garfinkel, H. (1967). *Studies in ethnomethodology.* Englewood Cliffs, N.J.: Prentice-Hall.

Garfinkel, H., M. Lynch, E. Livingston (1981). 'The work of a discovering science construed with materials from the optically discovered pulsar', Philosophy of the Social Sciences. 11: 131-58.

Garfinkel, H., H. Sacks (1970). 'On formal structures of practical action'. In: J.C. McKinney and E.A. Tiryakian, eds. *Theoretical sociology: perspectives and developments.* New York: Appleton-Century-Crofts: 338-66.

Gee, J.P., Michaels, S. and O' Connor, M.C. (1992). 'Discourse analysis', in M.D. LeCompte, W.L. Millroy and J. Preissle (eds), The Handbook of Qualitative Research in Education. San Diego, CA: Academic Press. pp. 227-91.

Have P ten (1999). *Doing conversation analysis*. London: Sage.

Heritage, J. (1989). 'Current developments in conversation analysis'. In: Roger and Bull, eds.: 21-47.

Heritage, J (1995). 'Conversation analysis: methodological aspects.' In Quasthof U (ed.) \Berlin/New York: Walter de Gruyter. 391-418.

Hyland, K.(2004). *Genre and second language writing*. Ann Arbor, MI: University of Michigan Press.

Posteguillo, J.F. Coll (eds.). Genre Studies in English for Academic Purposes, Bancaixa, Fundacio Caixa Castello (15-28).

Sacks, H (1992). Lectures on conversation. Jefferson G (ed.), Introduction by Schegloff E. Oxford/Cambridge, MA: Blackwell.Schiffrin, D., Deborah Tannen, and Hamilton, H. E. (eds.). (2001). *Handbook of Discourse Analysis*. Oxford: Blackwell.

Swales, J.(1990). *Genre Analysis: English in Academic and Research Settings.* Cambridge: Cambridge UP.

27

Case Study Method

27. Case Study

Case Study is usually used by social scientists (social interaction and the social construction of meaning). In education, it may be a 'case of innovative practice', or a 'case of curriculum development' for a child with learning disability, or a 'case of depressed child', a 'case of low performance in mathematics', or a 'case of effective teacher' or a 'case of an effective institution'. In other disciplines such as, medical science, criminology, psychology, emphasis is on studying the 'the case'. What is common across all disciplines is in-depth study of case. A case study derives much of its rationale and methods from ethnography and its constituent theoretical discourses-symbolic interactionism, phenomenology and ethnomethodology (Atkinson *et. al.,* 2001). Case study is contextual analysis of a limited number of events or conditions and their relationships. Focus is on understanding the case rather than generalising to a population at large. Case study thus is particular, descriptive, inductive, and ultimately heuristic- it seeks to 'illuminate' the reader understanding of an issue. (Parlett and Hamilton, 1972).

Case study is a research design rather than an approach to the collection or analysis of data, and case studies involve utilisation of a wide array of different data sources and a number of different analytic strategies. Second, the case study examines units of analysis that are not drawn from well-demarcated population. Finally author must, therefore, be prepared to defend his /her methods against the slings and arrows of their critics.

27.1 Cardinal Principles of Case Studies

Three cardinal principles of the field research in context of a case study are:

- Every research question- regardless of field or discipline- is uniquely defined by a specific set of circumstances.
- There can be no attempt to answer a question without deep knowledge of the specific contextual parameters defining those circumstances.
- Such deep knowledge comes only to those who have paid their dues.

When is a case study an appropriate method of research? In this context number of situations exist:

- When it promises to yield fundamental insight into a rare but important process or event that offers no obvious point of comparison (March, Sproul and Tamuz, 1991; Adams, Clemens and Orloff, 2005).
- When it addresses an ambiguous, obscure, or otherwise inhospitable population that is difficult to reach through traditional methods (Geis, 1991).
- When it explores a crucial, deviant, or negative case that will shed light on an established theory (Emigh, 1997).
- When a case study approach is used in conjunction with a large-n statistical study to flesh out underlying causal mechanism (Kurtz and Barnes, 2002).
- When it is combined with a small-n comparative approach to asses necessary causal conditions or conditional theoretical statements (Paige, 1999).
- When it can be evaluated against an established body of theory that offers multiple observable implications (Campbell, 1975).
- When adequate body of theory exists, and the relevant hypothesis or control group is therefore unclear (Walton, 1992).

27.2 Identification of 'a case' for Study

Sometimes we experience that a particular institution is not performing to the expected level, or an individual performance in is very low in the organisation, or there is high level of attrition among teachers, or in other words, a particular institute has edge over other institutes in the similar area or a particular teacher gives good learning results as compared to others. Each case requires in-depth study to find tangible solution of problem. In order to identify a case study, it is essential to go through the plethora of literature specific to the case under investigation. This will enable the researcher aware about the existing problem that needs solving or you may come across new interesting idea.

A case study is an empirical enquiry that is conducted within a localised boundary of space and time (i.e. a singularity). All essential variables specific to a case are examined in natural setting observing ethical norms or codes. Objective is to inform the judgments and decisions of practitioners or policymakers, or of theoreticians who are working to these ends. Substantial evidence or data is gathered to enable researcher to explore *significant* features of the case; create *plausible* interpretations of what is found; test for the *trustworthiness* of these interpretations; construct a *worthwhile* argument or story; relate the argument or story to any relevant research in the literature; convey *convincingly* to audience this argument or story; and provide an audit trail by which other researchers may validate or challenge the findings, or construct alternative arguments. Inevitably the terms 'interesting', 'significant', 'plausible', 'worthwhile' and 'convincingly' entail value judgements being made by the researcher.

At least three types of case studies can be conceived:

- *Theory-seeking and theory-testing case studies*: particular studies of general issues - aiming to lead to fuzzy propositions (more tentative) or fuzzy generalisations (less tentative) and conveying these, their context and the evidence leading to them to interested audiences.
- *Storytelling and picture-drawing case studies:* narrative stories and descriptive accounts of social and educational events, projects, programmes, institutions or systems, which deserve to be told to interested audiences, after careful analysis.

- *Evaluative case studies:* enquiries into educational and social systems, projects or events to determine their worthwhileness, as judged by analysis by researchers, and to convey this to interested audiences.

27.3 Selection of the Cases

- Cases should be selected in the same way as the topic of an experiment is selected.
- Developed preliminary theory is used as a template with which to compare the characteristics and empirical findings from the case(s).
- Selected cases should reflect characteristics and problems identified in the underlying theoretical propositions / conceptual framework.

27.4 Research Design

Queries need to be satisfied while designing research study are: statement of the case; what are the boundaries of the case under study?; time framework- how much time can be spent in each field work; what methods of investigation to be employed?; the logic of case study approach-depth verses coverage; whether exploratory or explanatory or descriptive, and holistic i.e., single unit of analysis or embedded i.e., multiple units of analysis.

There are some generic demands that must respond to, namely:

- **Transparency:** The logic by which theory, evidence, and methods are connected must be explicit.
- **Causal logic**: It explains variations in the attributes of different units of analysis. This approach is frequently grounded in, and draws strength from positivism.
- **Phenomenological logic:** It assumes that social reality is constructed by and through symbolic and cultural interpretations. It is customarily associated with field observations of real-life situations, participant observations, and ethnographic and the interpretation of key texts. Lubeck and Alford note that the open-ended, negotiated, self-conscious character of social interaction means that causation is not linear, relation are contingent and subject to continual change.

- **Historical-Dialectical logic:** It assumes that all relationships and processes are interdependent and change over time in relation to one another. The essential concepts is totality, conjunctures, and chronology.
- **Clarity:** Refers to internal logic or architecture of the study. The clarity question can be tested by asking two or three people to read proposal and explain to you, in a few sentences, or the central problem and central claim.
- **Methodology precision:** Asserts the importance of focusing on the 'how' question. How large must the sample be? How will the sample be selected? How can one assume the reliability and validity of the data? How exactly can evidence be collected?, etc.
- **Theory driven expectations** are perhaps counterintuitive and somewhat controversial. But theoretical tradition provides something more than a context for the research during review of literature.
- **Doability:** Highlights practical considerations and collects substantial evidence for the policy implications.
- **Research Design:** Considers overview of the study project (objectives, issues, readings, literature and research); Field procedures (access to field sites, sources of information); case study questions posed to Investigators; key classifications; suggestions for likely sources of evidence (not the literal questions to be asked), and a guide for the case study report.
- **Methods:** The most commonly employed methods are: (a) interviews-structured or semi-structured (b) documentary analysis-video or audio and (c) observation-participant or non-participant.

27.5 Conducting a Case Study

27.5.1 The investigator: Good knowledge of the phenomenon, sensitivity for novel and unexpected issues in data collection; knack of asking good questions; a good "listener", and addictiveness and flexibility are basic skills that have to be developed by the investigator.

27.6 Collecting the evidence: Six sources of evidence namely (i) Documents (letters, agendas, progress reports); (ii) Archival records (Service records, organisational charts, budgets etc.); (iii) Interviews (typically open-ended, but also focused, structured and surveys are possible); (iv) Direct observations (formal or casual; useful to have multiple observers); (v) Participant observation (assuming a role in the situation and getting an inside view of the events), and (vi) Physical artifacts, are to be used.

27.7 Analysing the Evidence: Analysis of evidence is one of the most significant aspects of doing case studies. Most important is to have a general analytic strategy, which helps to choose among different techniques. Preliminary techniques – matrixes, tabulation of frequencies, temporal schemes etc. can be tried out to get the analysis started. Analytic memo are used to draw interpretations. Relationships among variables are analysed. Sometimes theoretical orientation guides the analysis. In descriptive case studies, a descriptive framework for organising the case study is developed. Analysis is done on the basis of the general characteristics and relations of the phenomenon in question. In explanation building, a set of causal links is identified on the basis of result of series of iterations.

27.8 Characteristics of Good Case Study

Building blocks of case study are (i) historical in-depth analysis of a case, (ii) intervention/s, (iii) impact analysis. Methodology should take into account (i) control procedures in absence of process of randomisation of selection of sample, (ii) comparison, (iii) natural setting and (iv) ethical code for researcher. Prolonged engagement with data sources, persistent observation of emerging issues, internal and external validity and reliability of raw data, triangulation, testing story against the analytical statements, effective countering the challenges of findings, and audit trail have to be observed and defended with substantial evidence. An outcome of the research must be that it says something significant to someone (teacher, manager, policy-maker, parent, learner, etc.), thereby informing her or his work and potentially helping to improve it.

Case records regarding the agreed interview transcripts or reports and observation reports, the final versions of analytical statements, the interpretative writings, the final draft of conceptual background statements, the day-by-day journal of the research, etc. This compilation of working records, edited to be suitable for public access, shows in detail how the researcher has collected data, analysed it, interpreted it, tested findings and so on. The case report which in principle should be subject to peer scrutiny by academic referees to vouch for its trustworthiness and probity.

27.9 Limitations

- The weakness of case study is that it is not possible to generalise statistically from one or small number of cases to the population as a whole, even though good case studies appeal to the capacity of the reader for 'naturalistic generalisation'. (Stake, 1994).
- A case may not be statistically representative of the population as a whole.
- Drawing boundaries of a case is not straightforward and involves crucial decisions i.e. what to include and what to exclude and, thus, what is the claim to knowledge that is being made.
- Case studies lack scientific vigour and reliability in case of social science.
- Case study is sometime coloured or influenced by subjectivity of the researcher.

Further Reading

Bassey, M. (1981). *Case Study in Educational Settings*. Buckin gum: Open University Press.

Bennett, Andrew. (2001). "Case Study: Methods and Analysis." pp. 1513-1519. in *International Encyclopedia of the Social and Behavioural Sciences,* edited by Neil J. Smelser and Paul Baltes. Amsterdam, The Nneitherlands: Elsevier.

Murphy, R. and B Torrance, H.(eds) [1987]. *Evaluating Education: Issues and Methods.* London: Paul Chapman Publishing.

Ragin, C. and Becker, H.(eds) [1992]. *What is a Case?* Cambridge: Cambridge University Press.

Reynolds, J. (1981). *Case Method in Education: A Qualitative Guide for Effective use.* International Labour Office, Geneva.

Stake, R. (1995). *The Art of Case study Research.* Thousand Oaks, CA: Sage.

Stenhouse, L. (1984). The conduct, analysis and refooting or case study in educational research and evaluation; In R. Murphy and H. Torrance (eds) *Evaluating Education: issues & methods.* London: Paul Chapman Publishing, pp. 74-80.

Walker, R. (1974). The Conduct of Educational Case studies : Ethics, Theory and Procedures, Buckingham: Open University Press.

Yin, R.K. (1994). *Case Study Method- Design and Research.* New Delhi: Sage.

28

Sociometric Techniques

28 Sociometry

The word *sociometry* comes from the Latin "socius, " meaning social and the Latin "metrum, " meaning measure. As these roots imply, sociometry is a way of measuring the degree of relatedness among people. Measurement of relatedness can be useful not only in the assessment of behaviour within groups, but also for interventions to bring about positive change and for determining the extent of change. For a work group, sociometry can be a powerful tool for reducing conflict and improving communication because it allows the group to see itself objectively and to analyse its own dynamics. It is also a powerful tool for assessing dynamics and development in groups devoted to therapy or training.

A useful working definition of sociometry is that it is a methodology for tracking the energy vectors of interpersonal relationships in a group. It shows the patterns of how individuals associate with each other when acting as a group toward a specified end or goal (Criswell in Moreno, 1960, p. 140). Moreno himself defined sociometry as "the mathematical study of psychological properties of populations, the experimental technique of and the results obtained by application of quantitative methods" (Moreno, 1953, pp. 15-16).

In order to study group conflict and interpersonal relations, Bogardus (1928) and Moreno (1934), developed quantifying measuring techniques, which were later to be called 'sociometrics'. Sociometry is a technique used for measuring the social relationships that exist among the members of a group. It is a study to measure social choices that people make. Subjects can also be asked to rank others members of the group using sociometric technique. Members of a group or organisation can be asked to rate each other using one or more criteria. It is also used to identify communication and interaction patterns of individuals in groups. It has also been called a means of studying the attracting and repulsions of members of groups. In brief, sociometry is quantitative study of social relationships and interactions, social attitudes, and social preferences.

According to Helen Jennings (1952), sociometry may be described as a means of presenting simply and graphically the entire structure of relations existing at a given time among members of a given group. The major lines of communication, or the patterns of attraction and rejection in its full scope, are made readily comprehensive at a glance.

For example, a person is asked to choose one or more other persons according to one or more criteria supplied by researcher. With whom would you like to work? With whom would you like to play? He then makes one, two, three or more choices among members of his own group or of other groups. This method works well for kindergartners as well as for atomic scientists. Such techniques are used in various educational situation to study social adjustment, group dynamics, learning, motivation, discipline, leadership behaviour, social interaction and development, and index of popularity.

Sociometric techniques have been used in the studies of mainstreaming of differently-abled children and their integration in regular classroom; social, economic, and cultural discriminations among students; peer relations- issues in assessment and interventions; classroom climate and its effects on academic achievement; children as being 'socially at risk'; interaction pattern of sub group, cliques and specific friendship and group conflicts; study of academic culture in higher education; identification of level of friendship, and anxiety; and evaluation of teachers on sociometric scale.

28.1 Some Principles of Criterion Selection

- The criterion should be as simply stated and as straightforward as possible.

- The respondents should have some actual experience in reference to the criterion, whether *ex post facto* or present (in Moreno's language, they are still "warmed up" to them) otherwise the questions will not arouse any significant response.
- The criterion should be specific rather than general or vague. Vaguely defined criteria evoke vague responses. (Note for example that "friendship" is actually a cluster of criteria.)
- When possible, the criterion should be actual rather than hypothetical.
- A criterion is more powerful if it is one that has a potential for being acted upon. For example, for incoming college freshmen the question "Whom would you choose as a roommate for the year?" has more potential of being acted upon than the question "Whom do you trust.?"
- Moreno points out that the ideal criterion is one that helps further the life-goal of the subject. "If the test procedure is identical with a life-goal of the subject he can never feel himself to have been victimised or abused. Yet the same series of acts performed of the subject's own volition may be a 'test' in the mind of the tester" (Moreno, p. 105). Helping a college freshman select an appropriate roommate is an example of a sociometric test that is in accord with the life-goal of the subject.

"It is easy to gain the cooperation of the people tested as soon as they come to think of the test as an instrument to bring their wills to a wider realisation, that it is not only an instrument for exploring the status of a population, but primarily an instrument to bring the population to a *collective self-expression* in respect to the fundamental activities in which it is or is about to be involved." (Moreno, 1953, pp. 680-681).

As a general rule questions should be future oriented, imply how the results are to be used, and specify the boundaries of the group (Hale, 1985). And last, but not least, the criteria should be designed to keep the level of risk for the group appropriate to the group's cohesion and stage of development.

28.2 Application of Sociometry in the Work Setting

The typical process for a sociometric intervention in an organisation follows these basic steps: (1) Identify the group to be studied, (2) Develop the criterion, (3) Establish rapport/warm-up, (4) Gather sociometric data, (5) Analyse and interpret data, (6) Feedback data, either: (a) to individuals, prior to group meeting, or (b) in a group setting, (7) Develop and implement action plans, (8) Post-test (optional).

Numerous sociometric techniques are used to measure social interaction within groups, but sociogram, sociometric matrix, guess-who technique and social distance scale are most frequently used in educational research. Methods of sociometric analysis include:

1. Sociometric matrices,
2. Sociograms, and
3. Sociometric indices.

28.3 Sociometric Matrix is a rectangular array of numbers or other symbols indicating the choices made by the members of a group. Choices or preferences are ploted in columns of the matrix. It is convenient to write sociometric matrices. For example, suppose a group of five members has responded to the sociometric question. With whom you like to work? The responses to the sociometric question are of course, choice. If a group member chooses another group member, the choice is represented by 1 and 0 i.e. '1' indicates a member choose other member in a group and '0' in case member does not choose another. Sociometric Choice Matrix is shown in Table 28.1.

Table 28.1: Sociometric Choice Matrix

	A	B	C	D	E
A	0	1	0	0	1
B	1	0	0	0	1
C	0	0	0	1	1
D	0	1	0	0	1
E	1	1	0	0	0
Σ	2	3	0	1	4

Criteria : Each member has to make two choices out of five members of the group on a specific question.

Three kinds of choices will emerge as given below:

A simple	-	One way choice: 'A' chooses 'E' does not choose 'A'
Mutual	-	Two – way choice: A chooses 'B' and 'B' chooses 'A'
No choice	-	Zero choice to member of a group: for instance 'C' chooses 'D' and 'E' but 'C' fails to get choice from other members of the group.

E. gets maximum choices (4). Two mutual and two independent.

'B' gets 3 choices two mutual x one independent.

'A' gets two mutual choices.

D gets one choice.

C could not figure on the choices.

Evidently C is not at all popular because no one chooses him. D is not popular because he receives single choice.

In this matrix we find 'most popular' on one hand and 'isolate' on the other, isolates having least social interaction. This gives rise to the in-depth study of isolates so that effective strategies can be evolved to bring about desirable behavioural modification. Variables of 'most popular' individuals can further be studied in relation to leadership development theories.

28.4 Sociogram

Sociogram is a map of interpersonal relationships and interpersonal lines of communication. Sociometric choices may be represented graphically on a chart known as a sociogram. There are many versions of the sociogram pattern. For instance, it can be presented in different symbols indicating boys and girls or teachers and boys. A choice may be represented by a single-pointed a arrow and mutual choices by an pointing in opposite directions. Those chosen most often are referred to as stars, those not chosen as isolates. Small groups made up of individuals who choose one another are cliques or cohesive group.

Sociogram is a diagram or chart of the choices made in groups. This is shown in Figure 28.1.

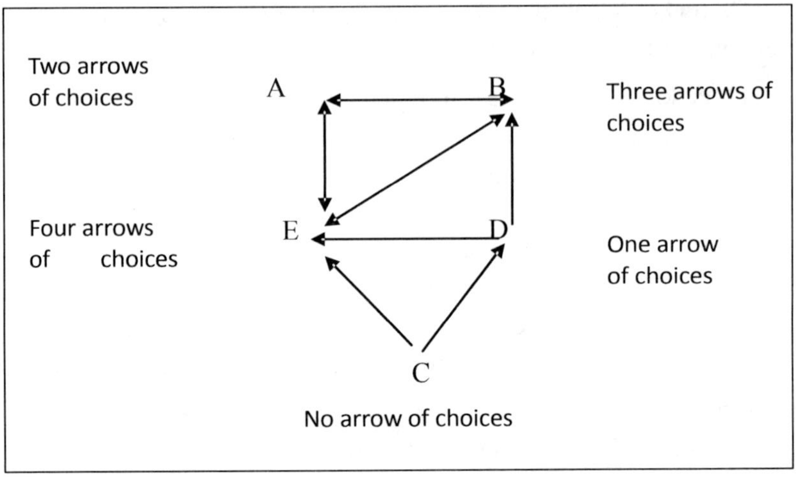

Fig. 28.1

- E got maximum choices (4). Therefore, E is the centre of choice. We might call him leader.
- Move important, A B and C choose each other. This is a clique. We define a clique as three that A B E choose each other.
- 'C' is not chosen it reflects that he is either isolate or neglected.

Number of sociograms can be constructed at different period of time to identify changes in interactions or relationships from time to time in order to bring isolates or individuals at social risk into the mainstream or to transform cliques into more general group membership. Peer group interactions and relationships help in understanding the nature of the members of the group.

Sociogram is feasible only for small group for descriptive purposes or graph and is E excellent means of summarising group relations. For larger group (larger than 20 members) and move analytic purpose, it is not suitable. It becomes difficult to construct and difficult to interpret.

28.5 Sociometric Indices

Sociometric indices reveal the choice status of Person, and Group cohesiveness.

A simple but useful index is:

$CS_E = C_E / M\text{-}1 = CS_E = 4/4 = 1.00$

CS = Choice status of 'E' person

C_E = choice given to E

M-1 = Total number – 1

Similarly Ca = Ca / M-1 = 2/4 = .50 and

Cb = Cb /M-1 = 3/4 = .75

Cc = Cc /M-1 = 0/4 = 0 (zero)

Cd = Cd /M-1 = 1/4 = .25

Group sociometric measures are perhaps more interesting. It is a measure of the cohesiveness of a group. Group cohesiveness is represented by sum of mutual choices or mutual pairs. This useful index is the proportion of mutual choices to the total number of possible pairs. It is a five member group, the total number of possible pairs 5 things taken 2 at a time.

Total number of possible pairs = 10/2 =5

There were three mutual choices in case of B, therefore, group cohesiveness is:

= 3/5 = .60 a substantial degree of cohesiveness.

28.6 Applications of Sociometry

1. They are useful in classifying individual and groups.
2. In studying the manifestation of prejudice against SC/ST urban/rural students.
3. In identifying the leader or popular student in the class.
4. In identifying group cohesiveness.
5. In identifying isolates or rejected.
6. In devising strategies to bring isolates or rejected into mainstream.
7. Mainstreaming of differently abled children and their integration in regular classroom.
8. Identifying social, economic, and cultural discriminations among students.
9. Peer relations-issues in assessment and interventions.
10. Classroom climate and its effects on academic achievement.
11. Identifying children as being ‘socially at risk’.
12. Interaction pattern of sub group, cliques and specific friendship and group conflicts.

13. Study of academic culture in higher education.
14. Identification of level of friendship, anxiety, cildren at risk, and
15. Evaluation of teachers on sociometric scale.

Further Reading

Hale, Ann E. (1985). *Conducting Clinical Sociometric Explorations: A Manual.* Roanoke, Virginia: Royal Publishing Company.

Kerlinger, F. (1986). *Foundations of Behavioral Research.* 5rd edition, Orlando: Harcourt Brace.

Kothari, C.R. (2004). *Research Methodology: Methods & Techniques.* New Delhi: New Age International Publishers.

Koul, L. (2009). *Methodology of Educational Research.* Vikas Publishing House, New Delhi 14.

Leedy, p., Ormrod, J. (2010). *Practical Research: Planning and Design.* 9th edition, Needham Heights: Allyn Bacon.

Paneerselvam, R. (2004). *Research Methodology.* New Delhi: Prentice-Hall of India.

Punch, K. F. (2009). *Introduction to Research Methods in Education.* New Delhi: Sage.

Rolfe, S.A. (2001). 'Direct observation' in G. Macnavigaton, S.A. Rolfe and I. Siraj –Sanger, Jl(1996). *The complete Observer?* A Field Guide to Observation, London: Falmer Press.

Unit - 6

Analysis and Evaluation

29

Analysis of Qualitative Data

The term data refers to the raw information researcher collects from the world they are studying. Data are both the evidence and cues. Gathered carefully, they serve as the stubborn facts. Data ground investigator to the empirical world. It motivates researcher to think deeply and creatively about the aspects of life he/she is going to explore. Qualitative data include narrative and visual data. Focus group discussion, field notes, interview transcripts, diaries, official documents, newspaper articles, photographs, videos, and films are used as instruments for the collection of data. Trustworthiness and authenticity of qualitative data depend on the creditability and seriousness of the researcher. Self-delusion, biases and subjectivity should not creep into data. Substantial evidence derived from researches makes way for good public policy planning.

29.1 Elements of Qualitative Analysis

A summary of the recurrent elements in qualitative research is given below (Miles and Huberman, 1994)

- Qualitative research is conducted through an intense and/ or prolonged contact with a 'field' or life situation. These situations are typically 'banal' or normal ones, reflective of the everyday life of individuals, groups, services or organisations.

- The researcher's role is to gain a 'holistic' overview of the context under study: its logic, its arrangements, its explicit and implicit rules.
- The researcher attempts to capture data on the perceptions of local actors 'from the inside' through a process of deep attentiveness, of empathetic understanding, and of suspending or 'bracketing' preconceptions about the topic under discussion.
- Reading through these materials, the researcher may isolate certain themes and expressions that can be reviewed with informants, but that should be maintained in their original forms throughout the study.
- The main task is to explicate the ways people in particular settings come to understand, account for, take action, and otherwise manage their day-to-day situations.
- Many interpretations of this material are possible, but some are more compelling for theoretical reasons or on grounds of internal consistency.
- Relatively little standardised instrumentation is used at the outset. The researcher is essentially the main 'instrument' in the study.
- Most analysis is done with words. The words can be assembled, sub-clustered, broken into semiotic segments. They can be organised to permit the researcher to contrast, compare, analyse, and bestow patterns upon them.

The whole phenomenon under study is understood as a complex system that is more than sum of its parts. Focus is on complex interdependencies and system dynamics that cannot meaningfully be reduced to a few discrete and linear, cause-effect relationships. Its richness and complexity mean that there are different ways of analysing social life, and therefore, multiple perspectives and practices in the analysis of qualitative data.

Processes and procedures are to be adhered for the collection, analysis and interpretation data in the field.

29.2 Processes and Procedures

- At first, collect data widely, pursing different subject, exploring physical and social spaces to get a broad understanding of the parameters of the setting, subjects, and issue in which you are interested. Develop a research focus, based both on what is feasible to do and what is of interest to you, narrow the space of data collecting. Do this after three or four visits or some initial interviews. Make decision concerning the type of study you want to accomplish, for instance, ethnographic, case studies, grounded theory, life histories, and so on. Decide what type of study to pursue.
- Develop analytic questions. Assess which of the questions are relevant and which should be reformulated to direct your work in light of new experience in the field.
- Plan data- collection sessions in light of what you find in previous observations. You will have to think about what you know already and what shape your study in taking.
- Write many "observer's comments" about idea you generate. Research records his or her own thoughts and feeling. Exclusion of formula hunches, record important insights that come to you during data collection before you lose them. Whenever you feel strongly about an event witnessed or a dialogue engaged in, note the image that come to mind. When words, events, or circumstances recur, mention it in observer's comments and speculate about meanings. If you think you have a breakthrough in understanding something that was previously obscure to you, record and elaborate on it. If you notice that certain subject have things in common, point it out in observer's comments. The idea is to stimulate critical thinking about what you see and to become more than a recording machine. Try to relate what you are observing to ideas and finding in the literature.
- Write memos to yourself about what you are learning. After you have been in the field five or six times, force yourself to read over your data and write a one- or two-page summary of what you think in emerging. Develop links is that summary between observer's comments. Continue this practice of memos writing or summarising regularly.

29.3 Analysis of Qualitative Data

Data analysis means the process of systematically searching and arranging the interview transcripts, field-notes, focus group discussion, and other materials that researcher accumulates to enable him to come up with findings. Analysis involves working with data, organising them, breaking them into manageable units, coding them, synthesising, and searching for patterns. Data interpretation involves ideas about your findings and relating them to literature and to broader concerns and concepts.

There are variety of ways of handling analysis and interpretation. In one approach, analysis and interpretation are concurrent with data collection and more or less completed by the time the data are collected. This approach is generally followed by experienced researcher. It is most efficient and effective. The other mode involves collecting the data before doing the analysis and interpretation. Therefore, the researcher needs to follow the procedures as such given below:

- A repertoire of analytic techniques thus characterises qualitative research, and different techniques can be applied to the same body of qualitative data, illuminating different aspects of it.
- Methods for the analysis of data need to be systematic, disciplined, and transparent.
- The concept of 'audit trail' through the data analysis is now realistic for much qualitative research.
- Induction is central to analysis of qualitative data for generation of theory. But deduction is also needed for the verification of the theory. This sort of data analysis is a series of alternating inductive and deductive steps, whereby data-driven inductive hypothesis generation is followed by deductive hypothesis examination for the purpose of verification.

29.4 Interactive Model of Data Analysis

Interactive model of data analysis is most comprehensive, the main components are:

- **Data reduction:** The objective of data reduction is to reduce the data without significant loss of information.

- **Data display:** Organise, compress and assemble information. There are many different ways of displaying data- graphs, charts, networks, diagrams of different types (Venn diagram, causal models, etc.).
- **Drawing and verifying conclusions:** Conclusions will be in the form of propositions, and once they have been drawn, they need to be verified.

29.4.1 Coding

Codes are tags, names, labels against the pieces of the data. There are two types of codes- descriptive codes and inferential (pattern) codes. Descriptive codes are very useful in summarising the segments of data, and which provide the basis for inferential codes. Inferential codes are more interpretive, and focus on pattern codes. A pattern code is more inferential, a sort of 'meta-code'. Pattern codes pull together material into smaller and more meaningful units. A good way to understand pattern codes is by analogy with factor analysis in quantitative research.

The task of coding is more tedious because (i) the settings are more complex, (ii) the materials to be organised are not as easily separated into units, (iii) the setting is not void of people, nor are the classification systems as self-evident or clear-cut.

Developing a coding system involves several steps:

- Search through your data for regularities and patterns as well as for topics your data cover.
- Write down words and phrases to represent these topics and patterns. These words and phrases are coding categories.
- Sort out the descriptive data you have collected so that the material bearing on a given topic can be physically separated from other data.
- Jolt down some coding categories coming across while you are collecting data.
- Develop a list of coding categories ready to mechanically processing. Under each coding family, we will define what we mean by the type, discuss what kinds of data can be sorted by it, discuss when this family of codes is most often used, and then provide an example of a unit of data that might be appropriately coded under categories representing the family.

29.4.2 Setting / Context Codes: This term refers to codes under which the most general information on the setting, topic or subjects can be sorted. Material that allows you to place your study in a larger context is found under such codes. In most studies one code is sufficient to cover this material. Under such codes much of the descriptive literature (pamphlets, brochures, yearbooks) produced about the setting, subject, or topic can be placed, as well as local newspaper articles and other such media coverage. In addition, general statements that people make describing the subjects, the setting, and how the setting fits in the community can be coded here.

29.4.3 Definition of the Situation Codes: Under this type of code your aim is to place units of data that tell you how the subjects define the setting or particular topics. You are interested in their worldview and how they see themselves in relation to the setting or your topic. What do they hope to accomplish? How do they define that they do? What is important to them? Do they have a particular orientation that affects how they define participation (religious, political, social class, feminist, right-to-life)? You may be looking at various participants: students, pupils, and administrators, as well as parents. You might have a coding category for each type of participant. There may be other distinctions between participants that could be the basis of coding categories. Some "Definition of the Situation" codes in a study of women's perceptions of their own elementary school experiences included "Feminist Awareness, " "Image of Present Self, " and "Influence on Interpreting Past" (Biklen, 1973).

29.4.4 Process Codes: Process codes are words and phrases that facilitate categorising sequences of events, changes over time, or passages from one type or kind of status to another. In order to use a process code, the researcher must view a person, group, organisation or activity over time and perceive change occurring in a sequence of at least two parts. Typical process codes point to time periods, stages, phases, passages, steps, careers and chronology. In addition, key points in a sequence (e.g. turning points, benchmarks, transitions) could be included in the family process codes (see Roth, 1963).

29.4.5 Activity Codes: Codes that are directed at regularly occurring kinds of behaviour are what we call activity codes. These behaviours can be relatively informal and lead to codes such as a "stable management," "competitions", or "showing films," or regularly occurring behaviors that are a formal part of a setting, such as "handling equines, " "visits and tours", "camps", "workshop, conference, and fairs."

29.4.6 Event codes: These kinds of codes are directed at units of data that are related to specific activities that occur in the setting or in the lives of the subjects you are interviewing. Event codes point to particular happenings that occur infrequently or only once.

29.4.7 Strategy codes. Strategies refer to the tactics, methods, technique, maneuvers, ploys, and other conscious ways people accomplish various things. Researcher, for example, employs strategies such as developing new techniques and practices through interface with stakeholders to ensure maximum change and welfare.

29.4.8 Narrative Codes. Narrative codes describe the structure of talk itself. When informants tell you their stories, they offer an account of their lives framed in a particular way. If it is in narrative form, what is the structure of the narrative? Where does the story start, what story does it tell, and where does it conclude?

29.4.9 Memoing

Memoing is the second basic operation of qualitative data analysis. Memoing begins at the start of the analysis along with coding. Memoing is recording of ideas whatsoever may be. These memos can cover many things. They may be substantive, theoretical, methodological or even personal. Ideas may lead to new patterns and higher level of pattern coding. They may also elaborate a concept or relate different concepts to each other. This last type of memo produces propositions.

29.4.10 Abstracting

Like factor analysis in quantitative research, numerous ideas or indicators are reduced to first order concept, and then second order concept. Or it is proceeding from first level abstraction to second level abstraction. It is continuum from concrete-to-abstract and specific-to-general which is remarkably similar in both approaches.

29.4.11 Comparing

Comparison is fundamental to systemic inquiry, whether data are qualitative or quantitative. Comparison is the intellectual activity in the analysis of qualitative data. Comparing is essential to conceptual development. Comparison helps in going from the first level of abstraction to higher level of abstraction.

29.4.12 Rapid and Rigorous Qualitative Data Analysis (Daphne C Watkins, 2017).

The RADaR is in-depth and naturalistic technique of analysis of qualitative of data. The RADaR technique, uses Microsoft Word and/ or Excel. It provides an expedited and user-friendly way of organising, reducing, coding, and analysing qualitative data to obtain findings from qualitative project and disseminate these findings to relevant stakeholders. It allows users to begin with the raw qualitative data from transcripts or case records and end with a streamlined list of quotes that can be incorporated into tangible products such as presentations, papers, and final reports. The RADaR technique is rigorous because of the systematic strategies employed during each step of the process, and it is accelerated because the time required to produce each phase of the data table shortens as more condensed presentations of the textual data are completed (Daphne C Watkins, 2017).

Step-wise Analysis of Qualitative Data

Step-1: Qualitative data can come in many forms, such as in-depth interviews (e.g., one-on-one or focus groups), direct observation (e.g., field notes, video recordings, and audio recordings), and written documents (e.g., archival records, newspapers, case studies, magazines, books, websites, memos, reports, transcripts). The RADaR technique involves all of the qualitative data (e.g., transcripts, reports, or other text data) and is formatted similarly. For example, focus group data transcripts include details about the focus group (e.g., date, time, location, type of group) at the top of the first page or in the page header. The name of the participant(s) speaking is placed in bolded font, or all "caps" and their words are either in plain text or italicised. If the qualitative transcripts all have similar formatting, this can speed up creating the RADaR Phase 1 data reduction table.

Step: 2 All-inclusive "Phase 1 data table" is placed into a series of data reduction tables.

Step-3: The next step involves the all-inclusive, "Phase 1 data table" to produce a shorter, and more concise "Phase 2 data table". This process requires the analysts to eliminate chunks of texts, or data, leaving "the Phase 2 table" with only the text that is relevant to the overarching research question. This moves the analysts toward a narrower focus on the data and encourages their progression from the development of open codes to more specific, "focused codes" (Grinnell and Unrau, 2011; Watkins, 2012).

Step-4: In this phase, areas of commonality across groups or between participants (e.g., transcript numbers, income groups/gender) is discussed. Opinions about the relevance of certain quotes are generated in relation to the objectives of the study. This process can be performed iteratively. Close assessment of each analyst's reviewing, reducing, and coding styles is carried out. Disagreements among the team are thoroughly discussed and resolved. This data reduction process moves the team/individual from Phase 2 and to Phase 3, and so on, of the data tables.

Step-5: In the last stage, the researcher/analyst proceeds from drafting language to the final project deliverables. These project deliverables can range from a final project report to a conference presentation, thesis/dissertation, or peer-reviewed manuscript. In this process, the researcher/team gets answer of research questions. The Major codes and/or quotes from the final phase of the data table that helped them to define, refine, and illustrate those themes are identified.

29.5 Grounded Theory Analysis

Grounded Theory as an inductive process is guided by specific guidelines as outlined by Corbin and Strauss (1990):

- Data collection and analysis are interrelated and concurrent processes.
- Concepts are the basic units of analysis. Conceptualisation of data rather than description is central emphasis of Grounded Theory.
- Categories must be developed and related. Concepts are grouped together to form categories, and must be of theoretical significance to contribute to the development of categories.
- Sampling in Grounded Theory proceeds on theoretical grounds. Sampling is guided by ideas generated from the phenomena under study.

- Analysis makes use of constant comparisons. The comparison of incidents results in the development of concepts. Comparisons are drawn throughout the research process and as concepts are grouped into categories. The process provides verification as the researcher compares concepts and categories with new data.
- Patterns and variations in data are accounted for.

Three steps are involved in the analysis of grounded theory

- First step is to find conceptual categories in the data,
- The second is to find relationships between these categories,
- The third is to conceptualise and account for these relationships at a higher level of abstraction.

Therefore, there are three general types of codes:

- Substantive codes (produced by open coding), which are the initial conceptual categories in the data.
- Theoretical codes (produced by axial coding), which connect these categories. Axial coding is the process of relating categories to their sub-categories. The coding is termed 'axial' because coding occurs around the axis of a category, linking categories at the level of properties and dimensions.
- The core code (produced by selective coding), which is higher order conceptualisationof the theoretical coding around which theory is built. Selective coding is done on the data to find the central or core category. Selective coding is the process of integrating and refining the theory. Core category represents the main theme of the research. The criteria followed for choosing the core category as proposed by Corbin and Strauss (1990) are: (i) the category must be central; that is, all other major categories can be related to it; (ii) it must appear frequently in the data. These are indicators pointing to the concept; (iii) the explanation that evolves by relating the categories is logical and consistent. There is no forcing of data; (iv) the name or phrase used to describe the central category should be sufficiently abstract that it can be used to do research in other substantive areas, leading to the development of a more general theory.

Diagrammatic representation of grounded theory analysis is given in Figure – 29.1

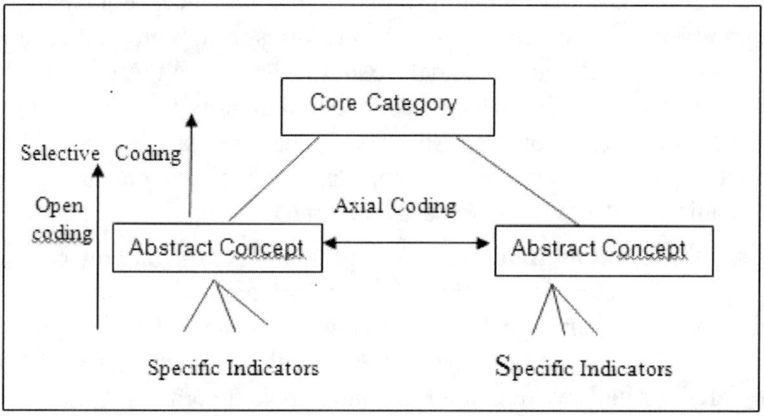

Figure 29.1: Diagrammatic Representation of Grounded Theory Analysis.

29.6 Other Analytic Approaches in Qualitative Analysis

29.6.1 Narrative analysis

It may seem unlikely, but Aristotle, the same philosopher who gave us the scientific method, also set out methods for creating methods for creating compelling narratives. In *The Art of Rhetoric* he describes a system of persuasion that has three drivers:

- **Ethos:** The will and character to change the current situation. To be effective, the author of the narrative must possess credibility and authenticity.
- **Logos:** The logical structure of the argument. This must provide a rigorous case of transforming problem into possibilities, possibility into ideas, and ideas into action.
- **Pathos:** The capacity to empathise. To be capable of inspiring movement on a large scale, the author must understand the audience.
- **Metaphors:** Good stories are anchored by powerful metaphors. Aristotle himself observed, "ordinary words convey only what we know already; it from metaphor that we can best get hold of something fresh." In fact, he believed that mastery of metaphor is key to rhetorical success.

In narrative analysis, form and content can be studied together and a concern with narrative can illuminate how informants use language to convey particular meanings and experiences. For example, Connelly and Clendenin (1999) present stories from both teachers and administrators. The authors analyse and reflect upon these stories to make links between knowledge, context and identity for both teachers and administrators. Cortazzi (1991) examined important aspects of 123 primary teachers experience and through their stories a clear picture of is built up of how teachers are teaching.

29.6.2 Ethnomethodology: The primary focus is on how central features of a culture, its shared meanings and social norms, are developed, maintained and changed rather than on the content of those meanings and norms (Feldman, 1995). With so much of social life mediated through written and especially spoken communication, the study of language is at the heart of ethnomethodology.

- **Discourse Analysis:** Discourse encompasses ideas, statements, knowledge that are dominant at a particular time among particular sets of people...and which are held in relation to other sets of individuals...Implicit in the use of such knowledge is the application of power. However, it is not restricted exclusively to verbalised propositions, but can include ways of seeing, categorising and reacting to the social world in everyday practices. (Jupp, 1996). Coulthard (1985) has many examples of micro-level discourse analysis I the language teaching context.
- **Conversation Analysis:** Conversation analysis focuses more and more on the formal analysis of conversations. It is an empirical research investigation of social interaction. Moreover, it is a continuing process of producing and securing meaningful social order. The elements of social order are present in the local scenes in which interactions take place. Conversation analysis has helped to map out a distinctive and original field of inquiry.
- **Genre Analysis:** Genre is a term for grouping texts together, representing how writers typically use language to respond to recurring situations (Hyland, 2004). A genre comprises of a set of communicative events, the members of which share some set of communicative purposes (Swales, 1990). For example,

a genre exhibits various patterns of similarities in terms of structure, style, content and intended audience. In social science, genre is a social action and a speech event that has communicative goal shared by the members of a particular discourse community. Genre in literary studies for instance includes film, anthropology, folklore and music.

29.6.3 Semiotics: Semiotics, or a science of signs, lays out assumptions, concepts and methods for the analysis of sign systems. There are many sign systems (for example, mathematics, music, etiquette, symbolic rites, and secret signs) to which semiotic can be applied. Semioticians identify mechanisms by which meaning is produced (the most common ones are metaphor, metonymy and opposition), and have devised techniques using these mechanisms for interpreting qualitative data. Mavers (2007) conceptualises writing as a process of design to study how meaning is made by a 6-year old child who uses semiotic resourcefulness in email exchanges with her uncle.

29.6.4 Documentary and Textual Analysis

All documentary sources are the result of human activity, produced on the basis of certain ideas, theories or commonly accepted, taken-for granted principles, and these are always located within the constraints of particular social, historical or administrative conditions and structures (Finnegan, 1997). Words and their meanings depend on where they are used, by whom and to whom.. Woods (1979) analyses school reports, and shows the concepts and categories teachers use to make normative judgments about pupils.

29.7 Interpretation

The whole phenomenon under study is understood as a complex system that is more than sum of its parts; focus on complex interdependencies and system dynamics that can not meaningfully be reduced to a few discrete and linear, cause-effect relationships. Here are some additional ideas that can help you move your interpretation of the data along.

- Revisit writings that helped you understand the basic ideas behind qualitative research. Start by going back to the basic theoretical orientations underlying the approach. What are the basic assumptions of symbolic interaction, for example, and how do the findings in your own data relate to those premises? Is the way you are thinking reflective of these ideas or are you at- tempting to use another theoretical scheme? What scheme are you using?

- Read published studies related to your own research. Study them to figure out how the authors explain their approach and contribution. How is your data similar to and different from that in the books and articles you are reading? What concepts, ideas, and theories do others use to frame their data? What is missing from their findings? From their analysis?
- Purposely try to be evaluative of your subjects and the situation you are observing! Although qualitative researchers usually avoid saying something is good or bad, for the purposes of getting a deeper sense of your own relationship to your data, ask: Is what I am seeing good or bad? What values, assumptions, and criteria do I use when I am evaluative? What do my subjects use?
- Ask: What are the implications of my findings for practice? For current events? For the theoretical orientation I think I am operating from?
- Speculate about the assumptions that the audience you are writing for might have. Strategise about how to interpret to them what you have come to understand.
- Is there a story of an incident from your research that captures a major insight or understanding you have derived from your work? Tell that story. Try to work with it and think creatively about where and how you should tell it. How does it relate to theory, your findings, and so on?
- Work on writing a clear paragraph summarising what it is you want to tell readers.

29.8 Software for Analysis of Qualitative Data

ATLAS.ti

Hermeneutic Unit is researcher's project and documents, codes, memos, and other files associated with it. The Hermeneutic Unit Editor is main workplace area and main menu provides access to different components of the Hermeneutic Unit (HU). The researcher can view the documents through Primary Document Pane. Main Tool Bar provides easy access to primary documents, quotations, codes, memos.

- First of all the researcher has to ensure that data must be in text-based, electronic format.
- Next step is assign or import the files you plan to analyse.
- Open textual primary documents and assign codes to them. Researcher can select one of four types of coding techniques namely, open coding, code-by-list, in-Vivo coding, quick coding. Researcher can assign multiple codes to the selected text.
- Quotations in ATLAS.ti are segments of primary documents. Researcher can choose to code these segments.
- Store different kinds of objects in Families. (i.e. Male or Female). All procedures for displaying, editing, and creating families are found in the menu of their object types.
- Use different search options for Simple search, Category search and GREP search (i.e. search for all years between 2000 and 2011).
- Retrieve coded texts, graphic or audio segments that match your specified criteria and Interpret the data accordingly.

Researcher can export and import qualitative data for analysis to other soft ware (for example, SPSS). In addition to textual documents, researcher can work with graphic files and other audio and video formats (like WAV, MP3, WMA, SND, AVI, MPG, WMV, MDV, etc.).

NVIVO 9

NVIVO 9 helps researcher to easily organise and analyse data in documents, pictures. Surveys audio and video, so one can deliver robust findings quickly. NVIVO9 delivers simpler, flexible analysis with greater insight. Themes as 'nodes' are stored in containers. Nodes that represent anything at all like people, places and organisations and assign any demographic data can be created. Researcher can assign his or her colours to nodes sources, attribute values and can see themes in coding strips, charts and models. Sub-nodes can be rolled up into the parent node.

Researcher can identify the most frequently materials (sources) or nodes and display results in a word tree. Connections between items can be explored and displayed visually with 'connection map' which help researcher to see pattern and convert the graph to a model. Cluster analysis can be conducted to visualise the similarities and differences. Researcher can conduct Framework analysis using NVIVO9's new Framework matrices.

MAXQDA 11 is a high-performance program for professional social science-oriented data analysis, ideal for researchers from social sciences, education, economics, and many others, who work with and analyse text in their professional capacities.

29.9 Identification of Most Significant Change

29.9.1 What is MSC?

The most significant change (MSC) is identified through participants (actors). Participants are inspired, informed and involved both in deciding the sorts of change to be recorded and in analysing the data. Most Significant Change is also a form of monitoring because it occurs throughout the programme cycle and provides information to help people manage the programmme. It contributes to evaluation because it provides data on impact and outcomes that can be used to help assess the performance of the programme as a whole.

Essentially, the process involves the collection of significant change (SC) stories emanating from the field level, and the systematic selection of the most significant of these stories by panels of designated stakeholders or staff. The designated staff and stakeholders are initially involved by 'searching' for project impact. Once changes have been captured, various people sit down together, read the stories aloud and have regular and often in-depth discussions about the value of these reported changes. When the technique is implemented successfully, whole teams of people begin to focus their attention on program impact.

Steps for Implementation (Davies, R. and Dart, J., 2005)

1. How to start and raise interest
2. Defining the domains of change
3. Defining the reporting period
4. Collecting SC stories
5. Selecting the most significant of the stories
6. Feeding back the results of the selection process
7. Verification of stories
8. Quantification

9. Secondary analysis and meta-monitoring
10. Revising the system.

29.10 Methodology

Motivate & involvement of the actors in the problem situation.	→	Consensus between actors & researcher on theme/themes	→	Small group responsible for research cycle	→	Formulation of Research Design by the actors & researcher
						↓
Outcomes Most Significant Changes Significant Changes		Analysis of data jointly by actors & researcher	←	Identification & weight-age of indicators of change	←	From Qualitative understanding to quantification

Sustainability

29.11 What are domains of change?

Domains are broad and often fuzzy categories of possible SC stories. In CCDB, participants in MSC were asked to look for significant changes in four domains:

- Changes in the quality of people's lives.
- Changes in the nature of people's participation in development activities.
- Changes in the sustainability of people's organisations and activities.
- Any other changes.

29.12 How to capture SC stories

- Fieldworkers write down unsolicited stories that they have heard
- By interview and note-taking
- During group discussion
- The beneficiary writes the story directly.

29.13 People's Own Analysis of Empowerment

The participants are asked to share their experiences of their social movement. Each group is asked to prepare notes: the first illustrating life before association with the movement, the second illustrating the current situation, and the third depicting their aspirations for the near future (around 2-3 years). Apart from this framework, the groups are given no other guidance, hints, or input from researchers/investigators. The intention is to enable the groups to express themselves freely and spontaneously. The narrations are to be based on real experiences on specific theme or themes.

29.13.1 From Qualitative Understanding to Quantification

The Process of translating this complex qualitative understanding of change into quantified indicators is done by the participants. This is process entirely driven by and for the movement members. The self-assessment is done in a trusted space. Purpose is benefiting the future of the group and shaping its future plans and demands from service providers. There is no sense of competition between groups. Each group undertakes the reflection exercise for themselves. The process of evaluation is in itself empowering. The results of the self-assessments are collected and are aggregated and processed to provide analysis for programme. The data are categorised and weighted to enable trends, distribution, and correlations to be reviewed.

29.14 Criteria for Selecting Significant Changes

There are several ways of reaching a decision about Significant Changes in people's lives.

- **Majority rules:** A simple way of coming to a decision by the participants vote on the theme.
- **Scoring:** Instead of voting, participants can rate the value of a Significant Changes in the domains. The rating for each of the theme is then aggregated and with the highest rating is selected as the most significant.
- **Scoring by a group vote:** This method is suitable for groups who are short of meeting time. Prior to the meeting, participants are asked to read Significant Changes in theme and rate their significance. These ratings are summarised in a table and presented to the participants when they meet face-to-face. Participants discuss the scores and cast their votes.
- **Secret ballot:** Each person writes their choice of Significant Changes on a slip of paper, and then the total votes are presented.

The broad domains of Significant Changes identified by the actors (actual users) are given below:

- Significant Changes in the quality of social life of people (mutual support, trust, respect, and equality, interaction and participation, and social mobility) have been observed.

- Changes in income of people and sharing of economic resources (equity in income and resource sharing, and upward shift from below poverty line) have been observed.
- Significant Changes in formal and informal decision-making and participation in political activities have been observed.
- Changes in the sustainability of people's organisations and activities have been observed.

Technology, Sydney, New South Wales. Juliet's meta-evaluation examined four aspects of the use of MSC, described as follows:

- **Efficiency:** How well MSC was implemented using the resources and time available, and how the benefits of MSC compared with the cost.
- **Efficacy:** To what extent the purposes of using MSC were achieved.
- **Effectiveness:** To what extent the use of MSC enabled ADRA Laos to facilitate programme improvement.
- **Replicability:** To what extent differences in context, staffing, programmes and donors might limit the ability of other organisations to replicate ADRA Laos's use of MSC.

References

Corbin, J. and Strauss, A.(1990). Grounded Theory Research: Procedures, cannons, and evaluative criteria. *Qualitative Sociology*, 13(1).

Daphne, C. Watkins (2017). Rapid and Rigorous Qualitative Data Analysis: The "RADaR" Technique for Applied Research. *International Journal of Qualitative Methods,* Volume 16: 1-9. Sage.

Davies, R. and Dart, J.(2005). The 'Most Significant Change' (MSC) Technique: A Guide to Its Use.www.mande.co.uk/docs/MSCGuide.htm

Feldman, N. (ed.) (2001). Strategies for Interpreting Qualitative Data. Thousand Oaks, CA: Sage.

Fernandes, W. and Tandon, R.(1981).*Participatory Research and Evaluation:Experiments in Research as a Processof Liberation.* New Delhi: Indian Social Institute.

Freire, P.(1970). *Pedagogy of the Oppressed.* New York: Herder and Herder.

Gayfer, M.(1981). Participatory Research, Development and Issues. *Convergence, 14 (3) 5.*

Hall, B.L. (1981). Participatory research: Popular Knowledge and Power: A personal reflection. 14 (3), 47 *Convergence.*

Huberman, A.M., and Miles, M.B.(1994). Quality Data Management and analysis Methods. In N.K. Denzin and Y.S.Lincoln (eds). *Handbook of Qualitative Research.* Thousand Oaks, CA: Sage.

Korten, D. and Klauss, R. (eds) (1984). *People Centered Development: Contributions Toward Theory and Planning Frameworks*. West Hertford, CT: Kumarian.

Laue, J. (1978). Advocacy and Sociology, in G, H. Weber and G.J.McCall(eds), *Social Scientists as Advocates: Views from the applied disciplines.* Beverly Hills: Sage.

Lemann, T. and Young, R. (1975). From conflict theory to conflict methodology: An emerging paradigm for sociology. *Sociological Inquiry*, 14, 15-28.

Miles, M.B. and Huberman, A.M. (1994). *Quality Data Analysis.* 2nd edn. Thousand Oaks, CA: Sage.

Rajesh, T. (eds) (2008). *Participatory Research: Visiting the Roots.* New Delhi: Mosaic Books.

Further Reading

Feldman, N.(2001). *Strategies for Interpreting Qualitative Data.* Thousand Oaks: CA: Sage.

Huberman, A.M. and Miles, M.B.(1994). Data Management and Analysis Methods. In N.K. Denzin and Y.S. Lincoln (eds). *Handbook of Qualitative Research.* Thousand Oaks, CA: Sage.

Marshall, C. and Rossman, G.B. (1989). *Designing Qualitative Research.* Newbury Park, CA: Sage.

Miles, M. B. and Huberman (1994). *Qualitative Data Analysis.* 2nd edn. Thousand Oaks, CA: Sage.

Feldman, N. (2001). *Strategies for Interpreting Qualitative Data.* Thousand Oaks: CA: Sage.

Huberman, A.M. and Miles, M.B.(1994). Data Management and Analysis Methods. In N.K. Denzin and Y.S. Lincoln (eds). *Handbook of Qualitative Research.* Thousand Oaks, CA: Sage.

Marshall, C. and Rossman, G.B. (1989). Designing Qualitative Research. Newbury Park, CA: Sage.

Miles, M. B., and Huberman (1994). *Qualitative Data Analysis.* 2nd edn. Thousand Oaks, CA: Sage.

Noncommercial sites

http://caqdas.soc.surrey.ac.uk/

http://www.lboro.ac.uk/research/mmethods/research/software/caqdas.html

http://www.qualitative-research.net/fqs/fqs-e/inhalt2-02-e.htm

http://www.audiencedialogue.org/soft-qual.html

http://www.socresonline.org.uk/3/3/4.html

Commercial Sites

http://www.qsrinternational.com

http://www.qsr.coma.u

http://www.qualisresearch.com/ethnograph_software

http://www.researchware.com/

http://www.atlasti.de.atlasneu.html

http://www.scolari.co.uk

http://www.socresonline.org.uk/3/3/4.html

30

Report Writing and Presentation

- Qualitative research is like a prism which reflects multiple images of 'reality', reflects complexity, and fractures certainty. It recognises multiple views and multiple voices. It is methodology of ideas, and the deconstruction and reconstruction of ideas (Atkinson, 2007). It is contextual and there is nothing outside the text (Derrida, 1976) and reality is perceived as socially and culturally constructed. The process of deconstruction is one which seeks to interrogate these constructed 'texts'. It is 'opening up new imaginaries' in research and interpretation (Scheurich, 1996).

Qualitative research is a critical and systematic enquiry aimed at informing understandings of phenomena which are pertinent to the discipline. Thus, sociologists study sociological phenomena, psychologists psychological phenomena, economists economic phenomena, etc. (Bassey, 2005). Qualitative research is "to explore the complexity of the apparently simple, and uncover textual silences beneath the noise and splendour of social, political and educational rhetoric. It offers interpretations that are diverse, uncertain and polyvocal" (Atkinson, 2005).

Qualitative research is like a prism which reflects multiple images of 'reality', reflects complexity, and fractures certainty. It recognises multiple views and multiple voices. It is methodology of ideas, and the deconstruction and reconstruction of ideas (Atkinson, 2007). It is contextual and there is nothing outside the text (Derrida, 1976) and reality is perceived as socially and culturally constructed. The process of deconstruction is one which seeks to interrogate these constructed 'texts'. It is 'opening up new imaginaries' in research and interpretation (Scheurich, 1996).

Qualitative research is a critical and systematic enquiry aimed at informing understandings of phenomena which are pertinent to the discipline. Thus, sociologists study sociological phenomena, psychologists psychological phenomena, economists economic phenomena, etc. (Bassey, 2005). Qualitative research is "to explore the complexity of the apparently simple, and uncover textual silences beneath the noise and splendour of social, political and educational rhetoric. It offers interpretations that are diverse, uncertain and polyvocal" (Atkinson, 2005).

Qualitative research involves the collection, analysis, and interpretation of data that are not easily reduced to numbers. These data relate to the social world and the concepts and behaviours of people within it. Qualitative research can be found in all social sciences and in the applied fields. Qualitative research is like a prism which reflects multiple images of 'reality', reflects complexity, and fractures certainty. It recognises multiple views and multiple voices. It is methodology of ideas, and the deconstruction and reconstruction of ideas (Atkinson, 2007). It is contextual and there is nothing outside the text (Derrida, 1976) and reality is perceived as socially and culturally constructed. The process of deconstruction is one which seeks to interrogate these constructed 'texts'. It is 'opening up new imaginaries' in research and interpretation Scheu Qualitative research is a critical and systematic enquiry aimed at informing understandings of phenomena which are pertinent to the discipline. Thus, sociologists study sociological phenomena, psychologists psychological phenomena, economists economic phenomena, etc. (Bassey, 2005). Qualitative research is "to explore the complexity of the apparently simple, and uncover textual silences beneath the noise and splendour of social, political and educational rhetoric. It offers interpretations that are diverse, uncertain and polyvocal (Atkinson, 2000).

Preparation and presentation of a research report is the most important part of research process. No matter how brilliant the hypotheses are formulated and how well research study is designed, they are of little value unless communicated effectively to others in the form of research report. Moreover, if the report is confusing or poorly written, the time spent on gathering and analysing of data would be wasted. It is, therefore, essential to design, write and communicate the results in a logical way in a research report. Qualitative research is "to explore the complexity of the apparently simple, and uncover textual silences beneath the noise and splendour of social, political and educational rhetoric. It offers interpretations that are diverse, uncertain and polyvocal (Atkinson, 2005).

The research report is presentation and reflection on the methodological proceedings, with all its narratives about access to and the activities in the field. It is documentation of various materials, with its transcribed observations, conversations, discourses, interpretations and theoretical inferences. (Lüders, 1995). It should present systemic relationship between goals, methods, and analysis of qualitative data for getting answers to the research questions. Research, then, includes not only the interaction between the researcher and the issue, but also the interaction between the researchers and their potential readers, for whom they finally write their presentations. This relationship—as well as the text produced for this purpose and the writing linked to it—is determined in multiple ways:"contextually…rhetorically… institutionally…generically…politically…historically" (Clifford 1986, p. 6).

30.1 Format of Research Report

The format of a research report comprises three main sections: (1) the preliminary section contains namely, title, acknowledgements, abstract, contents, list of tables and figures. (2) the body of the report or text includes- need and importance of study, review of literature, objectives and research questions, research design and methodology, analysis and interpretation and implications of the study and (3) the reference section comprises, research notes, bibliography, and index.

The text of the report should be divided into different chapters depending on the type of research. In the case of qualitative research, the different chapters are: (1) Introduction- should begin with the background of the research; discuss the motivation for the work that is being undertaken, explore the aims and objective and research questions; (2) Review of literature-focuses on the past literature in the field of research specific to the present research if any: the critique comparison of the past literature will narrow down the research topic and provide a base for further direction; make sure that you have read and understood cited work, organise your content according to ideas instead of individual publications to ensure the smooth flow of contents and make the chapter more readable. (3) this chapter should include-research design, methods, sampling, research tools for data generation. (4) Data analysis- should focus on data reduction, coding, identifying patterns and triangulation. (5) Presentation of data-may include- graphs, charts, diagrams and photographs, outcomes can be highlighted from the charts and graphs. (6) Analysis of data should take note of the following processes:

- *Reflection on method:* Materials contain procedures and strategies employed.
- *Reflection on ethical dilemmas and conflicts.* There are two sets of behaviour-subject's ideology, values, moral, and ethic on one hand and observer's comment on the other.
- *Reflection on the observer's frame of mind:* These preconceptions relate to religious beliefs, political ideology, and cultural background, position in society, race and gender.

Interpretation, Conclusions and Recommendations- the researcher should take note of reflection of analysis, reflection of methodology, reflection of research ethics and reflection on the observer's frame of mind:

- In interpreting the 'data' the researcher constantly asks how good evidence is for inferences which he/she is drawing. Data comes from what people say and feel, how they interact with others and what they do in different situations. The data are constantly crossed-checked as field work proceeds. In this process, the researcher develops an understanding of what is going on, or an explanation for something, alternative understandings and explanations are considered, incorporated or cast aside.
- The social picture is build up in painstaking way. The researcher explains processes in precise and lucid way. High level of validity is ensured through social audit, comparison and reflection on methodology.

Each section of the report should lead to number of conclusions. At the end of the section these are spelt out and the reasoning behind them explained. If there is a separate 'conclusions' section, these conclusions are pulled out and repeated as an ordered sequence, with reference back to the body of the report as necessary.

Not all reports present recommendations, some are merely required to present a set of information based on research. Where there are recommendations, these may be presented as a part of the report's conclusions, or in a separate section which may place towards the end of the report, after the conclusions, or immediately after the executive summary. Indeed, some writers prefer to make their recommendations part of the executive summary, since there are an important part of what the busy reader wants to know first. Most Significant Change (MSC) can be derived on the basis of analytical analysis of contextual data.

30.2 Appendices

The value of placing certain lengthy detailed information in a series of appendices (sometimes called annexes) has already been mentioned. The type of information that may go in appendices includes:

- A detailed description of the research methodology.
- The research brief and members of the team producing the report.
- Detailed research data.
- Case studies.
- Institutional Data in brief.
- Description of different models/approaches/techniques.
- It also contains those parts of dissertation that are either well known or does not contribute directly to the main text, but needs to be included for completeness.

30.3 Bibliography

Bibliography is an alphabetical catalogue of different literatures which are used in the research. The references can be classified into notes, books, journals, magazines, newspapers, research studies, and information retrieved from Internet, etc. these citation styles are illustrated in American Psychological Corporation.

30.4 Style of Research Report

Scientific knowledge is always presented scientifically. And the consequence is that "logic of presentation" has to be considered as well as "logic of research." How researchers' constitution of experiences is linked to the experiences of participants. How these experiences are organised, analysed and presented in such a way to satisfy the audiences. The text should add to new practice, or knowledge that remained underexposed up to now. Where knowledge is schematised as the production of text, as the transcription of discourse and practice, and the conditions of possibility for discussing ethnographic practices of representation are created. (Fuchs and Berg, 1993, p. 64). The research report with its presentation of and reflection on the methodological proceedings, with all its narratives about access to and the activities in the field, with its documentation of various materials, with its transcribed observations and conversations, interpretations and theoretical inferences is the only basis for answering the question of the quality of the investigation (Lüders, 1995, p. 325).

30.5 Reflexive Function of Writing

Research includes not only the interaction between the researcher and the participants on specific theme/themes, but also the interaction between the researchers and their potential readers, for whom he/she finally writes presentation. This relationship—as well as the text produced for this purpose and the writing linked to it—are determined in multiple ways: "contextually…rhetorically…institutionally… generically…politically…historically" (Clifford, 1986, p. 6). According to Corbin and Strauss (1990, p. 16), researcher should critically assess: (i) the validity, reliability, and credibility of the data, (ii) the plausibility, and the value of the theory itself, (iii) the adequacy of the research process which has generated, elaborated, or tested the theory and (iv) the empirical grounding of the research findings.

30.5.1 Strategies for Communicating Evidence

The researcher should build evidence on the field narrative and audio-visual data. Question arises how to communicate the evidence in write-up to convince readers. True picture or evidence can emerge through dissension, disagreement, discourse and discussion and comparison. Most Significant Change can be captured through participants' storytelling and focused group discussion. Substantial evidences provide inputs for designing and redesigning of public policy. The evidence makes the generalisations take hold on the reader's mind. Clifford (1986) argued that the writer can capture 'partial truths'which are shaped not only by the evidence but also by the language the writer uses.

30.6 Language Style

It an unpretentious medium designed to convey content as specifically and clearly as possible. It should mean that what a scholar writes can be understood at first reading by a reasonably literate and well-intentioned person. Oxford Language Reference (Law, 2007) has given some guideline for effective style as mentioned below:

30.6.1 Control sentence length. There are five main ways of dealing with overlong sentences namely:

- Split and disconnect
- Split and connect
- Use a list
- Cut verbiage
- Discard the sentence and start again.

30.6.2 Use words your readers will understand. There are two ways of removing jargon:

- Use simpler alternatives
- Where necessary, reconstruct your sentences.

30.6.3 Use only as many words as you really need. There are three main techniques to follow:

- Striking out useless words
- Pruning the dead wood and grafting on the vigorous
- Rewriting completely.

30.6.4 Use strong lively verbs. Good verbs give your writing its power and passion and delicacy. It is simple truth that in most sentences you should express action through verbs. Three types of construction are considered:

- Nominalisation linked to parts of *to be or to have*
- Nominalisation linked to active verbs or infinitives
- Nominalisation linked to passive verbs. For example,

An examination of the school records was carried out by Dr Raina.

This becomes, by the same technique:

Dr. Raina examined the school records.

30.6.5 Use vertical lists. Vertical lists have become a common feature of many documents in this process; complicated text is broken up in manageable chunks. For example, instead of writing this: Abstract gives the overview of the research report outlining the title of the research, research methodology i.e. method, sample and tools and main findings of the study and its implications.

30.6.6 Put your points positively when you can

When two, three or more negatives are gathered together in the same sentence, meaning may become obscure. Therefore, sentence containing more negatives should be replaced or to be reconstructed to make it more understandable and meaningful. Three cardinal principles of the field research in context of a case study are:

1. Every research question- regardless of field or discipline- is uniquely defined by a specific set of circumstances.
2. There can be no attempt to answer a question without deep knowledge of the specific contextual parameters defining those circumstances.
3. Such deep knowledge comes only to those who have paid their dues.

30.6.7 Avoid personal pronouns-I, we, you, my, our and us should not be used. For example, instead of saying "I used Focus Group Discussion tool to generate data" it should be "Data was generated through Focus Group Discussion".

30.6.8 Abbreviations: The use of abbreviations, except some acceptable ones such as I.Q., M.A., etc. should be avoided in the main text of the research report. In the footnotes, the table and the bibliography, some standard abbreviations are used to conserve space.

30.6.9 Quotations and references: Make sure that it is clear when you are quoting directly from another person. Short quotations can go into the body of your text, marked off by quotation marks. Longer quotations should be separated and indented.

30.6.10 Ellipsis: They are used to indicate omissions in quotations. It can occur at the beginning or at the end of a quotation. An ellipsis (...) is indicated by three full stops.

30.6.11 Footnotes: Footnotes are generally found at the foot of a page. The footnotes usually include the source of information-name of the author, the title of the source, exact page(s) of the source of reference, date of publication, and publisher and place of publication.

30.7 Typing of the Research Report

General rules for typing the research report are:

- A white bond paper of 8.5 by 11 inches size of 13 to 16 pound weight should be used.
- Material should be typed on one side of the paper
- left margin: 40 mm, top, bottom and right margins: 25 mm
- text font: 12 point Times-Roman or Times-New-Roman
- line spacing: 1.5 lines
- dividing of words at the end of the line should be avoided as far as possible
- throughout the manuscript an indent of seven spaces should be used at the beginning of paragraph and quotations.

30.8 Editing of the Research Report

The process of editing involves examining and correcting the typed materials of the report for its content, format and language.

- The purpose of editing is to critically and thoroughly examine the precision in the statement of the problem, it as objectives, hypotheses or research questions, methodology, analysis of data and their interpretation, drawing inferences and conclusions.
- There should be logical links between objectives, hypotheses, design of research, interpretations and conclusions. Make sure transitions are succinct, with one section naturally flowing into another.
- In case of any divergence between the established theories or findings, the report must provide substantial evidence to support the thesis.

- Structure of the report, presentation of figures and tables, writing of footnotes and references or bibliography should be thoroughly checked and rechecked to ensure good presentation.
- Ensure the proper use of language in the presentation of report. Guidelines for effective writing style should be followed.
- Correction in ink should not be done. In case of two or more mistakes, new corrected typed paper should be inserted in its place.
- Double-check and triple-check that your manuscript is as error-free as possible. It is necessary to go for proof reading twice or thrice to ensure error free presentation.
- Student should submit a full first draft for comment by supervisor before the final draft is begun.

30.9 Presentation

- Good quality presentation implies clarity, conciseness, coherence, and designing with appropriate formatting.
- Presentation should preferably be through power point.
- Brief introduction which may include-Need and importance of the study, objectives, limitations and delimitations (two slides).
- Substantiate the validity of approaches from a position of detachment (one slide).
- Concise and precise explanation of methodology- research design, sample (size and selection procedures), tools used (reliability and validity), statistical methods used for analysis of data (three slides).
- Present the significant findings of the study. Appraise the research work in the light of current theory and accepted practice (two slides).
- Compare and contrast, support or not a particular argument or line of thinking.
- The researcher has to provide supporting evidence for all his assertions. This usually takes the form of reference to the research literature. One should not make unsubstantiated claims.
- Present briefly the implications of the study (one slide).
- Make things explicit and open to scrutiny.

References

Bazerman, C. (1988). *Shaping Written Knowledge: The Genre and Activity of the Experimental Article in science.* Madisan:University of Wisconsin University Press.

Berger, A. A. (1993). *Improving Writing Skills: Memos, Letters. Reports and Proposals.* New Delhi: Sage.

Best, J. and Kahn, J. (2009). *Research in Education.*10th edn. Needham Heights: Allyn and Bacon.

Burton, S. and Steane, P. (2004). *Saving Your Thesis.* London: Sage.

Hart, C. (2005). *Doing your Master Dissertation.*New Delhi: Vistaar Publications.

Koul, L. (2009). *Methodology of Educational Research.* New Delhi: Vikas Publishing House.

Leedy, P. and Ormod, J. (2010). *Practical Research: Planning and Designing.* 9th edn. Needham Heights: Allyn and Bacon.

Madsen, D. (1992). *Successful Dissertation and Thesis.* San Francisco: Jossey-Bass.

Montagnes, I. (1991). Editing and Publication: Training Manual. International Rice Research Institute, Manila.

Mounsey, C. (2005). *Essay and Dissertation.* New Delhi: Oxford Press.

Paneerselvam, R. (2004). *Research Methodology*. New Delhi: Prentice Hall of India.

Richardson, L. (1990). *Writing Strategies: Reaching Diverse Audiences.* New Delhi: Sage.

Shah, V.P. (1977). *Reporting Research.*Allahbad: Rachna Prakashan.

Strunk, W. and White, B.B. (2000). *The Elements of Style.* 4th edn. Needham Heights: Allyn and Bacon.

Walliman, N.(2005). *Your Undergraduate Dissertation: The Essential Guide for Success*. London: Sage.

31

Evaluation

31.1 Evaluation

The increasing use of qualitative methods and information for evaluation purposes in public policy and social change or empowerment has been well recognised. Qualitative research involves evidence-based procedures. Evidence-based interventions connect to people's emotions, culture, experiences, and habits (Gibbs, *et.al.*, 2014). Second, qualitative research focuses on the meaning of the policy or programme for clients, target groups, and practitioners. How do the participants experience the support programme? Third, qualitative evaluation Information derived from the research aims to empower or educate those involved in the programme (participatory approach). The criteria of triangulation, member checking, and conducting an audit trail are essential. These criteria are most appropriate to avoid or detect spurious (causal) inferences and possible biases, which in itself are significant potential distortions when assessing the instrumental effectiveness of a programme or policy. (Fielding and Fielding, 1986; Maxwell, 1992).

Evaluation is a systematic, rigorous, and meticulous application of scientific methods to benchmark the processes, impact, value addition and outcomes in light of objectives of the programme. It is a resource-intensive process, frequently requiring resources, such as, evaluator expertise, labour, time and a sizeable budget. (Rossi, Lipsey, and Freeman, 2004). Evaluation calls for the best inputs, and the best processes to produce the best outputs and impact. The evaluators have to conform to standards at par with international standards. Institutions are required to keep pace with the growing knowledge and strive hard ceaselessly, to meet the benchmarked quality standards.

There is a general agreement among the experts and stakeholders that evaluation is a significant tool to assess the strengths and weaknesses in conduct of study. Insights and cues from the evaluation would provide substantial support to devise strategies to ensure good results. Academia in teaching and research realise that the institutions of higher learning engaged in research in social science should adopt more objective, more reliable and valid method of evaluation. Therefore, there is a need to evolve a more enlightened, integrated and comprehensive model of evaluation based on clearly defined dimensions of quality.

31.1.1 Evaluation Strategy

Evaluation strategies signify a broad overarching and encompassing perspective on assessment. Evaluation strategies can be further classified on the basis of methods/models adopted for evaluation or on the basis of the purpose of evaluation. Evaluation strategies based on methods can be further classified into three major categories as given below:

31.1.2 Scientific Method

Scientific method implies "a continuous process of rigorous reasoning supported by a dynamic interplay among methods, theories, and findings" (NRC, 2002). Scientific inquiry in social sciences including education is more descriptively oriented, more dependent on context, less cumulative, and more intuitive than the idealised model of experimentation. It recognises the importance of philosophical, historical, social and cultural context, participant involvement, political considerations, and ethical requirements as inherent features of the study of social and educational phenomenon. (Eisenhart and DeHaan, 2005). Scientific methods were probably the first methods adopted that provided an insight into evaluation strategy. Scientific methods are based on ethics and values laid out in the social sciences. They prioritise and evaluate the accuracy, objectivity, reliability and validity of the information generated. The scientific method includes experimental methods such as experimental and quasi-experimental designs; econometric-oriented designs, cost-effectiveness and cost-benefit analysis. Quality of the research is judged on the criteria of objectivity, reliability and validity of data and statistical inferences.

31.1.3 Project Management-Oriented Method

Project management-oriented methods are widely used nowadays in operations research, social research and even in development planning and management. The Programme Evaluation and Review Technique (PERT) and Critical Path Method (CPM), as part of network analysis, are probably the best-known management-oriented models. Some researchers also consider 'logframe analyses' as a management-oriented evaluation method.

31.1.4 Qualitative Method

Qualitative research is contextual. Selection of themes, identification of locale, formation of groups, procedures and techniques of sampling, collection of narrative and audio-visual data, generation of data, analysis of data, and validation of results are derived through active participation of actors. It captures meaningful picture instead its parts. It not only cuts across the commonalities, but is inclusive of unique features of each constituent of the phenomena under study. Truth is to be understood in systemic circular relations. It recognises multiple views and multiple voices to understand structure, order and facts of the society. Its subjective human interpretation in the evaluation process is propounded in 'grounded theory' (Glaser and Strauss, 1967). Quality of the research is judged on the criteria of authenticity and trustworthiness.

31.2 Evaluation strategies based on the purpose of evaluation can be categorised into formative and summative evaluation

31.2.1 Formative Evaluation

Formative evaluation provides the initial feedback needed to strengthen the intervention or policy formulation. It examines the programme's delivery process, quality of monitoring and implementation. It is continuous evaluation of the impact of organisational inputs on the desired outcomes. Formative evaluation usually requires the same data as summative evaluation, though the research design and methodology adopted for formative evaluation may differ. Formative evaluation uses qualitative research methods and techniques. Focus is on continuous monitoring as well as evaluation. The main difference is in the case of data analysis procedures. In the case of formative evaluation, usually complex analysis procedures are used to explore the impact of interventions but causal relationships are not performed. This is because the purpose of formative evaluation is to ensure that the programme is moving in the right direction in a timely manner and that there are no gaps between strategies devised and outcome sought. If there are gaps, it helps programme managers in addressing the gap through formulation of strategies. Formative assessment recognises substantial evidence. Policy planners, stakeholders act on the basis of evidence. The aim of formative evaluation is to improve upon what has been achieved.

Formative assessment is reflected in Figure 31.1

Figure 31.1 Formative Assessments of Policy/Programme

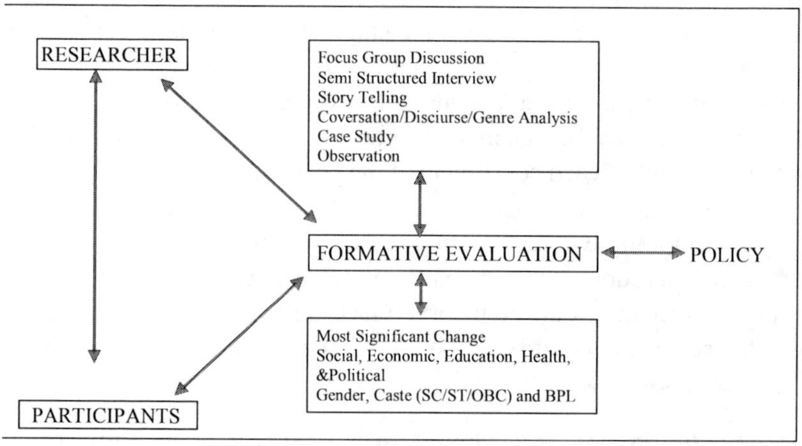

Formative evaluation can be specified into the following categories:

(a) Needs assessment*:* This determines the programme's needs from the perspective of all stakeholders.

(b) Feasibility assessment*:* It assesses the feasibility of a programme, policy or a concept for implantation. It analyses both the technical and financial viability of an intervention.

(c) **Process evaluation:** Process evaluation evaluates the impact of an intervention on process indicators. For example, whether an intervention targeted to increase family-planning awareness has any impact on group meetings between eligible couples is studied through process evaluation. It investigates the process of delivering the output.

31.2.2 Summative Evaluation

Summative evaluation is a cumulative assessment. It refers to evaluation as an end product. Evaluator/researcher tries to identify the impact of development programme on the lives of people, especially the vulnerable section of the society. It is activity based evaluation. It also tries to examine the effects or outcomes of a programme/intervention by ascertaining whether the outcomes are in consonance with the stipulated objectives. It determines the overall impact of the programme beyond the immediate target outcomes. Summative evaluation is quantitative or metric based assessment. Summative evaluation can also be specified into following categories:

(a) **Outcome evaluation:** It tries to analyse the impact of a programme's service delivery and organisational input on desired outcomes.

(b) **Impact evaluation:** Impact evaluation ascertains the project impact by analysing whether the project's activities and tasks have been successful in achieving the desired objective and goal. It, therefore, assesses the overall impacts of the programme.

(c) **Cost-effectiveness and cost-benefit analysis:** This assesses the benefit that is going to accrue from the project vis-à-vis the cost that is going to be involved in the project.

(d) **Meta-analysis:** Meta-analysis integrates the outcome estimates from multiple studies to arrive at an overall or summary judgment on an evaluation questions.

31.3 Guiding Principles

The American Evaluation Association (2004) has created a set of Guiding Principles for evaluators. The order of these principles does not imply priority among them; priority will vary by situation and evaluator role. The principles are as such given below:

- **Systematic Inquiry:** Evaluators conduct systematic data-based inquiries about whatever is being evaluated. This requires quality data collection, including a defensible choice of indicators, which lends credibility to findings. Findings are credible when they are demonstrably evidence-based, reliable and valid. This also pertains to the choice of methodology employed, such that it is consistent with the aims of the evaluation and provides dependable data. Furthermore, utility of findings is critical such that the information obtained by evaluation is comprehensive and timely, and thus serves to provide maximal benefit to stakeholders.

- **Competence:** Evaluator is equipped with necessary skills and expertise to conduct evaluation more effectively. Evaluator provides competent performance to stakeholders. Evaluation teams comprise an appropriate combination of competencies, such that varied and appropriate expertise is available for the evaluation process, and that evaluators' work within their scope of capabilities.
- **Integrity/ Honesty:** Evaluators ensurc thc honesty and integrity of the entire evaluation process. A key element of this principle is freedom from bias in evaluation and this is underscored by three principles: impartiality, independence and transparency.
- **Respect for People:** Evaluators respect the security, dignity and self-worth of the respondents, programme participants, clients, and other stakeholders with whom they interact. This is particularly pertinent with regards to those who will be impacted upon by the evaluation findings. Protection of people includes ensuring informed consent from those involved in the evaluation, upholding confidentiality, and ensuring that the identity of those who may provide sensitive information towards the programme evaluation is protected. Evaluators are ethically required to respect the customs and beliefs of those who are impacted upon by the evaluation or programme activities. Examples of how such respect is demonstrated are through respecting local customs e.g. dress codes, respecting people privacy, and minimising demands on others' time. Where stakeholders wish to place objections to evaluation findings, such a process should be facilitated through the local office of the evaluation organisation, and procedures for lodging complaints or queries should be accessible and clear.

- **Responsibilities for General and Public Welfare:** Evaluators articulate and take into account the diversity of interests and values that may be related to the general and public welfare. Access to evaluation documents by the wider public should be facilitated such that discussion and feedback is enabled.

The researcher is supposed to examine his or her research proposal on certain given criteria of evaluation before its submission. When a student submits a proposal for research, it is usually reviewed by a professor or a committee of professors. The usual criteria of a relevant problem, evidence of knowledge in the area, appropriate methodology, and good continuity in the proposal apply when a proposal is reviewed.

31.4 Criteria for Evaluation of A Research Report, Article, or Thesis

3I.4.1 The Problem

(a) Description and statement of the problem

- o Has the problem area- situation-significance been justified?
- o Has careful analysis of known and suspected facts specific to the problem been undertaken?
- o Has the logic underlying the selection of variables or themes been adhered?

(b) Review and Evaluation of the Literature Pertinent to Problem Areas.

- o Has the adequacy and relevance of the previous investigations cited with reference to the basic difficulty posed, methodology used, and analysis of data been incorporated?
- o Has practical or theoretical framework from the research studies cited with reference to the current problem under investigation.
- o Have the statements of the concepts, assumptions, or postulates underlying the problem been cited and discussed.
- o Are the statements of hypotheses/research questions precise and doable?

(c) Research Design and Methodology

- Is selection of research approach appropriate?

- Is design of sampling plan specific to nature of problem?
- Are the tools for the collection of data reliable and valid?

(d) Analysis and Interpretation

- Is in-depth analysis of contextually–bound data undertaken?
- Is narrative appropriate?
- Does it generate or create new data?
- Does it transform problem into possibility, possibility into idea, and idea into action/innovation?
- Is Interpretation of the results unbiased and based on current data?
- Whether it can make most of these conditions a reality and will take responsibility for doing so.
- What are the most significant changes that have been identified?

31.5 Evaluation of Project

Evaluation is review and reflection exercise conducted by the experts or specialists to assess what worked and what didn't? Has the project followed appropriate method, sample, and tools for the collection of data? Has the researcher gathered tangible and intangible evidences to substantiate his/her theses? It is to assess where we were (base-line data) before start-up of the project and what is the present status of the project? Has the project achieved what it set out to achieve? Is project passed through various processes of evaluation? Is project executed within the time framework? Is quality of work benchmarked? Has it added value to assets and human capital? Have people participated proactively in data generation, execution and evaluation of the project? To what extent the project met the perceived needs of the vulnerable section of the society? Are we within the helm of sustainability? What are the Most Significant Changes identified?

However, the periodical monitoring and evaluation of project go side by side. The process of concurrent evaluation helps to identify strengths and weaknesses at execution level. Are necessary actions designed and executed to achieve the stipulated objectives of the project? **Evaluation at the final end point** is to identify what we have achieved at the close of project. How **control and comparison** exercised to establish the authenticity and trustworthiness of outcomes.

Has the researcher followed the steps as mentioned below for evaluation of the project:

Step One: Do you understand what is your project? What are the objectives of the project? Are processes of evaluations clearly defined? What is the status of project with regards to stipulated objectives? Are the participants ready to participate in the process of evaluation of the project? What strategy is to be followed to inform, inspire and involve the participants (actors) in the process of monitoring and evaluation?

Step Two: Is the Project evaluation designed to assess the impact of the project on the participants? First, the researcher should identify the subject (participants) and locale for evaluation in consultation with the participants. Selection of participants needs to be through random sampling or purposive sampling whichever is feasible. Participants should know what is being evaluated and how is it be evaluated? At a minimum, evaluation findings need to be: reliable, accurate and of reasonable quality, easy to understand, relevant, not too critical; and above all else useful. The researcher needs to specify the types of evaluation to be undertaken, for instance: *Process Evaluations* – It is to assess the processes involved in organising and/or implementing the project. Are processes simplified? Are these processes brought down to the level of understanding of stakeholders or participants? *Impact Analysis*- assesses the benets in terms of changes in beliefs and attitudes, skills, behaviour and/or policies, structures and systems. *Outcome Evaluation* – The focus is on the measurement (value added) of (a) most significant changes realised; (b) Are outcomes commensurate with targets; (c) has knowledge base increased; (d) are the actors empowered (increased in their capacity and knowledge base) to participate in decision –making process. Has the participant level of confidence been increased? (e) What is the level of participant's sustainability?

Step Three: Information or data about a dened group or population needs to be collected through potential participants. If you are dealing with a small population it may be possible to obtain the data from each and every individual. However, when the potential population base is large, you may only be able to obtain data from a few people or sample of the total population. It is necessary to assess whether your sample is appropriate. When surveying a larger population, random selection needs to be taken.

Step Four: Collecting the Data, there are three important questions that need to be answered prior to choosing a data collection. Is your data specific to the objectives to get answer to your questions? What is the best way of doing this? Who should collect the data? The researcher needs to ensure that there is systemic relationship between research questions/hypotheses and analysis of data to capture the reality.

Step Five: In qualitative evaluation non-metric techniques are used for analysing data. In case of quantitative metric techniques are used for analysing data. Are the tools used standardised? Has your data revealed or captured truth? Essential elements are –reflection on analysis, reflection on methods, reflection on ethical dilemmas and conflicts, reflection on the observer's frame of mind.

Step Six: Reporting is very significant part of evaluation. It is, therefore, essential to design, write and communicate the results in a logical way. Reporting on and using of findings has to provide substantial evidence of significant difference established. Impacts, value added, outcomes are reflected in the mentioned in evaluation report. What is the life lived experience of the participants? Do they feel and experience change in their lives in light of execution of project in their area? Findings of evaluation provide the future roadmap to socio-economic-political and cultural development.

Impact Analysis

By 'impact' we mean the broad or long-term effects of a project or programme or policy. This can include effects on people who are direct users of a project or programme or public policy. It also implies effects on those who are "excluded", "marginalised" or "deprived". Across gender, it reflects empowerment of women. Quantitative design has seen by their advocates as being especially good for impact analysis. Qualitative design, on the other hand, has been advocated primarily in conjunction with other evaluative functions such as "Cause & effect"; "implementation analysis"; "process analysis"; "community self-analysis"; "the empowerment of vulnerable section of the society"; and "interpretation and understanding of life lived experience". Lawrence ( ). Impact evaluations are much easier to measure because they consider benets in terms of changes in beliefs and attitudes, skills, behaviour and/or policies, structures and systems.

Maxwell (1996) has explored the role of qualitative work in the assessing of the programme impacts. Although there have certainly been elaborate and emphatic defenses of the qualitative approach to programme evaluation, such defenses rarely attempt to qualify the approach explicitly and rigorously as a method of impact analysis (Stake, 1981). Of course, some proponents of the qualitative approach suggest that it is better than the quantitative approach precisely because its particular goals or functions have greater value than the goal of impact analysis (Guba and Lincoln, 1981). Impact is a matter of causation and a non- quantitative approach to design is apparently not well suited to the task of establishing causal relations. The root of the difficulty is located in the counterfactual definition of causality, which is our only broadly accepted formal definition of causality for social science. However, "physical causality," is widely used in practice and has recently been formalised. For example, "Modus Operandi" approach explains casual inference in evaluation. Under conceptualisation, a tailored case study design with a sample size of one in principle as strong a basis for making inferences programme impact as a randomised experiment. External validity can also be ensured (Lawrence B. Mohr, 1999).

Guiding Principles for Impact Evaluation

- **Impact analysis identifies gaps** between anticipated and actual outcomes and strategies to improve the effectiveness and accountability of development policy/programme/project.
- **Coordination and Cooperation** between institutions, stakeholders, and beneficiaries need to focus on impact evaluation in an integrated way.
- **Relevance:** Impact evaluations are done in ways that are relevant to policy/programme/project. This means asking the right questions, at the right time, but also answering why something worked or did not work, not just whether it worked or not. Combining qualitative and quantitative methods can help achieve this.
- **Ethical:** Impact evaluations need to be done in an ethical way. Having a counterfactual usually means having a comparison

group that has not benefited from a programme or policy. This raises ethical issues about denying coverage to some groups for the sake of evaluation.

- **Use the appropriate methodology**: To ensure that impact evaluations are high quality and therefore useful, it is important that they use the most appropriate methodology to answer the counterfactual (DFID: 2008).

Development agencies want to know 'what works, what doesn't, where and why', and want to identify who benefits from development assistance, including poor, vulnerable and excluded population. Mixed method of evaluation, for instance, Qualitative and Quantitative are used to identify impact of programme/policy on the lives of people. Reliable and valid or authentic and trustworthy tools are employed. Participatory approach for identifying the impact. Triangulation is also important, obtaining different perspectives on change; questions that directly ask stakeholders the role of the project also go part of the way. However, these approaches can be more consciously and rigorously applied to provide more plausible evidence of causality. Issues of causality are implicated as links between outputs, methods of delivery and perceived change – the effects – are established. Yet, only too often, organisations present data on outcome indicators as evidence of effectiveness without any convincing analysis to show the extent to which their intervention has brought about change.

The first question to ask when considering impact evaluation concerns the kind of evidence that will be acceptable to stakeholders and what will be done with evaluation findings. Second, organisation has to be clear about the resources they have for implementing programme/ policy/ project. Third, identify the level of confidence that is required by stakeholders in any assessment of causal link. Fourth, the control and comparison are necessary for identifying change by the participants.

Checking that results, support causal attribution. There are a number of ways of checking the results to see if they support causal attribution; with enough resources, these can be done in combination.

The three Gathering additional data Ways to gather additional data might include:

- Asking key informants to attribute causality (asking what was a trigger for specific actions or change, for example), providing evidence that links participation with observed changes.
- Drawing on the previous experience of experts and other stakeholders to determine what pattern of effects is typical for a similar initiative.
- Considering alternative explanations by looking at the processes and linking them to observed results.

Data analysis should also be able to reveal potential connections, such as:

- any link between results achieved and the extent of participation (for example, data showing participants attending activity sessions regularly for more than one year with more positive outcomes than those with irregular or short-term attendance) how overall outcomes have been affected by the positive or negative influence of individual participant characteristics external to the intervention (for example, young people in a drug and alcohol programme with strong family support achieving step changes more quickly than others).

The timing of change may also be important. Do changes relate to anticipated timelines for change? If outcomes have been achieved earlier, for example, this might be due to factors other than the intervention. Case studies can be compared to check how results might be affected in the event of differences in project implementation or individual participation levels. Can elements of practice be linked to more positive or negative results? Different cases may be analysed to identify how different components of the programme might produce different specific outcomes.

The Broad Domains of Significant Changes identified by the actors (actual users) are below:

- Significant Change in the quality of social life of people (mutual support, trust, respect, and equality, interaction and participation, and social mobility) need to identified.

- Significant Changes in income of people and sharing of economic resources (equity in income and resource sharing, and upward shift from below poverty line) has to be benchmarked.
- Significant Change in formal and informal decision-making and participation in political activities has to be assessed.
- Significant level of sustainability of change has to be identified.

Criticality is a key factor in assessment or evaluation of research work. Composition, reflection, context, transparency, enquiry, healthy scepticism, positiveness, and evolution in process are the basic elements of criticality. Research scholar should develop skills of critical thinking in order to develop a good thesis.

31.5 Allison Tong, Peter Sainsbury, Jonathan Craig ((2007) Checklist for the Evaluation of Qualitative Research:

Consolidated criteria for reporting qualitative studies (COREQ): 32-item checklist:

No.	*Item*	*Guide questions/description*
	Domain 1: Research team and reflexivity	
Personal Characteristics		
1.	Interviewer/facilitator	Which author/s conducted the interview or focus group?
2.	Credentials	What were the researcher's credentials? *E.g. PhD, MD*
3.	Occupation	What was their occupation at the time of the study?
4.	Gender	Was the researcher male or female?
5.	Experience and training	What experience or training did the researcher have?
Relationship with Participants		
6.	Relationship established	Was a relationship established prior to study commencement?
7.	Participant knowledge of the interviewer	What did the participants know about the researcher? e.g. *personal goals, reasons for doing the research*
8.	Interviewer characteristics	What characteristics were reported about the interviewer/facilitator? e.g. *Bias, assumptions, reasons and interests in the research topic*

(Contd...)

Domain 2: Study design		
Theoretical Framework		
9.	Methodological orientation and Theory	What methodological orientation was stated to underpin the study? *e.g. grounded theory, discourse analysis, ethnography, phenomenology, content analysis*
Participant Selection		
10.	Sampling	How were participants selected? *e.g. purposive, convenience, consecutive, snowball*
11.	Method of approach	How were participants approached? e.g. *face-to-face, telephone, mail, email*
12.	Sample size	How many participants were in the study?
13.	Non-participation	How many people refused to participate or dropped out? Reasons?
Setting		
14.	Setting of data collection	Where was the data collected? e.g. *home, clinic, workplace*
15.	Presence of non-participants	Was anyone else present besides the participants and researchers?
16.	Description of sample	What are the important characteristics of the sample? *e.g. demographic data, date*
Data Collection		
17.	Interview guide	Were questions, prompts, guides provided by the authors? Was it pilot tested?
18.	Repeat interviews	Were repeat interviews carried out? If yes, how many?
19.	Audio/visual recording	Did the research use audio or visual recording to collect the data?
20.	Field notes	Were field notes made during and/or after the interview or focus group?
21.	Duration	What was the duration of the interviews or focus group?
22.	Data saturation	Was data saturation discussed?
23.	Transcripts returned	Were transcripts returned to participants for comment and/or correction?
Domain 3: analysis and findings		
Data Analysis		
24.	Number of data coders	How many data coders coded the data?
25.	Description of the coding tree	Did authors provide a description of the coding tree?
26.	Derivation of themes	Were themes identified in advance or derived from the data?
27.	Software	What software, if applicable, was used to manage the data?

(*Contd*...)

28.	Participant checking	Did participants provide feedback on the findings?
Reporting		
29.	Quotations presented	Were participant quotations presented to illustrate the themes / findings? Was each quotation identified? e.g. *participant number*
30.	Data and findings consistent	Was there consistency between the data presented and the findings?
31.	Clarity of major themes	Were major themes clearly presented in the findings?
32.	Clarity of minor themes	Is there a description of diverse cases or discussion of minor themes?

References

Allison Tong, Peter Sainsbury, Jonathan Craig ((2007). DOI: http://dx.doi.org/10.1093/ intqhcmzm042 349-357

Best, J. and Kahn, J. (2009). *Research in Education.*10th edition, Needham Heights: Allyn and Bacon.

Cozby, P. (2009). *Methods in Behavioural Research.* 10th edition, Bemont: Wadsworth.

Dunn, K.E., and Mulvenon, S.W. (2009). *A Critical Review of Research on Formative Assessment: The Limited Scientific Evidence of the Impact of Formative Assessment in Education. Practical Assessment, Research and Evaluation.* Volume 14, Number 7.

Gibbs, A., Jewkes, R., Sikweyiya, Y., Willan, S. (2015). Reconstructing masculinity? A qualitative evaluation of the Stepping Stones and Creating Futures interventions in urban informal settlements in South Africa. Culture, Health and Sexuality: An International Journal for Research, Intervention and Care, 17, 208-222.

Goode, W.J. and Hatt, P.K. (1990). *Methods in Social Research.* New Delhi: McGraw-Hill.

Guba, E. G. and Lincoln, Y. S. (1981). Effective evaluation: Improving the usefulness of evaluation results through responsive and naturalistic approaches. San Francisco, CA: Jossey-Bass.

Guthrie, G. (2010). *Basic Research Methods.* New Delhi: Sage.

Martin, R.L. and Smith, T.G. (2017). Playing to win: How strategy really works. *Harvard Bussiness Review,* September and October 2017.

Laws, S. (2003). *Research for Development.* New Delhi: Vistaar Publications.

Leedy, P., Ormrod, J. (2010). Practical Research: Planning and Design. 9th edition in Needham Heights: Allyn Bacon Ozga, J. (2000). *Policy Research in Educational Settings.* Buckingham, UK: OUP.

Potter, C. (2006). "Psychology and the art of program evaluation". *South African Journal of psychology* 36 (1): 82-102.

Punch, K. F. (2009). *Introduction to Research Methods in Education*. New Delhi: Sage.

Rossi, P.H.; Lipsey, M.W. and Freeman, H.E. (2004). *Evaluation: A systematic approach* (7th ed.). Thousand Oaks: Sage.

Singh, J. (2008). *Methodology and Techniques of Social Research*. New Delhi: Kanishka Publishers.

Swann, J. (2000). How can research lead to improvement in education. *Prospero,* 6(3/4), pp. 130-138.

Wooding, S. and Grant, J. (2003). *Assessing Research: The Researchers' View.* Cambridge, England: RAND Europe.

32

Criteria for Evaluating Quality of Research in Education

The terms ***quality research*** and ***quality evidence*** are related concepts that have been at the centre of much debate in academic, professional, and public policy circles. The debate stems from the widespread belief that the quality of research in social science including education is often uneven and lacking in credibility, making it difficult to make a confident, concrete assertion or prediction regarding evidence for change or improving practice. (Shavelson and Towne, 2002). The debate is also due, in part, to the lack of consensus on the specific standards for assessing quality research and standards of quality for assessing evidence (Mosteller and Boruch, 2002).

It is a fact that all phenomena and knowledge have both quantitative and qualitative dimensions. The distinction between objectivity and subjectivity, normally associated with quantitative and qualitative research, is neither accurate nor useful. Standards for quality research, whether primarily designed to gather quantitative or qualitative data, typically emphasise the traits of objectivity, internal validity, external validity, reliability, rigour, open-mindedness, and honest and thorough reporting.

Quality of research depends on system, participants, researcher, and support. System calls for the best inputs, and the best processes to produce the best outputs and impact. The researchers have to conform to standards at par with international standards. Institutions are required to keep pace with the growing knowledge and strive hard ceaselessly, to meet the international standards in research. Research activities should also get adequate financial support from national and international agencies to improve its quality.

In general, research especially in social science including education does not have much creditability at the national and international levels. Part of the reason may be a lack of credible research models or quality paradigms. Another reason is casualness in evaluating research. Moreover, there are no reliable and valid criteria conforming to national or international standards for evaluating research. It is, therefore, essential for the research communities to identify more valid, reliable methods and a comprehensive set of norms to judge the quality in research. Quality needs to be assessed in the light of its contribution to the general quality of understanding and what it offers to the larger public and professional conversation over why and how educational institutions matter. The goal is to provide rigorous, evidence for one's claims. Hence, need arises for international cooperation and free flow of researches in different areas and at different levels in the field of research. There is also a need for assessment and accreditation of institutions engaged in research by the autonomous national and international bodies.

32.1 Models for Evaluating Research

A number of strategies and models have been proposed for evaluating the quality of research. However, a majority of these have been found to have some limitations particularly for evaluating research. Evaluation reports do not provide substantial evidences or consensus on the basis of which policy planners can make decisions. Because research quality means different things to different people and in different settings, developing a commonly agreed upon strategy for all purposes is desirable and challenging at the same time.

Commonly cited criteria for evaluating systems to rate the strength of bodies of evidence include (a) Quality (the aggregate of quality ratings for individual studies, predicated on the extent to which bias was minimised in the study designs); (b) Quantity (the number of studies, the sample size, the study design's statistical power to detect meaningful effects, and magnitude of the effects found or the effect size), and (c) Consistency: (for any given topic, the extent to which similar findings are reported using similar and different study designs). Typically, the overall study design, the specific research questions, methods, coherence, and consistency of findings influence the type and quality of evidence produced.

Evaluation has to address three questions namely what is to be evaluated? Who is to be evaluated? How is to be evaluated? The essential first purpose of evaluation is to address organisational issues in academia. It involves processes to optimise the quality of research outcomes, to reinforce the principles of accountability, and to develop explicit and rational criteria for policy planning. Secondly, the process of evaluation focuses on researchers, stakeholders, and financial support. Thirdly, evaluation needs to be linked with inputs, outputs, and impact. It has generally been observed that the evaluators are mostly interested in inputs and outputs while policy planners are deeply interested in the impact.

Inputs (resources) are the direct or indirect human, organisational or material resources required to implement and carry out the planned research activities. Processes are the clearly defined actions, which are required to produce results. Outputs are the immediate measurable results and are direct consequence of the implemented activities. Impacts involve changes in the quality of education and its impact on society.

Most of the developed countries use input, output and impact criteria for evaluating research. These countries also use internal and external methods of evaluation. National Research Council, University Consultative Committee, International Panel of Experts (peer review), National Assessment Exercise (UK), EERA, EAQA, AERA, are some of the agencies which provide mechanisms and expertise to evaluate quality in research. However, there are no uniform standards and norms for evaluation of research at international level. Table 32.1 reveals evaluation criteria used by most of the developed and developing countries.

Table 32.1: Criteria for Evaluating Research in Developed and Developing Countries

Category	*Criteria/ Methods*	*Agency*
Developed Countries		
USA, UK, Japan, Australia, Germany, Canada, Sweden, Norway, China	Internal and External Inputs, outputs and impacts Bibliometrics and Peer Review International standards and Bench-marking Provide mechanisms that realistically reflects research quality, rather than relying on quantitative surrogates.	International panel of experts, National Research Council Consultative Committee, ERA, EERA, EAQA, and RAE
Developing Countries India, Pakistan, Bangladesh, Iraq, Nepal, Tanzania Iran, Thailand	Inputs, Output Bibliometrics citations Simple publications count Internal and External No mechanism for quality assurance.	UGC, NAAC, NCTE

Most of the developing countries including India use input and output criteria. In practice, conventional bibliometrics method is used (number of publications) to assess the quality of research in education. In India, the system of evaluation varies from university to university. There is no uniform, reliable and valid method of evaluation of system, scholar and supervisor at different levels of research. Peer review by the experts is largely ignored while evaluating the quality of research in education. Impact of the study is also not generally considered in the process of evaluation.

32.2 Indiana University Model (1996)

The different criteria for evaluating research according to this model given by Frank K. Lester are the following:

1. Worthiness: relevance
2. Coherence: research questions, research methods, analysis techniques
3. Competence: research carefully, conceptualised, designed and reported
4. Planning and investigations
5. Creditability: claims made and justified on substantial evidences

This model lays emphasis on planning, competence, coherence and creditability claims made and justified on substantial evidences. Institutional initiatives, resources, processes and methods of evaluation are the other important variables of quality assurance. Competency also involves the role of supervisor as a guide and ultimately the status of the evaluator. This latter role is taken lightly and reduced to a bare formality.

32.3 The U.K.'s Research Assessment Exercise Model (1997)

The criteria for evaluating educational research given by Arnold and Guy in the above model are:

1. Appropriateness, Economy, Effectiveness
2. Efficiency, Process Efficiency, Efficacy
3. Impact, Additionality, Displacement, Process
4. Improvement, Strategy and Quality.

The above model of evaluation should also address the organisational issues in academia. In particular, evaluation should optimise the nature of the institution, reinforce the principle of accountability, and emphasise the application of explicit and rational criteria for decision-making and policy making.

32.4 Educational Research Evaluation Model (2001)

The different criteria for evaluating educational research according to this model given by E Fossey, C. Harvey, F. McDermott, L. Davidson are the following.

1. Congruence, Responsiveness,
2. Appropriateness, Adequacy,
3. Transparency, Authenticity,
4. Coherence, Reciprocity, and
5. Typicality and Permeability.

Biometrics, peer review, and impact analysis are done on the bases of above mentioned elements of quality. Moreover, institutional processes and programmes for the promotion of research are also needed to be evaluated to assess the quality in educational research.

32.5 The National Research Council (USA) (2002) has described standards that shape scientific understanding and that are frequently used to process the quality of research. This has lead to the term *scientifically based research* being used in some settings to address research quality. The different criteria for evaluating quality in educational research include the following:

- Pose a significant, important question that can be investigated empirically and that contributes to the knowledge bas.
- Test questions that are linked to relevant theory.
- Apply methods that best address the research questions of interest.
- Base research on clear chains of inferential reasoning supported ajustified by a complete coverage of the relevant literature.
- Provide the necessary information to reproduce or replicate the study.
- Ensure the study design, methods, and procedures are sufficiently transparent and ensure an independent, balanced, and objective approach to the research.
- Provide sufficient description of the sample, the intervention, and any comparison groups.
- Use appropriate and reliable conceptualisation and measurement of variables.
- Evaluate alternative explanations for any findings.
- Assess the possible impact of systematic bias.
- Submit research to a peer-review process.
- Adhere to quality standards for reporting (i.e., clarity, cogence, completeness)

32.6. National Assessment and Accreditation Council (NAAC) (India-2004). Criteria for Evaluating Quality in Educational Research

The different criteria for evaluation of educational research given in the above model are the following:

(1) Institutional Infrastructure and Learning Resources and allocation for promotion of research activities.

(2) Research Output: Ph.D., M.Phil. and NET Produced.

(3) Bibliometrics: Research Publications (articles and books) and Research Project Completed.

In the above criteria, peer review and impact of research studies have been found missing in the process of evaluation. A little weightage (5 per cent) is given to research activities. Scholars participation in evaluation of quality of research programme and system have also not been given due consideration.

32.7 University of Washington Model (2006)

The criteria for evaluating qualitative research in education in the above model by Michael Watts include the following elements;

(1) Transparency,

(2) Clarity,

(3) Methodological precision,

(4) Theory-driven expectations,

(5) Doability.

Supervisor, peer review expert while examining or evaluating the research evidence should consider transparency, clarity, methodology, theory- base and doability.

Benchmark for evaluating the above given variables need to be specific, objective and measurable.

32.8 Model for Evaluating Qualitative or Quantitative Research in Education (2006)

In this model, Kadriye Erickan and Wolff-Michael Roth have given an integrative framework for evaluating research in education.

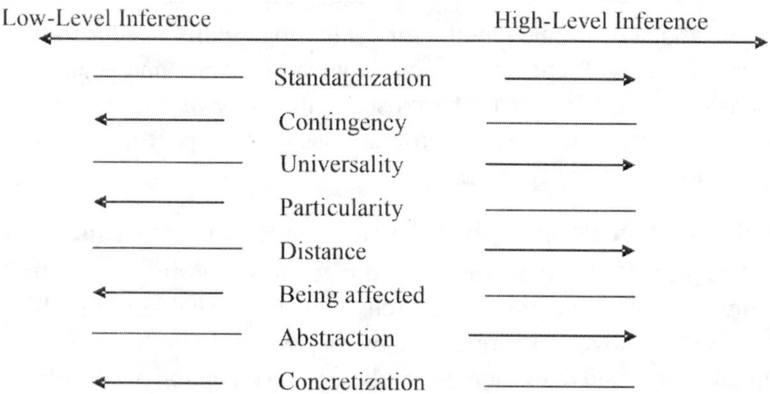

The aim of evaluation in this approach is to assess research results that are characterised simultaneously by high and low inference levels.

Instead of dichotomising research as quantitative or qualitative, we need integrative approaches that provide appropriate forms of knowledge needed by decision makers.

32.9 Quality-Based Research Model (University of Machigan, 2007)

The dimensions and sub-dimensions for evaluating quality in educational research given in this model by Berliner, G., are summarised as follows:

Dimensions of Quality			
Epistemic: Methodological and Theoretical robustness	**Technological**	**Capacity development And value for people**	**Economic**
Trustworthiness	Purposivity	Plausibility	Marketability and Competitiveness
Builds on what is Know + contribution to Knowledge	Salience/timeliness	Partnership, collaboration and Engagement	Cost-effectiveness
Explicitness	Specificity and accessibility	Reflexivity, deliberation And criticism	Auditability
Propriety	Concern for enabling Impact	Receptiveness	Feasibility
Paradigm-dependent Criteria	Flexibility and operationalisability	Transformation and personal growth	Originality
Scientific robustness	Social & economic robustness		

The above mentioned model for evaluating quality in educational research deals with epistemic, technological, capacity and economic dimensions of quality. It is the most comprehensive and integrated approach to evaluate research programmes on the specific variables for the assessment of research.

32.10. A Systemic Approach for Evaluating Research in Education

The present global strategy is dedicated to supporting interactive public access to educational research. This could enable users of its resources to move from research overviews and syntheses to the original studies and relevant meta-analysis, with an option of consulting the research instruments and perhaps the data as well. Such a system could connect research studies not only to related work but to the relevant curriculum materials, teacher reflections, media reports and policies. Educational research could augment the intelligibility of these research connections as well as their practical implications at national and international levels, by developing an open forum, an op-ed page, in readers to post commentaries and join discussions (Bostein, 2000).

Universities throughout the world today are expected to be both efficient and accountable and have reasonable standards in educational research. For more than two decades, there has been growing concern at national and international levels 'about the increasing cost of funding university-based research and the need to obtain "value for money" for public expenditure on higher education'. In response, many governments have implemented mechanisms that attempt to relate funding to performance. Evaluation has thus emerged as key issue to ensure reasonable and measurable standards.

32.11 Variables of Evaluation

Many institutions of higher learning have been observed using the word "research" in India but there is hardly any worthwhile research activity. Need therefore arises that institutions virtually engaged in research should also be assessed and accredited on the basis of infrastructure, learning resources, processes, profiles of faculty members, professional ethics among professionals and scholars, exposure to research designs and techniques, awareness about the practical implications of the problem, autonomy and space for independent research. It should also include quality norms for professionals and researchers. Their services as external evaluators can be utilised for evaluating the quality of educational researches in universities and other centres of higher learning. Uniform criteria conforming to international standards for the purpose of evaluation need to be developed and put to use at all levels of research in education.

32.12 Evaluation of Research Programmes and Publications

1. It is essential to evaluate research programmes in order to assess their quality. Research programmes need to be evaluated on six criteria namely, integration with long-term research programme; collaboration and cooperation in research effort; extramural support; dissemination, generation of new knowledge and changes in practice.

2. The current research effort's integration within a long-term research programme involves identification of priority areas, clearly identified target audiences, short-term and long-term goals, objectives, and strategies, and a well-focused, clearly articulated vision for the future.
3. Collaboration and cooperation includes interdisciplinary partnerships and joint publications; consensus on regional, national, and/or international research teams (where applicable), and sustained involvement of scholars and supervisors.
4. Extramural support is seen in terms of over all pattern of sustained support, awards, and fellowships for research programme.
5. Dissemination of research to the professionals focuses on research publications and presentations, referred articles, publication outlets, acceptance rates and conference papers and presentations.
6. Dissemination of research to stakeholders includes overall pattern of sustained dissemination efforts to stakeholders, educational programmes, trials and demonstrations, mass media releases, electronic products, and books, journals, and other print formats.
7. The contribution of research programme to new knowledge and changes in practice are assessed from substantial evidences in the above fields.

32.13 Institutional Assessment and Accreditation (Research Activities)

Universities and other centres of higher learning are regarded to be assessed and accredited on the basis of value added modalities. This implies assessment in terms of institution's progress on longitudinal basis in building research capability, delivery system, research outcomes and their impact. Value Added Modalities for evaluating research are reflected in Figure 32.2.

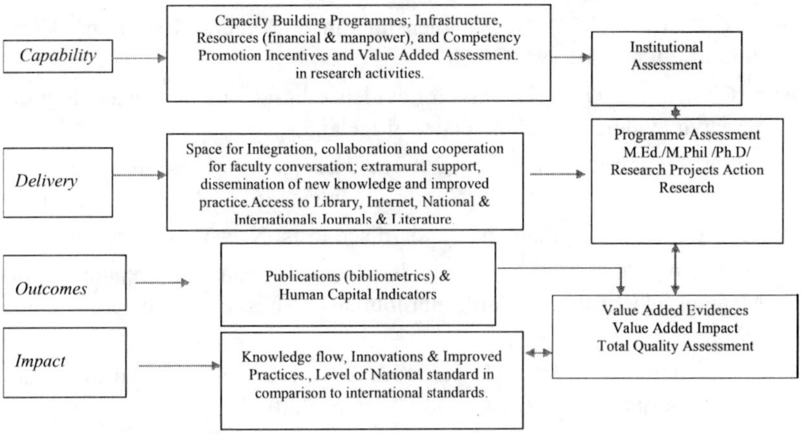

Figure 32.2: Value Added Modalities.

Quality norms or standards in research, therefore, have to be evaluated at each stage, (i.e. at inputs, processes and outputs). Inputs evaluation may pertain to infrastructure, expertise, skilled manpower and financial support and incentives. Processes may refer to delivery system with focus on efficiency, effectiveness and good governance. Outputs may be in the form of value addition, outcomes and impact. Evaluation of Institutional environment is essential where scholars are inspired, informed and involved to achieve excellence in their field of study. Evaluation also analyses the data on how innovative ideas are being transformed into practice. Adoption of quality norms alone would make research institutions responsive, accountable and quality oriented.

Quality in research, of late, has attracted the attention of research community across the countries. There is a general agreement among the experts and stakeholders that research quality articulates vision for future. Insights and cues from the evaluation would provide substantial support to devise strategies for achieving excellence in research. Research results (at micro and macro level) and meta-analysis need to be integrated to get substantial evidence that can be used for policy planning. It is high-time that International research community should come together and cooperate to evolve a more integrated and comprehensive model of evaluation based on clearly defined dimensions of quality.

References

Alvin C. Eurich (1962). New Dimensions in Educational Research AERA, News Letter, April 1962. 4-10.

Anne Clyde, L. (2005). The basis for evidence-based practice: evaluating the research evidence, the University of Iceland.

Bleakley, C. and D. MacAuley (2002). "The quality of research reports in journals", British Journal of Sports Medicine, 36(2): April, pp. 124-125.

Bostein, L (2000). A tyranny of standardised tests. New York Times & WKI.

Coladarci, Arthur P. (1954). "Are Educational Researchers prepared to do Meaningful Research?" California Journal of Educational Research, 5 (Jan 1954): 3-6.

Coladarci, Arthur P. (1960). 'Towards More Rigorous Educational Research' Harvard Educational Review, 30 (Winter 1900): 3-11.

Dahiya, L.N. (2001). Quality of Doctoral Research in India: Some Monitoring and Control Issues, University News 39(45) Nov. 5-11, 2001.

Dave, P.N. (2007). The Decline in the Quality of Research in Education. Perspectives in Education, Vol. 23. No. 1.

Day, A., and J. Peter (1994). Quality Indicators in Academic Publishing, Library Review 43 (7): pp. 4-72.

Fred M. Kerlinger (1960). Gersten, R., Baker, S. and Lloyd, J. W. (2000). Designing high-quality research in special education: group experimental design. *The Journal of Special Education, 34*(1), 2-18.

Gupta, A.K. and Kapoor, D.R. (2009) Criteria of Quality Research: An International Perspective. MIER Center for Educational Research (J&K).

Gupta, L. (2006). Raising Accountability and Valuable Input through Reports. *University News, 44(9).*

Hugh Burkhardt and Alan H Schoenfeld (2003). Improving Educational Research: Towards a more useful, more influential and better – funded Enterprise. Educational Researcher, Vol. 32, No. 9.

John Wlllinsky (2001). The Strategic education research program and the public value of research, Educational Researcher, Vol. 30, No. 1, pp. 5 -14.

Kapoor, D.R. (2009). *Dynamics of Learning Organisations.* New Delhi: Regal Publications.

Kapoor, D.R.(2014). *Research Methodology: Methods and Techniques*. New Delhi: Regal Publications.

Khanka, S.S. (2002). Declining Quality of Doctoral Research in Indian Universities. University News, Vol. 40, No. 9, March 4-10.

Levin, J.R. and O'Donnell, A.M. (1999). What to do about educational research's credibility gaps? Issues in Education, 5(2), 177-230.

Michael l. Kamil. (1994). More on the Quality of Educational Research: Respose to Pressley and Harris. Educational Psychology Review, Vol. 6, No. 3.

Michael Watts (2006). Essentials for Research Design. In Ellen Perecman and Sara R. Curran (Eds) A Handbook for Social Science Field Research. Sage Publications, New Delhi.

Mosteller, F., and Brouch, R. (Eds.). (2002). *Evidence matters: Randomised Trials in Education Research.* Washington, DC: The Brookings Institute.

National Research Council (1999). Improving students learning. A strategic plan for educational research and the utilisation.Washington, DC: National Academy Press.

Odom, S.L., Brantlinger, E., Gersten, R., Horner, R.H., Thompson, B., and Harris, K.R.(2005). Research in Special Education: Scientific Methods and Evidence-based Practices. Execptional Children, 71(2), 137-148.

P.K. Rajan (2006). Research in State University, University News, Vol. 44, No. 9.

Pring, R.(2002). False dualisms: Quantitative & Qualitative research. Journal of Philosophy of Education, 34(3).

Reddy, D.Obul. (2000). Supervisor's role in improving the quality of research. Unpublished paper at the National Seminar on Supervision of Research in Universities. New Delhi.

Robert, E. Slavin (2002). Evidence-Based Education Policies: Transforming Educational Practice and Research. Educatonal Researcher, Vol. 31, No. 7, pp. 15-21.

Shakeel Ahmand (2008). UGC-NET: A measure to Maintain Quality in Teaching and Research, University News, Vol. 46, No. 21 May 19-25, 2008.

Shavelson, R.J., and Towne, L.(Eds).(2002). *Scientific research in education.* Washington DC: National Research Council, National Academy Press.

Singleton, R.A., Straits, B.C., and Strait, M.M. (1993). *Approaches to social research.* New York: Oxford university Press.

Slavin, R.E (2002). evidence based education policy: transforming educational practice and Research. Educational reasearcher 31(7).

Sudarshan Mishra (2004). Process Issues for Organising Research in Distance Education, Indian Education Review, Vol. 40, No. 1, Jan 2004.

Vardharayan, P. (2003). Issues in Quality Research: Quality vs. Quantity. University News, Vol. 41, No. 12.

Wooding, S., and Grant, J.(2003). *Assessing research: The researchers' view.* Cambridge, England : RAND Europe.

Index